Giving Care,
Writing Self

Studies in the
Postmodern Theory of Education

Joe L. Kincheloe and Shirley R. Steinberg
General Editors

Vol. 132

PETER LANG
New York • Washington, D.C./Baltimore • Boston • Bern
Frankfurt am Main • Berlin • Brussels • Vienna • Oxford

Joseph Schneider and Wang Laihua

Giving Care,
Writing Self

A "New" Ethnography

PETER LANG
New York • Washington, D.C./Baltimore • Boston • Bern
Frankfurt am Main • Berlin • Brussels • Vienna • Oxford

Library of Congress Cataloging-in-Publication Data

Schneider, Joseph.
Giving care, writing self: a "new" ethnography /
Joseph Schneider and Wang Laihua.
p. cm. — (Counterpoints; vol. 132)
Includes bibliographical references and index.
1. Aged—Care—China. 2. Aging parents—Care—China. 3. Care of the
sick—China. 4. Caregivers—China. 5. Intergenerational relations—China.
6. Sex role—China. 7. China—Social conditions—1976–. I. Wang, Laihua.
II. Title. III. Counterpoints (New York, N.Y.); vol. 132.
HV1484.C62 S35   362.6'0951—dc21   99-053061
ISBN 0-8204-4864-8
ISSN 1058-1634

Die Deutsche Bibliothek-CIP-Einheitsaufnahme

Schneider, Joseph:
Giving care, writing self: a "new" ethnography / Joseph Schneider and Wang
Laihua. –New York; Washington, D.C./Baltimore; Boston; Bern; Frankfurt am
Main; Berlin; Brussels; Vienna; Oxford: Lang.
(Counterpoints; Vol. 132)
ISBN 0-8204-4864-8

Cover design by Lisa Dillon

The paper in this book meets the guidelines for permanence and durability
of the Committee on Production Guidelines for Book Longevity
of the Council of Library Resources.

© 2000 Peter Lang Publishing, Inc., New York

Printed in the United States of America

for Nancy Claire, Li Mei,
and Xiao Xue

Contents

Acknowledgments

Thanks are due to many who over the course of almost a decade gave to and cared for us in diverse ways that helped bring this book forward. The seventeen families in Tianjin who, for the most part, welcomed us warmly into their homes and allowed our return visits and continuing conversations in 1990–1991 and several subsequent summers are at the heart of several chapters. The doctors and nurses at Main Hospital and in the sickbed unit in particular more than once saved us from foolish mistakes and helped us forge relationships with their patients that facilitated the field research. The Tianjin Academy of Social Sciences and, in particular, the support by the then president, Wang Hui, made our connections to and meetings with people in Tianjin possible. Wang Hui, in this and much else, exceeded his considerable reputation as a friend and champion of sociology and social science in China. His personal trust in and endorsement of our project at all its China stages sustained its life.

The Drake University Center for the Humanities and the Drake University Research Council provided crucial funding at various points. The Humanities Center and the then directors Robert Hariman and Richard Abel were important in this regard.

Four people Joseph met early in his initial trip to China and with whom he has sustained friendship and from whom he has learned a great deal about China and Chinese people's lives are Carsten Küther, Pang Bingjun, Sun Binghe, and Zhu Hong. Sun, in particular, has offered a keen eye on various drafts of chapters and has been an invaluable but always friendly critic.

We owe a particular debt to Patricia Clough for her critical reading of an earlier draft of the manuscript and for her encouragement and intelligence; and many thanks go to Norman Denzin for his generous support and helpful critical insights beginning early in the project. Others who helped importantly are Nigel Bruce, Cai Qing Lian, Susanne Chan Siu

Shan, Peter Conrad, Bronwyn Davies, Avery Gordon, Barbara Ho Pui King, Barbara Hodgdon, Jim Holstein, Hua Qing Zhao, Huang Ying, Charlotte Ikels, John Kitsuse, Kuah Khun Eng, Peter LaBella, Kelly Lee, Li Ying Hui, Liu Kaimin, Gilbert Mattos, Laura Mattos, Pan Yunkang, Ron Troyer, and Eric Tsang. We have benefitted in particular ways from both the critical eye and sense of aesthstics of Min-Zhan Lu.

Joe Kincheloe's and Shirley Steinberg's endorsement of the manuscript for their series came at a crucial moment in its long life.

We thank each other for the hard work, support, friendship, affection, and commitment to a project that sometimes seemed never likely to produce the two books that it finally has.

And we thank Nancy, Li Mei, and Xiao Xue for their unflagging patience and belief in what we set about to do. Their good-natured love and support have carried us over the difficult bits and have made the joyful ones all the more so.

We thank Maggie Chan Wing Yin for allowing us to reprint the segment of her journal she wrote about the story of Hua Mulan, and we thank Arts Publishing Company of Hong Kong for permission to use the translation we asked Pang Bingjun to make of this story as found in their school book for children edited by Lin Yu-ming, *Zhongguo Ertong Gushi Xuan*, copyright © 1985. We thank John Minford for his permission to reprint selections from the writing of Sun Lung-kee as contained in the edited volume *Seeds of Fire: Chinese Voices of Conscience*, copyright © 1989. Finally, acknowledgment goes to the following for granting us permission to reprint segments from other previously-published works:

R. David Arkush and Leo O. Lee, editors. *Land without Ghosts: Chinese Impressions of America from the Mid-Nineteenth Century to the Present*. Berkeley: University of California Press. Copyright © 1989. Reprinted by permission of the publisher. All rights reserved.

Patricia Ticineto Clough. *The End(s) of Ethnography: From Realism to Social Criticism*. New York: Peter Lang, Copyright © 1998. Reprinted by permission of the publisher. All rights reserved.

Ambrose Y.C. King and Michael Harris Bond. "The Confucian Paradigm of Man: A Sociological View" in *Chinese Culture and Mental Health* edited by W.S. Tseng and David Wu. Orlando, Florida: Academic Press, Copyright © 1985. Reprinted by permission of the publisher. All rights reserved.

Maxine Hong Kingston. *The Woman Warrior: Memoirs of a Girlhood among Ghosts*. Copyright © 1975, 1976 by Maxine Hong Kingston. Reprinted by permission of Alfred A. Knopf, a Division of Random House, Inc. Maxine Hong

Kingston, *The Woman Warrior*. Copyright © Maxine Hong Kingston, 1981. Reproduced by permission of A. M. Heath & Co., Ltd. All rights reserved.

Joseph W. Schneider. "Family Care Work and Duty in a 'Modern' Chinese Hospital." Revised and reprinted from an earlier version included in *Health and Health Care in Developing Countries: Sociological Perspectives* edited by Peter Conrad and Eugene B. Gallagher by permission of Temple University Press. Copyright © 1993 by Temple University Press. All rights reserved.

Paul K.T. Sih, editor, and M.L. Makra, translator. "Editor's Preface" and "Translator's Acknowledgments" in *Hsiao Ching: The Canon of Filial Piety*. The Center of Asian Studies, St. John's University Press. Copyright © 1961. Reprinted by permission of the publisher. All rights reserved.

Excerpts from "The Deep Structure of Chinese Culture," "The Long March to Man," and "The Deep Structure of Chinese Sexuality" from *Seeds of Fire: Chinese Voices of Conscience* edited by Geremie Barmé and John Minford. Copyright © 1989 by Geremie Barmé and John Minford. Copyright © 1986 by Far Eastern Economic Review, Ltd. Reprinted by permission of Hill and Wang, a division of Farrar, Straus and Giroux, LLC.

Margery Wolf. "Chinanotes: Engendering Anthropology" in *Fieldnotes: The Making of Anthropology* edited by Roger Sanjek. Ithaca: Cornell University Press. Copyright © 1990. Used by permission of the publisher, Cornell University Press. All rights reserved.

Joseph Schneider
Wang Laihua

April 2000

Preface

In a recently published interview, Trinh Minh-ha (1996) discusses some of the complexities of naming positions in the world of postcolonial studies. Annamaria Morelli, her interlocutor, credits postcolonial theory and practice with deconstructing many of the familiar categories in terms of which various "others" have been defined, studied, and located relative to a center or, as Trinh puts it, a "site of domination" (16). But Morelli goes on to wonder if perhaps the most tenacious of these centered categories, "the West" itself, is often spared the full power of this critique, thus insuring that its "others" remain fixed by a unitary image of the dominant, "center" category in this core binarism.

Trinh responds that this deconstructive work on the West or the center must be engaged "on both sides" of the various versions of this divide. She agrees that those who speak from subordinate positions should take care not to overstate the unity of the dominant center (thus further cementing their own marginality). But she wants to give more attention to what those who speak from that place of privilege and power, claiming to be allies of the deconstruction noted above, have to say. To work *against* the continued dominance of this privileged place even as one speaks *from* it, it is not enough only to disavow dominance, she says. One also should offer a critical analysis of how that site of domination came to be and continues to seem, to be, so unitary to its others. She reminds us how the self-characterizations coming from the center today so typically and strategically embrace images of a "mobile, changing, flexible, complex, and problematic" subjectivity; qualities of subjects that are, as she puts it, "safe for democracy." By contrast, images of the center's others in its own media remain "uncomplicated, unsophisticated, unproblematic, verifiable, and knowable"; as "incapable or undeserving of 'democracy'" (15).

To pay much attention, from the margins, to the complexity of those centers, she says, risks not only redundancy but is more likely to further their hegemony than their destabilization. While appreciating that these centers can be complex, Trinh urges us to pay more attention to the ways "natives" still are represented in centrist media than to encourage more "appreciation" of the center's diversity. This is the preferred course, she insists, because these images of others continue to "assume the primacy and the centrality of the West, they exclude even as they include, consolidate and package" (15). In this practice of moving to embrace or refuse categories that name the center, she calls upon those who speak from these centers but who are committed to a critique of domination to disconnect themselves from its "most confident master discourses, and . . . [from] all imperialist undertakings" (16).

> Just as in the women's movement where, for example, it is important that women not be the only ones to solve women's problems and to deal with gender politics, it is also crucial that Westerners work with differences, and learn to rename and exile themselves so as not to be lumped together under a unitary label. They would have to participate, as an other among others, in the process of constant renaming and displacing that marginalised groups cannot afford to ignore in this moment of history. (16)

Those who speak from positions of privilege but are given to a critique of domination should "work with differences, and learn to rename and exile themselves"; to participate in processes of "constant renaming and displacing." Constant renaming and displacing; and exile. A constant critique of one's own and others' moves to found, to center, to make and mark a place from which to see and know and secure that which is not "here." And a movement away, an exiling from that familia(r) place.

In the same collection of essays on postcolonial analysis, Iain Chambers (1996) addresses this question of how to speak and write about, but, finally, how to listen for difference from the center or, rather, from what he hopes might become "a third space" beyond the center/periphery dualism: from which both "the West [authority] and its others emerge modified" (49). Chambers urges us to consider again the enormously appropriating and reductive power of Reason's most famous and inseparable twins, language and sight, as they have colonized the space of what is and what can be (kn)own(ed). With his indictment of these twins—language and sight—we see that this central question in postcolonial studies is also central for all social and human science work and, certainly, for sociology and one of its major enterprises: ethnography or fieldwork. That is, these questions from postcolonial studies bear directly on this book's project.

How to consider ethnography's (sociology's) familiar practices of observation, representation, description, and explanation in light of the deconstructive critique of "Western rationality" and its most compelling technology, that is, of science itself? Indeed, one of the things that makes postcolonial criticism so powerful is that it interrogates not only the literary representations of various subordinated and subaltern populations—the imperial and colonial self-characterizations storied by dominating governments, nation-states and classes—but also the once-thought "neutral" and "objective" descriptions and theories that the social sciences have traditionally offered about their objects of study (and of course about themselves, although only implicitly so). This is not to say that these criticisms originated with postcolonial studies, but rather, that this particular version of criticism is positioned to benefit from the earlier and linked work in Marxism, critical theory, feminism, deconstructive criticism, post-structuralism, science studies, cultural studies, and gay, lesbian, and queer studies (see, e.g., Clough 1994).

One of the several important consequences of the disturbances occasioned by these criticisms in the human sciences and their gradual movement into academic social science in the United States is an increasing attention to the positioning and voice of the one who presumes to know and speak about others, that is, the voice from the center. Another is an appreciation of the ways that power flows so unmistakably along these relays that are at the very heart of knowledge and its practices. Indeed, the bringing together of "power" and "knowledge" that is such a central theme of Foucault's (1980) work and also of much feminist criticism has contributed profoundly to the destabilization of the allegedly "neutral" and "objective," "detached" ways of knowing that have founded and continue to ground so many twentieth-century academic and scholarly careers and related subjectivities. Chambers marks the declining legitimacy of these conventional ways of seeing and knowing by suggesting a shift away from metaphors of sight and seeing to a metaphor of listening, of quiet listening for silences that say so much but that have been deemphasized by the conventional practices and personae of sociologists and ethnographers, among others. This notion of quiet listening is also an image that runs through Trinh Minh-ha's work and is often linked especially to practices familiar to women. For both Chambers and Trinh, "truth" is least likely to be appreciated when approached directly; it is more possible, they believe, from a practice of what she has called "listening nearby" (see Chen and Trinh 1994). But a quiet listening nearby calls for a more modest and humble figure than the canons of social science, and even of ethnography, have seemed to encourage.

I first went off to China with my wife, Nancy Schneider, who was going to Tianjin to take up a year-long position to teach English in a foreign languages middle school in the summer of 1985. I went as a spouse, not as a "professor," an "academic," or "expert" in anything. This, ironically, was supposed to be *her* position relative to *me*, a would-be Fulbright lecturer at a major university in Beijing. The materials for "a spouse who might teach English" had come along with the Fulbright application a year earlier, and I had encouraged her to apply, to "give you something to do" and a chance "to see more." But that Fulbright went to a more famous fellow sociologist, and the day I called Washington to find out this news Nancy received a call from China, inviting her to be their "foreign expert." Professionally, this was not the auspicious beginning of the intersection of "China" and me for which I had hoped, and although I was acutely aware of this, I decided not to let it stop me from going along. After all, it was either that or Des Moines, which I felt I knew all too well, having then called it home for as long as I could remember. I had tenure. I had written; and published. It all felt too comfortable, too easy. Whatever "China" was to be—and I knew scarcely little about it—I felt sure it would be very different.

At the time we went to China and I took a break from doing "American" academic sociology, the first rumblings of the criticisms and reflections in the human sciences in the United States from which Trinh and Chambers speak, above, already had surfaced in various small conferences and meetings, although I was then unaware of them. Somewhat later, when I began to hear about "deconstruction," "cultural Marxism," "feminist psychoanalytic criticism," "multiculturalism," "poststructuralism," and the name "Derrida," I found it difficult to see their relevance to sociology, and so paid them only slight attention. Still, because some colleagues who I respected highly seemed to find them so important, I felt these developments couldn't be ignored. A good friend provided a humorous defense under which I could shelter myself for a time. In the bar at sociology conferences, when others would begin to tell of their recent work, he would say, loudly, "Don't tell me if it means I have to know about Derrida!" We laughed, of course, but I suspected that we soon would have to know.

In writing this preface, I aim to provide some context as you begin the first chapter and continue, I hope, to the end of this book. I've been told this is a "hard" book for readers, less because of its content than its forms, which I am sure can try—even perhaps exceed—your patience. For me, it has come to be the only way I can write from the extended and diverse experience I have had with "China" since that summer of 1985. Although I did go to Tianjin as an unemployed spouse, and came to appreciate some of what that can mean when Nancy's school leaders had assumed that I too would teach middle school students oral English (which I did do for a time), before long I was teaching sociology at the local "key" university and enjoying, like my wife, the status of "foreign expert," a label we sometimes took—with pleasure—all too seriously. That one year stretched to two. And although I failed again that second year to receive Fulbright support, thanks to the 1987 Gramm-Rudman Act that cut funding for the award in Tianjin (I was told), the school leaders invited me back, supported by local funds, as did those who had hired Nancy. Wanting, that second year, to have "something to show" back home for my time "in China," I was able to gain access to a local hospital to study how family members cared for their relatives there. That work, more or less successfully done, then became grounds for annual summer revisits to Tianjin and a nurturing of the contacts that had enabled the earlier hospital project.

This currying of local favor put me in Tianjin and Beijing in the exhilarating late spring and fateful early summer of 1989, where disturbances of a different sort were afoot. Nancy was to arrive in Beijing on the evening of June 5, and I had come up from Tianjin to meet her. We were treated, then, to a particular sort of first-hand view of the Beijing "people's government" in action in its brutal suppression of the Tiananmen Square (and other) demonstrations. That view fit, more or less well, with one we had been developing for some time, built on personal tales from friends, students, and acquaintances about their lives during the years of the Cultural Revolution (1966–1976) and before. This image would come later to sit uncomfortably with the characterizations of developing and Third World governments that I found in much writing about postcoloniality. It was difficult to read the regimes of Deng Xiaoping and Jiang Zemin, and, of the post-1949 Mao Zedong as well, in the narratives of the "local" offered in that postcolonial writing.[1] Later, after living and teaching in Hong Kong, 1996–1998, during the much media-ted "handover" of the territory to China, it seemed even more clear that all stories of postcoloniality are not the same. Still, they all seem typically to involve figures of centers, peripheries, and domination.

The final negotiation of the research proposal I had made to the officials at the Tianjin Academy of Social Sciences for a year-long ethnographic study of family caregiving practices in Tianjin, oddly enough, took place in a suburb of Kansas City in the spring of 1990, with tensions from June 4 still very much alive in China and internationally. Nancy and I drove from Des Moines so I could meet with the president of the academy and a senior research colleague during their visit to the States. Although my proposed project did not seem to involve any obviously "sensitive" questions—I then thought—the larger political situation made me skeptical about success. But, over tea and small gifts exchanged, and more than a little anxiety on my part, they gave their final approval of my plan to supply a budget of $5,000 to their academy to support a series of proposed visits to between ten and twenty families, and which called for assigning a young researcher—of their choice—to work with me. Driving back to Des Moines, we commented on how surreal the meeting and final approval seemed. I remember thinking, as we sped toward the sharp horizon of rolling prairie and bright sky, that finally, I would have "something to show" from my by then considerable investments in "China." Mine would be a study few others would be able to match, I (naively) thought. Getting this kind of access to common Chinese people was not easy, even for those sponsored by the Committee on Scholarly Communication with the People's Republic of China.[2] I made this particular comparison because I had been unsuccessful—yet once more—at getting funding from that body for this project. It had, in fact, occurred to me that there was something of a collection of rejections around my foray into "China," and I had more than a few doubts about where it all would lead. But I pressed on. You shouldn't be impressed by that. I think it mostly was because the thought of giving it all up was too frightening to take seriously. At least, when I thought about doing that it made me feel more than a little depressed; like a failure. Inadequate.

During the time when I was laying plans for and describing this year-long project to my would-be sponsors in Tianjin, the various "post-" discourses that had come into the human sciences in the United States from Europe had caused a great stir in various "humanities" disciplines and were, by that time, beginning to be taken more seriously in the social sciences, including sociology. Anthropology was the most consequential early site of these debates, but by 1990 even "mainstream" sociologists could not be sure they would be able to avoid questions about this or that "post-" development or the implications of one or another "feminism" for the familiar ways of thought and work in their fields.

For my own part, back home, I had been teaching an undergraduate seminar on Foucault and reading feminist poststructuralism. Although I didn't often use the word "poststructuralism," I knew that Foucault's work was seen as central to it. My earlier grounding and faith in symbolic interactionist and social constructionist sociology had begun to fragment as I took an increasingly critical, reflexive posture toward my own "interested" defense of some of its centered positions. Through Foucault, and the critique of analytic philosophy and "scientific knowledge" by certain feminists as well as a few "radical" ethnomethodologists (and even a closetreading of Rorty), I had come to see the immemorial complicity of the preferred technologies for knowing, the sorts of subjects they require, the objects they produce, the interests they tend to serve, and the results of those practices and connections. These are precisely those that Chambers and Trinh link to colonial-imperial centers. My professional world and persona, once resting on a conviction that things were divided up more or less neatly into discrete bits it was then the mandate and duty of scientists to connect through empirical research and explanation or, "just good stories," began seriously to blur. I was, indeed, on a "slippery slope." It was a little frightening. More than that, though, it was exciting, even pleasurable.

But I had made a proposal to do a scientific field study of family caregiving in Tianjin, with details of questions to be asked, data collection procedures, interviewing strategies, home visits, note taking, translation, and transcription; of how we would use "theoretical sampling" to focus our inquiry, and about how the study findings could be significantly juxtaposed to existing policy-relevant work on structures of social security and welfare in China's cities. These were qualities I sensed my sponsors understood and found desirable. After all, they were an "Academy of *Social Sciences.*" I had shaped what I thought was a "safe" path of research into "China." I began to realize that it now was shaping me, and in ways I was not sure I altogether liked.

With funds from my home university, I found myself in north China in the summer of 1990, in an intensive course in Chinese language as preparation for the fall project. I was trying to write interview questions, in colloquial Chinese, and had made a weekend trip to Tianjin to meet with the young man assigned to work with me, Wang Laihua. Although enthusiastic and friendly, he knew nothing about fieldwork or ethnography, and had little experience asking the sorts of questions and managing the responses that I imagined we must have. When he said he was looking forward to learning English and sociology from me as we worked in the project, I knew I couldn't tell him about my own doubts about science, sociology, and the very project I had shaped and in which he seemed so excited to participate. And at that point, I had more than a few worries about just what this young man's position in the work would be—just who he would be working for. I knew I needed "an assistant"—my language skills and local knowledge were limited—but I didn't want an "agent" of the academy controlling what I could ask, where I could go, what I could see, all of which were standard fare for social science researchers in late-twentieth-century China.

It was only considerably later, well after our year of work together had ended and my suspicions about Laihua looked more laughably paranoid than practical, that I began to try to explain to him that the book I told him we would write could not be quite as I had described it. I couldn't expect him to understand the path I had taken toward "the English version" of "our China book." Just as he was learning how to speak "scientifically," I was doubting and distancing myself from just that, those, way/s of speaking, knowing, and being.[3] Indeed, it seems fair to say that the centered discourse of science was and, arguably, remains one of the only ways of speaking about contemporary Chinese society that need not necessarily be in service to official Beijing pronouncements and policies (although, it should be said, even that can be the case). I sensed that the critique of conventional notions of science and knowledge that seems to me so right here in the United States could be "counterproductive" to much that I—and probably Laihua and many of his colleagues—might want to encourage, there. My agenda and interests here, then, could not be his; nor his, mine.

Yet, the ostensible practice of "scientific research" had been the occasion for our being connected to each other in ways we could not deny, some of which we only vaguely could see, never mind speak explicitly about in English. The more I read poststructural and feminist critiques of knowledge and truth produced out of relationships between the ones who seek to know and the others who are the objects of those projects—and sociologists surely were to be included in that former category—the more I realized how the weight of the differences between Laihua and me, and the familiar frames in which they are read, could come to overburden this strange but powerful friendship. While I was trying to wander away from the center, without completely losing my way, Laihua was learning the pleasures of stepping into it, or, at least, a particular local version thereof. The book that I had decided could not be would begin to emerge as the "Chinese version," with Laihua as its first—in fact, sole—author and visionary: "a sociological study" of family caregiving and relationships in Tianjin (see Wang and Schneider 1998).

But what of "the English version"? Well. In ways I had never imagined, it has become a real ghost story; an occasion for me to retire the indelible

distinction between what social scientists sometimes call "doing the research," on the one hand, and "writing it up," on the other, with the latter
usually seen as a matter only of "being clear" about what was "found" in
the former. The more or less seamless narrative of social science and
ethnography became increasingly haunted by all or many of the "spirits"
inherited from its ordinary violences. In what follows you will see how the
writing, a certain sort of writing, has become primary, itself a productive
"method" that not only blurs this old distinction between research and
writing but that emerges as never merely an "expression" of the author's
"meaning" and "intent." It had long since become clear to me that taking
care of, giving care to, my own intimates was a part of crafting a certain
persona, a particular subjectivity (although I only much more recently
could speak of it that way). Only later was it apparent that human and
social science writing also provides—after all, it is "writing"—a considerably more expansive and artful space in which persons come to be than I
ever had imagined. In neither case, however, contrary to what I once
argued with such certainty, is this merely the conscious choice and intention of the one who cares or who writes. Rather than the control, clarity,
centeredness, and certainty that have been the measures of Reason and
vision in a science that seeks to tell true stories about others, then, this
"English version," this writing, seeks what might be called a "tethered
dispersion": a simultaneous moving away from while still linked to a "home"
of recognizably familiar practices of research and writing; it effects repeated disloyalties to that home and is seduced by recurrent, self-imposed
exile from it.

   The more I read the various "post-" writings that seek to deconstruct
the social science narrative I had promised to tell about family caregiving
in Tianjin, the more it became apparent that such a story could not, finally
and fully, be told at the same time that one takes seriously the kinds of
criticisms Trinh and Chambers, among many others, make. A slippery
slope is slippery. It takes one elsewhere. But the metaphor is not quite
right: that elsewhere is not necessarily "down." It is, however, surely "away."

   The linear and finely crafted ethnographic narrative that had become
the hallmark, especially, of symbolic interactionist-influenced fieldwork in
U.S. sociology—although perhaps seen by some as a "poor relative" of
the definitive ethnographies that long had stood forth in anthropology,
before "the fall"—and toward which I earlier had aspired, was, for me, at
an "end." In writing this book, I have moved increasingly to effect recom-
mendations such as those from Chambers and others that we remain in
"a space between" center and periphery, between "tradition" and

"progress," between speaking with conviction and remaining silent, between—and therefore both—subject and object, where this "we" would have to include not only the First-World writers of centered truths about "others" but those "others" themselves. And while Laihua may not have the resources, including time, books, encouragement, money, subjectivity, to dwell in this space in-between as do I, our work together, a play with fluid subjectivities in, and our friendship around, this project surely has been the occasion for him to reflect back on his own "home" in critical ways. The "constant renaming and displacing; and exile" that Trinh recommends for those of us at the "center" as a strategy to help undermine the human sciences' contribution to imperialism and domination may not be an appropriate goal for Laihua's "Chinese version"; it seems surely to be so for this one.

And so, this book tries to walk from the familiar ways of conventional ethnography in the human sciences to the edge of its own nonbeing. By turns, it speaks in a voice of certainty and clear vision, and then grave doubt about what these so-familiar resources can lead to in the production of knowledge about the Chinese people we met and interviewed and whose lives we partially story for ends quite other than their own. Sometimes it lets its object go in favor of doubting the subject's hubris to tell the object's truths. To rest in—that is, to "listen" quietly in—these uncertainties is, says Chambers (1996), "imperative": "Otherwise, my desire continues to reproduce the cycles of hegemony that subject the other to *my* categories, to *my* need for alterity. Then my recognition of difference merely becomes the prison for the object of my desire" (54). This is of course as true for Laihua the social scientist in Tianjin as it is for Joseph considering caregivers and a young researcher, there. Living and teaching for two years, near the end of this writing, in Hong Kong, sharing space with various others who take "China" as their beloved object of academic study, helped me understand why I would insist that this surely is not "a book about China," even while, of course, in quite particular ways, it is. Such willingness to let the object go, even to lose it, would seem itself to be something to which those friendly to postcolonial studies must be open. In that letting go, this book offers an often fractured and disturbed flow of images of another sort that might be part of the underbelly or unconscious of ethnography. While it does not seek the "end" of ethnography, although it surely seeks to elaborate some of what Patricia Clough (1998) has called its "end(s)," it refuses, finally, to enact ethnography in the familiar ways, which is, to be sure, a rejection of those forms. Its truths, I hope, are more likely available from, in Trinh's words, "a listening nearby" than a "compelling," or "convincing" and quite familiar voice. The book's being, at minimum, is a claim of legitimacy for some "new" things in the politics and practice of a more mobile and responsible human science in the worlds' new millennia.

1

Closure/Openings/Writing

If ethnography is indeed autoethnography—ethnography of the self and the subject—then the perspective of the formerly ethnographized supplements it irrevocably with the understanding that being-looked-at-ness, rather than the act of looking, constitutes the primary event in cross-cultural representation.

Rey Chow, *Primitive Passions* (1995)

In a perforated history, therefore, the visual field is broken up so that elements of the narrative are experienced as uncanny, a haunted realism. What is thereby made possible is the experience of something for the first time that at the same time seems to be already known, known before—what Freud describes as "the return of the repressed."

Patricia T. Clough, *The End(s) of Ethnography* (1998)

While representing the self implies a pregiven self that is expressed in the writing, *writing* involves a becoming of the self, a making of a self that is not already all of a piece, but, rather, is in process. In writing and in other practices, then, there is the potential for self-transformation . . .

Ann Game and Andrew Metcalfe, *Passionate Sociology* (1997)

Sweaty and winded, I sink into my seat just as the train begins to move out of Tianjin station toward Beijing and our flight home. The air-conditioning in this soft-seat car feels so good. On this trip to China I finally have been able to admit to myself just how much I depend on it to create a private space of comfort.

5 August 1993. So many feelings come at once. We've made a mad dash to number 16, the first-class passenger car that always is just behind the engine and freight car, and always furthest from the entrance to the platform. Nancy sits across from me looking backward, wiping her forehead, tears in her eyes, as I look forward out the window.

"What's wrong? . . . Don't be sad," I say.

"Oh, you know. I hate leaving all our friends behind. It's such a wonderful place. It's such a terrible place. They deserve better. I just want to bring all of them together in one place and live there."

"Yeah, but in what place? And for whose pleasure?"

We've had this conversation before. The particular quality of these friends and our relationships aside, it always seems to say more about the differences between us and them, and our desire to erase or elide those differences into an image of sameness, but on our terms: we, the white, privileged and highly educated Americans from the United States, and they, the variously privileged Chinese intellectuals whom we have come (again and again) to feel so close to over the course of the past decade. I, the American researcher; they, the Chinese researchers and administrators in the Social Sciences Academy that hosts my "research visits"; we, the Chinese and American (from the United States) sociologists, they, the people in the families we interview; we, the Chinese, (t)he(y) the foreigner(s); he, the younger, less experienced (but in what?), deferential . . . son?; I the older, more experienced (but where?, and in what sense?), authoritative . . . father? And we, men; they, women. A growing awareness of the endless play of fantasied similarity and difference in "our" links to "China" have made the notion of seeing things clearly, "the way they really are," seem increasingly quaint. "It's such a wonderful place. It's such a terrible place." What place is this, and seen from where?

But today's leave-taking, for me in any case, has a quality that sets it off. Sadness, of course. Most immediately because of the good-bye to Laihua (that's "Lie-Hwa," his given name, which means—all given Chinese names should have an auspicious meaning—"come to China!") to whom, along with his young daughter and wife, we have become so linked over the course of the research project and our collaboration on this book.

"I didn't get to say a proper good-bye to LH." I feel a catch in my throat and my own tears welling up.

"I know," Nancy sniffles. "I hugged him but you didn't."

"Yes. But I wanted to, you know. And I'm sorry now that I didn't. Men."

And I am sorry. For, more than ever before, my young colleague—"LH," as he began to refer to himself—and I seem to have grown deeply comfortable with each other. But with only fifteen minutes before the train was scheduled to leave as we pulled up in front of the station, and so far to run with our too-heavy bags, it seemed there was no time to linger over a careful good-bye. It was a quick, firm handshake and look; a "thank you so much," and then we were separated by walls and corridors, off toward car 16.

Memories of that moment brought back memories of other separations from him: after ten months of his and my fieldwork and deepening friendship, we three then stood fighting back tears in the lobby of the Beijing-Movenpick Hotel. 17 July 1991. Once apart, the tears came to each of us and marked again what we had by that time taken to be a special connection. And then later, after seven months of his living with us in 1992 in Des Moines, to "continue our writing" and give him a chance to "see America": more tears and sadness. And again in the fall of that year, after less than a month's visit occasioned by his presentation—his first ever in English—at an international conference on caregiving, punctuated by some misunderstandings and turmoil between the two of us: I wanted him to commit to a State-side Ph.D. program, with all the personal and family disruption that would entail; he resisted (rejected?). I pressed. Then: still sadness at good-bye, but no tears; we each perhaps read relief in the other's eyes.

That is what I feel now. I am really glad to be going home this time, unlike the many good-byes we have said to Tianjin since 1985 when Nancy and I first came to China. Relief at a successful five-week visit to re-interview the seventeen families LH and I had visited so many times during our 1990–1991 project on the work and complexities of family caregiving for elderly parents; relief that we managed another period of bike riding, bus riding, eating local foods—just living a piece of everyday life in China—with no apparent mishaps or illness. It's a "developing country," after all. And China is an "other" place. And you never know if you will be able to get the data you need and want. All sorts of things can go wrong.

And it all seemed more physically demanding this time. Perhaps it was the heat and humidity; perhaps my age—then fifty—made it harder not to depend on taxis and Chinese hosts for various conveniences. Or perhaps I was beginning to acknowledge how inevitable such dependence is.

There is a particular sort of relief that comes when you begin to feel closure and an ending to a story that has wandered on for a very long time. And this one had. As I told and retold it, to friends, colleagues, and myself—the story of why I went to China and what I was doing there and what might come of it—I could hear a set of repetitions that I began to like. And I had since learned something about taking and giving pleasure in narrative closure itself. Perhaps this summer trip was another return to enact these fantasies. Whatever it is, it feels so good.

The mystique, exoticness, difference that had so intoxicated me when I first came along to China with my wife when she was hired to teach English in a foreign languages middle school in Tianjin in 1985 had begun to lose their appeal. What had once seemed so foreign and strange, so impossible for me to know, not to mention "write knowledgeably about," was beginning to seem quite familiar. Even my inability to understand Chinese had given way to surprisingly easy talk and hearing, although I still could read and write only a few characters.[1] I had more or less successfully convinced myself that this latter wasn't absolutely necessary to my research. After all, I was not and never will be a sinologist. I'm a U.S. sociologist who has studied some small part of contemporary Chinese life—family relationships around caregiving for elderly parents at home. And given this, the summer's revisits to the seventeen families we earlier had studied went so smoothly and seemed so easy that the sense of accomplishment I had enjoyed two years earlier, just getting into their homes and lives, had faded.

And more researchers studying all aspects of Chinese life, past and present, were coming to China; more cooperative projects had begun, involving famous scholars from famous universities in the United States. It wasn't any longer so strange or unusual to be doing social science research in China rather than interviewing refugees in Hong Kong (see Madsen 1987). And I had always felt self-consciously not famous and not from a famous university. I could hardly even speak Chinese. All of these—I was sure—along with a research design that was probably seen as insufficiently "scientific" and too "personal," had kept me from winning the several grants for which I had applied from the major funding agencies on China research in the United States.

The more deeply I had gone into this project, the more multiple my positioning as an outsider here—and even there, back home—had become. As I sought to inhabit the margins, I indeed experienced marginality, and I didn't like it. But margins always exist relative to, indeed, help to construct, centers. And centers can look different when viewed from the margins, especially if one has long enjoyed the privileges of living in those centers. They even can lose their luster and obvious superiority.

Sometimes I feel suffocated by this project and the relationships, around it; unable to get free of them and unable to succeed with them. I am not at all sure that I can gain closure, can "make something" out of it; be the "hero" of this ethnographic narrative (see Clough 1998, 15–28; Atkinson 1990, 106–110). Be . . . a "real man"? But that you are reading this, now, should dissuade you from worrying about that too much (of course, that line was written well before your reading was a "sure thing").

And there are many more "foreigners" in China now who have other sorts of profits in mind: to take advantage of, indeed to create, vast commercial markets and/or similarly vast pools of cheap labor in a state only gradually given to controls and regulations to protect people and the environment. The urban landscape had changed, even in the two years since our last leaving. Endless restaurants, stalls, sellers, concerns about money, street-wise beggars, uncontrolled enterprise, cellular phones, McDonalds, and even Cadillacs. *Caveat emptor!* These are all too familiar. After all, we are Americans, from the United States. China, Tianjin—the strange, alluring, and slightly sinister, "Communist" place—has been had. And part of the relief I was feeling seemed linked to a growing sense that I too could have a piece of the action. Finally, I was beginning to feel that I could actually write author-itatively about it too.

*****

Discipline frowns on such writing for a "scholarly" work that does not announce itself explicitly as fiction or autobiography. More particularly, social science canons frown on fiction and autobiography, both of which have too much of the author in the text, texts that are, rather, to be about "the world," not about the author, as though the two could be treated as completely separate. Much too self-absorbed; self-indulgent; narcissistic; feminine; not objective. *Ergo:* this is not a scholarly work and it certainly isn't social science (it certainly isn't sociology). Still, the announcement reads: academic sociology. This text, its very existence in your hands, is then something of an "intervention," as it is fashionable in some circles to say, into, in resistance to, precisely the discipline that frowns on it. But it is a resistance from within that very discipline. And it is allowed and put together only in the current moment of change in the "Western" academy that may be defined broadly as a critique of convention and canon itself, and an insistence on the centrality, indeed, constitutive quality, of language, of writing, to what the human sciences do and are.[2]

But what about the "Eastern" academy? What about these kinds of challenges to discipline, to the "law" (of . . . ?) in China? The ironies here further the shifting and multiple positions. These same desires to question, to doubt, to challenge discipline and authority—in the name of "other" knowledges if not scrutiny of knowledge practices themselves—can be found in contemporary China, albeit not so publicly. But the universities, and particularly the social sciences and what in English would be called the humanities, seem not to be the places to look for them; at least not today. In fact, discipline seems to be the order of the day in Chinese universities, and especially among those departments in which the social, the literary, and the critical might be expected to exist. Since the most recent repression of intellectuals and social criticism following 1989 (*"Liu si,"* or 6/4, or June 4, as those sympathetic to these events call it; those not—or careful to display a "not" in practice—call it *"luan"* or disorder), sociology has become something of a pariah discipline, having been identified as one of the main sources of student and faculty protest and criticism during May of that year (see, e.g., Calhoun 1994).

Instead of thoughtful, reflective criticism, new students at key Chinese universities in the wake of June 4 were investing most of their first year in military training, the details of which are the essence of discipline. Military training from within the very heart of the place where a critique of certain versions of discipline had struggled to be heard and joined. So while a theme of this book is explicitly to push against discipline, to disturb it (albeit with comparatively limited risk), discipline in the key universities of China—and perhaps even in the United States—likely would be scandalized by its form and aim; by its seemingly gratuitous disrespect.

But more immediately, what might LH's "leaders"—his bosses—think of such a work and his co-authorship?

"I think that is no problem. Anyway, not a big problem."

And the kinds of disciplines in China that are incomparably old compared to those of the very recent government long since have begun to change and to be challenged: the disciplines of the father (which are of course in some senses also the disciplines of the recent government and past governments and past dynasties) and of the family. Such changes in and challenges to the disciplines of the Father are ones that Americans, from the United States, are very familiar with, which, of course, shouldn't be taken to suggest that they are simply being "replayed" in a delayed evolutionary development in China. Nor does it suggest that "we" in some sense "know about," "understand," what the local truths that accompany the cracking of these family and fatherly disciplines in China might look like in their lived particulars because "We've been through it"; or, what the significance of these changes might be said to be when written in the narratives called "History," if they are written there at all (Duara 1995).

But in the "Western" academy it is a moment in which orthodoxy is under critical scrutiny, a moment inviting a discourse privileging heterodoxy in the strategies for producing knowledge and allocating space and time and voice to diversity over uniformity, to movement over stasis; indeterminacy over surety, the partial over the total. It is a moment when one sort of discipline is being challenged by others that—in their best incarnations—even as they imply an orthodoxy turn quickly to undermine it. A moment of heterodoxy in which, ideally, each position admits of a humility and acknowledges that only by speaking of multiple truths and by speaking *with* those whose lives and selves these truths story, can productive and a more ethical scholarly and academic speaking take place at all. Truth and objectivity can be spoken only insofar as their partiality and the social locations and bodies from which they emerge are foregrounded.[3]

Oh, God. But what if the "center does not hold"? We Chinese know disorder, *luan,* all too clearly and painfully. It tracks us. Cycles of order and disorder. It goes back very far with us. You Americans—I should say you white middle-class Protestant Americans from the United States—don't know. Perhaps you highly educated professors can't even imagine it. The "pleasure" of disorder? Spoken from the center? Still . . .

Here in the United States, "family" has become explicitly rather than just implicitly politicized; a site for struggles over the very notion of what an intimate, sustained "we," even an "I," can look like; over what words like "commitment," "duty," "love," and "responsibility" can possibly mean; over who can love and/or exploit whom, and how strong "family ties" can be. Discipline in this space of the family is being challenged to its very core, and it also mightily resists these challenges, usually with the help and endorsement of the State and its law (of the father?).[4]

But perhaps I am being too black-hearted about discipline. As Foucault helped us see, power also has a productive face. It enables as well as prohibits; it does much more than simply say "No!" At the least, order, stability, canons, meta/master narratives, hegemonic processes—the "modern"?—mark a place of departure for these sorts of comments; they mark what one is not, or wants not to be; and what one seeks to change or resist. And I should of course say that such resistant speaking/writing itself requires a secure place in which to stand; from which to speak and write "about"; a slowing down of the endless play of signifiers that deconstruction has brought to our attention; a standpoint, perhaps; a positioning.[5] To speak, to write about is to constitute for us a centered, even if briefly so, embodied place; it is, indeed, to create an "I"; and it is thus to effect a flow of power and desire, topics the discipline of sociology and the social sciences rarely see as relevant to their knowledges and work.[6]

*****

In China, one's family long has been seen as the most important kind of insurance and support against the infirmities of old age and illness.

While family members today remain the primary caregivers for their sick and elderly relatives, a series of changes currently underway in Chinese society—perhaps most notably, here, the effects of the one-child family policy and the market economy—make these present family caregiving arrangements untenable for the future (see Ikels 1990a, b). There simply will not be enough people in the adult children's generation, nor enough state-supported social services, given present availability, to reproduce the present more informal and family-centered care. More supplements from outside the family will be needed.

Toward a clearer understanding of the implications of these changes, we studied some aspects of present family caregiving practices for such elderly and ill persons at home in Tianjin, China's third largest city located roughly 80 miles (124 km) southeast of Beijing. We used as a research site the family sickbed (jiating bingchuang), a hospital-based program where doctors and nurses make home visits to monitor and give treatment to chronically ill, mainly elderly, patients left in the care of their family members. In this paper we use data from that ten-month field study, supplemented by hospital and government documents and data, to examine how care for a small number of sick and elderly people was managed at home.

First, we briefly describe the field study and discuss the history and nature of the family sickbed program. The balance of the paper examines the central contributions family members made to home care, supplemented by neighbors, friends, and the patient's work unit. We close with speculation about possible future problems and developments in home care in China.

Wang and Schneider (1993, 331)

*****

That is how we began an article about our research that was published in *The Journal of Cross-Cultural Gerontology*. The form is more recognizably social science. It opens with a strong, declarative sentence about the world, made from nowhere, hence everywhere. It arrogates to itself the prerogative to speak about "China" and things Chinese in an authoritative way. It cites research-based truths and promises more. It pronounces change; an impending crisis is implied and important implications are suggested; and a glimpse into the future is to be offered up, yielding understanding and order in the face of the unsettled moment it has announced and will document. Rhetorically, the opening paragraph sets up both an historical and a textual tension that subsequent pages will resolve or, failing that, reduce. This story has a beginning and an end.

The second paragraph specifies the grounds on which this knowledge and understanding of the world rest: "data," facts. Invoking the muse of all science, observation, the authors assure the reader that they will tell the Truth of family caregiving in Tianjin, and, by extension, urban China, because they themselves were there; "collected" data; went into sick and elderly people's families to actually "see" what was going on there for themselves (but of course, these are not just any "selves"). They systematically interviewed the people who received and gave this care—over a ten-month period—and also gained access to restricted "hospital and government documents." Both the paper and the journal announce them as scientists.

This more proper, more disciplined, writing tells the reader what will follow, and what he or she should follow: details about research design and sample, the steps followed in carrying out the research; the research results—the "findings"—drawn together by conclusions and predictions. What was initially unknown or only vaguely known; strange, perhaps even exotic; at the least, once puzzling, will here be rendered familiar, linked to prior reasoned knowledge; understood; becalmed. These are the key elements of the rhetoric of science, and in particular, social science. It is a rhetoric that is extraordinarily powerful in its capacity to encourage readers to suspend disbelief through the claim that the practices of scientific research, if sufficiently sophisticated and refined, produce some sort of direct access to the world. Indeed, the very assumption of the world, always waiting patiently "out there" to be known, independent of knowers and observers, is at the very heart of scientific practice and thought.[7] What we will describe was going on before we arrived "there" and continues, now; but you will know about it, too, because we went there and have come back to tell you.

These claims rest on a view of the scientist—the carrier of knowledge about the world—as one whose most important particular influence in the search for Truth comes only in the selection of the research question or problem. After that, the influence of the researcher is couched primarily in terms of how skillful, disciplined—how well *trained*—he or she is in the conventional techniques of producing knowledge that one's science demands. To the extent that what might be called "the personal" enters into scientific work at all, it is to be limited to the choice of what to study.[8]

And this is especially true for the social sciences, where contamination of one's research by the personal is thought to be a greater risk than in the natural sciences. For instance, Robert might choose to specialize in "intergroup relations" and "ethnicity" because (as he might say if asked "Why this topic?") of his own experience as a Jew in a largely non- if not anti-Jewish world; or Racquel might choose to do research on the psychological differences between men and women because (again, as she might say if asked "Why?") of her sense of unequal treatment growing up as a girl/woman in a world where boys/men seem to count for more. But once Robert and Racquel began their research, they, according to the discourse of scientific method, should be interchangeable. Particulars about each of them are to disappear. That their "personal" lives (and we might speculate as to what is implied as the opposite of "personal") and experiences might influence their scientific work, once begun; that human being might intimately inflect and "infect" the very doing of science, can only be seen as an intrusion on the value and worth of the results. These things are extraneous; not "about the world" under study. Even more egregious is the move to explicitly and quite intentionally bring the personal of the would-be objective scientist into the text; to make the personal, the "private," an object for the reader's gaze. Beyond irrelevant and disruptive, it's almost unseemly.[9] It does indeed undermine objectivity as a practice, and the self/centrality of the reader as well.[10]

*****

Bill died on 23 April 1985, after almost twenty years living with heart disease and the medical interventions around his gradually worsening condition. He had a massive heart attack . . . well, we said that, anyway; whatever kind it was, the muscle could no longer do its deadeningly routine but vital work. He died on the bedroom floor of the Florida retirement home he and Sara bought after leaving Des Moines, late one night as fire medics worked over his body, and as Sara, knowing this was the end but so hoping it was not, looked on.

In an earlier version of this chapter I had written "father" and "mother" where I now have Bill and Sara. I have had two fathers and mothers, which allows a certain opportunity for a second try at some things as well as some much valued distance on the kinds of things that these relationships of family can produce. Bill was not and Sara is not my "real" father and mother, but he certainly was the father I never had while growing up in a white working-class family where my parents had divorced by the time I was five. Although my desire for this second father was great, I felt it rather than understood it at the time I became a ward under his and Sara's care. This came late, during the summer I turned eighteen, amid deep trouble between me and my "real" mother's second husband. Now, as I recall that triangular relationship, I wonder how Freud could have known the details of our lives so well. Perhaps not surprisingly, this mobility in "fathers" and "mothers," "mother's second husband," would-be and surrogate mothers and fathers has allowed a certain skepticism on the importance of "blood" or "real" relations in families and on the idea that families have to be put together only in certain ways.

Just Sara and Bill were at home when it began, my two brothers . . . well, their two "real" sons (I was an "only child" in my first family) and I were far away in Texas and Iowa; asleep, or about to be. Although she thinks he already was dead, there on the floor, they took him to the hospital. She rode in the ambulance; waited alone in the darkened and quiet corridor outside the emergency room, and when her worst fears were confirmed by the ER doctor on duty, she went in to take her last good-bye kiss.

I always insisted on having the phone by my side of the bed. Although I didn't put it this way to Nancy, I felt this is what I should do. *"Zhe shi wo yinggai zuode."* Which is what so many adult Chinese sons and daughters said to LH and me about what they did for their sick parents. "This is what I *should* do." It is my duty. This comment came especially when I— not LH, for he knew the answer already and thus didn't ask the question—wondered why they worked so hard, or did so much for their parent's care; or when we praised them in any way for what they had done and were doing. It always resonated in a very particular way when I heard it. *"Zhe shi wo yinggai zuode."* What I didn't allow myself to see so clearly when I was insisting on the phone's location, along with so many other elements of the performed "what I should do," was that what I was doing for my father, the "care" I was doing was ever so much for me as well.

The phone had to be there because what if my mother called me during the night to say that she had just spoken to the doctor and the ambulance was on its way to take my father to the hospital? What if my wife, Nancy, answered and didn't handle it right? What if I didn't hear the phone, and she didn't either, even though it was just beside her? No. In order for me to be able to do what I had to do, the phone had to be there, beside me; just in case. I really *needed* it that way. In fact, it had worked just this way several times in the past.

But when *that* call came, early on the morning of 24 April 1985, with words that simultaneously haunt and free a son, what could be done? Nothing.

"Hello. Hello?"

"Oh, Joey." I knew the voice at once, but it was not the same. It was distorted by what it had to say. "Billy died last night."

"Oh no! Oh no! When? What happened?" But even as I asked that question, I knew it was just to keep a footing; just to have something to say. I listened without breathing. Billy died last night.

"He said he was having chest pains. . . . Got his pills . . . was having a very hard time breathing. . . . I called the . . . but I knew."

And I had so loved being a son to this father (although it wasn't always easy—I was "a good boy," even as an adult). It was actually the space within which I came to re-create myself as someone different from the Joe King of my "real" family. Well, of course, it wasn't a wholly "I" accomplishment, but there was a great deal of willfulness in it (it's easy to feel embarrassed by how skilled I became at speaking and embodying what I much later learned to call "patriarchal discourses"; but then I remember how embarrassment can discipline subjectivity to keep messiness and contradiction at bay, and so I try to let those feelings go). In the working and reworking of memory, I can see "Schneider" emerging to mark a space of opportunity to be a new kind of person; a one who "Joe King" was not; a some body who I never was when I was a son the first time. And what he, Bill, gave me—I'm sure it is what feminists call the "Law"— were resources to "be somebody," indeed ways to be in the world, to move through it with confidence; to "make things happen"; to speak and be listened to. Indeed, the right to speak and be listened to, and a way of seeing myself, all finally underwritten by his Name (quite literally; I became Joseph Schneider, taking his name and "correcting" the working-class ignorance [I thought, wrongly] of my "real" parents in not knowing "Joe" was diminutive [an apt word] for "Joseph"). His gift, among others, was the hubris and confidence of white upper middle-class masculinity.

All of this I came, later, to repay in care given (although the metaphor isn't quite right; I don't know where one finds the "balance sheet," or how to decide if it is indeed balanced), but not out of a sense of duty. *"Zhe shi wo yinggai zuode."* Not. In fact, other family members—especially Sara's— thought it strange that I was so attentive, so ready to please. After all, I was not a real son. But I did want so to please him. And when he got sick and then sicker and sicker, I saw more chances to show just what a caring and loving person, son, I was, although mostly only in intense, short stretches of time rather than in everyday, deadening routines. That care was the burden Sara dutifully took on, and which she did so well. It feels important to say that my care for Bill was a physical care, not just being a go-fer; not just a "taking care of business." I touched him; rubbed his back, his feet; clipped his toenails; helped him turn in bed after his heart and abdominal surgery; helped him shower; combed his hair; held him up as he tried to catch his breath in one or another of the many emergency hospital stays. Touching him seemed like a particularly good way to care. A natural thing to do. Although he gave me resources for performing a more convincing masculinity, my positioning in giving him care was—and perhaps this is what unsettled without being actually spoken—quite feminine. I loved him very much.

But I also came, finally, to feel that love as a burden. *Zhe shi wo yinggai zuode.* Yes. More and more I saw that in trying to please him I had to "give in," to submit to this way of seeing, that way of doing—his way—the weight made heavier by his vulnerability and illness, which he was not above using to control the smallest of details of speech, dress, time, and physical environment in this circle, this container, of care. Being different from what the Father wanted seemed less and less possible. Alas. What I always thought I wanted to be, a "real" son to this father, but wasn't, gradually felt less like a burden and more like an excuse for distance. Of course, I didn't put it so baldly, certainly not to others, nor even to myself. As attention to the expectations for my two younger brothers, the "real" sons, seemed to grow, I sat more quietly and with some comfort, on the margins. This is not a new story. It is all too familiar. Can we call it oedipal? Yes, at least partly so, although I didn't, then.

*****

The fundamental fact of Confucianism is that it is primarily a secular social theory, the foremost purpose of which is to achieve a harmonious society. Indeed, harmony is the most treasured social value (Bodde 1953, 19–80). But how is a harmonious society possible? To this question, Confucians invariably answer that if *every* individual were to act towards others in a proper way, then an orderly world would be achieved. The proper way is prescribed by the dictates *li* (propriety), a set of rules for action (Fingarette 1972, 53). In sociological terms, Confucianism perceives the ideal society as a massive and complicated role system. The conception of role is in fact embedded in the doctrine of *zheng ming* (rectification of names; Mote 1972, 49).

"Let the ruler be a ruler, the father a father, the son a son," and so forth (Lau 1979, chapter 12, paragraph 11). The guidelines for instantiating these various roles are defined by *li,* which can be conceptualized as the grammar of relationships.

In a thought-provoking article, Francis Hsu (1971, 23–44) argues that personality is a Western concept rooted in individualism, and he proposes that the central ingredient in the human mode of existence is man's relationship with his fellow men. Accordingly, Hsu proposes the *ren* (human-heartedness) approach of Confucianism in contrast to the Western approach, which focuses on anomic individuals and their intrapsychic dynamics. Indeed, it seems to us that the Confucian conception of man cannot be neatly characterized by Western concepts of individualism or holism and should be considered in its own terms (King 1981).

In Confucian social theory, the individual is never conceived of as an isolated, separate entity; man is, by Confucian definition, a social, or interactive, being (Moore 1967, 5). Using the words of Hu Shih (1919), the late contemporary Chinese philosopher, "In the Confucian human-centered philosophy, man cannot exist alone; all actions must be in a form of interaction between man and man" (283). Not unlike Emile Durkheim, Confucians (at least, Confucians of Hsun-Tzu's persuasion) see society as a humanizing agent: to them, being human is conditional on a man's being obedient to social norms in daily interactions (Bauman 1976, 26–57). It is no accident that the Chinese character *ren* means two men. As Lin Yusheng (1974–1975) put the matter, "*Ren* can only be cultivated and developed in inter-human relationships in a social context" (193).

Indeed, Confucius, the founder of Confucian School, is concerned with the nature of *humanity* rather than the polar concepts *individual* and *society* (Fingarette 1972, 72–73). Liang Shu-ming (1974, 94) presents a perceptive thesis that the traditional Chinese society is neither individual-based nor society-based, but relation-based. Liang writes that in a relation-based social system, "the emphasis is placed on the relation between particular individuals" (94). The focus is not fixed on any particular individual but on the particular nature of the relation between individuals who interact with each other (see also Solomon 1971). Put differently, in the Confucian paradigm of man, man is socially situated, defined, and shaped in a relational context. In brief, man is a relational being (King 1981, 19–24). A relational being is sensitive to his relations with others, above, below, or on equal footing with him. He sees himself situated symbolically in the web of a relational network through which he defines himself.

It must also be acknowledged, however, as De Bary (1970) correctly notes, that "the relations alone . . . do not define a man totally. His interior self exists at the center of this web and there enjoys its own freedom" (149). Confucians recognize and attach great importance to the *ji* (self). While stressing, on the one hand, the importance of relations between and among individuals, Confucians emphasize, on the other, that the individual is not simply a being shaped and determined by his role-relational structure. Ultimately, the individual is more than a role-player mechanically performing the role-related behavior prescribed by the social structure. To use Meadian terminology, the individual consists of a self (*ji* in Confucian terms) that is an active and reflexive entity. Confucians assign the individual self the capacity to do right or wrong, and, ultimately, the individual alone is responsible for what he is. This voluntaristic view of the individual is crystallized in the unique Confucian concept of *xiu-ji* (self-cultivation). Self-cultivation is a process that involves a subtle interplay between role and identity. And in the process, the ideal of sincerity is essential. The attainment of sincerity is the way of men. The Doctrine of the Mean says, "He who attains to sincerity is he who chooses what is good and firmly holds it fast" (Legge 1960, 324). For Confucians, sincerity is indispensable to the achievement of true self. In the eyes of Confucius, nothing is more unbearable than a *xiang-yuan* who was condemned as "the thief of virtue" simply for his lack of moral autonomy and courage in being unable to hold a consistent stand towards right and wrong (Legge 1960, 324).

The Confucian paradigm of man, in short, is sociological but not sociologistic. It basically sees man as a relational being, who achieves his humanism through interaction with other particular individuals. His self-image and character are shaped by his role in this relational structure. But the individual is not merely a player of roles prescribed by *li*; he has an active self that is capable of shaping the role relationship he enters.

King and Bond (1985, 30–32)

*****

"Zhe shi wo yinggai zuode." But this time not for its meaning, its substance. Rather, for the sound of Chinese language rendered in Romanized letters, enabling some formation or imagined formation of speech, of words said and exchanged elsewhere; of difference. Once these words are sayable, then said, various meanings might follow. Can you do it? In fact, what do you usually do when you read up against words from languages you cannot speak? Perhaps you can "speak Chinese" (but Cantonese or Mandarin? And what about dialects?) and thus it isn't a problem, isn't a sticking point in the flow of reading pleasure. You can understand it all, can't you? But once you couldn't. What did you do then? I'll bet you just black-boxed it, treated it as something you couldn't make out and that, in any case, likely would be reiterated in translation into *your* language in the next moment. It's strange and undecipherable. Foreign. Too slow. Let it go. It's not important, and if it is important, worth knowing, the writer will tell you what it means. If she doesn't, then you can't be bothered with it. Full stop. After all, the text is in English. But can you do it? Try.

The first word is *zhe*. In a kind of "folk-phonetics," you say the word choke without the k while curling your tongue back as if to make an "r" sound—but don't round your lips into an "o."[11] Then *shi*, which is like saying "sir" with an *h* between the *s* and *i*: "shir" (not "sheer"; but sir + *h* after the *s*: sh-ir; but without the "sir" perhaps it should be "sh-er," said in one sound). *Wo* is an important one, especially for us Americans, from the United States. It means "I." It's like this: "Woooooaaah," with a "long" o and a single, smooth sound. Say it. Out loud. "Woooooaaah." The next word, *yinggai*, is pretty easy. The *ing* is just like "our" *ing*; singing, hiking, caring. *Gai* is in this case a second syllable of this one word, *yinggai*. In fact, it also is a separate word, *gai,* with a meaning that is the same as the first part of the compound, which is also a free-standing word, *ying* (and both words mean "should"). The sound of *gai* is not "gay." Chinese people sometimes insist that there are no homosexuals in China, and that if there are, they are victims of spiritual or some other kind of pollution from the outside (but you should read Hinsch [1990] on this point). *Gai* is pronounced quite like (just like, as far as I can hear it) "guy" (but remember, no dogs or gay guys allowed!). *Yinggai;* pretty easy. Finally, *zuode*: it looks strange, I know. Think of it in terms of its two parts, *zuo* and *de*. Suddenly it looks manageable. The first word, actually the only real word here, is troublesome because of the *uo,* which is easily mistaken by native English speakers as a diphthong-kind of mark, something that gets rendered in one unitary sound. Here, it's a little like the *wo,* above, in that it is a smooth movement of sound that is approximated by "zoowoah." Then you just add the *de* (not a long e but a short one): *zuode* zoo-woah-de. Now, all together: *Zhe shi wo yinggai zuode!* This is what I should do. Literally: "this is I should do."

Perhaps you think it is silly to spend so much of your valuable time here trying to urge you to make sounds that are unfamiliar to you; to read and say a sentence in Chinese. It's beside the point. I've told you what it means. What more do you need to know? But then perhaps you should consider that I haven't mentioned the four spoken tones that are another part of Mandarin Chinese words, and that differentiate meaning and produce proper sound. And of course there is something else. Here is another version of *"Zhe shi wo yinggai zuode."* Can you do it?

这是我应该作的

And here it is in my own best hand:

这是我应该作的

Are these differences that matter? What do they matter? Is it all just a question of translation?

If you are willing to linger over this word *ren* that King and Bond underline, it can illustrate how even Chinese language points to the importance of links *between* people; of relationships, they say. This word is relatively easy to say, *"ren"* (try it, please), but apparently not so easy for those of us who move in a late-capitalist, "postmodern" society to embody. King and Bond (1985, 30) juxtapose Confucian "human-heartedness" to what they call "Western . . . anomic individuals and their intrapsychic dynamics." The view from King and Bond is a (mostly implicit) critique of the "Western" and an affection for the Confucian or "Eastern." This latter conception is of a society rather than of individuals; of propriety rather than self-indulgence; of responsibility and duty to one's others rather than a self-centeredness; of a search for the ideal self at the center of a web of connections to others, a self that should "do the right thing": ". . . the central ingredient in the human mode of existence is man's relationship with his fellow men" (30); ". . . the individual is never conceived of as an isolated, separate entity; man is . . . a social, or interactive, being" (31). And: ". . . man cannot exist alone; all actions must be in a form of interaction between man and man"; ". . . being human is conditional on a man's being obedient to *social* norms in daily interactions" (emphasis added). Indeed, King and Bond point out: "It is no accident that the Chinese character *ren* means two men."

But, King and Bond argue (especially after one variety of Confucian thought), this does not mean the absence of an "inner self." Confucian-inflected thought is not "sociologistic": "the relations alone do not define a man totally. His *interior self* exists at the center of this web and there enjoys its own freedom" (De Bary 1970, 149; emphasis added). These men can do the wrong thing, and of course regularly are so tempted (often, as the familiar story goes, by women). But what women do in this vision of "Chinese Society" (other than tempting and distracting men) is harder to fathom in these texts. The self here might even be seen as similar to that described by G.H. Mead (1934), that is, as "active *and* reflexive" (King and Bond 1985, 31; emphasis added). *"Zhe shi wo yinggai zuode."* But it's a "man's world." What about women?—A question that has been raised to embarrass more than a few "Western" social philosophies and that now can no longer be ignored, at least in U.S. public academic circles.

*****

Surely, one of the most eloquent and powerful voices of this century on women and gender in China is that of Maxine Hong Kingston. Her book, *The Woman Warrior* (1981a), and the later book, *China Men* (1981b), are unparalleled for the moral vision and emotional power they offer about women's lives in the postimperial, prerevolutionary period from 1912 to 1949, and of the experiences of Chinese women and men in the United States (and in "the Golden Mountain" of California, in particular). We draw on Hong Kingston here to suggest what she might say to the question, "What about women?" in this world that, arguably, still is "of men."

My American life has been such a disappointment.

"I got straight As, Mama."

"Let me tell you a true story about a girl who saved her village."

I could not figure out what was my village. And it was important that I do something big and fine, or else my parents would sell me when we made our way back to China. In China there were solutions for what to do with little girls who ate up food and threw tantrums. You can't eat straight As.

When one of my parents or the emigrant villagers said, "Feeding girls is feeding cowbirds," I would thrash on the floor and scream so hard I couldn't talk. I couldn't stop.

"What's the matter with her?"

"I don't know. Bad, I guess. You know how girls are. 'There's no profit in raising girls. Better to raise geese than girls.'"

"I would hit her if she were mine. But there's no use wasting all that discipline on a girl. 'When you raise girls, you're raising children for strangers.'"

"Stop that crying!" my mother would yell. "I'm going to hit you if you don't stop. Bad girl! Stop!" I'm going to remember never to hit or to scold my children for crying, I thought, because then they will only cry more.

"I'm not a bad girl," I would scream. "I'm not a bad girl. I'm not a bad girl." I might as well have said, "I'm not a girl."

"When you were little, all you had to say was 'I'm not a bad girl,' and you could make yourself cry," my mother says, talking-story about my childhood.

I minded that the emigrant villagers shook their heads at my sister and me. "One girl—and another girl," they said, and made our parents ashamed to take us out together. The good part about my brothers being born was that people stopped saying, "All girls," but I learned new grievances. "Did you roll an egg on *my* face like that when I was born?" "Did you have a full-month party for *me?*" "Did you turn on all the lights?" "Did you send *my* picture to Grandmother?" "Why not? Because I'm a girl? Is that why not?" "Why didn't you teach me English?" "You like having me beaten up at school don't you?"

"She is very mean, isn't she?" the emigrant villagers would say.

"Come, children. Hurry. Hurry. Who wants to go out with Great-Uncle?" On Saturday mornings my great-uncle, the ex-river pirate, did the shopping. "Get your coats, whoever's coming."

"I'm coming. I'm coming. Wait for me."

When he heard girls' voices, he turned on us and roared, "No girls!" and left my sisters and me hanging our coats back up, not looking at one another. The boys came back with candy and new toys. When they walked through Chinatown, the people must have said "A boy—and another boy!" At my great-uncle's funeral I secretly tested out feeling that he was dead—the six-foot bearish masculinity of him.

I went away to college—Berkeley in the sixties—and I studied, and I marched to change the world, but I did not turn into a boy. I would have liked to bring myself back as a boy for my parents to welcome with chickens and pigs. That was for my brother, who returned alive from Vietnam.

If I went to Vietnam, I would not have come back; females desert families. It was said, "There is an outward tendency in females," which meant that I was getting straight As for the good of my future husband's family, not my own. I did not plan ever to have a husband. I would show my mother and father and the nosy emigrant villagers that girls have no outward tendency. I stopped getting straight As.

And all the time I was having to turn myself American-feminine, or no dates.

There is a Chinese word for the female . . .—which is "slave". Break the women with their own tongues!

I refused to cook. When I had to wash dishes, I would crack one or two. "Bad girl," my mother yelled, and sometimes that made me gloat rather than cry. Isn't a bad girl almost a boy?

"What do you want to be when you grow up, little girl?"

"A lumberjack in Oregon."

Even now, unless I'm happy, I burn the food when I cook. I do not feed people. I let the dirty dishes rot. I eat at other people's tables but won't invite them to mine, where the dishes are rotting.

If I could not-eat, perhaps I could make myself a warrior like the swordswoman who drives me. I will—I must—rise and plough the fields as soon as the baby comes out.

Once I get outside the house, what bird might call me; on what horse could I ride away? Marriage and childbirth strengthen the swordswoman, who is not a maid like Joan of Arc. Do the women's work; then do more work, which will become ours too. No husband of mine will say, "I could have been a drummer, but I had to think about the wife and kids. You know how it is." Nobody supports me at the expense of his own adventure. Then I get bitter: no one supports me; I am not loved enough to be supported. That I am not a burden has to compensate for the sad envy when I look at women loved enough to be supported. Even now China wraps double binds around my feet.

Kingston (1981a, 47–49)

*****

人 ren 1. human being; man; person; people. . . . 2. adult; grown-up. . . . 3. a person engaged in a particular activity. . . . 4. other people; people. . . . 5. personality; character. . . . 6. state of one's health; how one feels. . . . 7. everybody; each. . . . 8. manpower; hand. (Beijing Foreign Languages Institute 1983, 571)

The above entry from *The Pinyin Chinese-English Dictionary,* compiled by a committee of "over fifty people, both Chinese and non-Chinese" focuses on *"modern* Chinese" usage and *"modern* English" translations (emphasis supplied; from the foreword). One searches in vain for "human-heartedness" here (but, of course, *that* is a different *ren,* but you wouldn't know unless it is written: 仁 [two men, two people, meaning "human-heartedness"]). Please note the publication date: 1983.

The entry that immediately follows *ren* in this dictionary is *renbenzhuyi,* humanism; and the one after that is, apparently, "an old Chinese saying": *ren bu wei ji, tianzhu di mie* —"unless a man looks out for himself, Heaven and Earth will destroy him; everyone for himself and the devil take the hindmost." Perhaps the exotic is more familiar than we think.

*****

"Human-heartedness" (*ren* 仁) may be less and less easy to embody for those of us who move in a "rapidly developing state socialist market economy." Today in China, it seems that everyone is interested in making money. This is something we heard, I hear, often as we talked to friends and acquaintances and family in Tianjin. From the space of post-1997 Hong Kong it is a deafening and very familiar roar. The newspapers, and certainly neighborhood and work unit gossip, provide stories of people who challenge the propriety not only of *li* but of the state's own rules. Many of these stories turn on money: the demand for it; resentments and hatreds over not getting it; greed; and the price, the costs, of getting and having it. Officials take bribes, ignore laws designed to "serve the people." Indeed, "Serve the People!" is more likely as a gag line in popular culture these days than a solemn commitment. Primary and secondary schools now exact huge sums from parents who want to send their children to "the best." (What would Chairman Mao say? Who cares?) Doctors take *hong bao* or "red packets" of money, under (and sometimes even on) the table and against regulations, for doing their jobs. College students post bills on the street advertising their services as tutors for young children whose parents want them to pass difficult entrance exams. Prostitution grows (Hershatter 1997, 327–392). And so on. Of course, not all and every, but not rarely, either. Young adult children leave their elderly parents to go abroad for study and work—or to go to Shenzhen or Hong Kong, if they can, for more "opportunity"—less common, apparently; but the stories circulate to mark the anxieties. "Humanheartedness" can suffer under these circumstances. You in America have some experience with this (albeit perhaps you are not so monolithically selfish as the figure King and Bond conjure).

In any case, before the recent return of repressed capitalism in China, the Communist Party had done a good deal to put and keep humanheartedness in its place, even as it endlessly reiterated a public discourse that placed "the people" at the center. As part of the many campaigns launched after Liberation (from capitalism and other evils) in 1949, but especially from the late 1950s until the late 1970s, Confucius's notions of how society should be, and of how relationships should work, were attacked as "feudal" and "backward." Precisely the kinds of loyalties and expectations that were to bind people together—"Let the ruler be a ruler, the father a father, the son a son"—were attacked by the state and the party as "old" and as obstacles in the way of socialist progress.[12] Rather than loyalty being properly paid to one's elders, one's ancestors, one's parents, and to one's friends, to the propriety that was society, loyalty was to the state, which took as its central aim to "serve the people" as the glory of socialism. And since the state was the "voice" and the "will" of "the People" (thanks to the supposed operation of the "mass line"), one's loyalty was then to "the People," who, strangely enough, easily could not include those in one's own family. During the years of the Cultural Revolution—which can be read as a distillation of some very familiar Maoist notions rather than as an aberration from them—displays of "humanheartedness" could be grounds for attack from one's ever-vigilant peers, not to mention superiors, and even occasionally from one's closest relatives.[13] Human-heartedness suffered then too.

But before we bleed excessively for this Chinese humanism and the particular harmony and inclusiveness—the family—of "the East" that seem to be such desired yet elusive objects in our postmodern, "Western" lives, we should look more closely at the structure of that harmony, at least as it exists in texts like King and Bond's, and in those on which they rely. And we should look in other texts as well—in those, for instance, that tell the lives of the people in the pages that follow. What one finds can complicate the desire for harmony and unity.

*****

Youngest brother took my father to Second Hospital at about noon on 1 August 1985. I arrived at my father's house from my own home, where I lived with my wife, just a little after they left. A neighbor friend told me my father had vomited blood that morning and that my brother, with another neighbor's help, took him to the hospital. I rode my bike there as fast as I could. I was very worried inside although I think I acted calm as I rode through the crowded noontime streets. Father had been getting sicker and sicker at home, where he lived with my younger brother who had just turned twenty-three, but we had no way to stop his sickness. As I rushed in the emergency room door I saw a doctor about to give father an IV. I could see that my brother, who was standing nearby, was very upset and had been crying. I walked toward him and put my hand on his shoulder.

"I went home and the neighbors told me," I said. "Things don't look so good. Why don't you go back home and get some things we'll need when father goes to the ward. I'll stay here."

"No, no. I should stay here and help," he said with a sob.

"There is nothing for us to do right now. The doctors will do their work now. We will need those things—a washing pan, a thermos, some clean cloths. You go."

"Okay, okay. A pan, a thermos, and some cloths. I'll hurry right back."

As I watched my younger brother walk away I realized how difficult father's illness had been for him. After all, he was still a young man and had no experience with sickness and dying, or with taking care of someone who was almost completely paralyzed. I thought sending him on the errand would give him some time to calm down.

But as I turned to sit down beside my father's bed there in the emergency room, I felt my own calmness dissolving. I looked down at his pale, thin face, and at the familiar but now dirty quilt my brother had brought from home to cushion his body in the cart they had used, and I couldn't hold back my tears. He looked so pitiful lying there, motionless, his blank eyes unable to focus, staring at the ceiling. Father only had my younger brother and me to depend on since my mother died in 1982. And while I had tried my best for more than two years since his stroke and paralysis to take care of him, I knew I had not done a very good job. At least I knew I had not been as good as I should have been. I held my father's hand and cried.

I cried for him, of course. But I think I also cried for myself. I felt so alone. It all seemed to depend on me.

Before mother died it was she who mainly took care of him. Then, before he got really sick, he continued to work in his factory. I lived at the university in a dormitory far away from our home, and could do almost nothing for my father. About seven months after mother died, he got much worse, and so I moved back home to help my brother take care of him. I was a graduate student then, studying for a master's degree. Younger brother just had taken a job in a pharmaceutical factory and couldn't ask for leave to help. He went to work each day and I stayed home with father, took care of him, and studied. I also took care of him at night. In January 1985 I married Li Mei and we moved to into one very small room, near my parents' house. After I got married, my younger brother stayed with father during the night while I continued to look after him during the day.

I did most of the caregiving work for my father and couldn't expect my younger brother, my wife, or even my elder brother who lived in Tianjin but in a district rather far away to do more than they did. I love my father and wanted to do as much as I could to help make him better. During this time, taking care of him took most of my time and energy, but I still felt what I did was not enough. I needed help, and quietly hoped that the others would do the same as I did. But my younger brother could not; my wife could not; and my elder brother could not be like me. After all, my father wasn't his real father. All of them had their own reasons, of course. But I needed help. I often thought of my mother and I knew if she were alive she would have done a lot for my father. I would be helping her.

I really felt so lonely.

It must have been about eighteen days and nights that I spent at the hospital beside my father's bed. I didn't go home at all. We were so lucky because my wife, who is a nurse, was working in that hospital and helped father get a bed in her ward. It was hard to get into the hospital then because there were not enough beds . . . actually, it is still not easy. People had to, as we say, go by a "back door" to get in. Joseph writes about this more in the next chapter. Because my father was Li Mei's father-in-law, that hospital agreed to admit him to the department and ward where Li Mei worked. That was good, but about twenty days later they wanted my father to leave, saying that twenty days was quite a long time. In fact, for someone as sick as my father, it was not a long time. I looked after my father there as a *"peiban"*—someone who stays with a patient—and my wife took care of him—along with other patients—during the day. The doctors provided medical treatment and diagnosed his problem as one of the alimentary canal. They gave him a lot of IVs every day. I fed him a little soup, helped him go to the toilet, and kept a hot compress on his arms and hands to make the next day's IV easier, and so on. Mainly, I tried to make him comfortable and keep him from worrying more.

With time, my father got a little better and I felt more relaxed. My two brothers came to the hospital from time to time, but I stayed there most of the time. But before long, he got worse, and the doctors found out he had cancer. It became more difficult to be hopeful.

One of the worst things I remember was that the doctors and nurses had a very hard time finding a good blood vessel for the IV needle. That meant it was more important to keep the hot compresses on his arms and hands at night, after he had the IV. I would put a small piece of towel into hot water, wring it out, and wrap it around my father's arms and hands.

I tried my best to help him. When I saw him get worse and worse, I felt so sorry. Finally, one night when things looked very bad, I cried for a long time beside his bed. Then Li Mei and I went out to buy some new clothes for his burial. I knew my father soon would die.

I called my brothers together and we talked about how to take father to his hometown 500 kilometers from Tianjin. When mother died father asked us to take her body to the same hometown. Father wanted to be buried there too, next to her.

I told my brothers that the only thing we could do for our father now was to be sure this wish was fulfilled. They agreed, and so I asked them to share taking care of father in the hospital while I began to arrange for the trip. I contacted some of my own friends and some of father's, trying to find a car or truck. It was very hard when we took mother's body there three years ago. We used bikes then—my older brother's, my friends' and my own—and I had decided that this time we had to find a car or truck, although I knew that would not be easy either.

I spent a day and a half doing nothing else but looking for someone to help us. Finally, a good friend and former colleague of father's agreed to help. He arranged for a small truck from his unit to take some machines of his factory to Jinan, which was near my father's hometown, and he asked the two drivers to go through father's village on the way. I was very grateful! I thought, this is the only thing I can do for him now! I will never forget that colleague's help.

I spoke with the two drivers and told them father was in the hospital. I was afraid they would change their minds if he died before we started out. It was risky for them to take a dead body anywhere without official permission. After we talked I gave each of them 40 yuan and thanked them a lot. As we said good-bye I decided that if father died before they set out for Jinan, I would kowtow and beg them to take his body.

I then went to the hospital to tell my brothers about the arrangements. After we talked, my younger brother went home to pack some things to take. My elder brother also went home. I sat beside father's bed alone. I remembered a brief conversation we had earlier, soon after he came to the hospital and when his condition had improved. He asked me to take him home.

"Go home!" he had said softly as I knelt beside him.

"Yes. Okay! We will go home after you get better," I said. But I wasn't sure just which home he meant.

"You mean back to our own home or back to your hometown?" I asked.

"Our own home!" he whispered.

He expected to go home from the hospital, to get better. More than anything, I had hoped for that too. But now I had to tell him he was going to his hometown, to be with mother and his ancestors. I had to tell him he was going to die.

As I looked at his familiar face, now gaunt and pained, his body struggling for each breath, again I could not control my tears. I put my hand on his forehead and stroked his hair. "Can you still understand me?" I said. He nodded slightly. With tears running down my cheeks I said, "I have found a truck to take you back home." Again, he tried to nod, but he suddenly stopped breathing. I waited a few moments, not sure he was gone. His chest did not move. It was about 7:30 P.M., 2 September 1985, half an hour before the two drivers were supposed to arrive at the hospital.

When youngest brother arrived back at the door of the ward and realized that our father had died, he sobbed and cried so much that my friends had to hold him up. A little later, my elder brother and his wife also came. I knew the drivers were coming and that it would be best to dress father in his new clothes before they arrived. We—my brothers, some nearby visitors, and I—hurriedly finished just as the drivers came. I took them aside and told them what had happened and asked them please to continue with our agreement. They didn't seem to think it was a strange thing, and went to back the truck up to the department's outside door. My friends and I put father's body into the back of the truck. We three brothers and two of my good friends got in with his body, and we set out for my parents' hometown.

Eight or nine hours later we arrived. It still was dark as we lifted my father's body down from the truck and thanked the two men again for their help. I gave them 20 yuan for their breakfast when they got to Jinan and they drove off. The long trip was over. Our relatives there greeted us and we began to prepare to bury father. On the following day, we laid him next to my mother, burned paper money as a tribute, and told him good-bye for the last time.

*****

The text fragments you have just read aren't arranged randomly, although you shouldn't assume there is a compelling logic tying them together in just this way. Perhaps they, along with the entire book, would better be presented as a hypertext you could read in your own ways than in their somewhat uncomfortable present linear string. You well may ask what is the point of this kind of writing. Why not simply tell our story or whatever it is we want to say in as "direct" and "clear" prose as possible,[14] be it a story of the new ways to think about and write ethnography and sociology; of our feelings and experiences while doing the research in Tianjin and writing the book; of various disciplines named and resisted; of fathers and sons and the age-old tensions between them; of the complex dynamics of family relationships around duty, responsibility, and care; or of how gender, masculinity, and occasional attempts to deny them seem so interwoven through all these? Surely, such a set of linked stories could be told in a sufficiently familiar way, within the confines of conventional qualitative sociological writing, without having to resort to the disruptive devices in evidence here thus far.

Actually, it isn't that we haven't tried that way of writing this book during the more than ten years since the idea of the fieldwork in Tianjin was conceived, proposed, endorsed, and begun. We certainly did not intend to write a book in quite this way, or, even quite this book, when we began to work together. There were the earlier texts, beginning in 1988, that came from Joseph's 1986–1987 study in the intensive care unit in a Tianjin hospital, texts that strained to be conventional but just barely managed to be so (some editorial comments demanded more discipline from even that text—a version of which you see written over and around as chapter 2). And there is a very fat envelope in a file cabinet in Des Moines that contains a first draft of this book that Laihua wrote in 1992 during his stay in the United States. It is a straightforward descriptive text that details the research site, methods, focus, and sets out the elements of the world of family caregiving around the family sickbed (*jiating bingchuang*) that it claims to have discovered. Laihua is its first author. And there is Laihua's conference paper, which turned into the published article referred to earlier in this chapter, which is a brief overview of that longer descriptive text. And now, there is also the "Chinese version" of the book noted in the preface that Laihua shepherded through to publication in Tianjin.[15]

The problem here, what produces this strange text, comes from Joseph and his entwined desires for a different kind of writing, a different kind of sociology, and a different sort of subjectivity. And all at a time in his career and life when he might be expected to go along, quietly writing the kinds of papers and books he'd been reasonably successful at doing before. Laihua's voice is heard relatively rarely here, and while he spent the same hours interviewing people, making notes, and then working through the transcriptions into English as Joseph did, the angst and peculiarities of this book are much less his.

But too much has been said, written, and read about the intimate connections between knowledge and power and subjectivity, between the will to know and the practices of scientific research that link the "First-World" observer to the "developing" or "Third-World" observed and the texts written out of those connections; too much has been made of the masculine foundations of knowledge, of science, of sociology and their dependence on the containment and negation of the feminine both without and within to write as though feminism and Freud and Derrida never existed, or, at least, as though they are relevant only to "literary disciplines." And there has been too much detailed and elaborated criticism of science as a local, social, and ideological practice—a rather different story from that typically told by and about science—to simply treat "social facts as things" that exist independent of those who create and use them. The intimate, productive connections between sociology and the "social" have been too widely and consistently discussed and described to continue to act as though they were distinct.

It only takes a few sentences of writing before you are back in the thick of all these issues of knowledge, subjectivity, desire, power, epistemology, ontology, and gender; and this is especially so for ethnography or field-work, where the distance between those embodied others about whom one writes and one's own body is diminished. And, as noted, some warn that taking all of these strands of contemporary criticism seriously means one simply will stop writing such realist stories. Arguably, it is more likely that the familiar sort of representational writing, given its hegemony in the social sciences, will just go on as though nothing has happened. ("Okay. Reality is socially constructed; 'language games are played.' Let's get on with studying them!") Both are possibilities. Indeed. I have moved away from writing those familiar sorts of True stories in which writing is seen as a more or less direct representation of things outside and prior to it, in those familiar ethnographic ways that try to offer a sociological explanation of empirical pattern and process, although I am sure there will be sections of what follows that will feel all too conventional and not at all "new." This mix that you no doubt will note speaks of the peculiari-ties of Joseph and Laihua in historical context, at the particular intersec-tion of their personal and intellectual biographies. The text surely is not internally consistent and without contradiction; not unitary; not as sure as you might like or be accustomed to find.

There is a sense in which the choices made in this book, and the way it is done, represent a will to live, to be alive, rather than to "be good" by sticking to canon and convention, or to write bureaucratic documents and reports rather than what I want to call an open sociological text. The former writing feels increasingly like being a little, bit by bit, dead.

Although perhaps it sounds too dramatic, a friend, an academic who shares her own sense of this—and is of about the same age—and I once exchanged the sentiment that there is a kind of "writing to live" feeling in what we each have been doing. This might mean, among other things, a kind of writing toward another space and to another subjectivity or subjectivities, which then lead to movement and dispersion, and displace-ment, with various strategic pauses here and there; on to more move-ment, pauses, subsequent movement. Perhaps this movement, which is not, surely, a sense of transcendence or "getting beyond" or (god forbid) "progress" in a disciplinary or knowledge sense, is a fantastic hedge (a fantasy, of course) against death. But if it is so I would make no apology for that. Instead, we might better try to understand how writing sociology could be a matter of life and death (see Game and Metcalfe 1997, 105).

These comments then point to one sense in which this text is highly "personal." It is not so much that it "reflects" us, Laihua and Joseph—although that sort of discourse is easy to find here too, in spite of wanting to get away from it—as it is a piece of each of us, a *doing* of us cut out of and thus frozen in time. We certainly don't write in the ways we have here as a recommendation for you to follow; it is not a "model." You are a body written by a different matrix of histories and biographies, including the important familiar ones of race, class, gender, and sexuality. Rather, this way of writing is the way we are doing, have done, it; now, here, at the end of the twentieth century in American—of the United States—sociology, a key audience for this book. Like hypertext, it could have been and could be done in many, many other ways, all of which would be peculiar to the writers/readers involved, and none of which would guarantee an enduring correspondence between the writing positions displayed and a transituational, embodied self of author-ity.

Beyond the move toward a transformative rather than solely a representative kind of writing,[16] the personal of this text is also about our relationships with and desires for our fathers and the Father. It was only after Laihua had been assigned by his leaders at the Social Sciences Academy to be my "assistant"—a positioning that quickly became laughably inadequate to represent what he was doing for the project and for me—that we began to see, to create, parallels in our biographies that sounded the importance of father, of parents, and family to each of us; and of ourselves as caring and caregivers, with no apologies or professed ineptness to protect our masculinities.[17] We each began to story ourselves as reflections of the other. Our fathers each died in 1985, after being sick for a long time. We both were involved deeply in caring for these men, although in sheer hours spent and bodily energy expended, Laihua's care work far exceeded my own. I began also to see that whereas my enactment of "caring" was so often in terms of feelings recalled and reiterated in a set of caring tales I would tell, his tended to be elaborated less in language and to point more to embodiments of care.

Although there were moments when I tended to see these ways of caring as vaguely "the same," and to see Laihua as "like me" (a sentence more common in my memory than one seeing me like him), such a mirroring and unity are precisely the fantasies reiterated in our separate relations to Fathers; fantasies that, finally, began to look less desirable to me. So, Laihua's voice here on fathers is limited. I cannot speak for him; my words do not speak him, although they sometimes try. The ambivalence around Fathers and their Law that you find in the text is mine, although I would like to think that he shares some of that. Indeed, I would like to think that all of the Chinese sons I met and spoke to share some of that, but that is my projection onto them. There is, after all, an encouragement of a discourse of resistance to the father in the West that, while present in Chinese cultural space, may be less readily available as a way to mark who one is or would want to be, even today. Fathers "in China"—which doesn't mean only within the geography of its physical/spatial borders—are still much respected, in/as a practice.

And the recurrent critique of the gender order is also something that Joseph presses into the text. This is a theme Laihua did not especially pursue in the draft of the book he early wrote in English, but it is one that he and I have discussed a number of times. While I think his book or his version of "the book" would not locate it as such a central theme, I convince myself that Laihua's own life, with his wife and daughter and women colleagues, is a life that seeks, in context, an equitable and open space for women relative to men. This convincing takes little effort, based on my experience with him and them, but this, again, is my inscribing of him and not his own, and I have not pushed this line of discussion with him very far.

And the personal here is also about our own relationship that emerged on the occasion of the project being accepted by the leaders of the Tianjin Academy of Social Sciences in the spring of 1990. It has grown into what feels like a long and trusted friendship; and of which this book is indeed a piece or a particular weave. It is difficult to write this relationship between us in a way that is neither too grandly abstract nor too tediously mundane. And it is written in memory and fantasy, of course. There is a sense in which I and we write the friendship, create it—at least in part—in this text, as part of it, the friendship's, material existence. In the beginning, it seemed that we both wanted to write a book about the details of caring for others whom one loves, or to whom one has a duty for care. That we seemed to share a commitment to this, that we thought behaving this way was "a good thing," seems to have been an early bond between us. Again, it is the mirror of the "good son," writ large.

For me, the desire to write that text has diminished as the desire for a critical and self-reflexive commentary on the doing of the "research" and the writing of the texts linked to it has grown. In a sense, my reading and writing on the above "questions that no longer can be ignored" in the social sciences has written over possible and actual texts of a book "about caregiving by adult children for their elderly parents at home in Tianjin." That "object" and its related "objects" often are displaced in what follows, interrupted, because continuing to write descriptions, representations, of them as though detached from me and from diverse other aspects of their lives was not pleasurable. But that displacement also sometimes is effected to make the very point of how much we depend on linearity for our usual narrative reading (and writing) pleasure. That is, we desire the story itself. Laihua is written here as author, as informant, as object, and occasionally as subject. And although I attempt to write Joseph as other to him, mostly he is given this position for Joseph (by me). The people we spoke to mostly are here written as others for us, even when they are written as speaking "their own" (translated) words (after all, whose text, finally, can it be said to be?).

One of the aims of postcolonial criticism, little of which would be called academic sociology, is to destabilize the very dualism between white, Western, male, observer, on the one hand, and the observed, often persons of color, women, local persons of "Third-World" or "developing" countries; the position of lack, on the other. The aim is not to reverse the prior dualism with the subordinated now giving the former dominant his "just desserts," drawing on all-too-familiar practices of domination, but rather to work toward seeing difference not as other but as intimately linked to self, both across subjects-and-objects and within them; as indeed something vital to the self but not to be "explained" as, finally, the Same. The other as an intimate yet strange part of the self. A tension that is a pleasure, that moves but is never finally resolved.

Joseph's travel to China made these questions harder to ignore, perhaps, than if his ethnographic others were more easily read as, finally, the Same. And getting to know the other, for him, meant both getting to know Laihua as well as those whom we met in their interviews along with some of the others "in" him. After living those relationships, with some few still being lived, I hope some are written here less out of a desire for my self-certainty through knowledge about than a desire for the other that need not be reduced to the Same, that is not premised, finally, on a stronger "I."[18] It of course would be gratuitous to claim success in this. Surely, that former and all-too-familiar kind of possessive desire is written here—to "get in," "get the data," and "get out" with Truth. I hope that a less destructive, more open connection between desire and the other in knowledge might also be glimpsed.

What follows is then a collection of fragments, quite intentionally so, that is not meant to offer an explanatory narrative of the search for the truth of caregiving by adult children for elderly parents at home among seventeen families in Tianjin, China, over the course of the 1990–1991 and subsequent research years. It is not meant to fit into any developing or existing research literature on caregiving, although it might be read by some as relevant thereto. It speaks more, of course, to the criticism of conventional human science work and a hope for other ways of doing sociology. It does not attempt to cohere; it does not offer up the "correct" interpretation of this slice of life in urban Chinese families. It does not seek to be True, although it does hope to offer diverse truths for thought and consideration. It wants to provoke and to encourage your readings and writings, much as an encounter with a "real" hypertext might, although in considerably less "fast" ways.

We want through this book then to say something very modest: at the present moment in the human science practice of writing true stories about others, this is one legitimate way to do that work, which necessarily means not to do that work in quite the same way as before.

Peiban and Care in a "Modern" Chinese Hospital

陪 *péi* accompany; keep sb. company: *Wo pei ni dao nong chang qu.* I'll accompany you to the farm./ *Pei wai bin canguan gong chang.* Show foreign visitors around a factory./ *Pei bingren.* Look after a patient.
陪 伴 *péibàn* accompany; keep sb. company.
The Pinyin Chinese-English Dictionary (1983)

This chapter occupies an important place in the story of this book. First written in 1988 for a conference, then later revised for inclusion in a collection of research papers on health care in developing countries, it marks one moment in a transition from a more conventional writing practice of ethnography, in which the writing remains focused on the there of the field site and the objects for analysis, operated by the distanced and largely dispassionate eye/voice of the objective observer. Its heritage is evident in its (a) description of the "natural" social world of family caregiving in the hospital—as though it were a unity—using excerpts from the detailed fieldnotes and interview transcripts Joseph made during and after his visits to the hospital wards over the course of several months; it thus presents "empirical patterns" for examination and analysis; (b) selection of some segments of that natural world (which are in fact segments of text "written about" it) and the presentation of them as "puzzles," the sociological analysis of which promises insight both about that scene and a "larger" set of scenes of which the immediate one is taken to be one iteration; and (c) offerings of limited-range "explanations" of those patterns deemed "interesting" and "important."

At the same time, the text offers critical comments on the very writing practices that effect this description and analysis, thus linking it to some of the issues we already have raised. Many, although not all, of these "meta-" comments come in footnotes, a place where, even in conventional writing, one can often find provocative (and not fully intended) reflection on what is said in the "main" text. In this we invite some ambiguity as to which text is more important, the "body" of the chapter or the footnotes.

But the further into the chapter you read, the more silent the interrupting voices fall as the main story seems increasingly to take over the space, both in the body and the footnotes. That relative quieting, here and in the chapters that follow, speaks to various desires and pleasures of the text itself. Some are in the form of subjectivities we want to effect here, ones that hold dear certain notions of caring, giving, serving, loyalty, and duty to others. Others are in the writing/reading of the story itself, not always written over pages but sometimes only within a few lines or in a single paragraph.

This is not to be disingenuous. We could have continued the interruption and deconstruction rather than the narrative, but as Joseph tried this it *felt* less and less like what he wanted to do. Hence, he stopped. We think you will be able to see where and perhaps why. The story here begins, as usual, "there."

*****

From December 1986 through early April 1987, I did fieldwork at a hospital in a north China city where I lived and taught sociology at a local university. I had proposed to hospital and host authorities that I examine how Chinese family members and friends help take care of patients in the hospital (cf. Strauss et al. 1985).[1] My own past experience as the son of a father who died after a long illness, my research on the experience of people with chronic illness (Schneider and Conrad 1983; Schneider 1988), and the stories I had heard in China about how much care work Chinese family members do in the hospital made the question both personally and professionally interesting.[2]

Although the research project seemed a politically safe one—that is, it did not seem to touch what I thought local authorities saw as "sensitive"— I had read enough about foreign academics doing research in China to know that gaining access—"getting in"—would not be easy (cf. Wolf 1985). After all, I was a foreigner wanting to observe and write something about life in "New (that is, revolutionary) China" rather than to search archives for evidence from the dynastic or republican periods. I made a point of telling officials that my aim was to scientifically describe, not to criticize, Chinese practices and people. And I suggested that perhaps we Westerners could see our own high technology, highly rationalized, and often impersonal system of health care delivery in a critically helpful light as a result of my research; in short, that "we Americans" might indeed be able to learn something from "you Chinese" in these matters of giving care. I hoped such a characterization would "work."

As I began to see the municipal and hospital officials endorse and repeat to me and to each other descriptions of my work as "scientific," I appreciated as never before the legitimating power of this ultramodern discourse in the face of skepticism about motives and ends. While subsequently I would applaud the deconstruction of scientific realism and epistemology back home, I then still could use it uncritically to get what I wanted—access—and to assure them of my "objective" methods and "progressive," "enlightened" aims.

Yet I knew, even as I repeated and elaborated this story of "my proposed research," that once I got back home and began to write, it would be easy to criticize what I saw "in the field"; how easily non-evaluative "description" could be read—could be written—as (that is, could be) highly critical (see, e.g., Ellis 1995a). Moreover, since I had decided to privilege the perspective of family members by (at least in part) telling *their* story about carework, it would be easy to sympathize—"take sides"—with them, possibly running afoul of various official/policy perspectives in the hospital and elsewhere.[3] While I could perhaps use Chinese faith in "Western science" (see Goldman and Simon 1989; Anderson 1990), "facts," and "modernity" (cf. Rofel 1999, 1–37) to "get in," questions of the authority and power of my own voice and positioning would re-emerge each time I began to write (Schneider 1991; Fabian 1990; Clifford 1983a). And while I could enter the hospital ward only with permission from hospital leaders and doctors, I would try to tell a story about the work family members did and the care that they gave, work and care that from a "modern" or Western point of view are properly done by hospital staff. What postures would I effect in all this (then, there, and here, now)? How much of my own "I/eye" would I reveal (see Yeatman 1994, 27–41)?

Obviously, as noted, these complexities rarely keep us from writing. But they can offer serious disturbance and a critical review of practice that may have enduring effects on how sociology and human science writing is done. And since these dilemmas are so fundamental to the positioning and practice of social science—for how could "social science" be done without observation and "the observer"?—it seems at this point better to make such tensions more rather than less visible as we write; critiquing and seeking to loosen some of the conventions rather than abandoning the writing altogether or ignoring the challenges. Accordingly, in this chapter and in some of those that follow we use conventional practices of ethnographic or fieldwork reportage to create realist scenes about care work in the hospital and at home, along with self-reflexive commentary that seeks to point to our own presence *both* in the story the text tells about "that place" as well as in the construction of the text as vehicle for that (still quite "modern") story (see Kondo 1990, 7–9).

Below, I first describe the hospital I most often visited—the field site—and the kinds of work family members and hospital staff did around and for their patients (the "you are there!" effect). I proceed then to organize segments of conversations (interviews) and observations I made—data—into a story about how, in doing the work of giving care, these family members took up positions in a complex web of often contradictory and always power-saturated discourses that characterize urban China in the late twentieth century. This latter move is where we most often see "theory" invoked explicitly in this sort of work, ostensibly providing links to the "larger" understandings of what is "seen" in the data. Sometimes I saw these family members as victims of power; at other times they seemed to be skillful wielders of power. Mostly they appear as working to defend themselves and their patients against what they saw to be much greater forces inclined not to operate in their interests. The story begins, again, with helpful section headings.

At the Hospital

Over the course of four and a half months I visited three general hospitals, but I went most often to the critical care unit (CCU) of one 500-bed hospital. Officials told me this CCU was "one of the best" of its kind in all of north China and that it had received many foreign visitors. Since, officially, only Western medicine was practiced in this unit, I took this to mean it was offered to foreigners, to Chinese, and to me as an example of China's progress in "modern medical care" (see Henderson 1989).

My first visit to the unit was in the company of a doctor-official from the city public health bureau who introduced me to hospital and ward leaders and displayed the necessary certified papers specifying who was responsible for the decision to give this foreigner access.[4] After I explained my interests and research procedures, in a well-rehearsed speech (albeit in English and translated by the official accompanying me), the leaders invited me to "come any time" and "see whatever you like." I repeated these invitations to myself many times—perhaps naively—during the course of my visits, especially when I felt unsure about whether or not to move into a certain space, to observe and ask questions.[5]

In the proposal I wrote for the project, I had offered to provide an interpreter to accompany me. Public health bureau leaders were hesitant to allow a Chinese "outsider" chosen by me to do this. And they found it difficult to secure a bureau person who had the time and English skills. After two visits with a bureau-supplied interpreter, I began to go to the unit by myself. As a result, I suffered not understanding most of the conversations I overheard, and was unable to converse with most of the patients and their *peiban*[6]—usually family members who spent large amounts of time beside their patients and who, only rarely, could speak English.

But since such an interpreter-official likely would have further constrained the range of conversations I hoped to have with these people, I felt that loss was also a gain of sorts. In consequence, I decided to rely on my own observations and those conversations I could have in English, supplemented by any information I could get from simple questions asked in Chinese. I also spoke to many English-speaking Chinese not connected to the hospital but whose experience of their own hospital caregiving was informative.[7]

Posted visiting hours in the unit were 4:00–7:30 P.M., Monday, Wednesday, Friday, and Saturday. Unit doctors told me that family members and friends who wished to visit at other times were required to obtain a *peiban zheng* or visitor's card from the head nurse, who would write on the card the reason for their visit, such as to bring the patient "delicious food" or to "serve the patient." This discourse of modern medical administration to the contrary, it seemed that at almost any time of the day or night there were some *peiban* on the unit. This was perhaps the first of several contradictions between what I was told and what (I thought) I could see.[8]

The critical care unit consisted of the first floor of a two-story wing at the hospital, a building probably dating from the early 1950s. Patient and staff rooms of various size opened from either side of a single corridor. The largest ward was called the "monitor room" and contained nine beds reserved for the most critically ill patients. Moveable fabric screens separated the beds, and one end of the room had storage cabinets and several wooden desks pushed together as a place for doctors and nurses to sit and write. Two smaller rooms, one ten-bed unit for women and a six-bed unit for men, were called "convalescent wards" and often received patients from the monitor room as well as from outside the unit. Two additional rooms housing various machines and equipment were reserved for treatment. The doctors' room, nurses' station, unit director's office, and wash room and toilet were on the facing side of the corridor. Often, two or three additional patient beds were placed against one wall in the corridor, along with cabinets, equipment, oxygen tanks, and carts.[9]

I spent most of my time in the monitor room, standing along the wall near the door (I really did entertain the fantasy that I was less conspicuous there) or, during "slow times," sitting at the desk where I could strike up quiet conversations with doctors as they sat and wrote in charts or chatted. I also had a full view of the room, the patients, and *peiban*. Such positionings of course located me quite visibly "with" the doctors, which certainly may have given patients and their families pause about what they could say to me. Still, I was thankful for (my conjured sense of) the "we" of those moments when I felt quite alone.

I made a few visits to an obstetrics ward and an internal medicine ward at two other general hospitals, always in the company of a public health bureau or hospital official. One of these hospitals was new, and both were larger than the one containing the CCU. In neither case did I have the same freedom to move and look around as I did at the CCU.

The Work of Giving Care

A bourgeois Western sociologist familiar with the complex specialization and control of work in U.S. hospitals, I was immediately struck by all of the physical labor family members were doing in the CCU.[10] This was notable in contrast to the considerably more constrained repertoire of such activities for their U.S. counterparts. I noticed a lot of washing and cleaning, bringing and taking; work that seemed routine and thus largely unnoticed by most local eyes, but which I saw as deeply felt family duty displayed and/or responsibility ignored by nursing and maintenance personnel.

Washing and Cleaning

Emblematic of this physical work are notes I made when watching a young woman, perhaps a daughter, who, having served supper to an older woman in the convalescent ward, went out into the hall and returned with a large steaming mop and began cleaning the floor around the woman's bed. None of the *peiban* or patients took much notice of her, but I did. As she finished the floor near her patient's bed, she proceeded to mop under and around the bed of the patient nearby, with *peiban* for that woman helpfully moving stools and shoes out of the way. Before finishing, she had mopped all of the central floor space in the ward. I saw similar mopping by both men and women *peiban* in this ward and in the monitor room. In the two cases where I specifically could take note, there seemed to have been nothing spilled on the floor to occasion the mopping. Nurses and doctors were regularly in and out of the room and they seemed to take no note of this work. For the *peiban* involved it appeared to be simply a next project in the evening round of bringing food, serving it, chatting, washing the supper cups and bowls, packing these away to be taken home, changing the sheets, and ministering to the patient—all proper practice for those who were responsible.

Bringing and Taking

Some of what was brought and taken included the patient's "favorite food" from home, soiled bedpans and urinals, thermoses of boiled water, supplies of medicine and materials from outside the hospital; large and heavy oxygen tanks put next to a patient's bed; doctor-written orders for lab tests on one's patient, delivered to the appropriate offices; and even patients themselves, taken to other departments in the hospital. So much work was done by people who themselves were not part of the official hospital workforce, and on tasks that in the United States usually are done by employees.[11] I was deeply impressed by what I read as "the Chinese sense of family duty." Being part of and contributing to my own family, and being able to care for my father, had been so important to me. (I couldn't help imagining myself doing all of this work in the many hospital rooms I had spent time in with my father. I could identify with these *peiban*, but I also sensed how onerous it would be for me if I had to do all this work. Where would I find the time? What would I have to give up? Could I? Would I?)

I noticed a patient's wife bring an X-ray film into the ward for a doctor to examine. Later I asked the doctor why she rather than a hospital worker had brought it. He said that she had gone to another department and gotten it. "Is this something that *peiban* often do?" I asked. He said, "Yes, family members like to do this kind of thing, and sometimes the doctor and nurse are too few and cannot take time to get these things."[12]

Peiban sometimes carried doctor-written requests for lab work to another part of the hospital. One night I watched as one doctor filled out such a form and gave it to a man whose young sister had just been admitted. After the man left I asked this doctor and his colleague, sitting nearby whose English was a bit better, "These forms. You gave that man three of them. What are they and where is he taking them?" Together they offered the following:

> Maybe observe this at night. Two labs, one outpatient and one inpatient. All doctors use outpatient lab at night because inpatient lab closed. *Peiban* take to outpatient department and this would probably cause technician to come to patient and get samples and take back to laboratory. Sometimes *peiban* go to lab to get result back. Or, doctor may call. If doctor and *peiban* do nothing, maybe tomorrow lab will send.[13]

Although one senior doctor in the unit told me that according to "modern" hospital administrative procedures, *peiban* were definitely not allowed to get lab reports and bring them back to the ward, there seemed to be a good deal of energy given over precisely to this kind of work (another contradiction inscribed). As the doctors quoted above implied, it was not so much that the lab would not come to do the tests or fail to send the results. Rather, *peiban*, doctors, and nurses alike saw this kind of taking and bringing work as expeditious and sensible—as something expected—for family members to do. *Zhe shi tamen yinggai zuode!* What otherwise might take three days thus could be accomplished in one or two. And besides, "they like to do this kind of thing," said the doctor. (I remember making a note to myself at the time about how this was surely a mark of "the Chinese sense of duty," not to mention simple "good sense," with which I was so impressed.)

Other examples of this "Chineseness" (this otherness, difference) were easy to find. For instance, if a patient had to go to another hospital for a special test, the work of contacting that hospital, making an appointment, and arranging transportation via some work unit's car all might quickly be taken over by a family member. I spoke to one man who had done this for his father:

> The doctor here suggest to us that you should have an exam for your patient . . . CT-do you know? (Yes.) But if you want to have, you must contact with that other hospital by yourself. (How?) My brother-in-law have a classmate who work at CT department there . . . so my father went very soon. Otherwise, you wait a long time because there are so many people need and so few hospitals—only two—that have that equipment. It is often broke down and the technicians can't repair it. Perhaps some of that machines are imported from America. [We share a laugh.]

Although not officially responsible for making these arrangements, neither this son nor the doctors could be sure just how long it otherwise might take. To rely on such slower institutional channels and the people whose job it was to activate them would be considered, I think by all parties (even by me), both foolish and lazy—falling short both of commonsense and proper filial duty. And to criticize directly those institutionally responsible would be folly, for that would only likely lengthen the time required to obtain the service. And besides, "family members like to do this kind of thing, and sometimes the doctor and nurse are too few and cannot take time" to do it, the doctor said. Yes, yes, I thought. This is precisely what it means to be a "good" family member. (I always thought of myself as a good, disciplined family member.)

One man in his early thirties described how he got the peritoneal dialysis fluid used in his father's care. We had been discussing the intravenous (IV) drip going into his father's stomach as we stood near the bed. Because I had heard other *peiban* describe how they went outside the hospital to get scarce medicines, I asked him how he got this fluid. Our conversation went on like this:

He: Yes, I go to medicine box . . .

I: What do you mean, "medicine box," what is that?

He: At the factory, not far from here . . .

I: Wait. You mean you go to a factory to get this medicine yourself?

He: Yes, it is not far from here. This kind of medicine all people here go get themselves. The other kind of medicine the doctor has to give.

I: How much do you get at one time?

He: Three *yuan*, two *jiao* a bag. Each time [father] must use two bags. One day, four times. He uses eight bags a day.

I: How many bags do you buy at one time?

He: There are ten bags in a box. At one time I buy twenty boxes.

I: You buy twenty boxes?! Do you have to take a bicycle?

He: (Smiling) No, my father's factory provides a vehicle . . . what shall I say, a simple truck.

I: And a driver?

He: Yes, a driver, and he helps me bring the medicine here to the hospital.

I: Where do you put the medicine when you bring it here?

He: Outside . . . I am going to use a long sentence now. When there is a flat and it is second or third floor, outside there is sometimes a place (makes motions with his hands) . . . what is it called?

I: Balcony? A balcony?

He: Balcony, yes. There is in the third building a balcony and I put the medicine there. Other people put their medicine there too.

I: So, each time you need the medicine you go there, four times a day?

He: Oh, no. I put some boxes under the bed, three boxes under the bed here. When it is time for the medicine, I give it to the nurse . . . .

Each time I read this dialogue I am tempted to modify it so that I don't appear so naive, so impressed by such a "straight man" account. This underlines for me the distance and closeness of their and my experience and, more generally, of the Western bourgeois social scientist in the "exotic" place. It also points to my (our) presence there as an occasion for such accounts and performances (cf. Clifford 1983b), and thus confounds simple notions of social scientists gaining "entrée" and "trust" as vehicles toward making "valid" characterizations of "the setting," as though the setting were made up of inert, inanimate objects.

Ministering and Monitoring

Another kind of carework *peiban* did seemed to demand greater judgment, such as in watching the patient, noting any changes in his or her condition, and reporting same to hospital staff. It turned mostly around intravenous (IV) drips, routine reports of fluids taken in and passed, temperature readings, foods eaten, frequency and volume of bowel movements, and the operation of various machines attached to patients.

Late one cold January afternoon as I sat in the monitor room, a sixty-five to seventy-year-old man was brought from surgery, where he had been operated that morning for pancreatic cancer. After a few minutes I asked a doctor about his condition. He said, "He is jaundiced, in shock, has lost a lot of blood, and has respiratory failure." Over the next hour, *peiban* did a good deal of ministering and monitoring work around this patient. Here is an excerpt from the notes I made as I watched:

A middle-aged woman, not a nurse, comes in, slightly breathless, and unlatches the other swinging door and props both doors open. Slowly, a bed is wheeled to the center of the room—there is very little space here—pushed and surrounded by eight or nine people. I assume they are family members. They are accompanied by two doctors in blue surgical clothes. Two of the *peiban* are carrying, and holding high, IV bottles, one with blood and another with a clear solution. As doctors and nurses begin to attach the patient to machines and put the IV bottles on stands, the relatives cluster around the bed, their attention focused on the man and the doctors and nurses. I am standing a foot or two below the end of the bed when a nurse comes in and seems to ask most of the *peiban* to go back out into the hallway, leaving three people beside the bed. The middle-aged woman and a man are on either side, crouched on the floor, each with one hand on the patient's knee and the other holding down a hand. As the patient tries to move his legs, these family members—his children?—push the legs back down straight. They look haggard and worried. The man lets go of the knee and hand to check the blood drip going into the patient's wrist. He flicks the IV line with his fingers. Another *peiban* comes in from the hallway and they both examine the bottle and tube. One adjusts the valve and looks closely at it. He makes no attempt to conceal what he has done. Apparently not satisfied, he says something to the nurse, who has calmly noticed him doing this. She turns, examines the valve, adjusts it and goes back to her work. I can see the other drip is connected to the man's right ankle as the woman moves the blankets to examine the place where the needle is placed. Every few minutes one or two of the other *peiban* in the hallway come in, stand for a moment at the foot of the bed, say something to the woman or man there, and then go out.

Another patient in the monitor room, a young man in his late twenties or early thirties who had suffered brain damage in a truck accident, was unconscious and tended to regularly by his sister. She seemed to be in the ward every time I visited, over the course of one month. The doctors told me her brother had been in the hospital three months. He had a tracheotomy and was fed through a tube inserted in his nose. Another quote from my detailed notes (these really are data, carefully collected):

> Patient 9's sister comes in and goes to the bed. She pulls the covers back, lifts the man's left arm up and then does the same with his right arm, pushing the blanket up under his armpits as she does. She touches the back of her hand against the man's cheek and looks down at him, steps away from the bed to a small stand at the head of the bed and appears to be pouring something that looks like honey into a cup, followed by some white liquid, mixing the two. Then dry powder goes in; more mixing. She puts this down and takes the thermos out into the hall, returning moments later. She pours some of this water into a basin, testing it with her hand and on her own face, wets a cloth, squeezes it out and proceeds to wipe the man's face, hands, forehead, neck, holding the nasal tube carefully to one side. She resticks the tape against his upper lip, rearranges the gauze pad covering the opening, and then takes a large syringe from the stand and draws some of the mixture into it. She connects the end of the syringe to the tube and pushes the plunger to empty the syringe into his stomach She repeats this 2–3 times until the mixture is gone.

And I watched one evening as a middle-aged son repeatedly reattached a ventilator connection taped over his father's mouth. Each time the son would have the tube in place the father would pull it out. This went on for twenty minutes before I left. Two nurses, sitting at the desk, from time to time looked toward the patient's bed but did not move to help the son. He looked very tired. I, too, felt tired, and wondered how long this test of wills could continue. I thought of my father when he resisted what we and nurses did to him "for his own good." How hard it would be, I thought, to force my father to keep that tube in his nose.

The Burden of Duty and
the Opportunities from Care

Family members were often called upon by doctors to sign permission forms for emergency procedures, tests, or surgery—to embody, in short, a piece of "the person responsible." These sons, daughters, and spouses were for the most part quite experienced in being responsible, but this particular performance was one with which they had little experience. It was an institutionally mandated responsibility that marked and marks—in the "modern" hospital—a line of fault between the patient and family, on the one hand, and the institution, on the other. These *peiban* were being asked to "be responsible," but to accept responsibility for something that they could not control. It was a burden that they accepted with great hesitance, in no small part because they seemed to have little confidence that this kind of "carework" by others would be done carefully and well. (This hesitance and anguish often expressed at the moment of signing a permission form made me think of how much we trust our experts in the United States—at least those of us who are, like most of them, white, educated, usually male—to "do the right thing." If we looked more carefully at this ritual, I wondered what we might learn about trust and responsibility, about morality in the "modern" hospital.)[14]

The doctors on the unit had become quite skilled in taking up their own positions as protectors of the hospital against subsequent possible claims by family members if procedures went badly. When I asked three doctors, during a conversation completely unrelated to such forms, "What is the most important thing *peiban* do for their family members?" they all said "to sign permission forms," especially for patients who were seriously ill.

I observed such a permission-form signing by a middle-aged man whose father had suffered a cerebral hemorrhage and was having trouble breathing. The doctors decided the patient needed a tracheotomy. I stood at this man's shoulder, outside the closed doors of the monitor room, and watched several doctors and nurses bent over the patient. Suddenly, a doctor and nurse turned toward the door and motioned for the man (us?) to come into the room. (Did they want me, too? Oh, no. Of course not.) The nine doctors and nurses who had been around his father's bed gathered around the son as one doctor spoke, making a downward thrusting motion with his hands. This talk at the center of the huddle of white coats went on for a few minutes, with the man and doctors talking in turn. They moved to the desk and the son was given a permission form, which, after some hesitation, he signed. He came back out into the hallway and stood near the wall, looking away from the door. He had behaved like a good son, at least in the doctors' modern script.

Family members' own sense of duty was considerably more diffuse than this signing coerced by doctors. It seems captured succinctly by a proverb one man cited when I said he was working very hard to care for his father, who suffered a cardiopulmonary problem. He replied: "There is a saying, if a father lay in bed for a long time, his son not care well for father" (*jiu bingchuang qian wu xiaozi*). He gave it to me in English; I asked how it sounded in Chinese, carefully writing down both versions.

I was immediately struck by how unreasonably demanding this seemed; what, after all, was a son expected to be able to do? Quite a great deal, apparently. I couldn't avoid thinking of my own father's long illness and time in bed and the care I gave him. He was, so often, such a long time in bed. I felt this Chinese wisdom was unreasonable. How could *we* be held to be so responsible?[15]

Another, older man, when discussing the routine practice of *peiban* spending the night beside a patient's bed and the importance of being vigilant, told me the following story passed on to him, likely not in innocence, by a member of another family on the ward:

> Some *peiban* told me there were two *peiban* here with a patient who was very serious and couldn't breathe. The . . . [he points to his throat] sput . . . (Sputum? Yes, I know) . . . the *peiban* were sound asleep. The patient died, and the doctor said that if the *peiban* paid more attention, the patient would not die so soon. If the patient is so serious, like in bed 4, the *peiban* [should] never go to sleep.

Here are complex moral instructions indeed. They draw on the son's sense of duty and responsibility (felt by him and fully understood by the doctors), the authority of the doctor in the modern hospital, and they rest on and shore up the political and economic conditions of contemporary Chinese urban life.[16]

The unasked question (so that I now can ask it) seems to be who really is responsible for the proper in-hospital care of the patient. On the one hand, children—perhaps especially sons—are quite familiar with and feel the weight of the discourse of filial duty; the proverb offered by the other son specifies the scope of this work (even in the more correct translation). The "doctors" indexed in the story reaffirm the nature of this duty while eliding what one might read as their own responsibility and that of the nurses. The family member's task seems impossible to fulfill; yet acceptable options seem not to exist (*"meiyou banfa"* —I have no choice). Arguing in the local context that it is, rather, the doctors, nurses, and hospital who failed the patient would have to be a private discourse, which would be foolish and shortsighted for a *peiban* to offer publicly. To ignore one's duty would seem an even less available option, although some do just that, of course. In any case, to ignore one's duty likely would be seen as more egregious than ignoring the responsibilities that come with a job, even with a highly responsible one such as doctor and/or nurse. Family members reaffirmed the traditional discourse, shoring up, paradoxically, a system of hospital care that they often privately criticized. (Note that here in the text and there in the world it now has become "a system" of care.)

Even when a patient was "not so serious," a family member might not sleep. The man who told me the preceding story said his father suffered a gastric ulcer but was "not so serious." A few moments later he said that he routinely spent the night awake at his father's bedside, reading English books. Having heard the prophetic and chilling tale about irresponsible kin, as had he, I felt I could understand why (or, why he would story himself thus).

Moreover, there was both cultural and institutional support for sons' and daughters' in-hospital care work. *Danwei*,[17] or urban work units in China, as a matter of policy released some sons, daughters, and spouses from their duties at work, usually with full pay for a specified period of time (such as one month), so that they could be at the hospital doing various caregiving tasks. If family caregivers were few, work units also might send fellow workers to the hospital to help care for a patient, especially if the patient had a good reputation at his work unit or if the illness was clearly due to an accident or dangerous circumstances at work. Although this could provide needed extra hands, *danwei*-supplied caregivers could bring more burdens. One middle-aged man said he was glad he and his only sister had not accepted the offer from his father's work unit to send "a person to assist us." When I asked him why they had not, he said, "because that person is not as . . . serious as a family member in care." He added: "Even if some unit person come here, it's that person's job to look after the patient. But also that person feels he does something for the family and so he thinks we should do something [for him or her] . . . like take him out to eat . . . in a restaurant. So, we don't like that idea." This reflects an intersection of traditional conceptions of proper family responsibility and good everyday politics. And from the *danwei*'s side, such policy might be cheaper than paying the additional fees for special nurses. But that these conceptions do not always fit together well is indexed by the family's refusal of such help. Here the son invokes the traditional discourse of reciprocal exchange to block what might be seen as good socialist practice. The official discourse and the policy, however, remain relatively intact.

Caregiving needs could also provide a fine opportunity to demonstrate oneself as a suitable candidate for marriage while also serving the official discourse of "revolutionary humanitarianism" (*geming rendao zhuyi*; see Wang 1986) in the hospital in the face of "too few doctors and nurses." One man and I had the following conversation:

I: Last night when I left I noticed that there was another man sitting here [by
      the bed] after you had gone. Who was that?
He: That was the boyfriend of my sister.
I: Oh, really? Why did he come?
He: In our society, if a young man see a young girl, if father or mother is ill, that
      boy or girl must take much care. It is a good chance to express kindness
      [chuckles and smiles broadly].

Moreover, not only was this care work a "good chance" to show oneself as a proper potential husband, it was a good chance for anyone to do what might be called "the good person," as described in chapter 1 by King and Bond (1985).

As I watched and was impressed by all this effort, I found myself recalling scenes from hospital waiting rooms and corridors back home, scenes that I had come to read as sometimes "contests of character," in which various degrees of sacrifice and selfless work could be displayed among relatives in what seemed almost a competition to take oneself up as, to perform oneself as, the son or daughter or grandchild "*closest* to," "caring *most* for," "loving and loved *best* by" the patient. And I felt ever so virtuous in displaying the various caregiving tasks I did for my father.

The concern for face and the proper display of traditional duties and responsibilities in today's urban China, coupled with the official discourse of scarcity, a collective responsibility for "modernization," and the then still quite alive remnants of what Henderson (1989) has called the "Maoist model of health care" would seem to render this work a terrain to be sought out and, if necessary, struggled over. That I could so easily make this reading and link it to my own experience of taking and giving care back home suggests that quite aside from the larger political and economic differences in which these *peiban* and I found ourselves around our patients' beds, what we were doing had very important resonance for just who we thought we were.[18] (Ah, yes. Did you feel that sigh of closure?)

Connections and Care

As Mayfair Yang (1986, 1989, 1994) and, more recently, Andrew Kipnis (1997) have noted, establishing, nurturing, and using social relationships—*guanxi*—to solve life's routine but important problems is arguably a signature of whatever it might mean to call a social and cultural space "Chinese." Problems of allocating and obtaining "scarce resources"—a theme in both official and personal discourses—often occasion discussion of "going by the back door," *zou hou men[r]*, as necessary to get what is needed.[19]

And one of the most needed "objects" a family member might obtain for a sick relative is a back door that would open into the intensive care unit I visited. It could, literally, be a matter of life or death. Or, it could mean the difference between more and less comfortable care. In either case, opening such back doors was an important way to demonstrate just what a good son, daughter, or spouse one was. The energy and effort I watched them give and heard them tell about seemed easy enough (at least for me) to understand, but I lamented the ingratiating and what felt to me as the groveling it sometimes required. In any case, there was little choice. What else could they do? ("*meiyou banfa!*").

Early in my visits to the CCU I began to understand that many, if not most, of the patients there had gained admission in this way. Of course, some patients were admitted because they suffered the conditions the unit was designed to serve. But *guanxi* and back door admissions seemed easily as common. The best—and luckiest—patient was perhaps one who both fit the admission protocol *and* had good connections, providing everyone a chance to behave properly: the official discourse of modern medical administration could be invoked, pointing to this patient as exactly the sort of case the unit could serve; the doctors could work hard for this (special) patient, invoking the discourse of selfless, perhaps even socialist, medicine; family members could hope, with varying degrees of certainty, that their patient would be given good care by doctors and nurses at the same time that they could see their own activities as successful, and themselves as properly responsible family members.

Different sorts of connections are named differently. For instance, if a patient or *peiban* and one of the doctors or nurses had some personal relationship, it was called a "friendship connection," *pengyou guanxi*. Speaking one afternoon about a newly arrived patient, a doctor said: "He has stroke and myocardial infarction. That patient's relative knows some doctor who work in our ward, so we receive this patient. The patient's relative wants the patient to have better care, so he came here from . . . [another] hospital." Later, when I asked whether all unit doctors and nurses could provide such an avenue into the unit, this doctor said:

> I will say yes, because we help each other. We have to work together. We have a rule in the CCU. The doctors' and nurses' direct relatives—father, mother, child, brother, sister, if they are ill, we receive the patient immediately, even though the patient suffers from things like advanced cancer and chronic renal failure [conditions officially not treated in the CCU]. We accept them immediately. Why do we have this rule? We want to make our doctors and nurses happy. We want to let them feel warm to work here.

This kind of family or *qin* connection is called *qinqi guanxi* and seemed to be a certain ticket into the unit. One man I spoke to explained his father's access to the unit by saying that his sister was going to marry a young doctor who worked in another department in the hospital. When I asked him if he thought it would have been difficult to gain admission without this contact, he said, "Yes, very difficult. I think many patients are more serious than my father . . . [but] have to stay at the emergency room . . . or not even there. Just give some medicine and told to go home."

When I heard these stories I thought what an asset a doctor-friend in China would be. To put him or her in your debt could be a kind of insurance against the terrible moment when one's parent or child needed medical care and/or hospitalization. This of course was not lost on doctors themselves. Speaking of one patient nearby, a doctor told me:

> This patient was introduced by some of our doctors [for admission] because the patient give our doctors some help. Two doctors ask me, two or three times a day, urge me to receive this patient. I thought about it. This patient helps these doctors get new houses. If I not receive, these doctors may not be happy. . . .
> I want to keep things peaceful and quiet, so I admit this patient.

Doctors often explained to me that the unit's scarce renal dialysis resources, for instance, were more wisely used for patients suffering acute renal failure. But, like other instances of modern administrative discourse, this could be matter of factly juxtaposed to an explanation that this patient, having suffered a cerebral vascular accident (CVA)—what one doctor called patients "waiting to die"—had "connections" and was thus admitted.

Another kind of back door, the object of more public criticism since the beginnings of the 1980s reforms, opens to allow officials—"important people"—entry. A man in his early forties had suffered cardiac arrest that produced brain damage. One doctor told me, "The father of patient is the head of . . . [a city] district. If his father not this kind of man, this patient we not receive in our ward." Another man about sixty-five, who suffered from liver cirrhosis linked to an earlier hepatitis infection, was described to me by another doctor as a "police official" to account for why he was on the ward.

Personal connections between important people in a work unit could yield a kind of *guanxi* between that *danwei* and the CCU (cf. Yang 1986, 136–190). Since for most higher cadres in a unit, and for some "model workers," the *danwei* then bore some or all of the costs of hospitalization and care,[20] work unit leaders can become rather directly involved in negotiating not only admission to the unit of one of their members but also their continued treatment. If one were an important leader, a loyal and valued worker, or if the unit were somehow liable for the injury or illness, such connection could be invaluable both to the *danwei* and the patient.

One afternoon I sat in the director's office and watched the leader of a factory plead with the CCU head to admit one of his workers, a man in his thirties with chronic renal failure, a condition not officially treated there. At the same time, such admission can become a costly proposition for a *danwei*, and work units were interested in striking a balance between proper care and cost. Family members whose patients required a good deal of special care, paid by the patient's own unit, were of course often happy to stay in the hospital as long as possible. As one man said, "Because the cost is supported by my father's unit, we are in no hurry to go back home. Here my father get good care and good look after."[21]

If a work unit were responsible for a worker's injury, the expectation seemed to be that they would pay all expenses, including hotel room costs for out-of-own family members and fellow workers who came to give care. One young man had been seriously injured in his work at a factory in another town. His *danwei* leaders seemed to assume responsibility: they came to the unit to encourage the doctors to "save this patient" or, as one doctor told me, "they would be seriously criticized. They have many accidents there." Not only was the work unit paying for all the care of this patient, who had been there for more than one month, they continued to pay his salary; they paid for all his brother's expenses to come to the city where the hospital is located; and they paid the expenses of seven fellow workers who came to share the care work. When I asked this brother how the patient came to the unit, he said, "the . . . [*danwei*] has a connection to this hospital." And in the work unit leaders' view, that this young man's father was the Party secretary of the *danwei* could only strengthen their case before the hospital's leaders.

At another hospital I visited, there was a patient who had suffered chemical poisoning at work and never would regain consciousness. His unit paid for a private room, for one shift of a private nurse, and for two eight-hour shifts of fellow workers' care at the hospital. He had been a patient there for three years. I asked if his family members—a wife and two children—came to see him often. The nurse said, "not so much any more."

Such situations involving work units and costs can put doctors and the hospital in a difficult position relative to the patient and family members.

Two doctors said that one of the reasons there is so much trouble between doctors and nurses and family members is that while work units
want to keep care costs down, family members and patients want as
much care as they can get. After invoking the supply and demand discourse—too few nurses and resources—one doctor said: "The doctor have
trouble with patient and with patient work unit director. For example, if
patient suffer from some disease, this patient need many money. The
patient unit director don't hope do, so this is controversy. If patient spend
money, unit must pay this money." And here, the family members may
draw fully on the *danwei*'s responsibility—using socialist discourse—and
on strongly held notions of harmony—the traditional Confucian discourse—
to try to keep the patient in the hospital. The harmonious image produced by the official discourse that the doctor, nurse, *peiban*, and *danwei*
all, as one senior doctor said, "work toward the same goal," seemed hard
to sustain in the face of these diverse efforts and interests. I doubted that
any of the *peiban* I had spoken to would take it seriously as a description
of the circumstances of care.

Peiban and Medical Staff:
Strains in Managing Care

Contrary to handing over responsibility for care to the specialist or expert, a position that family members in the United States might find more
familiar, these Chinese sons and daughters were more likely to see their
relationships to medical staff as requiring ongoing complex and crucial
management work. One should not, I came to see, merely assume that
doctors and nurses would do their jobs well and give good care. In fact,
the assumption seemed to be that if giving care indeed were a "job," one
could count on it *not* being done well. The outcome of caregiving had to
be managed by a range of interactions, offers, and deference directed
toward positively influencing people with authority—doctors, nurses, unit
or even hospital leaders.

This, however, is not to say that the doctors and *peiban* I met had in
fact behaved badly or irresponsibly. Rather, it is that the operative assumption—under the circumstances of "scarce resources," the practice of
using "back doors," and the importance of filial duty—was that without
the requisite display of appreciation and/or "help" to those in power,
without concerted attempts to marshal both symbolic and material resources to influence the course of events, one's patient's care likely would

go badly. This then could weigh heavily indeed on those who had ignored or failed in this kind of work.[22]

Next to these efforts, my assumption that such care work is primarily a question of professional training and responsibility—requiring little "intervention" and "connections"—has since come to feel more than a little naive. Indeed, it now feels ideological, pressing me to think more critically about the discourses that bring that naive subject who still trusts "modern medicine" into being. But at the time, in that hospital, thinking about "their" strange assumptions, I recall standing firmly and uncritically on my Western bourgeois modernist "truth," quietly thankful to be "an American" consumer of medical care (even after more than a little experience at seeing it operate and writing about it).

But for "them," to ingratiate oneself to doctors and nurses was an abiding and serious question. This was explained by a doctor who himself had received such help. I had asked him to translate one of my questions to the son of one patient, asking how he knew when he would be permitted to come into the monitor room after posted visiting hours. The doctor, answering the question himself, said:

> You must understand the psychology of the *peiban*. In this ward, *peiban* are forbidden but in other wards they are more. Strictly not allowed in this ward; must stay in hall [outside the unit]. Many *peiban* try many times [to come in]. If the nurse is kindhearted, easy to talk to, peiban will try and maybe nurse will criticize or let go in or pretend not to see *peiban* come in. (So, the *peiban* should be sensitive to the nurse's and doctor's idea?) Yes, to clean the floor, to ask if this or that is easy for you, can I buy something for you—if you need movie tickets? There are many ways maybe to make a doctor happy. There are many things that can help with, and different things from different people and different occupations. For example, if I want to have heat in my house, they may help with the tube . . . and this kind of thing. Everything. I am the person here who can help him.

With so much emphasis on calculated help giving and receiving, and the inevitable careful "keeping of score" that accompanied this, it was not surprising to hear the criticism that "some" doctors and nurses received gifts from patients—although this seemed to be a sensitive subject and has been officially prohibited. This was mentioned, in anger, by one *peiban* who criticized a doctor that he and his family did not like. After saying the doctor was "cold," he added, "And he receives gifts from his patients."[23] Clearly, for this criticism to be made, those who gave had to have a sense that the recipient had in some sense "cheated" them—had taken a gift but had still behaved "badly," or in a less than "responsible" way. In short, it

was not so much the giving of gifts and/or services that was being de-
cried, but rather the sense of a lack of propriety by he or she who had
accepted, a lack of balance or reciprocity.

For their part, while doctors and nurses usually acknowledged the importance of *peiban* labor in Chinese hospitals (note how we have moved
to such generalization), and agreed that they themselves certainly would
want to monitor their own family members' care in the hospital (the traditional discourse), they felt *peiban* could be a nuisance to their work as
professionals, and even troublesome to the patient (the discourse of modern hospital administration; again, see Henderson 1989). If a patient were
seriously ill and required constant attention, they reasoned, perhaps *then*
it was important to have a family member available most of the time.
There simply were not enough nurses and "conditions were poor" (the
discourse of a developing country, struggling to "modernize" but still falling
short).

One senior doctor at another hospital said, bluntly, "We doctors don't
like *peiban* because they interfere with . . . work and some treatment.
But patient very like to have family member stay with him." One young
nurse said, "Most of the *peiban* do not understand the treatment and care
in the hospital and are very worried sometimes and angry when nurse
uses treatments. They think that if we use a machine on the patient, the
patient be die . . . do not want us to use the machine." Although nurses
acknowledged *peiban* labor, they usually were quick to point out that
"today" nurses themselves were able to do all the necessary care work. I
asked one young nurse about this. She said that even when she was very
busy, she did not like having *peiban* on the ward "because the relative ask
the nurse many questions and this take time. Sometimes this kind of
condition has a bad influence on the patient." This discourse of modern
medical administration casts family members, although well-meaning, as
in fact not serving the best interests of the patient, necessitating intervention by the medical staff (whose interests are thus held up as one with
those of the patient) to curb these negative effects—that is, to restrict and
coerce the presence of *peiban* in the hospital. (This sounded quite familiar to me from my own experience in hospitals back home. My mother,
brothers, and I for the most part tried not to "get in the way of" or
"bother" the doctors and nurses who worked around my father.)

In a hypothetical but I think telling account of how doctors might effect
this coercion, we can appreciate how the tensions between doctors and
peiban easily could build. The following comes from a longer conversation about permission-form signing:

Dr.: The most important thing a relative can do is to sign the paper!

I: What if the relative says no, won't let you do it?

Dr.: We continue to work until . . .

I: What if the patient says yes and the son says no?

Dr.: We ask the son, why do you not agree? Is it because of money? We tell him it is not important to worry about the money. We may try to bring public opinion or family opinion against him. We may go to other members of the family to try to force him to agree, or, even tell him I will tell his father in the bed that his son won't agree to pay for the treatment we want to do. This public opinion and the opinion of other family members is very important in China. We don't want criticism. We might even go to the unit where the son or daughter works and say, "How do you educate your workers? This son does not want to pay money for a treatment his father needs. You should do better!" This way we try to force the son.

I: What if the patient or the father says no and the son says yes?

Dr.: That is no problem. We do it.

"Harmony" can thus be achieved coercively, using diverse discourses in quite artful ways.

And doctors and nurses did sometimes describe *peiban* to me as people who might "make trouble" for them of a more consequential kind. They did seem to consider the resources a chastened or disappointed *peiban* could marshal in possible retaliation. For instance, the truck driver-patient who had been injured in an accident in the countryside and suffered brain damage had become a problem for the unit. His condition was medically stable and there were no treatments available to him save routine maintenance care. The doctors wanted the patient to leave, but the patient's sister and family members would not agree to a transfer. One of the doctors said in our conversation about him:

This patient is give me a headache. He is a driver and there was a car accident . . . in the countryside. . . . During his stay there [in a small county hospital] the patient's condition became worse and worse. He had ARDS syndrome, so we received this patient here . . . three months! I would like this patient to go away. He was discharged [once] . . . and went to . . . [another hospital in town] but that hospital refused to accept the patient because they have no special treatment for such a condition. He stayed only at emergency room for three days, then nowhere to go so the relative came back and met me and the head nurse. My opinion was we should receive. The head nurse said we should refuse. I was afraid the relative would have some quarrel with us if the patient died. The patient's relative has a lot of trouble with us. The trouble is the accident occurred in the countryside and the patient stayed at [the small hospital]. Came here from there, so [that hospital] refused to receive this patient too. The other side is the [city hospital in patient's home town]. We want to transfer [patient] to [that] hospital, but the relative doesn't believe in that hospital. . . . She refuses to transfer.

(Could you just send the patient there, to that city hospital even if the sister says no?) No. The patient relative must agree with the opinion.

I asked this doctor what sort of trouble this sister might be able to cause. He said: "She maybe go to the health bureau or find the hospital president and say that the patient is severely ill but Dr. [his name] refuse to receive the patient. Patient die. I will be criticized." While this doctor here considers his own and the hospital's liability—something certainly familiar in the West—he also gives great attention to *peiban* opinion and refuses to directly override their position (a posture certainly less familiar in the United States).

I heard stories about family members beating doctors when something "went wrong" in their patient's care. Asking direct questions about this usually brought chuckles and asides spoken in Chinese by these doctors. During a conversation with three doctors in which I explained something about malpractice suits and insurance in the United States, one middle-aged doctor quipped, "In our country, relatives always beat the doctor, not sue the doctor." Two doctors I spoke to actually had experienced physical assaults by relatives and patients. One was attacked when a patient died unexpectedly during a delicate cerebral vascular procedure; the other was beaten by a patient and his wife when he worked in the emergency room during the Cultural Revolution. Writing in the English language *China Daily* about a possible shortage of doctors in China, one journalist reported that one reason for a "lack of enthusiasm" for the job was the "lack of necessary legislation to protect medical workers from harassment and even physical assaults by family members all too ready to accuse them of medical malpractice" (Chen 1987).

Nurses, because they were largely responsible for managing *peiban* in the hospital, often were criticized by both *peiban* and doctors (something that nurses in the United States would find all too familiar). While praising "these nurses here," *peiban*-critics typically connected the presence of *peiban* to "too few nurses." Some family members added that nurses didn't do their work well, that they were "lazy," and treated relatives and *peiban* badly. In the strongest explicit condemnation of hospital care and, especially, nurses that I heard, one *peiban* said, in English:

> The trouble is they play with you in the hospital. They do not provide adequate service, not to say good service, but they play on your anxiety for the comfort of your sick family member by telling you the patient needs a companion and giving you the I.D. card, as if they were bestowing a great favor. In the intensive care unit you're told to go home and take a rest by the head nurse because there are three nurses on duty day and night for eight or six patients, but the minute you're out

of the room the nurses demand to know where the family is or tell some other companion to call you because the patient wants to urinate or something. In fact, they're always right and you're always wrong. The nurses never tell you that a seriously ill patient can do without a companion. They won't do the work! What I can't understand is why they can't do their jobs by themselves like everybody else. I believe that if the hospitals provided something like normally decent service nobody is such a sucker as to want to stay by a sickbed day and night, going without proper meals and sleep. There may be such suckers but they certainly are not in the majority.

Nurses and medical officials I spoke to were sensitive to such criticism and usually countered it with the modern medical discourse that separated nurses' and *peiban* interests on the grounds of the former's expert knowledge and training and the latter's ignorance and emotion.

One head nurse in another hospital, whom I spoke to through an interpreter early in the project, clearly spoke this discourse. When I asked her, a woman in her fifties and who said she had been a nurse for thirty years, about *peiban* on her floor and in the hospital, she said:

There has been a directive from the public health bureau that the hospitals had to be managed according to correct managing principles. This means not so many peiban. (In the past, what did these peiban do in the hospital?) They would feed the patients, clean the wards, carry urine and blood samples to the laboratory, get food from dining hall, wash the patient's hands and face, help them eliminate urine and go to the toilet. Sometimes they were also responsible for watching the solution for injection [IV] because they would tell the nurse when the bottle was empty. If patient had a high fever, they could wash the patient with alcohol to bring the fever down. This is now forbidden because this work belongs to the nurses and nurse assistants. Before there was disorder, during the Cultural Revolution, and now there are new standards for the management of the hospital. We have the responsibility system. Everybody has his or her work to do and even if you want to, you can't ask the patient's family members to do this work. This is the work of the staff.

This is the "modern" Chinese hospital. It leaves little space in which to enact the more traditional discourse on caregiving typically spoken by family members and patients. In fact, family members appear in "the modern hospital" only at visiting hours, ask few questions, stay out of the way of the staff, and are available to staff and patient when needed. Moreover, this sort of hospital assumes adequate numbers of well-trained ("modern") medical personnel. This is the image of the Chinese hospital that makes good the promise of modernization, and seeks to demonstrate China's advancement in an international community of medical care. That all of what this senior nurse described as part of a disordered past was precisely what I would soon witness in such great variety and detail helped me understand the importance and power of the official view, and the resentment of the unnoted *peiban* who in fact did such a great part of this work.

Modernization and Hospital Care

It is of course wonderfully convenient that, as one doctor put it, "family members 'like' to do this kind of thing"—this caregiving work—because, as another admitted, "If all the *peiban* in the hospitals in China were removed, that would be a social problem." That this contradiction of modernization in China—relying on a traditional discourse to shore up a considerably less established, "modern" one—is also recognized by the Chinese health bureaucracy is indexed in a brief article, entitled "View on Visiting Patients in the Hospital," that appeared in a 1986 issue of the *Chinese Journal of Hospital Administration* (see also Zhong 1985). The author, arguing that it is of course necessary to place certain limits on "companionship" in the hospital, writes that without more resources, such tight controls on *peiban* will "only create difficulties for the patient":

> Generally speaking, the patients tend to be in low spirits, particularly the severely ill ones. Some are depressed and worried, some anxious, some in dark moods, some lonely. Most of them wish to have someone from their families at their sides. This not only assures them of better care, it also reduces the patients' tenseness. It has the effect of providing them with solace and contributes to their sense of security and is helpful to medical treatment and the patients' recoveries. . . . Many patients feel unaccustomed to nursing care from anyone who is not a family member. Some feel embarrassed or uneasy. . . . Clearing the hospitals of companions often gives rise to arguments that affect the relationship between the patients and the medical staff. . . . In order to be at the patient's bedside, family members sometimes force their way into the ward, which causes rows and fights. . . . [T]he hospitals have made great efforts toward reducing the number of companions and controlling visiting hours. A large number of people have been employed to guard the entrances. In addition, measures have been taken, such as sudden inspections, which involve a large amount of man-power and resources. . . . [All of] this means there perhaps is not such a great advantage in exercising a tight control on companions and visitors. . . . (Wang 1986, 192)

Indeed, from this description one might ask what the benefits of such controls in fact are, save greater consistency with the image of the "modern hospital."

What this characterization clearly doesn't begin to acknowledge is the complex and endless *guanxi* work the family members I met did in order to get their patients into the hospital, not to mention efforts toward helping ensure what they hoped would be good care, once in. And the deeper tensions that define the complex relationships between hospital staff and *peiban* are also ignored. In the hospital, doctors, nurses, and officials have authority in the official discourse they use to try to gain *peiban* conformity with stated "modern" hospital rules. At the same time, they draw on traditional discourses of filial duty and harmony to coerce coop- eration and carework by *peiban*, work that then goes largely unnoticed and, most recently, even is repudiated by official regulations. Yet the doc- tors themselves are interpellated by traditional discourses of filial propri- ety as well as by a kind of "negative control" that keeps them mindful of their own debts to and transgressions against traditional and even social- ist codes of behavior. While invoking discourses of bureaucratic authority and "modern medicine," these doctors and nurses cannot afford to forget that not only are they "Chinese," but also that their official political line is a communist one—a line that, as has so often been the case in the past, can be effectively invoked by those below and beside them against all manner of "feudal," "counter-revolutionary," bourgeois, individualist, and "liberal" conduct.[24] The possibilities of making trouble for others seem to proliferate on both official and traditional grounds. And finally, to compli- cate the picture further, family members themselves use the traditional discourses of filial responsibility in the hospital, perhaps sometimes in spite of themselves, as a way to create and re-create themselves as proper and dutiful Chinese sons, daughters, and spouses.

But you will have noticed that I here have moved into a more totalizing, analytic voice, one common to narratives' endings, where authors are hard put to slip off the stage unnoticed and leave a pleasurable feeling of order and understanding—even if critical—among the audience about the object of study, in this case, "how family members care for their relatives in urban Chinese hospitals." Yet even as I began this ending I want to step away from it, to leave the story open, uncertain; not one that claims to tell you what was "really there," even as I have done just that through the familiar tropes of ethnography.

And although in the beginning I justified the project using my status as an experienced U.S. social scientist, from the earliest days on the CCU my own personal experiences as an American, and recollections of virtue and guilt connected to my family and to my father's long illness and death strongly influenced what I saw. After initial drafts of this paper sat quietly for some time, a colleague, Min-Zhan Lu, helped me see in the paper a sentimentality and nostalgia for duty properly done; personal sacrifices made; and for a sense of family and connectedness in social relationships that, to me, often feels quite absent in our "(post)modernized" lives. Readily available to help me fall into this trap were other familiar notions of "the Chinese" and of "Chinese duty." The real risk, a risk greater than being critical of things Chinese, was nostalgically to valorize the dutiful and seemingly never-ending care work family members in China did while neglecting the contexts of power and coercion in which this work was done; to, in effect, affirm the doctor's assessment that the way to understand this work was to see it as the product of what "[Chinese] family members 'like' to do." It was to make them out as fools, "suckers" (*shan yao dan*), as the one *peiban* put it so shatteringly. The Western bourgeois social scientist going to urban China in the late twentieth century to find parts of a cherished and fantasied past at home, and a "mirror" of his desired subjectivity in the other tamed, is an image now increasingly familiar in the deconstructive reexamination of past human science work. What falls away, as my Chinese colleague gently suggested, are the "irrelevancies"—what I couldn't see as reflections of me/"us." This kind of vision affirms, at the expense of the difficult and coerced lives of the natives, imaginary selves and lives seemingly lost by privileged outsiders not subject to these complexities. That these desires for self-affirmation via selective versions of "difference" typically operate under the surface of such ethnographic texts makes them sometimes more difficult to see.

But mine and ours is only one small instance of the endless dilemma of speaking from a centered place, from a discourse that is not simultaneously subjected to criticism and destabilization, and as such easily becomes universal. A sense that the ground in modern(izing) China is itself full of contradictions and complexities, even as we try to make it cohere in a "scientific story," provides a space of pause and transfer.[25]

3

Gao Changping 高畅平:
Prosperous, Smooth

[I]n its narrative construction of the subject, ethnographic realism functions not so much to suppress the voices of the researcher or the subjects of research, as many criticisms of ethnography would imply, but rather embodies voices as statistical personations, events, situations, and perspectives.

In making vision a distribution, a delegation, a substitution in desire, ethnographic realism provides sociological discourse with a capacity or agency for making visible. Thus ethnographic realism provides sociological discourse with a kind of vision that even in the eighteenth century, Fried . . . argues, deserved to be called cinematic.

Rather than making up what is lacking in any individual's imaging, cinematic realism disavows lack in and for the subject. In conflating subject positionalities with the gaze, cinematic realism offers the viewer an imaginary unified subject identity, constructed in a fantasy of visual mastery over what the subject seemingly lacks. Condensing a desire for a lost wholeness or completeness, the figure of the spectator elicits the viewer's desire for a unified identity.
Patricia T. Clough, *The End(s) of Ethnography* (1998)

Zhi zu chang le:
You'll Stay Happy If You Face Facts

It was a beautiful spring day outside. The humid air of Tianjin summer had not yet arrived. The cool, May morning breeze moved softly through the second-floor flat, with its southern and northern exposures; one face to the sun, *yang mian,* one to the clouds, *yin mian.* Gao Changping's apartment building was typical of many built in Tianjin in the 1950s, taking up the full width of the building and thus allowing good air circulation, and one "cool side" in the summer and welcome warmth from the winter sun, on the other. Now, in the spring of 1991, it still is a good place.

"Gao *lao*," the young man began. From the start of this project with the older, American sociologist, he had adopted the polite, honorific *"lao,"* preceded by the patient's surname, when addressing the elderly respondents in the families they visited. The American, "Mr. Shi," as Laihua called him—using only the sound of the first syllable of his German name—followed this lead. In general, he relied on his young colleague to take the lead when they met with their "cases." "Please tell us about your illness, about your family, and your work. Give us some introduction, please," Laihua said as he slowly looked up from his notebook, meeting the old man's eyes with his last words of invitation.

The two sociologists were beginning their first interview with Gao Changping, sixty-six, and his wife Huang Yushu, sixty-seven, although these of course are not their real names.[1] Each was highly educated, having graduated from university as classmates in 1948, the year before the People's Republic of China was founded. They had been together a long time; in fact, they were acquainted as children and no doubt came from a "bourgeois background." Mr. Gao, the patient, had just retired from his job as a senior accountant shortly before this first interview. He suffers several chronic conditions, and had begun to receive the services of a sickbed doctor from the local and well-known cadre sanitarium in the spring of 1987. Sanitarium leaders had included his name on the list they gave the two sociologists in response to their request in the fall of 1990 for sickbed families to visit.

Although we saw Gao Changping's name on this list, by December we already had contacted several families in which the patient was a privileged male senior cadre.[2] And although Laihua had made an initial visit then, in May, when we looked back over our list and at his name, we almost eliminated him from our last set of interviews. When we met him briefly, a week before this interview, we told him that after hearing some initial details about his situation we might not continue the interviews. We explained that we didn't want to collect the "same information" we already had obtained from other senior cadres.

If you think about it, that could have sounded very odd to him and his wife. We were saying that because we had collected information from other men who were relatively privileged in education and job, we then would have known something fundamental about him; that what he might tell us would be redundant; would provide us "nothing new" in our attempt to understand the workings of home care. It must have sounded at least strange.

But, aside from whether or not we should have told them this, it is not strange to the world of social science methods. Laihua and I both had learned in school, although separated by some 15 years and 18,000 miles, that we were sociologists and not historians. *They* were concerned primarily with the details of particular and usually "important" people's actions and "historic" events. They were not scientists. We sociologists, by contrast, were concerned with social patterns; with structures and processes that were pan- or transindividual, which exist independent of any individual; qualities that the experiences and characteristics of "anyman" or "anywoman," given the proper category, might speak to. We learned that we should be concerned with "the social" rather than "the individual." We learned that we were more interested in studying "average" or "typical" social types who had no particular names or faces that might distract attention from the form. We were *social scientists*.

Even in the midst of a qualitative study specifically aimed at appreciating the *details* of people's lives around illness and family caregiving, we were still trying to be good social scientists; trying to maximize the diversity of *types* of people and situations in our sample; trying to focus, finally, on the general, not the specific. We had in effect told Mr. Gao and his wife that as far as we were concerned, the *really* interesting thing about them was the extent to which they did or did not share certain "characteristics" in common with others in similar and different situations.

If they heard this, if Laihua expressed it in Chinese as bluntly as I put it to him in English when we were preparing for our first visit, which I suspect he did not, perhaps they thought it just one more foreign peculiarity. More happily, perhaps they didn't quite understand what Laihua said, and, themselves a little uneasy at the beginning of this new adventure with sociologists, including a foreigner, chose simply to let it pass. In any case, they said they understood, and so we went on. Although we did not then know what we later would write about Gao, Huang, and their family, we knew that the prime aim in good fieldwork was a sharp eye, open ears, mostly a closed mouth, and lots and lots of recorded detail.

The four of us sat in the larger of the flat's two rooms, Laihua and I in armchairs against one wall, separated by a small, glass-topped table; Gao across from us on a sofa with a large white crocheted doily along the back. Huang was to our right, sitting at the foot of the bed she and Gao shared. They both wore bright white, short-sleeved shirts that set off their open, alert faces. She of course smiled more readily than he, and right away we noticed that one side of his mouth was slightly immobile, but not so much as to affect the amount or clarity of his speech. In fact, we came to think of him as one of the most articulate and thorough chroniclers of chroniclers of his illness and family life. And his eyes conveyed a wit and humor that put us somewhat at ease. Laihua especially appreciated the way he spoke, the care he took with words.[3]

The rest of the room, with its deep-red painted wood floor that was beginning to show the wear, was just large enough for the tall armoire to the right of the sofa where Gao sat; a low table stood to our left under the window that looked down onto the sidewalk and street, and a chest with a small television on it was against the wall next to Laihua. Everything was very neat and clean; almost Spartan in feeling. Can you see it? Can you see them? Like television. Can you imagine yourself sitting there with us? It helps if you try.

Across the narrow entry hallway from where we sat was another, smaller room where Huang sometimes did sewing and other projects. We could see a single bed and a chest to one side. On that same side of the flat were a small kitchen and bathroom. All those rooms on the north side had windows looking out onto a rear courtyard, ringed by similar buildings and a drive.

Excuse me. I realize I'm disrupting the story a bit by jumping in here. I guess I'm supposed to say only what I actually said, or, what you wrote down in your notes when we met. But your description of my old house makes me think of it. I really do miss that place. Now, in the summer of 1993 as we all sit here in my new house, I am really thinking about my old house. My wife and I lived there for so many years; over forty all together. My two daughters were born when we lived there, and they grew up in those two small rooms. Moving to this new apartment—we've been here about two years now—seemed like such a good idea. It's much bigger and has enough room for one of my children and family to come and live here when we get too old or sick. And a telephone. We have a telephone now. Wang Laihua, you know that—you called to make this appointment. That makes many things much easier.

"Yes, yes. It is very convenient. My wife and I now have one too, and we like it very much."

"Of course, this is a very good place. My oldest daughter and her husband moved into this same building. But sometimes I ride my bicycle back to that old house and look at our building and the yard in back. I stop in the park at the corner where we would meet our neighbors in summer evenings after supper for a chat. There are so many big trees there that give cool shade. That was really a good place. I didn't realize it would be so hard to adjust to the move. Here it's much less convenient to go shopping for vegetables and food; and I don't know any of the neighbors. Outside, around the building is a terrible mess."

"The mosquitoes are *lihai*—terrible," said Huang, "and the smell from the factory and garbage behind the building almost makes us sick."

When LH and I came into the building downstairs, we each commented on how messy and unfinished the grounds and entryway of the new building were. Now, as she spoke, Huang motioned us toward the rear balcony that connected the TV room where we were sitting to the back hallway of the flat.

"Come and see for yourselves," she said. We followed her out through the screen door and looked down over the hazy adjacent lot.

"*Aiya!* It is so ugly!" said Mr. Shi in Chinese. He was especially good in short sentences and expressions that didn't invite subsequent questions.

Large rectangles of chemical-laced water, rutted mud paths, scattered piles of all sorts of refuse, and a long, low industrial building with a smokestack belching amber clouds greeted our view. Even on the fourth floor at 10 o'clock in the morning the mosquitoes were, suddenly, everywhere.

"Yes. It's bad," said Laihua. "Perhaps when these three towers are completely finished they will clean all this up. At least as much as they can."

Thoughtfully, which I had come to see as his signature, Laihua didn't open the question of the factory's presence, which would yield to no amount of cleaning and tidying. Nor would the endless stalls of sellers and little eateries that had sprung up along that once wide and quiet, shaded street where Gao and Huang had lived. Surely part of the economic reform, such scenes reminded me of the dense back streets of Kowloon, or of a proto-strip mall—two images (especially the latter) about which I felt more than a little ambivalence.

As we walked back into the room, Gao sank into his chair and wiped the beads of sweat from his forehead with a handkerchief. It had been a particularly still and muggy July morning and we all were feeling it, despite the fans, our bare legs, sandals, and the cool drinks we had been served.

"When you finished your work in the summer of 1991 I was feeling quite good. But before long I got depressed. It's elderly depression, *lao nian yiyu zheng*, I know. I read that book you gave me, Laihua, the one you and your colleague wrote (Wang and Wang 1990), and I remember the part about how old people sometimes have difficulty passing the period when they first retire their jobs. When I read it I thought, 'I have failed to pass that period.' I had and still have a real sense of loss, and I feel like there is nothing to do. Before I retired I didn't think about this, that I would have trouble adjusting to retirement. Remember, you first came to our house, Laihua, just a few months after I had formally retired in January

1990. I just didn't realize. And I haven't dealt well with the move to this new house. Didn't anticipate how the new place would affect me, how my relationships with my friends there would change. In fact, everything has changed. But I hadn't expected it. Now, although my living conditions are better than before, I always think about the past.

"And I also got sick again since I last saw you. A neighbor at my old house was redecorating his apartment, the one above ours. He set up a saw in his place and made a lot of noise. Then he caused a leak in our ceiling, which really upset me. I couldn't sleep at night. Just after we moved here, the same thing happened. The neighbors were fixing up their new houses and there was a lot of commotion and noise. It gave me insomnia. So, I went to the sanitarium."

"How long did you stay?" Laihua asked.

"Forty-five days. I had a single room and it cost my unit 2,600 yuan. If I did it now, it would cost 5,000! But I didn't have any response to their medicine."

"Yes," I said. "I hear that prices for all sorts of medical services are increasing. But have you had any problems redeeming your medical costs at your work unit?"

"None so far, but I think there will be some problems in the future. The prices are higher than ever before."

"How did you feel when you stayed at the sanitarium?" I asked.

"I felt bored, mostly; and depressed. All I could think of was the past— my work, my old home, my life—and how I missed it all."

"Gao lao, I wonder if you worry too much about yourself; your illness, and your situation. Perhaps it would be better if you didn't think so much about these things," Laihua suggested.

"Yes, you are right. He thinks and worries about his diseases more than other people," his wife insisted. "But it got even worse when he began to focus on being retired and then moving. He was the worst in 1992. He was always unhappy. I don't think he laughed once that whole time, even when he watched those crosstalk programs on television."

"We have the same sort of problem back home," I said. "Many older people have a lot of trouble adjusting to retirement, especially if their work has been an important part of their lives. Big changes also might be more difficult the older we get." Laihua translated my Chinese into more hearable Chinese for the old couple, who looked slightly bemused as I spoke. They nodded. Whenever I spoke about "life in the United States" I always felt I was conveying weighty truths, even though generally I am skeptical of precisely that kind of expert positioning. Nonetheless, such moments were occasions for me to clear a small space for myself and fully occupy it, even though, or perhaps because, I usually could do it, finally, only in English, with Laihua translating.

"After he came back from the sanitarium, though, he was better. He had begun, I think, to adjust himself to his new neighborhood. This year has been better," Huang hoped.

Laihua shifted in his chair, paused, and then asked what he called a "resting question." "Do you take some special medicine to help you now?"

"Yes. I have begun to take some new medicine for the insomnia that I really can't do without. I also take some for depression, but not very much. In my opinion, there are two kinds of *jingshenbing*—mental illness. One is mental illness and the other is *shen jing*—nervous disease. I think I have nervous disease, not mental illness. When I went to Anding Hospital last year, they called it a compulsion, and said that I still have the ability to realize when I am getting upset, and to understand some of the reasons why."

Laihua wrote furiously in his notebook as Mr. Gao raced on. These interviews always were long and yielded many pages of notes, first in Chinese and then, many more, in English. And, as we soon learned, Mr. Gao always had a lot to say.

"But there is good news in my family," Gao said with a smile. "My youngest daughter just had a baby. She is thirty-six years old and just had a baby boy. He is two months old."

"Oh really!?" we both said, smiling broadly.

"Yes," said Huang. "It was a Caesarean delivery."

"It's very good. Your situation is really good now," enthused Laihua. Your oldest daughter and husband live in the same building here. Your youngest daughter just had a baby. You can take care of him when he gets bigger. That will be really fine."

Although I smiled and nodded my head in agreement, I felt myself pulling slightly away from this sentiment. Was I so optimistic for Gao *lao*? No. But then I myself didn't have any children or grandchildren, so perhaps I was unable to imagine the joy that might come from such anticipations and the prospects that having a grandson would dissolve the frustrations and depression of aging, illness, and retirement. I thought to myself, this is one of those games I often see LH play; about how thinking/saying positive thoughts/words could make things better, or at least keep them from getting worse. Put a good face on it and it will be good. Sometimes his unshakable confidence in the powers of optimism was a little disconcerting. Could it be so easy?

"You are right. *Wo zong bu ren tou*—I never recognize my situation for what it is. For example, I didn't see how good my old house really was, so I moved here. I was wrong to move."

I smiled more broadly, but to myself. This man was still the worrier we had met two years ago; not given to wild enthusiasms. I appreciated that.

Huang said, with a trace of exasperation, "You have to face facts."

"*Zhi zu chang le!*" Laihua added quickly. "You'll stay happy if you face facts!"

"Yes!" chimed Huang. "*Zhi zu chang le!*"

I thought to myself, Gao *lao* is right. At least with worry and doubt about facts there remains the possibility that the facts one does not like might be changed.

An Introduction: The Facts of the Case

Wang Laihua asked me to tell you some of the details about my illness and condition. It's essentially what I told them, during some of our meetings. But before I do, perhaps I should say something about the way Wang Laihua and Mr. Shi have written this chapter and our words and us in it.

What you will read below is made up mostly of words and sentences we said in response to their questions and in subsequent conversation. Of course, these words have been translated into English, edited, paraphrased, and supplemented. You noticed, I'm sure, that there are no quotation marks at the beginning of this section, above. And they were absent when I interrupted what they were saying, earlier on page 64. That means those, and these, words didn't come from their interview transcripts or fieldnotes. They are not then what most sociologists usually call "data." You might see these words as more "made up" than those bearing the usual quotation marks (although those, too, are made up). You might say, using their terms, that these words were written in a different "field" than the ones they talk about as coming from or being written in "*the* field." I'm not quite sure which writing, which "-graphy," done where, that their word "ethno-graphy" refers to.

But even these latter words—the fieldnotes—are approximations to what exactly was said there, then and what was available to be seen. And even if we had an audio and video recording of what was said, that too would be an approximation. And so on. Moreover, they tell me that such records are virtually never presented verbatim or unedited in ethnographies and qualitative research. If you care about this kind of thing, perhaps you might want to ask what's the point, finally, in such a pursuit of literalness. They told me they were doing all that writing to be sure they got what we said correctly and accurately. Is it the Truth they want?

Well, it can't be that, at least not here, since they seem to be suggesting that literalness is not necessarily "the Truth" or even "the truth." What they write here, without quotation marks, they seem to want you to take seriously, that is, to take also as true. It does make one wonder what the word means, at least in this kind of writing. If it isn't literal, if we didn't actually say it, does that mean it's a "lie"? No, no. They say they are trying to tell true stories here. Well, let's get on with it.

When you *do* see quotation marks here, you can be pretty sure that we said something close to what you are reading—of course, it was in Chinese, so how would you know since you don't see *those* notes and perhaps you can't read Chinese anyway. They have added things we didn't say, in so many words, but I suppose we could have said them. And since what we *did* say is here all translated into English, I have no idea what they're telling you (even if they were to show it to me, which they have not). I guess you will have to trust them that it is true—that my wife and I and daughters and their husbands really said all these things, or that what we said and meant is accurately conveyed here in English. That's a lot of trust, isn't it? But then, I suppose we could ask what's at stake here; what difference does it make if they "got it right"? And what does getting it "right" mean? What would getting it "wrong" look like or mean?

During the late 1950s and then during the Cultural Revolution, I learned to trust almost no one. And to be very careful about what I believed—or at least what I said I believed. Then, if you got it "wrong" it could make a big difference. I mean, the stakes could be great, personally. But the issue is a bit different here. Perhaps one way to get by it is to treat what they say about me and my family as a true story, made from facts but fabricated nonetheless; certainly, what they write here is under their control; is put together to tell the stories they want to tell. They told me there were over 100 double-spaced typed pages of notes from the ten interviews they did with me and my family. Obviously, they have chosen what they want to say from those pages. Or, what they think they want to say. Even when others seem to speak in their own words, it's written, finally, by Mr. Shi and Laihua.

My wife tells me to "face facts" and I'll "be happy." But I wonder. I've learned some things about facts in my lifetime that always make me a little skeptical of them. I've seen them change, almost overnight. What I thought was true became false, and what was false became true. More than once. So I like not to believe in facts so much. Maybe I'm wrong, but it's my way. Anyway, you have to figure it out for yourself. Now, about my situation. This next part is really true.

"I graduated university in 1948 with a major in economics and started my first job in 1949, in a bank. That was the year we got married. I worked part-time as a clerk in that bank before graduation. All together, I've worked for forty-two years doing more or less the same kind of work—financial management, development, and planning. It's all brain work, and that probably is related to most of my diseases. I worked in that same bank until the Cultural Revolution, when, in 1967, I was politically investigated and criticized by a group of Red Guards. When things began to settle down a bit after 1970 I wanted to return to my bank, but it was not possible. So I worked in the financial planning department in another unit for several years, beginning in 1974, and finally started a job in a large investment company in 1980, where I took charge of setting up the company's financial operations. I worked in that unit until I retired.

"In the summer of 1969 I became what was called a *xiafang ganbu* or 'sent down cadre.' This idea came from Mao Zedong: that people in positions of administrative and other responsibility in government agencies should be criticized for their feudal and bourgeois thinking and then sent to do manual labor with peasants and workers in order to learn correct socialist thinking and practice. Actually, people in positions of authority in all sorts of units, including the universities and schools, were also seriously criticized and often 'sent down.' The then Party Secretary of Tianjin demanded *'wan min ganbu zhuan gongren!'* —that '10,000 cadres become workers!'—and the biggest sectors of the local government supplied enough of their cadres to meet this quota. I was one of them. They didn't send me to the countryside but to become a seller in a little shop—you might call it a convenience shop. We call it a *tang guo yan jiu dian,* one that sells sweets, fruit, cigarettes, and wine. It actually wasn't far from my home. Because I hadn't done manual work for such a long time it was a big burden for me, and my blood pressure was really high. By 1978, most of the 'sent down' cadres had returned to their old jobs or to other similar jobs. But the bank transferred my personal file to that shop, which they should not have done, and that caused me a lot of trouble in trying to get my old job back. I had done bank work all my life, yet there I was, still selling fruit. It really bothered me.

"Sometimes I wonder if my various diseases are related to those experiences in the Cultural Revolution. My wife, daughters, and their husbands have talked about it with me a lot. I think it was a condition for most of the diseases that I have, but not really the cause. Most of my problems are not the same as *waishangbing,* or the illnesses of those injured in the Cultural Revolution. My diseases run in my family. Three generations of my family died from hypertension and heart attack. The oldest was sixty years old, and the youngest was thirty. So inheritance is the root cause of my health problems.

"The beginning of these problems was in 1967. I found out I had hypertension. In about 1970 I was diagnosed as having an irregular heart beat. In 1976 I had a heart attack and was diagnosed with coronary artery disease. Then in 1977 I had a problem in my brain. I lost consciousness and vomited constantly. Two specialist doctors—Sun Lida and Jiang Tao at Main Hospital—diagnosed my sickness as Ménière's syndrome, which is a result of restricted blood flow in a brain artery. Another doctor, Liu Yucun, who was the head of the surgery department at Main Hospital, also examined me. Dr. Sun Lida was the head of a department there, and about a year earlier I had asked him to come to my home to examine me. That's how the first diagnosis and treatment process for this problem got started.

"Dr. Sun was a friend of my brother-in-law who worked in the Tianjin Party Committee, and that's how we originally contacted him. I have the habit of trying to find the best specialists to diagnose my illness. Later, I don't bother them as long as they examine me and make a correct diagnosis, tell me the dangers of my disease, and suggest what I can do about it. That's all I ask. I think when someone gets older, he or she should have good friends who are qualified doctors. This is what I have tried to do. I also want to know about my diseases in detail. *Wo xin kexue bu wei xin zhuyi*—I believe in science rather than idealism.

"The same problem—Ménière's syndrome—happened to me again in 1982, and I stayed in Pinghe Hospital for two months in the summer. In August I went to Main Hospital, and then in September I stayed in the sanitarium for three months to rest and recuperate. That was the first time I went there. During that stay I had a CAT scan at First Affiliated Hospital and the director there, Dr. Yu, found I had some atrophy in my brain. That test only cost 120 yuan. The sanitarium sent me by their car to another hospital where they had that machine. Their doctors and nurses brought my medical file and accompanied me there. Back then, senior cadres were treated wonderfully. It also was difficult to get into the sanitarium then. The party committee of my unit had to make a special request. That's all changed. Now they only recognize money rather than people. Anyway, the development of my diseases was hypertension first, then heart disease, and then brain disease.

"The second time I stayed in the cadre sanitarium was in 1986. Late in 1985 and into 1986 I had been doing some difficult work reviewing accounting procedures of various companies to try to detect corruption. The government wanted this kind of thing stopped. Also, my unit was setting up a sanitarium for its members in the resort area of Beidaihe, and I had to go there and work on those arrangements. There was a lot of tension and difficulty around that work. In Beidaihe I began to feel strange and had trouble walking. I couldn't pick up food properly with my chopsticks, and I would drop food out of my mouth and drool on the front of my shirt when I ate. My thinking was also a little muddled. It was all pretty frightening. I came home right away but didn't see a doctor. It continued and got worse, so I went to see Yin Fangzhi at the neurology department of a street clinic connected to Main Hospital. My blood pressure was very high. She arranged a temporary sickbed for me at home, and then a consultation at First Affiliated Hospital. That was all in March. In April I went back to the sanitarium here as a patient. The specialists at First Affiliated Hospital wanted me to have another CAT scan, and so we called on a colleague again to help us arrange it—the same man who helped us with the first CAT scan. He works at my unit and knows the accounting and finance department at that hospital, so we had the test right away. My company once loaned the hospital money to buy that machine."[4]

What? I can't hear you. Oh, yes. My wife wants to say something here.

"At first, they put his name on a list and said it would be at least two months before he could have that test. That was a joke. By that time, a patient could die. After we contacted our acquaintance, he had the test quickly."

"Yes. They took twenty-one small pictures and eight big ones of my brain and spinal vertebrae. It cost 960 yuan. Anyway, while I was staying in the sanitarium, I was also looking for specialists and hospitals to help me diagnose the problem. The sanitarium is just for general care and recuperation, not for complicated medical treatment. I had to depend on specialists because the CAT report was very brief and only reported the numbers. I had to find someone who could tell me what they meant.

"Dr. Yin Fangzhi said we should find Dr. Chen Baogang, an old man who was quite famous in treating this kind of illness. The two of them read the CAT report and diagnosed the problem as a weakness in some of the spinal vertebrae. They also told me tests showed I had recessive diabetes and too much fat in my blood. For the vertebrae problem there were two solutions: surgery or traction. Of course, I chose the second and went to Pingshan Hospital for it. A specialist there, Dr. Zhao Buo, helped me. Later, I bought a traction machine and used it at the sanitarium, where I did it every day for thirteen months. I went home on 16 May 1987, and after a short while I went back to work.

"Another thing that was supposed to be treated in the sanitarium was a problem I was having during my sleep, but the doctors and nurses there said they didn't know how to treat it. A few years before that I began to have something like little comas while I was sleeping, and I would stop breathing. Then I would wake up. The doctors there were concerned that perhaps one time I would not wake up and then I would die. The leaders at the sanitarium asked doctors from the Second Affiliated Hospital to come and examine me. One of those doctors called my problem 'temporary coma in the night.' This is something I knew doctors in foreign countries know about, but not very many doctors here understood it. Mr. Shi, you called this 'sleep apnea.' Right? I found a report in a magazine from America that said some elderly people who have this disease die from it. It scared my wife and me, but it scared the doctors and nurses at the sanitarium even more. I had several spells of this when I was staying there. The chief doctor asked me to leave. He said there was no way they could treat the condition. Actually, there was some medicine I took to help me stop snoring, which is related to that disease. I also knew that they were afraid that I would die there, and that I then would try to hold them responsible.[5] They asked the nurses to check on me four or five times each night while I slept."

"I want to add something more here," said Huang. "At that time, when he was in the sanitarium, the leaders there said that if he wanted to stay there again, his unit should *dan bao* or take responsibility for his death if he were to die there. I also went to the sanitarium and signed a form. By that time, his sleeping sickness had been diagnosed. That made the doctors even more worried because it meant his sickness is well-known in the world, and that many foreigners had died from it. They asked him to leave. I know about that sleeping problem well. He had it when he was younger too. Now I am not afraid of it so much. When I see that he is snoring strangely during his sleep, I wake him up."

"Yes. My wife has been my special nurse for all my problems. At one point, she would give me oxygen to help me breathe more easily."

"We have a blood pressure tester here at home. When his heart beats slowly and his blood pressure is a little low, we handle it. We ask him to take some medicine. The sleep apnea scares me, but, luckily, we have been able to get treatment for him in time when he needs it.

"And I also have tried to help him adjust and prepare psychologically for his illness. When a person gets older, his sickness will get worse over time. Everyone finally has to die. In the past, after his sickness reoccurred, others said they thought he had gotten worse. Later, he recovered completely. I think it is because he has had early and good medical treatment. I also prepare myself for it mentally. A person gets older. His sickness gets worse. This is inevitable."

There was a pause in the talk as Gao slowly put his cup down and took up where his wife left off.

"I think I was most worried in the spring of 1986 when I vomited constantly. I even vomited blood. Shouldn't I be frightened? I paid a lot of attention to it; tried to understand it, and then avoid things that made it worse. For example, I was a heavy smoker and I liked to drink a lot of strong wine. When I found out those things affected my diseases, I stopped them. And I have tried to eat less fat and lose weight and exercise since I have understood my heart problems. Knowing about my diseases makes me feel better, mostly. Although sometimes I do think a lot about dying.

"But yes, my wife is my special nurse. She is my major caregiver. The biggest help she gives me is to help reduce my worries, my anger, and my frustrations. When I have 'eaten' a 'big chunk' of something and it is bothering me, she helps me 'digest' it. She helps me get it down. Over the past several decades, she has played a big part in helping me control my anger. After I got sick, my spouse and daughters treated it as an important thing. They united and took care of me, both in the hospital and at home. They stayed by my bed; brought me good food; and made me happy.

"After my children got married and moved away, my wife continued looking after me in this same way. She has looked after me all my life—the whole course of my life. She has stayed beside me from the beginning to the end. I can't put it more plainly. When I couldn't move, she emptied my bedpan and wiped me. She has sacrificed herself for me. What she has given me is more than what I have given her.

"A spouse is the only person who can stay by your side all your life. There is a saying: 'A patient who is sick for a very long time will have no obedient son by his bed.' Sons and daughters can't do what a spouse can do!

"The doctors at the sanitarium—when I was there in 1986—told me I should lose weight and change my diet to eat less fat, so I started to exercise. I would walk three times around the nearby Water Park each day—that's about 18 kilometers—and I reduced the amount of food I ate by a lot. On 25 December I fell down in the sanitarium and then had a high fever. There was blood in my urine. Through a consultation with Number 800 Hospital doctors, they diagnosed it as chronic prostate inflammation. My wife went to the sanitarium and stayed beside my bed for a week. It was interesting. My unit thought the sanitarium did such a good job in taking care of me that they gave them gifts, including a decorative mirror, to express their thanks.

"Finally, on 16 May 1987 I went home. I am sure they were relieved. Soon after, they set up the sickbed for me with Dr. Liang that I am still enjoying. She comes here once or twice a month, tests my blood pressure and prescribes medicine."

Let me see what else I have written here in my notes to tell you. Oh yes. "Last year, on 12 January, I was getting ready to go to work and I looked in the mirror and noticed that my mouth was a little drawn to one side and my face looked a bit strange. It wasn't too noticeable, but I went to Pinghe Hospital, near here. They thought it might be caused by a cerebral embolism, but they also suggested that I see a traditional medicine doctor. I found an old man who is a well-known traditional doctor and who has a lot of experience treating this kind of thing. He said he thought it was facial nerve paralysis but suggested that I go to the neurology department of another hospital I had a connection with and ask them to test me. I did that, and asked the doctor there if I had an embolism. He examined me and said it probably was facial nerve paralysis. This kind of problem is often treated by acupuncture and herbal medicine.

"I went to that traditional hospital again and had treatment from a young doctor. After fifty-eight days of acupuncture, he said he had failed to treat me successfully, and that he needed to call in his master to treat me, which he did. The master, who is quite famous and has visited many countries, treated me both in the hospital and after I came home. He gave me *tou zhen*—pass through—acupuncture with long needles, and after three months my face got better. I also continued to use herbal medicine, one kind that I took internally and another that I used to wash my face. At the time I also was having an IV of medicine from that street clinic where Dr. Yin Fangzhi worked. Now my face is almost normal. I stopped the treatment because I was having a spasm from the needles. Perhaps if I were a young female comrade, I wouldn't have given it up! I'm an old man, and I'm content with the way it looks now."

So, that's my illness and treatment situation. I'll just briefly say something about my family. You know my wife and I have been together for a long, long time. "Not only were we classmates at university, but also when we were sixteen, in middle school. We were neighbors. We were married when we both were twenty-five."

"No. I was twenty-six."

"Oh, yes. I was twenty-five and you were twenty-six.

"Our financial situation when we got married was not good. We both started working right away, she as a teacher and I in the bank. My wife was a middle school teacher of Chinese literature all her life until she retired. We have two daughters, and so our family is a harmonious one. The first was born in 1952 and the second in 1958. Although there was no family planning policy at that time, we planned it on our own. Because we both gave a lot of attention to our work, we married a little later than usual, had fewer children than others, and took more time between them. Besides that, we only have two daughters, no son. According to Chinese tradition, that means we will have no one to carry on our family. We broke this old custom.

"My first daughter is a worker. In fact, she is a model worker at her factory. She went to the countryside for seven years at the start of the Cultural Revolution. This was supported by the same ideas that sent me to the neighborhood shop as a seller, except that young students were anxious to help support Mao Zedong's continuing socialist revolution. They were full of enthusiasm for that. Most of us cadres were not so enthusiastic. As a result, she missed getting a college education. The second daughter was luckier because she was younger. She was trained in her *danwei's* college as a design engineer and started working there in 1977. Just last year she inherited my kind of work, accounting, and actually works in my unit.

"Both daughters are married, and the oldest and her husband, who teaches in the university here, have a daughter of their own who is twelve and a half. She is studying the violin in the best music academy in China, in Beijing, and she lives there at the school. Her music and her studies have been very high quality. My wife taught her school subjects and morals since she was a little girl. Her parents concentrated on her music. She even was able to skip a grade because of her intelligence. Actually, I think she inherited her musical ability from me. I used to sing Beijing Opera—not on the stage but just for my own enjoyment. I knew two roles particularly well, and during the Cultural Revolution I was criticized for it. They said I was 'a trumpet for gifted scholars and beautiful ladies in romantic stories.' In Chinese, it's *'Wo shi cai zi jia ren de chui gu shou.'* Anyway, after that, I stopped singing. My second daughter still has no child. All together, including my sons-in-law, my family members number seven. And these children don't depend on their parents to support them. They live their own lives. When my daughters got married, they left. But they continue to look after us. Today this daughter comes here; tomorrow that one comes. When they come they do housework and other trifles. Although we have no children at our sides, it is as though we do, and so as an old couple we are relatively happy."

Privilege

Gao *lao* is of course right to suggest that we have made up this true story about him and his family, and that in it we have foregrounded what we choose, although it is likely that some of these "choices" we ourselves are only vaguely aware of making. In this section, we want to frame some of the "facts" about Gao Changping and his family that you have just read in order to offer a more sociological reading: how one can see privilege operating in their lives, how it has shaped his medical and health care, and, by implication, what a difference it can make. Social scientists often use the notions of privilege and power as analytical resources to "make sense" of the details or data they set forth. This sort of interpretive foregrounding—in this case, of privilege or power or class—is typically seen as of a "different order" than that involved in setting out the facts of a case under consideration. It is often called "theory" or "theoretical." Here it's an encouragement to see the details of Gao's life and situation we have just offered as "explained by," "evidence of," understandable as the workings of considerably more concerted social and historical processes and practices in the particular place and time at hand ("urban socialist/communist China at the end of the twentieth century"). This interpretive/writing technology relies on the separation of the *reading* from *that which is to be read*, and is a familiar piece of the (scientific) realism on which virtually all social analysis and commentary rests.

And while much of the recent criticism of social and human science writing has focused on realist interpretation—the claim, implied or explicit, that the scientist operates "the mirror of nature" (Rorty 1979) to show us "the truths of nature"—it is important to see that the very production of the "facts" that Gao's wife encourages him to face—things that she takes to be just the way it is—involves a similar creative process. Contrary to the popular aphorism, facts do not "speak for themselves." Indeed, "facts" have to be so named and framed in order to exist in the first place, and it is in this naming and framing that they do whatever "speaking"—and it is indeed often consequential—that they do. So seen, they are more like ventriloquist "dummies" than voices independent of those who appear to "let them speak"—those, in short, who are in the business of producing true knowledge.[6] We make the point then that it is not just the interpretations and analyses of "social and cultural phenomena" that are made up, but also the very facts that such realist analyses purport to explain (cf. Latour and Woolgar 1979). While one may respond with a slightly tired "of course," the complication is all too easily, and too often, elided or "forgotten" in the authoritative speech of social analysts and critics intent on "getting somewhere," including those of us smitten by various of the "post-" styles of writing and thought.

And the foregrounding move here that Gao notes is also often a move of criticism. This is sometimes made more apparent by a simple question: why talk about this? Or, why *this,* rather than *that?* Within conventional social science, this may be more difficult to see, in that the notion of criticism there often is framed more in terms of implications for theory and methodology, and of the priorities set out within a sometimes quite formal system of assumptions, hypotheses, and already "collected" facts; in short, within a theoretical paradigm or canon. "Good" critical questions contribute to theoretical advancement; "bad" or "unpromising" or "uninteresting" ones are those that are seen to offer little or no such advancement in knowledge. Among those working in the human sciences in more reflexive and critical ways, and in ways that make the very selection of a theoretical problem itself a matter of politics and values, however, the designation of questions or choices as "good" or "bad" is seen explicitly as a political/moral move.

That we want here to comment on privilege in Gao's story is to say that we want to offer up a criticism of the operation of that privilege, although not necessarily because that critique might have implications for "formal" theory. Nor does it necessarily mean we want to criticize him and his family personally, or that we will offer up an elaborate alternative to the arrangements that we criticize. It certainly does not mean that we think privilege operates more perniciously in the system of Chinese state-market-socialism than in U.S. late capitalism. And that we criticize this operation of privilege is not to say that we ourselves are not part of, and do not participate in, the very sort of thing we are criticizing. We—Schneider and Wang—in our own lives and jobs and families enjoy and exploit privilege. Making privilege an issue here is, rather, to try to specify how it provides Gao and Huang and their children and us and many others advantages that affect the way their/our lives are lived, and to suggest how its absence can make life more burdensome and painful. Finally, the move to foreground this privilege does want to show how, across ostensibly very different political economic systems and situations, climbing local hierarchies of rewards and accumulating resources can seem perfectly natural and normal things to do.

Gao and Huang, although confronted with diverse and complicated coping and management problems linked to his illnesses and the anxiety and fear that accompanied them, have had more than a little privilege in their lives together. As is typically the case, the advantages they have enjoyed from their education and then from his position as a technical expert in banking and finance are ramified in many, often quite mundane, aspects of their family and personal lives. Unlike the operation of privilege in the "democratic capitalism" of the United States, it is for the most part accurate to say that in China since 1949, privilege has been closely connected to political standing and position within the Communist Party.[7] This is not to imply that in the United States relationships of privilege are enjoyed only by those who "deserve" them, but more to mark differences in the access to privilege in China compared to the United States, and to its operation in twentieth-century, postimperial, precommunist China as well.

Personal material wealth and income in China after 1949 could much less easily be translated into the comforts and advantages it brought during the thirty some years between the fall of the empire in 1912 and the socialist revolution in 1949. With the new government led by Mao Zedong's Communist Party, there was indeed a significant change in the discourses in terms of which people figured themselves as good citizens and as loyal Chinese. Virtually all scholars of modern China note that the material conditions of "average" people's lives—and especially those who had been the poorest and the most exploited—did improve after 1949, but in ways differently inflected by diverse local circumstances. An important part of those new discourses inaugurated and encouraged by Mao Zedong and the party was that the suffering of "the people" of China was caused largely by the exploitation by fellow citizens who were landed and/or monied people, usually with "foreign connections." Those who had enjoyed privilege and respect under the republic and the particular historical mix of feudalism and capitalism that China was before "Liberation," became the objects of criticism and the bearers of responsibility for the suffering so many had endured. Although an oversimplification, it was as though the "best" of the old postimperial/feudal/capitalist system became the "worst" of the new socialist one, and the poorest peasants and laborers of the old became the most respected and revered figures in New China (see Billeter 1985).

The socialism that Mao Zedong ushered into China was of course ostensibly a government of and for "the people," not one that simply would reproduce the structures of privilege and advantage of the old society by putting new bodies in old structures. But since some of the people had been so exploited, so beaten down; and since they were for the most part uneducated and/or, according to the party, suffered the "false consciousness" that their and the landlords' and capitalists' interests were the same, they were unable to see clearly the proper politics and future of this New China. They needed, in short, to be led to see the truth.

It was into this void that the Chinese Communist Party would step, offering itself as that leader, a "vanguard" for the people, working to cleanse the society of the remnants of "feudalism" and capitalism; building a truly humane state socialist utopia.[8] But this "void" was also strategically and retrospectively created by the discourses of that party (see Anagnost 1997, 17–44). One source of these discourses, although it would be shaped to Chinese conditions as read by Mao and other revolutionary leaders, was the political writings of Karl Marx and V.I. Lenin and the experience and wisdom that was both sought by and pushed onto China by key figures and events in the Soviet Union. The party and the particular social forms it took in China would become the structure in terms of which privilege was to be figured in the ensuing decades, although the rhetoric that accompanied and helped create these changes certainly did not speak of it in these terms. Rather, whatever benefits party officials at various levels enjoyed were described in terms of their leadership contributions to the revolution and to "the people."

Scholars on China, as well as popular opinion, seem to agree on a characterization of the social atmosphere in the early years of the new government as euphoric and progressive, buoyed by a sort of unity around the discourses of people's socialism and the commonweal that Mao and the party offered. Gao and Huang, and several others we interviewed, spoke these discourses, including that of "scientific socialism." Especially in the countryside, egalitarian reforms in the allocation and use of land—which had been held by wealthy landlords—were to make notable improvements in the quality of life most people lived (excepting of course the landlords). In consequence, popular support for the government is described to have been relatively high during this period. This historical context is where we would like to place Gao Changping's story, and most of the stories that follow, since almost all of the patients we met were born in the early decades of the twentieth century and lived through and in these events and their official and unofficial stories.

Clearly, although he did not speak of it to us, Gao would had to have enjoyed diverse and important family and material resources in order to pass through the gates of a major Chinese university in 1944 as a new student. And Huang Yushu would have had to come from a similar social class background. Although he tells us that his and his wife's financial situation was "not good" when they graduated university in 1948, they were, statistically speaking, a rarely privileged Chinese couple relative to the vast majority of their fellow citizens, according to what might be called "modern bourgeois" criteria. And although during the Cultural Revolution Gao would suffer for this privilege and the "bourgeois economics" he learned at university, he was able to turn his education and family resources into a job in the local branch of the major state bank in China.[9] Over the course of his employment there, he rose in position and responsibility to a quite high cadre rank. Even after being "sent down" and criticized during the Cultural Revolution, Gao was able to regain a similarly high position in a new financial agency that he helped to establish and where he stayed until he retired. Gao and his wife were articulate and politically sophisticated in their conversations with us, and although we did not ask him directly about his relationship to the party, it would be surprising indeed were he not a long-time member in good standing.

One of the most compelling examples of how Gao's privilege operated in the mundane details of his life is in his access to and use of medical resources, which in turn considerably reduced the difficulties and burdens of his home care. He certainly drew on his sense of himself as an educated and knowledgeable person—someone able both to understand unfamiliar ideas and act on his understanding of them; and he took a managerial and quite "individualist" view toward his health and illness. But the benefit he took in these matters from his position as a senior cadre in an important state institution was by far the most important influence in understanding how he got the care and treatment he described.

In contemporary China, the *danwei* or work unit has been at the center of the flow of authority and influence in everyday urban life.[10] One's "employer," in short, has been the conduit through which the state and its policies have sought to influence everything from one's political thinking, to whom one could marry, to how many children a family can have, to how much flour and meat and oil one could buy in the market. This kind of control has lessened significantly in the last two decades, but in terms of life chances and outcomes, the work unit very likely remains for most middle-aged or older urban workers the single most important association the citizen sustains. Too simply, one might say that the more important one's unit in the state's scheme of things (e.g., a ministry or national bureau), and the higher one's place in that unit (e.g., administration), the easier one's life was. Gao Changping ranked high on both criteria.

According to what he told us, the volume as well as the quality of his access to medical resources were remarkable—from highly trained and experienced doctors, to hospitals and clinics, to referrals, to special cadre sections in those hospitals and to the cadre sanitarium itself and its sickbed service, not to mention the full reimbursement from his unit for these services. Perhaps more than any other patient we met, Gao's story is one of diverse, high quality care enjoyed in what was, for the most part, a timely and friendly way. And fortunately for us, he had made meticulous written records of this care and the chronology of his illness that he was willing to share with us.[11] We came to expect that he not only could tell us the dates of his illness episodes and visits to doctors and hospitals, but also the diagnoses, his doctors' names and their specialties, and the details of these doctors' reputations.

By the time we interviewed Gao, toward the end of the project, I myself had built some context within which to understand what he described. When juxtaposed to the earlier stories from others who had considerably less medical care, what he had received was stunning to me. You already have read some segments from stories of those less fortunate people and more will follow. We hope that as you encounter them you will think back to Gao's descriptions to get a sense of what this level of privilege could mean. Recall, too, that his benefits came not primarily from his material resources—specifically, money—but rather as part of the perquisites of his job under state socialism.[12]

From his diagnosis of hypertension in 1967, to one of our last visits with him in 1993 and his story of having to deal with "old age depression" by using drugs from the cadre sanitarium, Gao appears to have been able to get the medical attention and care he wanted when he wanted it, and, more or less, at a level that satisfied him. It is likely that during the early years of the Cultural Revolution he would have been less free to negotiate his medical care using his position in his bank and personal relationships. The kinds of special treatment higher cadres received in hospitals and clinics (and still receive) would have been attacked by Red Guards and revolutionary committees during that time. And attempts to use networks of friends and acquaintances as "back doors" would have been risky. But by the time he suffered his heart attack in 1976, and the first symptoms of Ménière's syndrome a year later, Gao knew how to secure relatively high levels of care.

Through his network of personal and work connections, he obtained the services of several specialists in both Western and traditional Chinese medicine, beginning with Doctors Sun Lida and Jiang Tao in 1976–1977. As he tells it, he first asked Dr. Sun, the friend of his brother-in-law and a powerful and prestigious doctor whose reputation we already knew independent of Gao, to come to his house to treat him. As a result of his examination, Sun consulted with doctors Jiang and Liu, also on the staff of Main Hospital, and together the three diagnosed and treated Gao beginning in 1977. These "best specialists" were "managed" to ensure that they would remain available for subsequent consultation and care, and Dr. Sun even became something of a friend to Gao and Huang, visiting their house for dinner and conversation. At virtually every hospitalization and consultation, Gao was able to receive the services of competent, experienced, and attentive doctors.

This might raise the question of what doctors receive in return for giving their attention to influential patients such as Gao Changping. This speculation has been part of an ongoing and ever-louder public debate in China since the early 1980s over the extent and misuse of cadres' and officials' benefits and perquisites. Indeed, it was one of a few central themes in the massive public demonstrations in Tiananmen Square and around China in the spring of 1989, and had long been the topic of private grumblings among the *laobaixing,* or common people. Not surprisingly, this use of one's position to bring personal advantage—no doubt extant everywhere there are hierarchies, although admittedly to varying degree—was becoming apparent in urban hospitals and in medical care more generally throughout the 1980s (see Zhong 1985). While the government has responded with sometimes vigorous campaigns denouncing practices such as giving money and gifts to doctors in anticipation of and in return for their services (rumors circulate in cities specifying just how much a family might have to pay doctors for various medical and surgical procedures), in all of our research on caregiving in Tianjin we heard only stories of "other families" and "other doctors" who had given and accepted such illegal gifts. Still, it was the occasion for a good deal of grumbling about "some doctors."

But there is a difference between what might most harshly be called a "bribe" or "payoff," and what might be considered a proper level of politeness and appreciation for help given or requested (see Kipnis 1997;

Yang 1994). This difference is perhaps more subtly drawn in China, where there is a long tradition of gift-giving as a way to mark propriety and one's own status as a person properly sensitive to the reciprocity that defines the social. Giving small gifts and/or inviting a friend or acquaintance for a meal (increasingly, in a restaurant) in anticipation and/or in return for a favor asked can perhaps too easily be seen from afar as disingenuousness, or an untoward reliance on material reward and benefit when "genuine 'human feeling'" would be preferred.[13] Perhaps especially in matters of interpersonal and family needs and resources, rather than, say, in dealings between work units and agencies, such gift-giving and use of connections might better be read as more sanguine than pernicious.

As for Gao Changping, he announced to us proudly that although he had been treated by many specialists and obtained a good deal of medical care, he had "never given money to a doctor" for these services. The most he had done, he said, was to invite some of these doctors to his home for a meal, and give "small gifts" as a token of his appreciation. Of course, he would be unlikely to tell us directly if he had given money illegally for his care, implicating both himself and his doctors.

While no doubt there are some doctors who do take advantage of the fears and anxieties of their patients for their own personal benefit, short of a careful investigation—which itself would be very difficult—it is impossible to say how common such practices are. In any case, people seem both to complain about it and to worry or strategize about how best to place oneself in the debt of a medical doctor. As Gao recommended: "when someone gets older, he or she should have friends who are qualified doctors." He added later that money now had to be added to acquaintances and connections. Of course, it is good advice, but not easy for everyone to follow.

Beyond access to specialists, Gao had access to hospital and sanitarium care. This particular sanitarium, in a large parklike setting, with peaceful walkways and beautiful, quiet ponds of fish and flowers, was open only to cadres of a certain rank and only on authorization by the party committee in one's unit. Devoted to convalescent and rehabilitative care, patients are treated by a large staff of variously trained medical workers, including doctors, nurses, aides, therapists, barbers, and recreation directors. For acute episodes, patients received consultations with the best Western and traditional doctors from city hospitals. Gao himself was taken by a sanitarium car, accompanied by sanitarium doctors, for one such consultation. This kind of treatment was common for patients there.

And as for payment of Gao's medical fees, his unit seemed to have set no limits on the services he could receive.[14] The high fees at the sanitarium are mentioned in our 1993 interview with him, and his success in scheduling and then gaining permission for two CAT scans in the period 1982–1986 marks both the privilege of his position and his unit's practice of fully supporting their leaders' medical fees (recall the very different experience of the CAT scan patient discussed in chapter 2).

Although the sheer amount of money Gao's unit spent on his care is notable, it is important to underline that this is one feature of China's past urban health care system that has not absolutely distinguished high cadres from common workers. As we learned in stories from some workers' families, not only did they receive 100 percent reimbursement for medical fees, but the actual amounts of money paid were in some cases relatively great. This fully socialized aspect of China's urban medical care system has given way to much greater "private pay" arrangements and restrictions on what hospitals can be used and for which particular services. At one point in our conversations with Gao and Huang, he acknowledged that without China's public health care he would have been in very serious trouble. He might also have noted that some of the "public" are in a position to benefit considerably more than others.

Beyond Gao's privileged access to medical care, we want to note two other details of his story that are relevant to privilege. These deal with housing and with the way a parent can pass on employment to a child.

Gao told us that his oldest daughter, thirty-nine at the time of our first interviews, spent seven years in the countryside as a "sent down" youth. As a result, she was unable to attend university (in any case, the colleges and universities were closed for a good part of this period). As a result, when she came back to Tianjin in 1978, already in her mid-twenties and married one year to a man who had spent ten years in the countryside, she was seen as too old to become a university student. She also no doubt would have been expected—and perhaps expected herself—to turn her attention to having children and raising a family, in addition to getting a job. As a result, she became a worker in a light industrial factory, a job she still held when we met her.

Although escalating costs and the sheer volume of the demand have threatened the practice, it has been common in urban China for *danwei* to provide living quarters for their employees. With Gao's oldest daughter's factory job, however, there was no accompanying housing. That could have been due to a number of factors, including very scarce housing resources in Tianjin exacerbated by the 1976 earthquake; her being a woman just married with no children; and the low rank of her job in the factory. In any case, she was not given housing. Her husband, who was both a teacher and a graduate student in a local university at the time, similarly was not supplied with housing. Not unusual in urban Chinese cities, this young woman and her husband could choose either to live apart, each with one's own respective family, or they could as a couple share space with one or the other family (see Harrell 1993). Since there was more space available in Gao's home than in the husband's family, and since both sets of parents seemed to care little about traditional residence expectations that the wife live with her husband's family (underwritten by the presence of several other available siblings who could give care in the husband's family), Gao's daughter and husband moved into Gao's flat, taking the smaller room and displacing the younger sister to a makeshift sleeping space in the kitchen. They lived there for seven years, giving birth to their daughter only one year after moving in.

Later, Gao was able to secure a newer, one-room flat for this older daughter and her family through his own work unit. It was allocated to him—no doubt after some negotiation—in addition to the "old" flat where he and Huang lived, and he in turn invited his daughter and family to move there. They lived in that one-room apartment until 1991, when they, along with Gao and Huang, moved to the new, high-rise building where they took up residence in their own space. When we asked Gao about this move, which was not anticipated at the time we completed our first set of interviews in July 1991, he explained that he "traded" the one-room flat along with his own house for the two new apartments. This sort of trading and negotiation for new housing was commonly storied, especially from those with economically robust work units. Clearly, the elder daughter and her husband benefited greatly from her father's ability to use his position on their behalf. We heard a number of stories of how adult children of higher cadres enjoyed such housing benefits, including in some cases being able to live in a very large, new flat with a single older parent for whom they cared, and whose house likely would pass on to that child upon their death.

Finally, Gao's description of his second daughter's employment situation indexes another practice whereby a parent's privilege could be turned to a child's advantage, even in a socialist state ostensibly designed to limit this perpetuation of hierarchy across generations. Unlike her elder sister, Gao's second daughter was able to take college courses and a degree, albeit not at an elite school. Hers was something akin to what in the United States might be called a technical school, where she was trained as a mechanical design engineer. After this training, she worked thirteen years in that unit's factory before changing jobs. We should note in passing that for most of the time since 1949 the opportunity to change one's job has been very limited in Chinese cities. While the present moment sees much less control here, the fact that she was able to move from an engineering job in a factory to an accounting position in her father's unit, a job very similar to his own early employment, calls out for explanation. Although he did not offer us any details of this negotiation and move, she acknowledged that it had been an unusual and difficult thing to do, and that now it was "very important" that she succeed in the new position.

This situation is not precisely the same as a government-mandated practice common at the end of the Cultural Revolution in which urban children who had been sent to the countryside were allowed to come back to their former cities if they could show that a job was waiting for them. Those jobs often were created by a parent opting for an early retirement, opening up a slot for their child to take. This practice, called *dingti*, literally, "replace," began in 1978 and continued until roughly 1985,[15] and was open to children of workers and cadres alike. In Gao Changping's case, the negotiations no doubt were what one might call "private" and specific to his own reputation and influence. While in both daughters' lives, significant benefits came to them through their father's work unit position, he told us proudly that his children "don't depend on their parents to support them. They live their own lives." That he wanted in particular to make this point suggests he believes there are children who do and that he disapproves of it.

Nuance

Having said all of this about Gao's privileges and how he and his family benefited from them, alluding vaguely to so many who had no such resources and whose care and life circumstances were considerably less desirable, it is important to reiterate a complexity here that so often can be lost in the "generalizing tendencies" common to sociology. Especially in instances where we sociologists examine privilege against a background of more general scarcity, difficulty, and suffering, we sometimes sacrifice complexity to our ideological sympathies (which is surely not to suggest that clear-cut and homogeneous cases of simultaneous privilege, domination, greed, and venality are impossible to find; or that such sympathies should be grounds for apology). Typically, when many "key details" of a given "case" can be read as illustrative of a "type," we often read it then as indeed an instance of that type, especially if it is likely to confirm our own sympathies and subjectivities. It isn't that we usually *try* to do this; it happens mostly without our thinking much about it and as part of who we are or have become as social analysts.

And although we well know that a type is not the same as an instance thereof, reification and synecdoche—treating the type as the instance and taking the part to stand for the whole—is not uncommon in human science writing. In Gao's case, we might pause a bit longer over his claim to have had a difficult time when he and his wife went to university, and when they got married, in spite of whatever resources they had.

In an expansive and philosophical mood, in a late, relaxed interview with his oldest daughter and son-in-law present, Gao responded to a comment I made and asked Laihua to translate. I said something about how their family reminded me of families I know in the United States; that Gao and Huang had created something of a "mixture" of Chinese and Western ways in their family. Before my comment, he had been talking about some of what he saw as the more "traditional" aspects of their family.

"We both are well educated, but we did not have an easy life. Sometimes things were very hard for us, very bitter. We couldn't even pay our tuition to the university. Perhaps you, Laihua, can especially understand. We did it by ourselves. We saw our marriage as one against feudalism. We were opposite our parents, and undertook our marriage on our own, we call it 'bao ban huyin.' Even in middle school, we were thinking of going to university. Our thinking was to rebel against old morality and tradition. I was more modern than others, and they criticized us. But now, it seems that I am conservative in my thinking and in the way I like to work. We have been left behind. I am afraid we are not like what Mr. Shi says."

Huang interrupted him. "I want to add something. In the past, we wanted to free our personalities, and that required a rebellion against feudalism. We liked very much the time just after Liberation. We were influenced by the 1950s. Then, we could work hard. Our children were small. But we can't stand the things that have come in the 1980s. In the past, we were influenced by the idea of selflessness—da gong wu si—or hard work and plain living—jian ku pu su. And because of that, you can find these things in our children, even in our little granddaughter. They are not like some children today who insist on being dressed in beautiful clothes and who are not practical."

Laihua added a comment here and reiterated a position that he himself might have spoken. "It sounds as if in the past, you were rebellious. You paid more attention to practical things, to content rather than form or appearance. But now there are some people who pay attention only to the surface. On the outside they wear very modern clothes, but there is not anything deep inside."

As I said earlier, we each were drawn to Gao and his family on various grounds. While we could see how he and his family were able to use his connections and position to secure health care and treatment open to few, we also appreciated how much time and energy he and his wife put into this use. Again, as we have noted, working or "pulling" one's connections is an operative and very apt phrase in colloquial Chinese—"la guanxi"—used to refer to the work one typically has to do to bring the potential benefits and privileges of connection or position—unless, of course, it were much higher than Gao's—to life. Recall the detailed although linear characterization he offered of what he and his wife actually did to get the care he had. And since most of you readers likely have not lived in a late-twentieth-century Chinese city like Tianjin, it is important to underline the nature of the benefits in question, compared to how you might think of "benefit" and "privilege" as manifested in your own lives: a doctor coming to one's house; the use of a *danwei* car to go to and from a hospital or doctor's consultation; access to a CAT scan and other technology; treatment by a well-respected specialist; admission to a hospital and convalescence sanitarium; *danwei*-supported medical expenses. While certainly important in Gao's situation and in Tianjin in the late 1980s, these are privileges of a different order than those most of us might associate with that word in other worlds. Obviously, there are privileges and there are privileges.

We also liked and were drawn to Gao because in spite of, but, more likely, probably *because* of these privileges, he and Huang were able to shape a life and web of relationships in their family that were, while unmistakably linked to certain traditional Chinese practices (namely, parental responsibility for raising and nurturing children paired with loyalty and responsibility returned by these children in their adult lives), also artful creations of their own, to which we easily found ourselves drawn. In short, they seemed to us to have used their resources—whether seen as bountiful or meagre—well; in a way relatively open to new ideas and ways of doing some mundane yet quite important things. They told stories of selves positioned against some of what they felt were the most stifling traditions of Chinese family and social practice. They wanted to and seemed to have been able to see themselves as individuals separate from their families of birth, able to oppose some of the parental expectations and demands that are storied to have been so iron-clad, and that denied children whatever Huang might have meant by her reference to a "free personality." They valued education and pursued it. They restricted the number of children they had, and stopped with two, and two girls at that. Although what care they could give their daughters was interrupted by the Cultural Revolution, they continued to value them as independent and worthy persons, and later routed that energy into their granddaughter and, no doubt, will do what they can for their new grandson.

In a conversation about the routine flow of money and material resources between the older generation and the two daughters' families, it became clear to us that Gao and Huang have sought an autonomy between the three family units perhaps consistent with what they themselves were trying to achieve when young. Their younger daughter, Gao Huan, then thirty-three, and her husband told Laihua in a separate interview that her parents handle money in what she called a "British style that treats money very clearly and seriously." The conversation went this way.

"They don't give us money—except for last Spring Festival they gave each daughter and family 100 yuan [about US$20]. So, if we buy something for them or give them something, they always want to pay us back."

"This is what I am not used to," Gao Huan's husband—who had said little up to that point—added. "Between parents and children, you shouldn't figure money so carefully."

"This is a Western way to do it," she responded.

"Well, it isn't done completely, or else they would pay us for the work we do there," her husband smiled. "I'm not used to it."

"We never buy things for them, even on their birthdays. We just go there and spend time."

Her husband added, "Twice in the past we bought something for them for their birthdays. They paid us! So we gave up that idea."

"It's true. My parents never make much over gifts and material things," she said, "and they don't accept gifts from us."

Laihua comments: "Some traditional habits are like that—where people do things just for show—gei bieren kan, as when someone gets married and they buy a lot of things that aren't needed."[16]

"But it was the same when we got married in 1987," she continued. "My family brought eight cold dishes to his family and they cooked eight other dishes. That afternoon we all rode our bikes to his parents' home; and after we had our big family dinner, his parents accompanied us to our new home. It was a borrowed room. The next day we went on a trip that was organized by his unit. We passed out some sweets to the others and they then knew we had just gotten married. My family suggested that it should be simple. It is useless to make it complicated and spend a lot of money."

In these comments we seek to complicate the critical tone of our earlier writing on privilege. They help us paint a more nuanced view of Gao and the ways he used the benefits that came to him from his background, job, and political position. There were higher level cadres we met and interviewed who had more privilege than he, but in their cases there was less complication to discourage the reification of the type. Gao Changping. Prosperous. Smooth.

4

Not a Small Happiness

From the earliest of times girls had been taught via the Confucian Classics that they were not the sun, the heaven or the lightness of day. These Classics had cosmologically enshrined those most basic of equations—of yin and yang, of earth and heaven, of moon and sun and of night and day—with female and male. Originally conceived as complementary, such oppositions were early arranged in a series of hierarchical relationships juxtaposing superiority with secondariness, authority with obeisance and activity with passivity. It was their cosmological foundations which removed these prescriptions beyond debate to apparently universal, natural and immutable status, so that gendered difference became integral to cosmic order with the preservation of harmony dependent on the maintenance of such complementarity and hierarchy.

Elisabeth Croll, *Changing Identities of Chinese Women* (1995)

[T]he function of modernist ethnography is primarily one of cultural critique, not only of one's disciplinary apparatus through an intellectual alliance with the alternative cosmologies and practices of one's subject, or of one's own society (à la Margaret Mead), but also of conditions within the site of ethnographic focus itself—the local world which it treats. This involves critical thought experiments whereby the ethnographer poses possibilities—the roads not taken, repressed possibilities documentable on the margins of cultures studied—to those that seem to be dominant, and explores their implications in dialogue with one's subjects. Indeed, this kind of critical thought experiment incorporated within ethnography in which juxtaposed actualities and possibilities are put analytically in dialogue with one another might be thought to border on the Utopian or the nostalgic if it were not dependent, first of all, on a documentation that these traces do have a life of their own, so to speak.

George Marcus, "The Modernist Sensibility in Recent Ethnographic Writing and the Cinematic Metaphor of Montage" (1994a)

In the wake of semiotics, post-structuralism, hermeneutics, and deconstruction there has been considerable talk about a return to plain speaking and to realism. But to return to realism one must first have left it!

James Clifford, "Introduction," *Writing Culture* (1986)

One day in early November the sickbed doctor made her regular visit to see my mother. I remember it was either a Monday or a Wednesday because those are my regular days to spend with mother when my sisters go to work. I'm the oldest daughter in our family and since I have retired from my job as a teacher and my own children have grown up, I have more free time.

After the doctor examined mother that day she told me an American professor and a Chinese researcher from the Social Sciences Academy were studying *jiating bingchuang* —family sickbed—in Tianjin. She showed me the letter and said, *"Mei shi. Mei shi."* It's nothing to worry about.

My family already has some connections with America. My second brother and his family, and my third aunt—mother's sister—live there; I have one nephew who is studying there; and my own son is a graduate student there. My husband once spent two years as a visiting scholar in America; my third sister works in an American joint venture company here in Tianjin; my father worked for an American company in Beijing, before Liberation. So, we have some connections with America. They sometimes brought us trouble, but now maybe things have changed. The door is open, isn't it?

Later that week, doctor Han brought Mr. Shi and Wang Laihua to meet us. It was late in the afternoon and my two youngest sisters, who live with mother, and I all were here. The doctor introduced them and said a few words. Wang *laoshi*[1] talked about their research plan and interests. He spoke carefully and was very serious and not boastful. There was a quietness and honesty about him that we liked, and we were impressed that he didn't use a lot of big words. Mr. Shi was older, perhaps nearer my own age—I'm fifty-two. He said a few simple sentences in Chinese, but he couldn't say much. He said he had started to study Chinese too late. He and Wang *laoshi* spoke to each other in English, but I could catch only a word or two. They were polite and seemed worried about disturbing mother—we all sat next to her bed that day—so they only stayed a short time before making an appointment to come back for a longer visit.

*****

This chapter has had a number of different beginnings. Now, almost six years after we first appeared, together with Dr. Han, at this family's door, it continues to shift. The problem, as before, is that it wants to be about several different things. Or, perhaps it is that these things all are linked, but not directly or clearly. "Women in China" or "daughters in China" is one thing it wants to speak about, and what they do as caregivers in family settings but don't seem to be credited with. It also wants to be a text that links that lack of note with certain features of what might be called the cultural text of "woman" in China today and in the past. And it wants to be critical of that text—of the practices and ways of thinking found there—but, of course, not just there but also in many, many other times and places; practices and ways of thinking that take woman's "difference" as natural grounds for devaluation and disallowance in diverse social relations and symbolic forms. The epigraphs by Elisabeth Croll and George Marcus, taken together, are intended to signal that, to in some sense warrant it.[2] It wants to use the details of caregiving for a now-bedridden mother, in what is storied as several generations of a family of strong women, to complicate other, more familiar, historically recurrent stories of "China" and "the Chinese family." And it wants to do these and other things in a way that foregrounds not only the family member-characters that we interview/create but the researchers as well, and, even, the text itself, here and there threatening to come apart. As such, it both trades on the general—"women," "daughters" and "what *they* do"—but suggests that such categories are impossible. It hopes to question realism's claims, even as it relies on them, as the epigraph from Clifford suggests.[3]

For several weeks (actually, months), the following text segment from an earlier paper we wrote opened the chapter:

Research and speculation about the impact of current economic and social change in China on the place of women in urban domestic space make studies of what women actually do at home an important project (see, for example, Chan, Law, and Kwok 1992; Croll 1995; Davis 1992, 1993; Davis-Friedmann 1991; Honig and Hershatter 1988; Ikels 1990a, b, c, 1993; Wolf 1985). In the context of a cultural mix of Confucian-influenced teachings about the proper place of women relative to men in the family and in society—daughters still can be marked as "a small happiness" (see King and Bond 1985; Tu 1985)—on the one hand, and a socialist discourse on gender that insisted "women hold up half the sky," on the other, we accordingly want to consider in some detail what could (perhaps should) be called the figure of the "filial daughter," the *"xiao nu,"* if you will, rather than that of the much more familiar *"xiao zi,"* or filial son.[4] The point to make again—for surely it is well known by those who study caregiving almost anywhere in the world (see Abel 1991; Gubrium and Sankar 1990; Moroney et al. 1998), and perhaps most fully appreciated if not spoken by these daughters themselves—is that women of all generations and in all family positions routinely make primary contributions to caregiving work for their own parents, often in deeply personal ways typically not expected of men. Yet compared to their brothers and husbands, they seem to appear less often as figures in the texts of classic stories as well as contemporary studies about family life and filiality in China, both ancient and modern.

Beyond greater propriety of form, opening has the advantage of focusing immediately on the absent image of the *xiao nu* or filial daughter in representations of China. But "absent" isn't quite right. Such filial daughters in fact have been storied as part of what China and the Chinese family are, but certainly less often than have sons and, typically, in ways that suggest that such expectations for daughters cannot and should not be held as seriously as for sons. Another thing this kind of beginning does is to cite other studies of women and daughters in China, seeking to benefit from situating this project relative to those already published, and lining up allies behind the "just thereness" of the object and question studied (cf. Latour 1987); and it promises we will tell you the facts of what women "actually do" at home.

But that beginning lost out to a rather different one, where we have again made up a text that three daughters of this Tianjin family *might*, and no doubt could, have written if we had asked them to. The speaking subjects in this text and the one that begins the next section are "the same" as the persons in the family with whom we spoke. Or perhaps a better way to put it is to say that the characters in this text are "based on" the same persons, there in Tianjin, that we met first on that early November day in 1990 and on many subsequent days. The facts about their family and the circumstances of our entrée into their home that we have put in their hands are the truth, but of course we have made that claim before. At least, they seem for the most part consistent with (they "correspond to"?) what these sisters told us (does that make this then "the truth"?).

*****

Hello. I am third sister Du. That's my father's family name, Du. I'm called Li Rong, Du Li Rong. I am forty-eight years old. My mother is Wu Yu Pei. She is sleeping in the next room there. I live here together with my young daughter and fourth sister. And right now we're also caring for my youngest brother's small son while his parents are in France. Mother, because of a serious stroke about three years ago, can't move and spends all her time in bed. Her thinking is pretty clear and she knows all of us when we come. She can speak a little and move her hands and arms, but that's about all.

This room here, next to mother's, we use as a combination sitting room, TV room, and sometimes as a bedroom for my sister, when she doesn't sleep with mother. My daughter and I sleep in the smaller room across the hall. It's messy right now so I've closed the door. The entry way there just inside the door serves as our dining room. I think by Tianjin standards, this is a pretty good flat. It has three good-sized rooms, a bathroom, kitchen, entry hallway, and balconies on the front and back sides—a bit less than 700 square feet all together. And it is on the second floor. This whole complex of apartments belongs to the Tianjin Public Health Bureau, and we have this flat through my mother's work unit, a local hospital. We have several conveniences here that many Tianjin people don't have—a telephone, hot water, heating from radiators, and many different appliances to make life easier. But now my mother is sick, and that is our biggest problem. When fourth sister and I go to work, and my daughter and nephew go to school, first sister, *dajie*, comes to stay with mother. We also have hired a woman to help us when *dajie* can't be here. In the evenings, fourth sister and/or I take care of mother.

After that first visit *dajie* told you about . . . well, perhaps I should say that she would have told you about if they had asked her to, Mr. Shi and Wang *laoshi* came here many times. I was here almost *every* time they came. I think they found our family interesting—Mr. Shi said that to me once when they were here—because they asked a lot of questions that were not just about the family sickbed for my mother, but about many other details of our family relationships and history. He seemed especially interested in the fact that my sisters and I have taken care of mother since she got sick, and that for almost all her life mother herself had taken care of people in her own family and in my father's family. I'm not sure what he expected, but he always asked about that. It seemed as though he was trying to compare my brothers to us sisters, and especially to me, as caregivers for mother, because he asked a lot of questions about when my brothers left home and just what they did for my parents after they each got sick. My father also had a serious stroke and my mother and we children—especially my sisters and I—took care of him at home for six years until he died in 1978.

Each time Mr. Shi and Wang Laihua came to our house they thanked us again and again for our help, and they apologized for giving us trouble. They even gave us a gift—that blue lamp there on the chest.[5] Youngest sister and I tried to be polite to them too. We always served them hot tea when it was cold, and cold orange drink or Coca-Cola when it was warm. I knew Wang *laoshi* was especially polite because at first he never drank even one sip of what we gave him and always insisted we serve the professor first.

By the time they finished their visits, it seemed as though we were almost friends. First sister and I once went to Wang Laihua's home to wish him and his family *"bai nian"*—"Happy New Year"—during Spring Festival.[6] And when Mr. Shi returned to Tianjin in the summers of 1993 and 1996, we invited him, his wife, and Laihua to come to our house for dinner. My daughter, Xiao Li, who studies English, talked to them about the TOEFL [Test of English as a Foreign Language] and about the possibility of studying in America. She has four cousins who are studying there. He said he would try to help. When the daughter of my second brother, who lives there with his family, graduated from university in the summer of 1996, she brought her American boyfriend to China and they stayed with us. Mr. Shi and his wife were in Tianjin at the time and they came here to meet them and have dinner in our home.

But in November 1990, the first time they came, they asked a lot of questions about my mother and her illness, and about the daily routines of our caregiving. I told them . . .

*****

Gao Changping, whom you met in the last chapter, once described to us, in response to our question, the practice called *chumenzi,* meaning that when a daughter marries she should leave her family of birth and move to her husband's family, or at least out of the ambit of her own (what social scientists call "natal") family and into his. Literally, it is *chu*, go out, leave; *men*, door, meaning home; *zi* or child: the child who leaves. The dictionary definition of this word is "to marry," but, as such, it obviously applies only to a daughter.

Gao suggested that this way of thinking and acting probably was more common in rural areas than in cities, that it was more common in the past than today, and that, in any case, it certainly was not true in his own family, where his two adult daughters—now at or near middle age—were still very much part of their parents' family and its routine, even daily, operation. And we will see in the story of Wang Su Min, in the next chapter, that if a daughter never marries, and stays in her family long enough, her presence can make the question of just whose family it is quite ambiguous. In the case of Li Yu Jie, whom you also will meet in chapter 5, we will see that a daughter who does leave her family upon marriage can return, as she did when she fell ill and felt that her husband was not taking proper care of her. Not only did that require major refocusing of her parents' lives onto her illness and care, but it also meant a reordering of priorities of support by those parents—especially her mother—for her three brothers and their families' children, who might have expected priority in this regard. Of the ten other families with daughters we met in Tianjin, but whom we have not spoken of specifically here, five told us stories of parental care in which the daughters were very much involved. Although they had married, they *still were there* (and see Judd 1989, 1994).

> She was the only daughter; her four brothers went with her father, husband, and uncles "out on the road" and for some years became western men. . . . They expected her alone to keep the traditional ways, which her brothers, now among the barbarians, could fumble without detection. The heavy, deep-rooted women were to maintain the past against the flood, safe for returning. . . . The work of preservation demands that the feelings playing about in one's guts not be turned into action. Just watch their passing like cherry blossoms.[7]
>
> Kingston (1981a, 15)

But *chumenzi* has been written and rewritten to such an extent and in so many ways that it has become part of what "the Chinese family" means and is. When a daughter is married, her parents and family may put up outside their front door a single red character for "happiness" (these are available in shops around town or in a village). When a son is married, this happiness is doubled, and two such characters may appear. His family has retained its son and heir, and has gained a son's wife—a person with an other, "outside" name who is called *waixingren* in Chinese. But it does not seem that the usual talk around "gaining a daughter" anticipates that she will bring her family honor in her own right, or even that she is to be a real member of that family, but that she will become one who *serves* her new family in some rather particular ways. Indeed, in "the Chinese family," daughter is inscribed as a "small happiness," if grounds for happiness at all.[8] And if she is not seen as grounds for a "double happiness" in her own family, her presence in her new family, for whom it was said she was raised, has provided historians, novelists, and social scientists alike with much material for writing stories of difficulty if not misery.

*****

> If I went to Vietnam [as my brother did], I would not have come back; females desert families. It was said, "There is an outward tendency in females," which meant that I was getting straight As for the good of my future husband's family, not my own. I did not plan ever to have a husband. I would show my mother and father and the nosey emigrant villagers that girls have no outward tendency. . . . No husband of mine will say, "I could have been a drummer, but I had to think about the wife and kids. You know how it is." Nobody supports me at the expense of his own adventure. Then I get bitter: no one supports me; I am not loved enough to be supported. That I am not a burden has to compensate for the sad envy when I look at women loved enough to be supported. Even now China wraps double binds around my feet.
>
> Kingston (1981a, 49)

*****

Wong Siu-lun (1985, 1988), a sociologist at the University of Hong Kong, has written a good deal on the particular mid- to late-twentieth-century intersection of "the Chinese family" and entrepreneurial activity in Hong Kong, Taiwan, Shanghai, and elsewhere in what is called "the Pacific Rim."[9] Wong argues persuasively that there are particular characteristics of this family form that enable and even encourage the hard work, loyalty, discipline, and self-sacrifice that make for capital accumulation and material success in the kinds of markets that exist there, among small businesses as well as quite large transnational enterprises. While Wong focuses attention on the activities of sons in these family firms, it is worth noting the location of daughters, relative both to their brothers and to their brothers' wives, in the picture he gives us.

In a public lecture drawing on almost a decade of this work,[10] Wong devoted most of his attention to characterizing the particular place of daughters and daughters-in-law in this material success story. His lecture was a fine instance of *chumenzi* reinscribed as central to what "the Chinese family" is and how it operates. For Wong, the focus on women in the lecture was a conscious attempt to "right" his earlier "wrong" of saying little—or at least not enough for some of his audiences—about women and their place in this story.

The point to make here, for of course there are many complex arrangements and connections that make up these intersections that Wong and others study, is that with few exceptions daughters are clearly marginal to the administration of these family business operations. This stems from the fundamental insecurity of their positions in their own natal families—they are expected to marry out, into other (competitor?) families—and their forever outsider (not to be trusted?) status in their husbands' families. This is not to say that as daughters-in-law, women are unimportant to the success of these family businesses. In fact, they are very important. But, their importance comes from marriage to a family's son and from their responsibilities as supporters of his natal family and then as mothers of the next generation of family business heirs, that is, of sons. Women as wives and daughters-in-law are here particularly important in the proper acquittal of their duties as coaches for educational and cultural accomplishments of these children, and as repositories of virtue to ennoble the morality of the family name in the face of the "harsh realities," even illegalities, of what men *must* do in the "outside world" of business. As Hong Kingston suggests, "They expected her . . . to keep the traditional ways. . . . The heavy, deep-rooted women were to maintain the past against the flood, safe for returning. . . ." But who is this "her" of whom Hong Kingston speaks? She more likely is a daughter-in-law than a daughter. Hence: "I did not plan ever to have a husband. I would show my mother and father and the nosey emigrant villagers that girls have no outward tendency. . . ."

Aihwa Ong (1993) also has written of the way family plays in the operations of transnational Chinese business, but in a rather different disciplinary discourse from Wong. Ong uses Said's (1978) well-known notion of orientalism to take up what she calls a "post-orientalist" position, from which she suggests not only that affluent Chinese speakers and writers themselves deploy and nurture such discourses when it serves their immediate material and symbolic interests—not to mention their subjectivities—but that an important piece of this discourse situates women very much as inscribed by *chumenzi:* daughters become daughters-in-law in other families, where their prime responsibilities are to produce, tend, and nourish male heirs and/or to ensure propitious marriages of daughters to men who can be groomed to become properly responsible sons-in-law in the family enterprise. With the development of an increasingly far-flung and economically successful Chinese diaspora in the last decade, where the family home of wife and minor children is in the West and the site of business activity for the male head is back in Hong Kong and/or China, Ong (1993, 759) writes that "the role of the wife and daughter-in-law has evolved into one of maintaining a far-flung family network." This "Chinese woman" is an anchor of family traditions, but as neither a full insider nor a full outsider to the world of Chinese men. A position of instability, indeed; but a position nonetheless, a space of movement in the flow of power.[11] Perhaps such positioning allows less movement than Hong Kingston envisions for herself outside marriage, but still more than allowed the "heavy, deep-rooted women" of whom she writes.

Although the kinds of mobile and fluid identities Ong writes about in reference to these privileged Chinese, positioned today "on the edge of empires," is very much part of what she calls postmodern capital, the way that women figure here is hardly postmodern; is hardly something new. This is the way of daughters; a resource of and in "the Chinese family."

*****

We first met Wu Yu Pei as an eighty-three-year-old woman who had worked virtually all of her adult life as a nurse, having studied in Beijing at "an American hospital" before Liberation, and then came to Tianjin in 1937 where she was a nurse and then a head nurse in a gynecology and obstetrics hospital until she retired. She spent her life taking care of other people, most of whom were her patients, but many of whom were members of her own and her husband's families. She and her husband, who died in 1978 after a six-year illness, had seven children—four daughters and three sons—named Du after their father, although one child, the second daughter, kept her mother's family name, Wu, as her own.

Fitting her status as an intellectual, and that of her businessman-husband, all seven children—born between 1937 and 1947—were well educated. The oldest and the youngest sons had graduated from the best universities in China. The second son had begun a similar course of study, but it—as well as his life—was irremediably interrupted by the Cultural Revolution, a point underlined by his sisters in their various stories of him, and, later, by him in his own words. And one of those sisters, the youngest, and her younger brother each spent over a decade in the countryside during that time. The four daughters, predictably, were less well educated than their brothers, at least in a formal sense, although all held what social scientists would call "white collar" jobs (an accountant, a buyer for a restaurant, and two teachers). The two youngest children, the fourth daughter and the third son, each had spent considerable time as sent-down youth during the Cultural Revolution. This fourth daughter, Li Fen, forty-four when we first met her, spent fifteen years in Xinjiang Province in the far northwest, returning home in 1979 at age thirty-three as a single woman, which she remains. The youngest son, who was abroad when we began our visits, spent ten years in Inner Mongolia and then in Northeast China, but had the good fortune of being included in the examination system that accompanied the reopening of universities in 1977.

Gradually, he worked his way into a medical school and is now a doctor at a local Tianjin hospital; is married, and he and his wife have a young son who lives with his two aunts, grandmother, and cousin.

Wu *lao's* husband had *guomindang* or Nationalist Party connections before 1949, and served as an officer in its army. Later, he served as a member of the *Guomindang* Political Affairs Committee. After 1949 he worked many years for an American medical supplies company in Beijing. Wu's own family, by contrast, had some notable Chinese Communist Party connections, with a beloved third aunt—"*san yi*"—helping underground Communists during the civil war; she was said to have known Jiang Qing, Mao Zedong's last wife and a leading "leftist" of the Gang of Four during the Cultural Revolution. *San yi* left China for the United States in 1948 to study, just when those fearing the effects of the revolution also were fleeing. Wu *lao's* third brother fought in the Eighth Army and was reputedly known and respected by Mao. And to add yet another twist, many of Wu *lao's* family members, as well as she herself, were Christians. All of this meant a complicated political standing in New China for the family and its children, none of whom had become—or been able to become—involved in the Young Pioneers or in the party. Wu's second son, age forty-nine when we first met his family, emigrated to the United States after the Cultural Revolution. Her third son and the youngest child, forty-three, is a doctor. When our research began he and his wife were temporarily in Europe where he was pursuing further medical study. The eldest son, fifty-three, is an engineer who, upon completing his Beijing college education, had been assigned to work far away in Shenyang, where he remained. Now, at the end of her life, Wu Yu Pei herself had gotten sick and required virtually total care. This is when we first came to her house, looking for another case in our study.

We each were moved by the women in this family, both those whom we actually met and spoke to and those of earlier generations about whom we heard in the stories these daughters told us. The more we knew of them, the clearer it seemed to us that, quite unlike many of the familiar stories and characterizations readily available about "the Chinese family" and women's place in it, here were women—here were daughters—who not only were central to maintaining their own natal family, but who saw this and their attention to these responsibilities as all quite unremarkable—as something they "should" and "wanted to do." Still, they conveyed a sense of themselves as different; as "not like a typical Tianjin family." Part of this characterization seemed to refer not only to their relatively high education levels, privileges, and connections to things foreign, but also to a sense that while they revered certain family traditions—especially those of filiality and children's responsibilities toward their parents and elders—they quite consciously had not been taught, and did not subscribe to others; especially those, they said, that seemed to privilege sons over daughters within family life. Yet . . .

*****

The complexity of speaking about "women in China" today is evident in a recent book by the anthropologist Elisabeth Croll (1995), *Changing Identities of Chinese Women: Rhetoric, Experience and Self-Perception in Twentieth-Century China.* Drawing on her own long field experience in China, from various other fields in which she moves, and from published sources—many of them autobiographical—she offers a critical rereading of the twentieth-century cultural text of women, and particularly daughters. Croll is especially interested in the way language, and the experience of its "dominant" discourses in this century (Confucian, state socialist, reform), has importantly shaped who woman is, to whom she (quite literally) belongs, and to what she might aspire. The book's three sections consider the early decades up to the revolution; from 1949 until the 1980 reforms; and the subsequent period of reform to the present.

In the first section of her book, devoted to texts written by privileged young women during the prerevolutionary and postimperial period—the time that Wu would have grown up in Tianjin and then moved as a young woman to Beijing—Croll offers a translation of a poem from the ancient *Book of Poetry,* which she calls "one of the richest and most authentic source materials depicting social life in ancient China," to help us see how the birth of a daughter, compared to a son, might have been said or read, still in the 1930s[12]:

> When a son is born let him sleep on the bed,
> Clothe him with fine clothes and give him jade to play with.
> How lordly his cry is! May he grow up to wear crimson,
> And be the lord of the clan and tribe.
> When a daughter is born let her sleep on the ground,
> Wrap her in common wrappings and give her broken tiles for playthings.
> May she have no faults, no merits of her own.
> May she well attend to food and wine and bring no discredit to her parents.

In this and similar pieces of what "the Chinese family" has been, daughters can hardly miss the message: they are, in Croll's words, "not the sun, the heaven or the lightness of day." Rather, woman was, and arguably remained, a if not *the* place of submission; always second to the male first:

> to be *obedient, unassuming, yielding, timid, respectful, reticent* and *selfless* on the basis of *"first others then herself."* A woman should *endure reproach, treasure reproof* and *revere her husband* for *"a husband, he is Heaven,"* "Heaven is unalterable, it cannot be set aside" and "if the wife does not serve her husband, the rule of propriety will be destroyed."[13]

Obedient. Unassuming. Yielding. Timid. Endure reproach. Treasure reproof. Pursue sacrifice. But, surely, these directives are not part of what the daughters of *modern* China have learned about themselves. Are they?

*****

In a seminar at the University of Hong Kong in the fall of 1996, a scholar from Australia talks about the medicalization of postpartum depression in women there. Most of the people in the room are not Chinese, and the research being reported has not focused on Chinese women. In the discussion, the question is refocused speculatively on Chinese women in Hong Kong and their symptoms of postpartum depression. A young junior colleague who is Hong Kong Chinese and is completing her research on conflict in relationships between fathers and adolescents in local families, suggests that aside from what might be considered "normal" depression after the birth of their new babies, such research among Chinese woman would want to be sure to consider any differences in such depression between women who had given birth to daughters and those who had given birth to sons. She speculated that a "longer-than-normal" period of depression among the former might be attributable to the sex/gender of their babies. There seems to be a shared nod among those present—most of whom are women—that this is a perfectly reasonable speculation. Mothers having daughters might reasonably be expected to be more depressed than those having sons. This is 1996 Hong Kong (and, we must ask, where else?).

*****

Croll draws on those few published autobiographical narratives written in the preliberation period by women of some privilege. Many of these women reflect critically on their own encounters with the figures of the "good and virtuous" daughter, sister, wife, woman in popular classics of instruction directed specifically to young girls and women.[14] These autobiographies also speak about the similar lessons taught, learned, and occasionally resisted in the mundane details of their own lives in families.

The Classic for Girls, the *Nuer Jing,* offered up one of the most familiar weaves of this text of Chinese family and personal life: *san cong si de* or "The Three Obediences and The Four Virtues." *Zai jia cong fu,* at home, obedience to father; *chu jia cong fu,* after leaving home, obedience to husband; *lao lai cong zi,* in old age (when the husband is gone), obedience to sons. As for the virtues, there should be an adherence to the general moralities of woman: know your place under Heaven and mold yourself accordingly. More specifically, speak little so as not to bore others; keep yourself and your body clean and effect a pleasing image (to men, although of course direct this only to your husband); and mind well your domestic duties.[15]

The popular short biographies of women collected in the *Lie Nu Zhuan,* said to have appeared sometime in the first century but, arguably, still familiar in their broad strokes in the twentieth, reiterated the importance of these virtues and practices, and offered unmistakable moral tales of "filial daughters, chaste maidens who would sooner meet death than dishonour, and [of] sisters-in-law, wives, mothers and widows whose chastity and devotion to duty was above reproach and worthy of emulation."[16] These principles were reiterated and even strengthened during the Sung, which spanned more than 300 years from the late tenth to the late thirteenth centuries, the period during which practices of spatial segregation of the genders, seclusion of women, and foot binding emerged.

For all her scientific even-handedness, Croll for the most part reads these and later versions of this cultural text against the grain, looking for evidence of the psychic and emotional costs of an ancient rhetoric of devaluation that has fixed daughters, compared to sons, as decidedly secondary; or, later, in a rhetoric of state socialist hyperbole, that declared equality between men and women, daughters and sons, but that barely could be sustained due to the weight of hypocrisy growing out of women's mundane experiences of subordination.

While it would be disingenuous in the extreme to imply that women who are "not Chinese" have lived their lives outside similar constraints and (could we say?) "comforts" of family, or that *all* Chinese women have lived within them, many of the stories these women told, in Croll's book/s and elsewhere, seem good candidates as exemplars of lives lived primarily in, through, and for relationships first to their own families, and then to their husbands' families.[17] And Croll says that at least in the prerevolutionary texts she consulted—written we should note by women whom she characterizes as "rebellious"—stories of what she calls "free girls"—and especially of free young women—were unusual if not rare.[18]

*****

When I read some of these ideas that come from ancient books, and that some people still believe in, it reminds me how much difference there is among Chinese people. You know, I have a daughter. She is our "one child." My wife and I love Xiao Xue very much. Her name means "little snowflake." I can't imagine having only a "small happiness" because we have Xiao Xue.

I know it is said that some people have a bigger celebration when a boy is born than when a girl is born, but this is not my own experience. In fact, we didn't have any celebration at all. I didn't even think of it. Maybe that is because I don't have very many relatives in Tianjin. Maybe it is because in my wife's family there are brothers. Perhaps their family had celebrations at the births of their children. I don't know. Now that I think of it, my own family never had this custom of having celebrations for most things.

But I do remember thinking that if we had a boy, that would make my father very happy, so I did think about that for a while after Li Mei and I got married. I also had the idea, then, that a boy in China may have a brighter future than a girl because of the influence of traditional ideas.[19]

Later, I changed my thinking a lot. I no longer wonder what it would have been like to have a son. From our research on family caregiving here in Tianjin, I now think that a daughter can look after her parents better, or at least as well, as a son can. She can be as filial as a son. And from the time I spent in the United States, I realize that a woman can do many more things than a common Chinese man like me thinks. With the development of life in the cities, I see less of the differences Croll and others have written about between having a boy and a girl, although these differences still do exist in many places. And I also hear other people say, to each other and to themselves, that you should love your child because you can only have one. What does it matter if it is a boy or a girl? You can only have one baby. I think most common people accept this idea.

*****

In response to our questions in an early interview, as we sat warming our hands with cups of steaming tea on a cold December afternoon, Li Fen, Wu *lao's* fourth and youngest daughter, recalled at length the day her mother fell ill.

"Three years ago, in 1987, mother had a serious stroke. I remember. It was on the morning of May 29. The woman we hired to stay with mother found her trembling and unable to move. She called third sister at work but she wasn't in. Then she called me. I hurried home, and when I saw mother I knew it was serious. I ran downstairs and asked a retired doctor friend to come. He tested her blood pressure, listened to her heart, and said we should take her to the hospital. Just then, third sister and youngest brother arrived. We decided to ask another doctor friend to come and examine mother. After the examination he said it appeared that she had a cerebral hemorrhage. At 3:00 P.M. we called the ambulance. Because mother weighs so much, we had to ask the man who minds the bicycles at the front gate to help us carry her to the ambulance."

The scratching of Laihua's pen fills the momentary silence. Li Fen talks very fast and knows this narrative well. "Please," he says. "Wait a moment." Fourth daughter apologizes and chuckles at herself. Mr. Shi manages to say, *"Laihua. Ta hen xingku le!"*—Laihua is having a hard time!—as he himself takes a sip of tea. The younger man looks up, smiling, and Li Fen continues.

"But when we got to the hospital with mother, there was no one there to help us carry her into the emergency room, and there was no stretcher in the ambulance that we could use. Finally, we found a stretcher from inside and my brother paid two boys five yuan each to help us. But when we got mother inside the emergency ward, there was no bed for her. I ran to find a friend who works as a nurse in the neurology department. She helped us find a bed there. The doctors diagnosed it as a cerebral hemorrhage. Mother could not move or sit up, and she could only say a few garbled words.

"I think it was about a week later that my brother was able to arrange for mother to have a CT scan. Since there was no CT machine at Main Hospital we had to look elsewhere. He knew the son of the head of another hospital's neurology department. He was in charge of the CT lab there. After third brother made these arrangements, we took mother for the test. He said it was a blood clot that affected most of the left side of her brain. He told us she didn't have long to live. We were so worried."

Li Rong sighs in unison with her sister. "It really was a terrible situation. We could do nothing!" Her sister goes on.

"When we got back to Main Hospital after taking mother for that test, a new patient had taken her bed in the regular ward, and so we had to go back to the emergency room. The doctors there gave her an IV of some medicines and we waited. Three days later we still were waiting for a regular bed, and mother had developed bed sores from the rough mattress.

The nurses and doctors there told us they had no way to deal with these sores, and so they got worse. My aunt, who also is a doctor, came to the hospital and brought several medicines for bed sores. After we used it for several days, the sores got better.

"Third sister and youngest brother fed mother water and milk. She began to swallow, and the next day she regained consciousness. The doctors said it was a miracle. Li Rong bought a foam rubber mattress for mother's bed. During this time in the emergency room, we three did a lot of running around to help arrange tests and get test results—sending urine and blood samples; going to get medicines. It took up all our time and energy.

"Actually, I should say, it was very difficult to get mother into a regular bed at Main Hospital—I mean, one in a ward rather than in the emergency room.[20] We contacted everyone we could think of to help us, including the president of another hospital. Even the party secretary of that other hospital called Main Hospital to urge them to let my mother go to a regular ward bed. Finally, our president friend went to Main Hospital and spoke to the director there. The leaders at Main Hospital were afraid that mother would die there and that they might be criticized for it. They still wanted her and us to leave. Finally, after ten days in the emergency room, they agreed to let her go to a regular ward, but only on three conditions: First, our family members—my first and third sisters, younger brother, and I—had to agree to take care of mother twenty-four hours a day in that ward; second, she could stay there only one month; and third, she had to do what the doctors told her. We had to sign a paper agreeing to these things. Then we four, including *dajie*, began to care for mother in shifts, night and day, in the hospital.

"The bed sores got worse again. My aunt again brought medicine and we bought a special lamp to dry them. After a month of this we left the hospital, just as we had agreed, but the sores were at their worst. We continued to apply ointment and use that lamp for five more months at home. We also continued the daily insulin injections we ourselves had started to give her while she was in the hospital. Soon after mother returned home, we got Main Hospital to set up a sickbed, and a doctor began to come regularly to see mother. That wasn't easy to do either. We had to find a doctor friend at the hospital to help us."

*****

While we sociologists and other ethnographers may worry about speaking with a too unified and homogenized voice about "women" or "daughters in China," others might hear this concern as misplaced. For it is only roughly in the last decade and a half that women's voices and/or a concern with women's experience has been taken seriously in social science research published in English.[21] Croll's book is one of a growing list of recent studies that draw on ethnography, life histories, as well as autobiographical accounts to tell true stories about women's lives and experiences in China.[22]

Interestingly, these writings can feel "messy" and "scattered" (cf. Marcus 1994b, 567), perhaps to some even "beside the point" when compared to the more grandly theoretic narratives on "China," its "Society," and its "History" (see, for example, Freedman 1958, 1966, 1970; also see Duara 1995). Absent the kind of quite intentionally fragmented writing we have tried to display here—which most of those texts have not used—this sense might come in part from the particular subject matter, that is, the mundane details and aspects of women's lives and the very otherness of these stories to the more familiar ones told. Such a reading, of course, can come only against the background of what "we" have taken to be the primary foci of the learned professional texts written about "the Chinese family" and "China."

Margery Wolf, another anthropologist who has written a good deal about the lives of women in mid- and late-twentieth-century China and Taiwan, marks her own sense of having—having crafted, we would want to say—and coming to want to tell stories about women that seemed to run quite counter to *the* China stories—*the* China?—she herself had learned about and learned to respect as a scholar; stories that in some sense had colonized the academic terrain one might call "Western anthropological knowledge of China in the mid-twentieth century."

In a short paper called "Chinanotes: Engendering Anthropology," her contribution to a critical reexamination of the institution of fieldnotes in anthropological work, Wolf speaks both about her own positioning "in the field" as a woman, the wife of a then more highly trained academic husband-researcher, and about similar positionings relative to "more important" men of those rural Chinese women she lived with and came to know quite well while doing research. Our text here links to and relies on hers.

As an institution, the Chinese family has been subjected to study for many years—in fact, one could say centuries without much exaggeration—by historians, philosophers, theologians, sociologists, social reformers, novelists, and even some anthropologists. That it is a male-dominated structure and male-oriented group is obvious; that it was primarily a male-studied subject was also obvious but deemed unimportant. The consensus seemed to be that Chinese women contributed to the family their uteruses, a few affines of varying degrees of influence, and considerable discord. Other than that, they were of minimal interest in any examination of the Chinese family's strengths, cycles, or romance. They added comic relief and provided support functions, but stage front was totally male.

I was vaguely aware of the invisibility of women at the time of my first fieldwork in Taiwan [beginning in 1959], but since my relationship to academia at that time was strictly marital, I was neither interested in nor constrained by the all-male paradigm. I hung out with the women, as did all women, and the understanding I acquired of the family was theirs. When I began to write, I dutifully read the important books about the Chinese family and then, turning to my fieldnotes, began the struggle in which I was ultimately defeated. In writing *The House of Lim* I assumed to some degree that the "unusual" influence of the women in the family resulted from the presence of some unusually strong personalities among the female Lims. But when I began to look at other families, my fieldnotes would not conform to the paradigm. Neither the words they recorded nor the voices they brought back fit the standard version of how things worked. At every turn of the family cycle, where the well-known anthropologists of China (see, e.g., Freedman 1961, 1970) debated the importance of the father-son relationship versus the solidary brothers against the father, my voices spoke of mothers-in-law in fierce competition with their sons' wives for the loyalty of the son-husband and, most important, of mothers and their children set in unflagging battle formation against what they saw as the men's family. I realized that I must either ignore my notes and see the Lim women as unique or ignore the received wisdom and let the women I knew give their version of the Chinese family and its cycle.

But that was only half the struggle. The other half was with my sisters, who were using their strong new feminist legs to stir up the mud in our pond and raise our consciousness. You will recall that during those years we were looking fiercely at women's situation, at our oppression, our subordination, our position as victims (e.g., see Gornick and Moran 1971). Once again, the women's voices in my fieldnotes gave me problems. Of course they were oppressed; obviously they were victimized. But victims who passively accepted their fate they were not. Nor did they seem to see themselves as victims, although when it was to their advantage to evoke their powerlessness and their lack of influence, they certainly did so. Moreover, the women in my fieldnotes seemed considerably more analytic than the standard texts on the Chinese family assumed women to be. Events in the family cycle that were described by social scientists (usually but not always male) as the result of male interests and needs were seen by women—and by this woman as well—to have been manipulated by women with very definite personal goals in mind. If men were aware of women's goals, it was only vaguely, and they certainly did not see them as relevant to outcomes.

The blinders Chinese men wear result from the centrality of their gender and their institutions in society. Chinese women, structural outsiders who participate only peripherally in the major institutions, are much cooler, much less constrained by those institutions, and hence freer to work around them [fewer ghosts?], within them, and eventually against them. My fieldnotes contain many examples of men solemnly discussing concepts such as filial piety and institutions such as ancestor worship. They are balanced by the voices of iconoclastic women, like that of one who advised another to spend her money on herself rather than save it for her funeral:

> So what are you worrying about? If they can stand to let you sit in the hall and rot, then you shouldn't worry about it. You will be dead. Hurry up and spend your money and enjoy yourself. If you die and they do spend all your money to pay for a big funeral, people will just say "Oh, what good sons they are. What a fine funeral they gave for her." They won't say you paid for it. If it were me, I'd spend every cent now, and if they couldn't stand to just roll me up in a mat, that would be their worry.[23]

Chinese men and perhaps some anthropologists dismiss these discordant voices as indicative only of women's ignorance; Chinese women would be quick to agree. They have found ignorance or the appearance of ignorance to be a valuable resource.

Wolf (1990, 347–349)

Wolf's story of the unsettling intersection of fields in the work of telling true stories is just the sort of text that seems to open up possibilities for the kind of critique that George Marcus encourages in the opening words of this chapter. She draws on the fields of her own experience as a woman and as a woman living in the United States during the emergence of an increasingly critical political discourse about women and their place relative to men in society. This discourse "back home" troubles her own personal and professional experience and place in anthropology and in Taiwan and China. But the latter also come to trouble the former when she cannot make her fieldnotes—a no doubt careful record of what she heard and what women told her—fit the passive, victim status she saw in some U.S. feminist readings of "woman's place."

In short, she offers both a critique of conventional anthropological (at the least) knowledge as partial and selective in the face of its claim to be "the whole Truth" about Chinese family; she critiques certain feminist images of women as passive victims when they are not; she also, but less explicitly, offers a criticism of the particular way that Chinese family life is put together. And by implication, she alerts us to the "blinders" that not only "Chinese men wear," but also to other blinders that men in her own field of anthropology wear with regard to what are the important, the serious, subjects for study and how they should be approached.[24]

*****

Wu lao depended completely on her children, especially on her two youngest daughters. Confined to her bed, she required substantial care including not only washing her hands, face, and body regularly, but preparing special foods, feeding her; changing and washing soiled sheets and bedclothes; detailed record keeping of medical expenses; the maintenance and activation of a diverse network of aging medical colleagues and personal acquaintances as valuable resources; getting various medicines, and actually securing the reimbursement ensured by Wu's work unit to cover the costs of her illness and care.

The effects of the stroke on her speech and thought had created barriers to the depth of emotional communication she and her children could have, although much could be read into a slight smile, a sigh, or look. Her children, especially those who were closest to her day to day—Li Rong and Li Fen—looked for, and for the most part found in the old woman's eyes and face, the mother they knew and loved, and whose care had become one, if not the, center of their daily lives.

As we listened to her daughters' recollections of their mother and her family, as we looked through the family photo albums that were thoroughly haunted by the presence of absent, incriminating photographs destroyed hurriedly before Red Guards could find them, we began to see her daughters' vision of a woman who had extended her caring to many relatives outside her immediate family, sometimes at considerable sacrifice and risk to herself and to her own children. When one of her brothers in a southern province died suddenly in 1944, leaving a wife and four small children who needed a home and support, she took them into her home and, according to her daughters, treated her nieces and nephews even better than her own children (for fear others would think she didn't treat them as well—*gei bieren kan!*). The newly joined families totaled eleven children and three adults: Wu, her husband, and her second sister-in-law. These nephews and nieces grew up with their Tianjin cousins, and their mother stayed on there until 1967. Wu's sister-in-law and a classmate once lived a short time with them, and her own third sister and a friend stayed with them for many months. Another of her brothers lived in her home to convalesce after the "Anti-America and Help Korea War" in the early 1950s; and second daughter-in-law and her small daughter spent six years living with them during the Cultural Revolution.

We heard a story, repeated in various fragments, of Wu as the center of her family; her husband lived and worked in Beijing from 1949 until 1961, returning to Tianjin once each month for a visit. Her daughters spoke of her as the "manager" of the family, and told stories of how she herself for eight years soon after she was married went daily to her parents' home to care for her sick and aging mother, a mother who, her granddaughters told us, had insisted—against her daughter's wishes—that she not have her feet bound as a young girl. It seemed that now all this care she was said to have given so freely was indeed coming back to her in the time of her own greatest need. If anyone ever hoped of having children in order to ensure care for themselves in old age and illness—and this was a common remark—Wu and her children would offer very strong encouragement.

"You know," her oldest daughter once said to us, "Chinese parents sacrifice a lot for their children. We children should repay this. This is the children's responsibility, a duty that we can't refuse. Since we were children we have been taught this. We have never complained about it, and we shouldn't." It was, as she said, a duty we can't refuse. But, of course, sometimes we do.

*****

"Love your parents" bid to halt abuse of the aged
Tom Korski in Beijing

China is promoting a "Love your Parents" campaign after complaints of widespread abuse of the elderly.

Authorities yesterday hailed an initiative in Zhejiang province to present awards to young people who "demonstrate praiseworthy respect for mum and dad," Xinhua (the New China News Agency) reported.

The establishment of a US$1,200 (about HK$9,300) award fund, privately financed by a local farmer, was prompted by public alarm over the decline of family values involving "members of the younger generation who show disrespect to their parents," Xinhua said.

The average age of mainland residents is 33, according to government surveys. Yet China is also home to the world's largest elderly population with 110 million senior citizens—a number projected to grow by 30 per cent by the turn of the century.

State demographers forecast that within 40 years one in four Chinese will be over 60.

Authorities have decreed that the first Chinese Senior Citizens' Day will be commemorated in September as part of a national effort being staged to promote care for the aged.

Government regulations outlawing abuse of the elderly were introduced last October after a National People's Congress (NPC) study cited numerous cases involving neglect of senior citizens.

Under China's Law on Protecting Rights and Interests of the Elderly, mainlanders must provide "economic and spiritual support" to parents and in-laws, under threat or court fines.

The NPC's Civil Affairs and Justice Committee noted that, "in recent years, a number of people have refused to provide for the elderly members of their families and sometimes even abuse or desert them."

State research last year also found most Chinese surveyed failed to regard their own parents as suitable role models.

The Beijing Research Institute of Youth study found that just 30 per cent of respondents considered their mothers and fathers as models of "honesty, responsibility and kindness."

South China Morning Post, 10 February 1997

*****

But it also was said that one couldn't count on daughters: "There is an outward tendency in females." Commitment to this proposition long has been the grounds on which Chinese parents have been so pleased to have sons. Sons you can count on. They stay; they add to a family's material and symbolic prosperity; they take care of their parents. They have a duty to their parents. But daughters? Well, you know daughters. They go with their men. Chumenzi. It's not clear whose family they're in.

We often wondered how Wu lao and her daughters managed their own senses of themselves, given these notions of what it means, among other things, to "be Chinese." We suspect they would not recognize themselves in these aspects of those traditional notions. Perhaps they simply bracketed off such ideas as, of course, there but not quite relevant.

Sometimes in conversation they would add, usually as an aside, that "in some ways" their family was "not very traditional."

"I am a little surprised," Laihua once said to these sisters when they were describing some of the details noted above. "According to traditional Chinese ideas, common people pay more attention to differences between family members, and especially between those related by blood and those not. But in your family this seems not as clear."

"Since my mother has managed this family," third daughter Li Rong, replied, "we haven't paid attention to these things."

After we got to know them better, we wondered aloud about their relationship to "Chinese tradition," rendered usually in terms of dualisms like "Chinese/Western," or "traditional/modern." And before a family dinner in 1996, where Joseph first met Wu's youngest son, the doctor turned and said to him spontaneously: "You know, our family is not a very traditional one. In a traditional family, the sons should care for their parents when they are old, but in our family it is the daughters, and especially Li Rong, who have done this—for both our father and our mother—while the sons were gone."

Indeed. For Li Rong and Li Fen, but especially for Li Rong, taking care of, giving care to, her parents had become a very important part of her life, although they did not say this to us in such a direct way. We want to go a bit further to say that it gave them a kind of "status" or honored position in their family, marked both inside and outside its gate. When Mr. Shi insisted on having LH ask a question that he had used so often in his previous research on chronic illness experience in the United States— "How do you *feel* about having to do all this carework for your mother?"— these sisters were at something of a loss for words (which was for them quite uncharacteristic). They in fact seemed not quite to understand what I was asking. For them, it simply was what one, what they, should do. *Zhe shi wo yinggai zuode.*

For him, for Joseph, it was a real question, one he had felt keenly in conjunction with caring for his father, and one that seemed to be live for many caregivers in the United States. There, it seemed to him that the verb "to care" is read or heard primarily not so much as doing—although of course this doing is not denied—but rather as *feeling*, as a state of one's mind and heart that had to be spoken or written to the one cared for (see, e.g., Moroney et al. 1998, 6–14; Tronto 1993, 101–124). But for the children Du, and for the other children we met in Tianjin, the proper performance of care seemed to give priority to *doing*, to committing one's body and time and energy in real, actual time and space; to the unmistakable physical *work* of care and the meanings it conveyed—meanings that were simply "understood" and need not be "expressed" in language (cf. Kipnis 1997, 104–115; and see Fei 1992, 45–59). In these terms, Li Rong, Li Fen, and her sister had performed their filial duty well; better, far better than their brothers.

* * * * *

After considering the pre-Liberation years and then the revolutionary period between 1949 and 1976, Croll turns her attention to the ways women have had available to them to think and talk about themselves in the time since the 1980s "opening" and reforms begun by Deng Xiaoping. She characterizes the experience of women in this period by the phrase, "not the moon," by which she means to suggest that women today realize that their own "light" is not produced by a reflection of the sun, which is to say of men, with whom they are linked in family and marriage relationships.[25] Some women, says Croll, hopefully, are beginning to embrace the idea that they are a source of illumination in their own right. But she and others suggest that the disillusionment over the gap between the official rhetoric of gender/sex equality (which remains the official discourse on this question)—"Women Hold Up Half the Sky!"; "Men and Women are Equal!"—and their routine experiences that are at odds with this language have left women unsure as to the nature of their own "light." Hesitant to embrace "Western" feminist models, with their implicit and explicit critique of traditional family, marriage, and motherhood ("So selfish!"), some Chinese women are searching for a clearer sense of what it means to be "a Chinese woman" (see Xu 1996).

In this search, inflected by a sensitivity to this "East/West" dualism, we should not be surprised to find women looking for "Chinese" sources. And, as Croll notes, "Chinese culture" is not without texts that have sought to inspire young girls to uncover woman's own "light." Still notable here is the quite ancient tradition of story and legend that speaks of strong, "warrior women," filial daughters who did distinguish themselves in lives outside their marriage bed and the hearth of their husband's family. These stories surely have been resources for young girls and women through which to imagine themselves as other than they were, or were about to become.[26]

One of the most often mentioned of these stories is that of the warrior woman Hua Mulan. Even Hong Kingston (1981a, 17–54) draws on this narrative as a source of strength and hope against a life lived as a disappointment, as a "bad girl," as a burden to one's family; as, indeed, one who leaves. It seems safe to speculate that the story of Hua Mulan has been an inspirational tale for generations of girls and young women. And indeed, its work continues as such today.[27]

In the fall of 1996, while teaching a course on media and society at the University of Hong Kong, I wanted to convey the idea that texts could be given multiple readings, and that one could set out to read a text "against the grain," which is to say in ways that its authors might not have intended or imagined. Wanting to choose something "Chinese" to include with various "Western" materials, graduate teaching assistant Susanne Chan and I went looking in the library for an English text of the story of Hua Mulan. We didn't find one, but she did find a recently published storybook for primary school children. I was more than a little surprised to find that this story had such durability, and that most of our students—almost all women—immediately recognized Hua Mulan when I mentioned the name. They all had read this story as primary or secondary school students.

The Story of Hua Mulan[28]

Hua Mulan was a young country girl from a family of six: her old parents, an elder sister, Mulan herself, a little brother and a little sister. For their livelihood the family depended on Mulan and her elder sister who wove cotton cloth for sale.

At that time, the country was in a state of turmoil. A war had been going on for six years. Farms and homes were deserted. Wherever one turned there was desolation. Yet the rulers of the empire still pressed the populace for taxes, grain levies, and military conscripts.

One year the Emperor issued another decree for conscription. Because there were too few young draftees to meet the quota, Mulan's father was also to be called up for service. The news worried Mulan's family. The idea of her old, frail papa going to war and dying on the battlefield filled Mulan with great sorrow. As she had no elder brother, and her little brother was much too young, she decided to disguise herself as a young man and enlist on behalf of her father. Having convinced her parents of her plan, she obtained the required horse and weapons. Then she donned the military uniform and left home to report to the army unit. Because of the urgent demand of the war situation, the new recruits were all sent out to the front line at once.

In battle, Mulan proved to be exceptionally courageous and was cited many times for her military successes. Indeed, her very name struck terror among the enemy soldiers. However, none of her own troops had the least idea that she was a young woman. In her twelve years of fighting she took part in eighteen major campaigns, not to mention numerous minor battles. Her name was recorded in the Book of Merits and she had been promoted twelve times, up to the rank of general.

When the army returned in triumph, Hua Mulan was given an audience with the Emperor himself, and was granted special awards for her illustrious exploits. Much impressed by her courage and loyalty, the Emperor wanted to appoint her as a *shangshu*, a powerful ministerial post at the imperial court. Hua Mulan declined the offer, however, and requested a leave to return home to visit her family.

Together with her armed escort, Mulan came back home after long years of absence. Her relatives and fellow-villagers all turned out to welcome the general's triumphant return, and Mulan's family members all were overjoyed. Pigs and lambs were killed for the occasion of the family feast.

On her arrival home Mulan hastened into the room she had occupied as a young girl. She took off her military uniform and changed into the attire of a young woman. She also took care to powder her face and put some flowers in her hair. When she came out to see her comrades-in-arms, they truly were taken aback: how could they have dreamed that the Mulan they had fought side by side with was actually a young woman! This was something they never had heard of before.

When the news reached the imperial court even the Emperor found it too extraordinary for words. He had her summoned to court immediately and, on seeing Mulan, he said he would never have believed a beautiful young woman with such a floral and jade complexion was none other than the same general who had killed so many enemy and achieved such great military success.

Thereupon, the brazen-faced Emperor offered to take her into the Palace and make her one of his concubines. Mulan replied: "Your majesty once made me a minister. Since ancient times it has been against decorum for an imperial minister to be taken into concubinage by the emperor. Please let me go back to my home." However, after she returned home, the Emperor sent his men to enforce his wishes. Mulan refused again, and that very night killed herself with her sword.

Afterwards, the Emperor granted her the posthumous title of "filial and chaste general."

Lin (1985, 1–2)

Although I remembered hearing about this story from my first reading of Hong Kingston's book, I never had seen a text of it. As I read it several times in preparation for class, I was struck not only by the possibility of reading it against its grain, but also by the way it offered an opportunity to consider not only multiple but actually contradictory meanings in a single text. I was impressed by how easily the students at first spoke their familiar readings—that girls could be brave and strong and successful warriors just like boys—but also by how they were able to imagine the plausibility as well as the political flavor of my own quite opposite impressions of the text as a guide for girls.[29] I had asked the students to keep reading journals of their reactions to all course materials. At the end of the term, as I reviewed these volumes, the comments of one student, Maggie Chan Wing Yin, stood out for me in the clarity with which she had put these points. Here is what she wrote:

11/29/96

Yesterday we read in class the Chinese tale of a young girl who went to battle as a man. This story is familiar to us. When I first came across this story, it already brought some messages to me. At that time I was told what this story wanted to tell us: women can have new roles; they are not necessarily just to be feminine and stay in the family. They can do what men do, and can be as brave as them. Now, I realize that this story, while trying to open up new roles for women, is actually reminding us what women should look like—feminine, and that they have to come back to the family no matter how successful they are in their careers. Therefore it is in fact a rather conservative story regarding sex roles. The girl Hua Mulan was very brave in the battles, but she did not continue to go to war. After some years, she eventually went back to her family and restored her identity as a girl. Why couldn't she continue to act like a man? Is it because men and women are actually different? A woman is a woman, she cannot do exactly what a man does. Why can't a woman fight in battles as a woman? The girl was brave and successful, but she was doing all these things as a man, in the identity of a man! Doesn't it imply that only men should be brave and fight for their country? If it is to open up new roles for women, the girl should go to the war as a girl! Moreover, she did not go voluntarily, but just had no other choices. She went to war just because her father was too old to do that. If her father was not so old, she would not have done what she did because it was men's job. The girl fought in war because of filial loyalty, not because she wanted to fight for her country. The intention is apparently different. A man would voluntarily join the army and may see it as a glory. But how about a girl? She does that because of other people. Is this what women should do?

The sense in which this text might serve as inspiration for young girls to believe in their own light, in the diversity of their own capabilities, and in worlds outside the familiar positions of woman in "the Chinese family" can be seen then as at least ambiguous (see also Dai 1995, 258–261). Despite her accomplishments, Hua Mulan's proper place remains as a filial daughter in her father's house. So committed to this end is she, at least in this text of the tale, that she kills herself rather than become a concubine for the Emperor, who has come at the end of the tale primarily to notice not her accomplishments as a warrior but rather her beauty and body as a desirable young woman. The faithful daughter: at home; or, as a wife; or, not at all.[30]

On the one hand, from the tradition of *chumenzi* we see a daughter as one who leaves, who cannot be counted on; whose filiality, while expected, cannot be taken as seriously as that of a son. Yet, on the other, there are the stories of warrior women who were fiercely filial and brave, who left only to defend and enhance their family's or nation's honor, but who returned to their proper place under their father's and then husband's roofs.

One well may pause over this latter choice as a model for young girls to emulate, just as Maggie and some of the other women in the class who read the story of Hua Mulan did. The daughters Du, however, did not speak to us of such ambivalence about their lives; they did not seem to pause. So, in some sense, we have paused in those places where we—or, at least I—wanted them to pause but where they did not; and we have done so without asking them.

*****

"You know," her oldest daughter once said to us, "Chinese parents sacrifice a lot for their children. We children should repay this. This is the children's responsibility, a duty that we can't refuse. Since we were children we have been taught this. We have never complained about it, and we shouldn't." It was, she said, "a duty we can't refuse."

And they did not. At least some of them did not. Her daughters; especially her two youngest daughters, Li Fen and Li Rong; and most especially Li Rong, who shared a room with her own teenage daughter Du Xiao Li—a daughter who also had retained her mother's family name—did not.

"*Dajie*," Laihua began, turning to the oldest sister and using a pause in the women's talk to change the subject a bit, "We have a question. In your big family here, who is the center of caregiving for your mother?"

"Third sister. Li Rong," she said immediately. "In this family, Li Rong is the nucleus. Everyone listens to what she says. If there are important things to decide in the family, she decides them."

This word nucleus or center came up later in the conversation when we asked her where the center of the family was for the twelve years that their father lived and worked in Beijing.

"The center of the family then was Tianjin. Our mother's family lived in Tianjin. The center of the family was here. In the past, women played more of a role in our family than men. My father's sister even once gave us money for support. Now the situation is the same."

Now the situation is the same.

Later we asked Li Rong directly about her position in the family. She of course denied she was the "center," but allowed how perhaps she did more "family work" than the others. She attributed this to her organizational skills, adding that she worked as an accountant. She insisted that what she did were "small things." Still, through the years, she allowed that she had come to know her mother very well.

"I have a good relationship with my mother because I have lived at home with her for all my life. After I graduated from college I came back to live at home; and I lived at home through the time of my work, my marriage, and then my divorce. And I helped mother take care of father during the six years when he was sick. My eldest sister used to live far away, in a distant district of Tianjin. Although now she has moved closer, her health is not very good and of course she is married. My youngest sister went to the countryside in 1965 and only came back in 1979, the year after our father died.

"My mother has often said to me, 'You are good.' When my youngest sister would playfully ask her about each one of us, 'Who is better—the eldest son, the second son, the eldest daughter?' and so on, mother always shook her head 'no' to each of the others, and then would say my name. 'Third sister is the best!' she would say. But maybe her thinking isn't so clear. After all, she can only say a few words."

"But, Du Li Rong, it's interesting to us—especially interesting to this American son who had heard so much about Chinese sons and what they do. You two sisters not only care for your mother regularly, but you also care for your younger brother's son who lives here with you now. You cared for your father when he was sick. In the past, your mother worked and lived here with all you children. She even took in other relatives who needed help. When people, both inside and outside China, talk about family life here, they often mention the idea that sons have and take more family responsibility than daughters. It's even said, still today, that daughters might become members of someone else's family. But in your family, it seems that you sisters take more of this responsibility than your brothers."

"Yes. You are right. There is a way of thinking in China that the care of old parents is the sons' responsibility, and that parents put more importance on their sons than on their daughters. There's a saying, *'Fumu zai bu yuan zou.'* It means, 'If your parents are alive, you shouldn't leave them.' It is one of Confucius's teachings. Of course, it means *sons* shouldn't go far away, since according to these same teachings daughters are supposed to marry into some other family and leave their parents. But our parents never taught us to think this way, and they never paid more attention to their sons than to their daughters.

"All three sons in our family now have left Tianjin. My oldest brother has lived and worked in Shenyang for more than twenty years. It is far away, and he can see mother only when he comes here on business. Of course, when he was assigned this work a long time ago he had no choice but to accept it. The other brothers are abroad now. After the Cultural Revolution, second brother wanted to go to America to study. My third aunt helped him. My mother was so happy that he could go. Later his wife and daughters joined him there. My youngest brother and his wife now are in Europe, where he is doing medical research. Perhaps they will come back. Actually, the three sons in our family never considered caregiving for their parents to be their responsibility."

Hmmm. It seems as though in your family, the daughters have stayed at home and have taken responsibility for the family while the sons have left to pursue their own futures. Perhaps your parents' teachings were taken too seriously by your brothers.

"Well, it's difficult to say. This family is a little unusual. My two younger sisters have had trouble with their marriages, but this happens to provide a convenience in caregiving for my mother. My youngest sister was more than thirty when she came back from the countryside. And she is very particular about a husband. So, she is not married. Third sister's situation . . ."

"Let me tell you about it myself," Li Rong interjected, or, would have interjected had she been there at that moment.

"I was married in 1972 to an intellectual from Beijing. That was during the Cultural Revolution you know. Not long after we were married, he was sent to work in Harbin. Does Mr. Shi understand that then people had no choice about their job assignments after school? You had to take what was assigned. And it was considered 'bourgeois' and not 'revolutionary' for a woman to want to follow her husband just because his work took him far away."

Yes, yes. I have read about that.

"And my own job and my family were in Tianjin, so I stayed here. I lived with my parents after my husband went to Harbin. That year—1972— also was the year that my father got sick.

"Two years later, in 1974, our daughter was born. Two years after that, my husband got his work transferred back to Tianjin. Before he came back, my daughter and I—as I said—had been living with my parents. My second sister-in-law and her little daughter also lived there; all six of us were in one small room. A larger, second room that we once also lived in had been taken over by Red Guards. After my husband arrived, we three people found a small room not far away and moved there.

"I had developed the habit of helping mother take care of my father, and so even after my husband came back I went to my parents' home almost every night after supper to help her. He had suffered a serious stroke—just like mother's now—and there was a lot to do for him, a lot of work to do.

"Father died in 1978. After that, I spent a lot of time finding a way to help my youngest sister come back from the countryside. Finally, we were successful, and she came home in 1979. In 1980 my husband and I were divorced. Actually, that guy was very bookish and I didn't really like him. He once criticized me because I gave so much help to my parents and not enough attention to him.

"After I got a divorce, my daughter—she was six years old then—and I came back to my family's house. And soon after that, we all moved here to this flat—my mother, youngest brother, youngest sister, my daughter, my second sister's son, my second brother's eldest daughter, and I. It's a pretty good place. It belongs to mother's work unit, and the rent is very low.

"In 1981, my youngest brother got married, and his wife joined us— they moved into this room where we are sitting—so the family grew larger. They actually had an apartment of their own, but they wanted to live here. My mother and brother asked me and I agreed to let my brother's family live with us. Three years later, they had a son and then there were nine of us.

"At that time, my new sister-in-law couldn't do housework. My mother managed the money, and I managed big events in the family. Mother made a mistake once with paying a bill, and after that she asked me to take over all the money matters for the family, and I took care of four children—two nephews, a niece, and my own daughter. By then, my second brother and his wife had gone to the United States. And, of course, I also went to work each day."

As we counted the growing number who lived under Li Rong's care, we found ourselves thinking how like her mother she had become. Like mother, like daughter.

Du Li Rong. "It occurs to us that the responsibilities of caring for your parents when they were ill, and perhaps the care you gave to your other family members, perhaps that affected your marriage badly. Perhaps I shouldn't ask you this, but have you considered marrying again? It's been more than ten years since you divorced."

"No."

"Maybe taking care of your family has influenced your thinking?" Laihua tried again, pausing.

Shaking her head again, she looks away, remaining silent for a time.

"After I was divorced, some people encouraged me to remarry. Some even introduced me to available men. But when I thought of my daughter, of how it might affect her, I didn't want to do it. And I thought to myself, my daughter respects me very much. I think she can . . . I think she would take care of me in the future.

"Actually, before my youngest brother left, he, youngest sister, and I agreed that we sisters and brother had to rely on each other in the future. But now my brother has gone abroad and he is not sure he will return. Now, youngest sister and I can take care of each other as we take care of mother and the children. I don't want to do something that would affect my daughter badly."

"So, it's possible that your family responsibilities and concern for your daughter influence your ideas about marriage?" Laihua invited.

"Hmmmm."

You know, Li Rong. There is a Chinese saying: *"Jiu bing chuang qian wu xiao zi."* You know what it means. Even a filial son can't be expected to stay by his father's bed if the illness is a very long one.

Yes. I have heard that. I wonder. What about a filial daughter?

*****

Today things have changed a lot for Wu *lao's* family. The loved and respected mother died from pneumonia in March 1992. All of her children,

except her second son in America, came home for her funeral. The youngest son had come home from France about one month before his mother
died; to stay, he said. He told his sisters that he felt his mother was calling
to him to return (against, his sisters were quick to point out, his wife's
protests that they remain abroad). Or, was it a ghost that called to him?
When he and his wife returned, they moved back into his mother's house,
joining their young son and the others. Wu's oldest son had come from
his home in Shenyang for his mother's funeral. Second son, Wu's sister,
and nieces and nephew, all in the United States, sent money.

Respecting their mother's wishes, the children—the daughters—planned
a Christian funeral service. Their work units had given them some money
to help with the funeral costs. Colleagues had given them traditional
paper wreaths to display outside their building. Li Rong and Li Fen
made the arrangements, including renting a small bus, draped with the
proper funeral cloths, to take the family to the crematorium with Wu *lao's*
body.

When we visited them in the summer of 1993, as we sat in the familiar
room next to where Wu had spent the last years of her life, the three
sisters—second daughter recently had moved to Tianjin by herself to live,
leaving her husband in the south—insisted on showing us the videotape
they had made of their mother's funeral. It already was positioned in the
VCR when we arrived.

Second son, now fifty-two—about the same age as Mr. Shi—was also
there that day, visiting for a few days from Beijing before returning to the
United States. It was the first time he had come back to Tianjin in many
years, and the sociologists saw his presence as a fine opportunity to talk
to this man who in their developing tale was coming to represent "the
sons who left," juxtaposed with "the daughters who stayed."

As we six—daughters two, three, and four; son two, Laihua, and Joseph—sat sipping Cokes and watching the video of what good and proper
children do, they pointed out this family member and that—"Oh! There's
big brother, and little brother is over here"—this minister and that, on the
huge Sony TV screen, something the youngest son was allowed to buy
when he returned from France.[31] Li Rong and Li Fen, talking over one
another, told how in preparation for the service they had taken all of the
furniture out of their mother's bedroom. Then, with their youngest brother,
they built a raised platform for her body, in the shape of a cross. They
draped it in white sheets, and bought two large green plants for each
corner of the room behind her. They dressed Wu in fine royal blue silk
pajamas. Her hair was lovingly combed for the last time and pulled back

from her face. They folded her hands over her chest, and hung a small cross on the wall behind her head.

Er ge, second son, was quiet as he watched. He had seen the tape many times before, but still, he watched intently. He was in the room, but he was not on the screen. "Oh! There is *da ge;* there is *xiao di*—big brother, little brother. Look, look!" But second brother was not there.

Someone knocked at the door and our watching was briefly interrupted. I sat closest to second son at the end of the sofa, slightly out of the center of conversation and we talked quietly to fill the moment.

"Your family has helped us so much in our research. We have been very, very impressed by the care for your mother. Your two youngest sisters have really done a lot."

"Yes, yes. My sisters have done all of the work. And now my third sister wants to send her young daughter to school in America. Of course, I told them I will pay for that if she can pass the test." He paused and looked at me. "But you are an American professor. Perhaps you can help her?"

"I can try. I can try. Of course." I had been asked this question, it seemed, hundreds of times before. And I will try, I thought, but there probably is little I can do.

"But you could pay for your niece's education if she could go?" I asked.

"I will pay. I have told them I will pay," he said, looking at me intently, and pausing again. "Because . . . because. . . ." Tears suddenly come to second son's eyes, and with a quiet sob he adds, "I owe her," motioning to Li Rong. "I owe her a lot." He lowers his head and tries to control his tears. I notice his sisters noticing this, but in silence.

In the fieldnotes I made of this moment I have written: "I put my hand on his hand and say, 'Yes. I thought about how you must feel, being there, in the States, and being the oldest son.'"

But he of course is *not* the oldest son, so I am not sure what I was thinking when I said that. I do know that the issue of what this son in America was doing or not doing for his mother was always in my mind when we visited this family and when I thought about them. What to make of what I said? Was I blaming him as a way of not blaming myself? Was it a mark of my own guilt and sense of not having done anything for my own mother during the many years she was ill with cancer, living alone, just across town; dying? I almost never called her; saw her less; perhaps I sent a birthday card. What kind of a son was I?

Later, as Laihua and I ride away from the interview in the dark, I ask him if he noticed second son crying and if he heard what he said.

"Yes. I heard," LH responded. "He owes his sister, it is true. But, in fact, it is really his mother who he owes. And he can never pay her back."

As we sat watching the TV screen, Wu *lao's* children, family, and a few close friends slowly filled the small room. Two priests, one old and blind, one young, said prayers for her soul and assured her children that their beloved mother had gone to heaven. They sang a hymn. Her children cried, as they should have. Especially her daughters cried, as they should have. And most especially Li Rong cried, for she had lost the most of all.[32]

5

Feeling, Duty, Care

Des Moines
19 July 1994

Dear LH:
   You have been such a good letter writer recently. Many thanks. Your latest one came the other day. By this time you should have received the chapter on Gao Changping. I am now working on Wang Su Min and family, so have a few things to say about them here. I have no very clear logic for moving from Gao to Wang, but if there is one, here it is: here we have another story about caregiving and family that involves issues of gender and that focuses on women. I don't mean that Gao's story did focus on women especially, but he does talk about the daughter/daughter-in-law and son/son-in-law business, and he does have two daughters who have been supportive caregivers.

   In chapter 3 on Gao Changping we criticized the generalizing logic common to social scientific investigation and totalizing ways of seeing and writing about others and ourselves. We implied it was better to focus on the particular details of an individual or a family in context than on how such individuals and their circumstances were similar to or different from some "average" or "typical" (or even "global"?) image. We want to sustain that criticism but we would be disingenuous to suggest that we here are uninterested in, or in fact do not depend upon, generalization; or that our crafting of particular stories is somehow done without regard for generalities about family life and caregiving practices in "urban China" (and note the "about women," above). Indeed, we write some of the people and scenes here primarily *because* they seem to be contrary to (or consistent with) the more general or common patterns or practices linked to the object, "the late-twentieth-century urban Chinese family." And choosing *against* a standard or type surely is something of a measure of the very importance of the type itself. Moreover, as the many citations to published academic work show, we take pains to link our various discussions to extant research on Chinese family life and how it intersects with caregiving, gender, politics, and so on, not to mention the vexed question of doing ethnography. Even the production of "the interesting," so common (not only) to academic work, relies heavily on sociology's and, in general, the academy's central trope of irony, foregrounding what ("in fact"?) *is* as at odds with what was/is *thought* to be (the general case).

In this chapter, questions of form stand forward again in our attempt to make the very making of a chapter itself an object of attention. That of course displaces the chapter that might have been. For in the creation of a "chapter," writing must be disciplined. Beyond perhaps the more obvious physical parameters, such as length and subdivision, footnoting, and type font and size, chapters are supposed to be "about" something; some "thing" that gives the words, sentences, paragraphs, and pages a linear coherence beyond their own boundaries (see Landow 1992, 35–70). Beyond the empirical details of "substance," this "something more" usually is theory or the theoretical, as we noted in chapter 3.[1] This is the promise of conventional theory in social science: it will make things "clear" by (ironically?) reducing complexity and difference to essence; it will bridge distance and time, and put unrecognized (or not fully appreciated) similarity into bold relief. There is both a politics and a morality embedded in this move to theory; and from its place of deployment—the theorizing subject—it may be seen as a centering flow of power (see, e.g., Latour 1988).

Writing the plural pronoun "we" is another centering and consolidating move. It implies a shared authorial/writing position and thus elides and leaves unexplored the gaps that separate the two (at least) of "us."[2] Which of the "we's" in this book could be broken open to display difference, disagreement; lack of precisely the shared "understanding" that they temporarily secure? They help create a smooth and seamless surface of the text to aid a "fast forward" reading, as though they were buttons on a tape recorder one could push to speed things up, get past the messy bits; to help "get on with the work." Moreover, the we's are mostly written by the older, U.S. professor rather than by the younger, more deferent Chinese researcher who continues to live and work at the Tianjin Academy of Social Sciences. Joseph writes a jointly authored text in which he has written most of the words. Laihua received drafts, we's written in; a shared position, for the most part, marked and closed. And the text is of course in English, Schneider's rather than Wang's "native language." So which, if any, of the we's here are more Laihua's than Joseph's? Which are more and which less fraught? How might Laihua resist? How will these two be differentially benefited, or harmed, by the publication of this book? While these surely are not issues peculiar to multicultural projects, they take on added importance when authors are located in contexts that are so discrepant not only in terms of what sorts of work and accomplishment are rewarded and how, but also, of how disapproval and even punishment for intellectual/ideological "bad judgment" is handed out. All the familiar issues linking "respondents" and "researchers" discussed in conventional ethnographic methods texts seem to bear on our "we," for Laihua and his "story" become data for this text in a way in which Joseph and his do not.[3]

But what about the way the chapter begins, with what appears to be a letter? In our work together, we often talked and wrote to each other about "what our book is or might be 'about.'" From what you have read thus far, you know this question might have been a more "open" one for *this* book than is usually the case. There are many sources of this ambiguity and fluidity. One is a conscious desire to resist the disciplines of realist science that we have noted thus far. It is less a claim that we could do, fully, without them than an attempt to use them perhaps less seriously than is required from "the inside." Although for students of literary studies, this desire might immediately call forth the name of Roland Barthes, one of a small number of enormously important "continental" scholars and intellectuals of mid-century. But for U.S. sociologists and social scientists who "grew up" under the influence of logical positivism in American graduate education, Barthes is not such a well-known figure. After all, he was "literary" and thus not thought to have anything relevant to say to those who considered themselves scientists (cf. Brown 1977, 1987).

But Barthes (1974, 3–16) wrote insightfully about precisely the kind of desire "we" (really, Joseph) have just noted: wanting to resist and encourage the resistance of reading and writing discipline. He distinguished what he called the "readerly" text from the "writerly," and he much preferred the latter. By "readerly" he means one that is primarily to be followed, attended to; known, mastered, and "copied." (Incidentally, we Chinese have a lot of experience with this sort of text and its power—maybe we even could call "Chinese culture" this kind of readerly text.) It is authoritative; it offers up Truths to be possessed, consumed; capitalized upon. Toward this end, the readerly text must become transparent so that what is "really important," this Truth, can come through clearly and directly. Readerly texts are especially useful in writing realism, that is, "True stories."

In contrast to these disciplines, Barthes urges the pleasures of the *writerly* text, wherein readers are encouraged, in the very reading, to become writers, or, more consistent with Barthes, readers/writers. This sort of text is full of marked "seams," "rough spots," *aporia*. It makes the reader more rather than less aware of how writing is a technology for producing meaning, closure, and smooth, tidy surfaces. Realism (the "masculine"?) criticizes the writerly text (the "feminine"?) for being "self-indulgent," "narcissistic"; for "getting nowhere" because it is too concerned with itself. In the face of such hard and smooth surfaces, says Barthes (1974, 4), the reader is "plunged into a kind of idleness—he is intransitive; he is, in short, *serious*: instead of functioning himself . . . he is left with no more than the poor freedom either to accept or reject the text: reading is nothing more than a *referendum*," a mirroring; the reader a reflection.

There are many seams left quite apparent in this book. And we sometimes resist telling you explicitly what is happening—what something "means"—in hopes that you will become more consciously a reader/writer of an other (your "own"?) text. But even this way of putting it obscures and postures—implying that we could tell you what some thing, indeed every thing, "means" but are simply withholding bits of this truth from you to make a point, for "effect." But it is precisely this posturing, this bluff, that we want to doubt . . . and use . . . and doubt.

This kind of writing, especially when it seeks to call itself "sociology," is seen by some as an egregious transgression against responsible scholarship, and a waste—at the least—of paper and/or electricity. "Why draw attention to you?! Given all we need to know about China (for instance, but "the world" would do in this space as well), tell us about what is really important." And "China," and "the Chinese family" are fine examples of important things "we" want and need to know about (but why?).[4] Some seem particularly offended by this sort of writerly, sometimes called "postmodern," text.[5]

But precisely toward appreciating such textual qualities, we have decided to use a series of letters, exchanged between us, in Des Moines and in Tianjin, during the summer of 1994, as the chapter itself. We were trying to solve a familiar dilemma: "now that we have finished *that* chapter, what shall we do *next*, and *on what grounds?*"

All bracketed text, along with the footnotes, are additions made to the original four letters we exchanged. In this, we strive somewhat to "have it both ways": to foreground the often submerged intertextuality and "rough edges" of virtually all (academic) writing, as well as to convey our then-nascent "truths" about these people and their families. In several earlier drafts of the chapter, we had left in much more of this "roughness" in the form of cross references to earlier letters and from one included letter to another. We also were going to include all of the details about Laihua's proposed pseudonyms for people and places, and his many specific answers to Joseph's questions about the exact *Hanyu pinyin* or romanized Chinese language that is part of the fieldnotes. Were this book an actual hypertext rather than a linear printed text, that would have been more possible. In the final edit we decided that such a strategy would too much risk losing your goodwill as well as making the chapter and book too long. What follows then we have edited, trying to leave in those bits from the letters that were or would have been most central to building the chapter that was not, finally, written.

But back to that first letter Joseph wrote to Laihua. Sometimes you may have to remind yourself that you are reading something not written first to you.

In this family, we have, as you say in our fieldnotes, "one of the most interesting and unusual stories" among those that we wrote. Things that stand out for me as I have now completed another careful reading of the fieldnotes: What does someone who has no children do for care when they fall ill? Given the great reliance on adult children in urban China as support and caregiving resources, how does one manage when there are no children? What does someone do who also has no spouse? It would seem to be the so-called worst-case situation.

To complicate matters, what if the patient is a woman? Again, I don't want to overstate the importance of gender here, but within the context of Chinese thinking and practice around gender, a woman patient without spouse or children might be expected to be in the worst situation of all. Single men, especially elderly men, might be more likely to be pitied and taken care of by women relatives, as we [just] saw in the case of Wu Yu Pei's family. This may be similar here in the United States, although I haven't looked at the research on it (surely, there is some).

So, here we have a case where the question is "Who will/does care?" Moreover, the dilemma is presented to the family in that she lives in/with that family in which she and her two sisters and brothers are the senior members.

The "case" here is a sixty-eight-year-old woman suffering severe em-physema, who requires an oxygen tube in her nose to breathe and lives "alone" in one of four separate rooms of a small compound that she and a younger brother and his wife share with another family. All these rooms have separate doors onto a small "yard"—a walkway, really—which once belonged to her parents, and that also had housed a second brother and his wife. Across the walkway from these rooms is a narrow enclosed storage space with a bottled gas cooker that serves as the kitchen. Cold running water is available in the outside walkway, but not in the rooms. The family shares a neighborhood public toilet down the *hutong* or lane outside. Because she is frail, Wang Su Min mostly uses a chamber pot kept by her bed.

At the time of the interviews, this family, or, what we took this family to be, consisted of Wang Su Min, the oldest child of her deceased parents, her two younger sisters sixty-five and fifty-two, and two younger broth-ers, fifty-eight and fifty-six. Her four siblings all are married with adult children. In addition to interviews with Wang herself, we met several times with the younger of the two sisters, of whom we spoke then and write here as "*lao meimei*" (literally, respected youngest sister), echoing LH's calling; the eldest (but third-born) brother's daughter, Wang Hui, age thirty-four, married with a small child and a fulltime job; the eldest brother's wife, who is retired and had been quite involved in the local neighborhood committee; the son of the younger brother, Wang Qiang, twenty-nine, who is married with no children, also working fulltime; and *lao meimei's* twenty-two-year-old son. We also briefly met with a woman from the countryside who the family hired through the *jiedao* or street committee to come in each day and help care for Wang Su Min. These people con-stituted Wang's network of primary caregivers during her worsening ill-ness, and it is from our conversations with them and observations that we draw in these letters.

I noticed as I read the interviews that we asked this question several times: who has the *responsibility* to take care of or see to the care of Wang *lao*? The family members didn't give especially direct answers. Getting a little ahead of myself, I think this question is brought forward clearly by the caregiving work and relationship of the niece, Wang Hui and Wang *lao*. On pages 9, 12 of the notes (the copy I sent you in the mail)[6]—at the end of visit #3 on 5/23/91—Wang Hui makes the point that it is primarily because of the "feeling" between her aunt and her that this caregiving work is done, *not because of her responsibility or duty to do it.* This then allows us to open up the large and important question of this distinction between feeling and responsibility or duty as grounds for care. See additional discussion on pages 19, 25, 32. Wang Qiang says that he does what he does for both feeling and responsibility.

According to conventional ways of thinking about and doing family in urban China today, I assume that it is more the brothers and sisters of Wang *lao* who would have the responsibility to see to her care. Just how much responsibility is not so clear. They don't have as much responsibility as a spouse or a child, but they have it nonetheless, especially since there is no spouse or child around.

And among the brothers and sisters, it would seem for Chinese this age that the eldest brother would be the more likely person to be most responsible. But I am not sure here, LH. You will have to think about this and give me some insight. A *da ge* [oldest brother, conventionally written as *dage*] surely is thought to have more responsibility to his parents than do the other siblings, at least according to traditional teachings. We see an example of this in Zhang Xiufang's family [chapter 6]. *But it's not clear to me what the traditions have to say about an elder brother and his responsibility for an unmarried and childless sister.* Perhaps in ancient times (or, not so ancient), such a daughter would have been killed or abandoned at birth, or perhaps later sent away, solving the problem of who is to feed and "be responsible" for her. Socialist thinking about the family and women has no doubt made this more complicated, while not completely removing the differences between men and women as valued kinds of persons. What are your thoughts on this, LH?

So, perhaps we have a situation here where the key dilemma is, as I wrote above, "Who should be/is 'responsible' to care for Wang *lao*?" If you agree that this is a kind of vacuum or ambiguous situation (and I would like to know if you feel pretty sure of this in terms of "Chinese culture and tradition" as well as on what basis you feel sure/or not), then we have an even stronger story about women, because the people who take up this caregiving are for the most part women. Now, on one hand, one could say that this is not surprising because the patient is a woman. But what if WSM were a man? Her being a man would not make us predict that the people who would take up his caregiving would be men, especially in the kinds of tasks, say, that *lao meimei* and Wang Hui do, not to mention the women from her [WSM's] unit who have been assigned to come in and help, and the *baomu* from Yangcun.[7] So, it seems we have a story about women on a number of levels.

This is not necessarily surprising, given what we know about traditional roles for women in Chinese and world society. What is of course
interesting is the particular way this family seems to handle things, and
the problems they confront in the process.[8]

So, the focus here may be how and who cares for this woman, given
this family make-up and their relationships. Key caregivers are *lao meimei*
and Wang Hui, with Wang Hui probably doing more routine and regular
work, and the sister being somehow more "responsible" for the over-all
arrangements of that work, including things like contacting [WSM's] unit
and so on.

In light of the above issues, it is interesting to note that *lao meimei*
says she has told the children, the younger generation that they should
shoulder the *responsibility* of taking care of their aunt. This way of thinking, of course, seeks to transfer the burden from the older generation's
shoulders to those of the young. Partly, and as you ask directly, these
children do what they do because of their own parents and in order to be
properly respectful and obedient to their parents. They also do it because
their own parents *are* the ones *responsible* but are themselves getting
old and/or sick. We have Wang Hui, thirty-four, Wang Qiang, twenty-
nine, *meimei's* youngest son, twenty-two, and some work done by *dage's*
son. But we agreed, the most important and regular of what might be
called the "second tier" of caregivers are Wang Qiang (his sister says that
she will care for their own parents and he can come and look after their
aunt—page 5; *dasaozi* [the oldest brother's wife—literally, "big-elder-
brother's-wife"] says that she looks after Wang Hui's children so she can
come and look after her aunt, page 23) and *meimei's* youngest son.
Okay. On to some more specific issues.

Compared to Wu Yu Pei's and Gao Changping's families, WSM's story
is one of less money and influence, less privilege, although it certainly is
not as difficult as Li Changhai's or Mr. Hu's or Mr. He's. WSM's own
retirement income is about 110 yuan a month [then about US$19], and
her family members say that they don't give her money but that they do
buy things for her, including food. They say she spends most of her own
income on food. *Dage* and wife pay Wang *lao's* room rent and utilities.
Wang Hui says that the two other aunts spend more than she or her
cousin do (10).

The family structure here should be noted. We have the real *"lao da"*
as WSM herself—she is the oldest child in the family and a good ten years
older than her oldest brother. The first two children in the family are

women (*er jie* [second sister] is sixty-five). *Dage* is fifty-eight. Given her age and her not being married and her own work record under socialism and "New China," this *dajie* [oldest, first, big sister] has been a powerful person in this family, even though she is a woman. In fact, her influence and "power" are no doubt more than if she had married and had a child. *Meimei* says (31) that when they all were children they "listened to" their *dajie*, which is to say they did what she told them. I feel sure that this history, although we do not know it in detail, has something to do with the current contradictions between her and her oldest brother and his wife.

In traditional terms, this is a situation that never should have been permitted to happen, but then traditional China was not a socialist state with an ideology of equality. I really do think that the impact of the forty-five-plus years of socialism in China is not small in terms of its effect on how people think about themselves and each other, and much of this is not consistent with ancient teachings about the family—most of these are called "feudal"; many of them stem from Confucius and his disciples. Interestingly, *meimei* refers to a cousin they have who also never married—their father's brother's daughter. She says of her: "She's open-minded and she influenced my oldest sister" (31).

On page 2, *meimei* calls her sister a "*lao chu nu.*" Could you please, LH, give me both a literal translation of that and a smoother one into English; along with the *Hanzi* [that is, Chinese characters]. We have it now as "old girl," meaning one who never married.

Another small item is the unit-supplied caregiver who came to take care of WSM from October/November to April 1990–1991. *Dasaozi* tells us (22) that the unit first assigned someone to come help care for Wang *lao* back in 1986. And we find out in our last interview in 1991 that they have just secured another colleague to come take care of her during the day. This apparently has been going on between the summer of 1991 when we left and summer 1993, since, when we made our last visit to them, there was still such a person caring for her (38). This is pretty amazing. This is perhaps not exactly "unusual," but it certainly is notable since there are lots of folks for whom this would be impossible and for whom it would be a wonderful thing. Wang *lao's* relationship to her unit and her good reputation there may also be part of this. Her unit in general seems to support her well and without resistance. This may be in part due to their pretty good economic condition (see page 33). They paid the 3,000–4,000 yuan for her last stay in the hospital without making it difficult, apparently (15).

Another thing that strikes me about this arrangement of caregiving is that *meimei* says that it has to be arranged and that she arranges it (5). Often when we ask this kind of question, the answer is "it just happened naturally." In fact, Wang Hui takes this position when we ask her about it. But *meimei* and others say that it had to be set up and it had to be decided and it had to be distributed. This is more "evidence" for our argument that this is a caregiving burden that falls not clearly on any one's shoulders, and so it has to be decided who will do it. And I don't think that *dage* allocated this himself. Even when someone says it happened "naturally," of course it also had to be "set up," but that likely is a reflection then of clear lines of *responsibility* (perhaps another word that might make sense here is "duty," which may have a more appropriate and meaningful Chinese language base). In interview with Wang Qiang (17), he says that keeping the caregiving for his aunt stable over a long period of time will be difficult—more of the same sort of point.

Like Zhang Xiufang's family [chapter 6], there is apparently some tension here over housing issues and who has priority. We only hear this from Wang Qiang directly—that *dage*'s son and wife lived in Wang *lao*'s room for two years after they were married, and she had to ask them to leave, making her brother and his wife angry, no doubt. This small yard and set of rooms once was owned by the father of this family, and they all lived there. The second brother and his wife moved out of one room, and gave it back to the unit in trade for a new apartment. Now, another family lives in that room, which no doubt was something those who stayed there did not like very much. Who will get the room Wang *lao* is in when she dies? Will *dage*'s children have first choice? Would they want it? It is not really a good place to live, and they have to use a public toilet. Anyway, this is not really a major issue.

Some contradictions between *dasaozi* and *dajie* make tension in this yard. *Dasaozi* (26) tells us that the *jiedao* once came to their home to ask about these contradictions—LH says this likely was informal visit since formal one would be pretty serious. *Meimei* and *dasaozi* both say that this is a result primarily of Wang *lao*'s illness. When she gets worse, they say, her temper and behavior get more difficult. Interestingly, they manage this by (a) not disagreeing with her, and (b) not talking to her about anything. This of course is a familiar sort of management strategy by younger people to deal with older people who are seen as "difficult." Unfortunately, it tends to isolate them further and make them more disagreeable in that they feel they are being closed out of and off from social contacts and family information—which they in fact are. A "vicious circle." See reiteration of this by *meimei*, page 30. *Dasaozi* says that she sometimes has lost her temper with Wang *lao*, but that she shouldn't because "she is a patient" (pages 26 and 36).

We have Wang Hui's husband who supports her in her caregiving for her aunt, both because of her feeling for this aunt and also because he himself had illness and caregiving in his family with which she helped him deal (she helped with his father, page 11). Wang Qiang says that sometimes this "brother"(-in-law) does the [oxygen] tanks when Wang Qiang can't; he also at first did the disconnecting of the tanks, and then Wang Qiang took them for replacement; now Wang Qiang can do it all (15).

This son [the patient's nephew], Wang Qiang, also was taking care of his parents after an explosion near their home that quite unsettled them, so he earlier had less time. But now, when Wang *lao* is sick and needs him, he can do.

Wang Qiang's wife's family is apparently yet another example of one where a daughter is an important caregiving figure, even though she is married and has her own new life (16). She takes care of her widowed mother who lives in a single room by herself. Not surprising, in a sense, except that it needs to be noted.

Both the *dage* and *dasaozi* were party secretaries in their respective work units. I am inclined to think that this might be reflected in the "face" they want to show to us, and also in the way *dasaozi* involved the *jiedao* in Wang *lao's* care (but see page 34 that *meimei* suggested should get *jiedao* woman). See a reference to "serve the people" by *dasaozi*, page 27.

See page 22: discussion of this family's "private" house, as in case #22.

So, these are the things I wanted to mention from WSM's family. Look them over and please answer the few questions and also think about what I have mentioned, and about the family, and see if there are things that you would like to add.

I am thinking of perhaps putting something together from this family and Li Yu Jie's situation to talk about this "responsibility and/or feeling" business as grounds for caregiving. Do you think this is important? In some sense I guess I do. Why? Well, in a culture like China where there have been such long-established notions of duty and responsibility, it is interesting to note the talk in the interviews that make a distinction between taking care of someone on the basis of "duty" on the one hand and then also, or, rather, on the basis of "feeling." On a superficial level, one might think that in America there is more caregiving based on "feeling" than there is on "duty," but I think we have to be careful about that. And we should ask ourselves what if anything these two—"duty" and "feeling"—have to tell us about the nature of social arrangements and connections between people in a society.

I don't know if one can, for instance, draw a parallel to the gradual reduction of the importance of family "duty" to follow one's parents' wishes in marriage, and the rise of "feeling" as the preferred basis for marriage. Certainly, it could be argued that the rise of the latter—a stress on "feelings"—is more individual-focused than is a stress on duty or responsibility, which puts a lot of stress on one's position relative to someone else in the social arrangements, quite independent of what one's "feeling" about them might be.

For centuries in China, an important resource for thinking about what kind of person one is, for both men and women but in somewhat different ways, was in terms of how well one conformed to what his or her "duty" was. No or little attention was given to questions of "feeling." So, like with marriage, perhaps questions of "feeling" are also markers of the rise in importance of the individual. This surely would correspond with the other changes that have been taking place in China since 1980. Anyway, things to think about.

Now I am going on to read case #23 notes to see if there are things there to draw together. Or, I'll first reconsider this and think about the other cases to see if there are ones where this issue seems important too.

I know we cannot have a chapter for each family, and I also want to make the structure of the chapters different—I don't want them all to be like Gao Changping's or the one based on Wu Yu Pei's family. By the way, I have not worked more on that Wu chapter because I want to get some new work done first—work on other families—before I go back to it. Clearly, one important chapter will have to deal with sons and fathers, because we know that is one important reason that we have done this project. For that chapter I am thinking the most important families are Hu, He, Li Changhai, Zhang Xiufang's family, and a bit of Liu Wen Bin. Oh, then there is Mr. An, too. Well, obviously, there is a lot about fathers and sons. We'll see.

Love to you all three,
J and N

*****

Tianjin
6–8 August 1994

Dear Joseph:

Hello! I hope that you have received the letter and the foot massage roller that I asked Ms. Shen to take to you when she went back to Minneapolis, Minnesota. I hope Nancy and you are enjoying it, if so.

It has been very hot and muggy since the beginning of July in Tianjin. It is one of the hottest summers here since 1928 according to the media. You are lucky not to be here this summer, just like you were lucky not to be in Des Moines last summer when it flooded there. It is raining very hard outside at this moment, and it will be another very muggy day tomorrow.

I want to answer your questions on the chapter of Gao Changping as well as the questions about Wang Su Min. In the letter that Ms. Shen took to you, I said some of my ideas about the chapter on Gao Changping.[9]

We always knew we would not use people's actual names in our writings. And I didn't want to rely on the familiar practice of using no names at all, speaking "one man said" or "a woman who," thus locating these figures as anonymous representatives for social categories to which we assigned them (see Clough 1998, 26, "statistical personations"). As papers became chapters and the possibility of presentation or publication increased, we had to choose pseudonyms. The new names had to sound "authentic" (remember, it's a true story), and since certain periods in twentieth-century China (and, no doubt, before) have been occasions for the meaning of given names to be inflected in one way or another (for instance, more or less "revolutionary"), these pseudonyms had to be chosen with a sensitivity to the age of the people and a knowledge of common names for that generation. As drafts of the chapters were prepared by Joseph containing the "real" names, Laihua then replaced all proper names of persons and organizations, concealing identities while retaining the verisimilitude of our stories. Laihua continues:

I have read the chapter again carefully and looked through my dictionary to know some of those English words. I think this chapter is really a great one. I like it very much, although there are still some parts that I haven't really gotten through. I think it is mainly because of my English and my knowledge about American sociological research. However, I feel I am going ahead in it more and more. That is due to my learning about our own research data. I appreciate your wonderful and hard work, and I feel quite good to answer those questions and contribute somewhat to this great book.

Okay, I would like to tell you first some of my thinking about the chapter of Gao and those parts of it [which have been deleted at this point].

After I read your letter of 7/19 I came to understand what you are trying to do with the data. It is going to be very good and I really appreciate it.

From your last letter of 7/22/94 I know you are reading case #23 and trying to find out how to write another chapter with the data of #29. Here I want to say that I think that your idea of writing about "feeling and duty" using the data from both #23 and #29 is okay! *Feichang hao!* Very good! But, my suggestion is not to put "gender" issue too much into this chapter. I think your thinking about feeling and duty must be another great one and has to have space to be discussed without other things interfering.

You could write another chapter based on #6 Wu Yu Pei and others to talk mainly about "gender." Is that okay? This is just my idea and it is for reference only. You also said that you would tell those stories about sons and fathers. Actually, when I read Gao Changping's story I thought about that. As you know, Gao doesn't have a son and depends on his daughters and spouse to take care of him. So, at least, you can give readers a chance to compare them. It is natural, isn't it?

As for Wang Su Min [case #29], I read your questions in the letter and I think your thinking about who has responsibility for caregiving and that the idea of duty is different from feeling is quite clear. What I should say is just to "open up this large and important question," please! Also, Wang's story really shows a contradiction between feeling and responsibility. Actually, it happens in every family we interviewed. But it is most clear in Wang Su Min's and Li Yu Jie's [case #23] families. Both you and I know that the responsibility of taking care of a patient is really something of a burden. If the responsibility is treated only as duty, like [#29's] first brother and [#23's] husband seem to do, the responsibility would be a complete burden. It would be very bad, done with no feeling between the patient and caregiver. But if such care is supported by feeling, it would become something like "feeling burden." Virtually, responsibility and feeling are always tied up. I mean that the two are different but often linked together.

They usually influence each other. I prefer to think of it as a triangle of responsibility, burden, and feeling. I just hope you let me see all of this in your great chapter. Of course, you have to face responsibility and feeling first and make it easy to recognize.

You are completely right. According to Chinese conventional ways of thinking, Wang's brothers (especially the eldest brother) and sisters (if there were any) would have responsibility for her. It's the same as the situation for #23's husband. As we know, Wang *lao* is still in her own family and is not *chumenzi* at all. So, morally, her own family members have to have the responsibility for her care. It should be more so because she is alone and ill. In her family the eldest brother is supposed to be a "family head" (*jiazhang*). He no doubt has the responsibility first, or has more responsibility than the others. And yes, we saw the same thing in Zhang Xiufang's family [chapter 6].

Actually, we have seen the difference between a man and woman here. I think socialist thinking is one thing, and what happens in Wang *lao's* family is another. I don't think socialism has an important effect here. I am trying to understand your thoughts about gender on this.[10] Even though big brother has the responsibility, I don't think that means that he actually does more than the others do. It's probably just the opposite. It is those women who do a lot of care for Wang *lao*. Usually, I think it is only a matter of convenience that one woman takes care of another. I like to see your way of thinking on this.

Moreover, talking about responsibility and feeling, you are going to draw a structure of Wang's family and their relationships. It is good and completely necessary to do this. It will make your view rich and sociological, I guess. I read your questions and I am sure you are right to do it this way.

In response to some of your questions:

About paying rent for a "private house." Actually, it shouldn't be called house rent (*fangzu*) because it is a private house and there is no rent for such a house at all. But of course they do pay something for that house, and it is called *zhandi fei,* which means rent for the land the house sits on. Usually, the amount of money involved is much less than house rent and has to be paid only one time a year.

About "*lao chu nu*" or "old girl": *Lao chunu* has the same meaning as "*lao guniang*" (old girl). *Chunu* means virgin; *lao* means old. So, literally, it can be "old virgin." Also, you know, an "old girl" who has never married means in China that she is a woman who never has had sex with a man. That meaning was especially clear in ancient China. Could this happen in America that a woman who never married also would not have had sex with a man? Of course, neither you nor I can be sure that Wang really is a virgin even though she never has married. But anyway, her sister called her "old virgin."

About the caregiver Wang's work unit sent: I think you are right in your views of Wang's relations with her former unit, but there is something you should think over. Her unit is *supposed to be* another caregiver according to socialist thinking. That is, she worked there for a long time, never married, and is childless. The unit has to help her. This is why her family always goes to her unit to ask for both money help and *peiban*. Morally, her unit can't resist this. Of course, that her unit is in good economic condition makes this easier for them. My question here is who is the most important caregiver in this case? It's still her family. So, you could give different weight here to a socialist way of thinking and a more traditional way of thinking about this.

About housing: as you know, a house in Chinese cities is really a kind of important inheritance, especially when people were—and sometimes still are—assigned houses by their units. Such a thing is really very hard to get these days. You know of this same situation in Zhang Xiufang's family [Chapter 6]. Although that small room lived in by Wang *lao* is not good at all, it still is a place to live or to store some things. Recently, such a space has become more important because it can be a resource to help get a new apartment when the old houses are torn down and rebuilt. Now, if you buy a new apartment with one living room, it will cost more than 50,000 Chinese dollars (one could buy it pretty easily) [roughly US$8,772, at that time]. But if you have a room like Wang's, and that old house is rebuilt (it would be an apartment in a new highrise building, not a single story building), you might just have to pay 10,000, more or less.

I think it is hard to say who in the family will get that room later. Because some of her family members contribute to her care, they will benefit from what they do when she dies. In terms of tradition, *dage*, the elder brother, should/could get it because he is supposed to be the family head. But they no doubt will negotiate with each other—"they" being *dage, lao meimei,* and the others. I mean that it is not at all certain that *dage* and his children will get that room since the others have taken care of Wang *lao*. I guess there will be a negotiable result, or even possibly conflict.

Okay! I haven't answered all of the questions about Wang's family. Some are not really questions, and others are ones that you understand

very well. But I will look them over again when I get the draft of this chapter, just as I did for Gao's chapter. Okay?

By the way, Li Mei and I also are working on the fieldnotes. I hope I can squeeze in time to do it well and quick like you are doing. Learn from Joseph!

Please tell me if you think there is something wrong with my answers. Thank you!

Best wishes to Nancy and you,
LH (Limei and Xiao Xue)

*****

Des Moines
24 July 1994

Dear LH:

Okay, here are some things from my careful reading of the notes from #23, Li Yu Jie and family. I am reminded again how complex this story is too. Aren't they all? Hope you and LM and XX are fine.

Case 23 [Li Yu Jie]

I think the idea that this case has to do with questions of responsibility and feeling is correct. It has to do with a lot more, of course, but it does have to do with this distinction and how we might see it at work in caregiving and family. This kind of distinction probably can be found in virtually all of the families.

To review the details. [In this family, we interviewed Li Yu Jie, the patient; her mother and father, her husband, her son, and her three younger brothers.] At the time of our 1991 interviews: LYJ is forty-four, lives with mother and father and son in parents' home.[11] Graduated high school 1966, just as CR began. Married 1975; son born 1976. Lived with husband (now age forty-five) and his "parents" (aunt and uncle) for about ten years after they were married (page 40; so, *chumenzi* here *was* observed). Says her relationship to husband's "parents" has been very good, but that her relationship with his real mother and sister lacks a bit (41). Her heart disease is probably congenital. In any case, her family knew about it when she got married, but neither she nor they told the husband-to-be. He found out seriousness of her condition when their son was born in 1976, and it was the doctors who told him at that time; they also said she was "not fit to be married" and that she should not have had a child (29). He apparently told her at some point after this that he felt "cheated" by her and her family in that they did not tell him. Some reference to the deterioration of their relationship beginning a couple of years after they were married, which would put it at about the time he found out about her health.

First serious heart problem—heart attack—in 1984, and her condition sort of went downhill after that. Her father says that the first really bad time was in 1987 when she had fibrillation (*fangchan*; page 8). Although she tried to continue working, she could not, and stopped in 1985 (13). The JC [family sickbed, *jiachuang*] she now has was begun in 1986 and continues. Since 1987 it is said she couldn't take full care of herself. Was in the hosp. at the end of 1988 and also at end of 1989 and into '90 (9). She is in effect on what we here in the States would call full medical disability. Her unit pays her 53.70 yuan [then about US$9.40] per month retirement wages, which is perhaps the lowest pay of any of the people we met. And we think these wages have always gone to her parents rather than to her own family. At least, they have for a long time gone to her parents. When the factory (an embroidery factory?) was having hard times, it paid her only a portion of this amount. Her unit also has trouble reimbursing her medical expenses, which are quite high. The most recent long stay in the hospital in 1990 totaled about 8,000 yuan [US$1,404]. The unit still owes the hospital and the family money that it should have paid but could not pay for these expenses (see 17).

There seem to be two stories about who paid the costs. At first, the brothers let us think that they themselves paid the 4,000 or 2,000 in question, but we find out on questioning that it is the old parents who paid 2,000 and LYJ's husband who paid 2,000 (see pages 17–19). This also links back to the bit about the great Chinese medical care system, noted somewhere here.

Her old mother, age sixty-four, is the center of her care and probably we could say the "center" of that family, although she of course makes way for the proper place of her eldest son, who often spoke with authority and displayed his authority in stories and actions about their family. Patient's father is retired and doing *bucha* or postretirement work.

LYJ is the oldest child in this family, and apparently took interest in and was involved in both taking care of her younger brothers and their affairs as they grew up. It sounds like this *dajie* was involved in dealing with her own family as her brothers grew up and got married. This aspect certainly is not consistent with a case of *chumenzi*.

While her connection to her parents and her mother and to their home apparently always has been strong, the intense caregiving work and responsibility did not shift to that place until she began to become gravely ill, in the late 1980s and then in 1990. From her and her mother's talk now, it appears that she will not move back to live with her husband as long as she has to depend on him for care, since she and her family think that he not only is not careful in his carework for her, but that he does not treat her illness as a very important matter (e.g., 42). There is a lot of tension and bad feeling here, especially between LYJ toward her husband, but also from him toward his wife and his mother-in-law. This also exists in somewhat more distanced form between the brothers and the husband, but there are efforts to keep them apart, to minimize the chance of conflict.

One interesting thing is that while the old mother criticizes him a lot, she does not want to foment a real break with him, which would happen if the contradiction were made face to face (47). At least not until her daughter dies, after which she has told her daughter that she will not be able to maintain the connection with him. This tension and conflict is something that made LH nervous because he thought there were some chances for us to become involved in making the conflict explicit, which might then affect our chances to continue our research visits to families in general. So, he—LH—managed this case very carefully so as to avoid our involvement in this family conflict.

And she [LYJ's mother] is really very critical of her son-in-law, even though she says he is not bad. She will not really cut him any slack (see 41, 47).

The *dage* talks of his mother as a "great," "model" mother and a virtuous wife, saying that she sets an example for how they, the brothers, should behave. This brother talks a very strong traditional line in terms of what their responsibilities are, and what Chinese traditions dictate. And he even uses this to talk about how, because his big sister is staying at his parents' home and is so ill, he and his brothers do not come so often with their families and do not ask their old mother to care for their own children as much as they might like to. We don't know how much this *actually* affects her caregiving for these grandchildren, but the brothers and she talk often about this. It is a kind of "sacrifice" theme that marks their own contribution of caregiving for their sister (5). And of course it is also an implicit criticism of their sister's husband who, according to the way things should be, should be taking care of his wife at their own rather than at his wife's parents' home.

One thing that comes out here is our own involvement in this family's life (pages 21, 22–23). This ranged from one interview at which one of the brothers asked us to help them deal with a reimbursement that had not yet been taken care of, to the more subtle ways in which LYJ and her mother wanted us to accept their characterizations of her husband as the "true" ones; to this husband's own efforts to offer *his* truth—sometimes quite different—to us. As noted, LH was very sensitive to this and worked hard not to make any mistakes that would alienate or offend (also see 28 re Mr. Yang [the patient's husband] and contacting him). LH also was very careful about our effects on the patient, given the seriousness of her illness. There is one instance where he insisted that we hesitate in an entry hall before going in to see the patient so as to avoid bringing cold air to her (46). She and her mother later note this, and bring it up to us to mark how we are even more considerate of her than her own husband.

In any case, this may be a theme, usefully illustrated here, along with their attempt to give a foreigner a positive impression of their family.

There is also an interesting dynamic here between a way of speaking in which the old mother and LYJ say, in effect, "We shouldn't say anything bad about her husband," usually followed by a good deal of bad words in fact said (see, e.g., 22). And toward the end of our visits, the mother says that what LYJ says are often trifles and that it is good for her to talk (44). The mother says at the end that when they found out she might die, although according to tradition the daughter is not of their family, they had to save her (page 46).

This mother is a very strong figure, and she also knows how to make and press her point. There is a story of how she actually went to LYJ's husband's former work unit to criticize him for the way he treated his wife as a patient (page 46). This is strong and serious stuff, and while they say that he changed work units because his reputation was bad in the old one (page 43)—contributed to of course by what they themselves did—he says that he changed so that he could be closer to where LYJ was living so that he could see her and take care of her more easily. Mother says another thing she hated was that he told LYJ directly before he told the other family members that the doctors said she would likely die (page 46). So, diverse stories.

Note how LYJ's son refers to his grandparents in terms of his grandmother, his *"laolao,"* rather than both of them (page 39 and elsewhere). In fact, others do the same. See pages 10, 11, 12, 20.

As for this diverse story and multiple truths point, this case might be an opportunity to raise the question of the "truth," and in how telling a "true" story, the scientist/analyst typically has to engage in a set of practices by which he or she *chooses* one version as the correct ("true") one and deprivileges the others. Keep this possibility in mind [and see Wolf 1992].

And, LH, here is a general question for you that you can think about and respond to as you can/like. I have a sense that in much Chinese literature and philosophy, there is not nearly so strong a difference or line dividing the truth from fiction or fantasy or imagination as is common in Western rationalism. In fact, this is I think one of the reasons often cited as to why it took Western science such a long time to get established in China (if it is in fact "established" now). I mean, according to an impression I have, Chinese "thought" and tradition and philosophy allow much more space or tolerance of shifting truths rather than just *one* truth, at least when it comes to complex social matters. So, tell me what your sense of this is, please. This is a little ironic, because, at the same time, in China there is this sense of certain moral rules that are not negotiable. That is, that these moral principles absolutely cannot be violated and that the truth as spoken or defined by a power or authority figure—the father, the emperor, the village leader, the party secretary, and so on, *is the (one and only) Truth*. So, another question you can perhaps help me with in understanding things Chinese is how it is that we can have these *two* kinds of things that seem so contradictory fit together in one cultural tradition of China?[12] In terms of the former point, I keep thinking of the ancient Zhuang Zi poem about the man who was dreaming of being a butterfly, but the question that the author raises in the poem is that it isn't clear if it is instead a butterfly dreaming of being a man.

See discussion of truth in our notes, page 38.

A lot of positive comments from family members to us about doctors and the hospital and JC, as might be expected. "Good hospital + good family = optimal care" (page 16). There is discussion of the last time when LYJ wanted to leave the hosp. so badly but doctors said it was not a good idea and that she likely would die [if she left]. But she was so unhappy and homesick there, they tell us. At first, the family resisted—especially 3rd brother who has medical connection—but then they relented and she came home. The story that they tell us is that the medical people were and are shocked to find not only that she is alive but that she is better. This, the family members say, is due of course to the good medical care of hosp and JC, but also of course to the loving and responsible and psychological/emotional care that the family members have given her that the hosp could not give (page 17).

Of course, if they thought we would repeat their criticism of the doctors and hospital, the family members would not offer them. In fact, I was trying to think of anyone who criticized the doctors and hospital or JC system. I do remember that Pan *laoshi* of Liu Wen Bin's family did offer some criticism, and I respected her for doing that. Can you think of any others of our cases who was even a little critical?

My sense of using this case as one from which also to talk about the feeling/duty issue seems right, although it is multilayered. LYJ is an adult who has returned as a child to her family, and rather late in her life at that. Her mother talks about her "love" for LYJ, and that she is her "only daughter" (pages 5, 10, 16 and before, 21). There is another sentence in which the mother refers to her daughter as her only "good," or *huo*, which I didn't fully understand. Can you help me with that meaning, LH? It's on page 43. It seems clear that there is a language of feeling between the two of them rather than just talk of duty or responsibility. Mother tells of last time her daughter left the hospital that she was very sad because doctors told them there was no hope. At this point in the interview she cried, which is something she did more than once (page 10).

Similarly, it seems clear that there is a lack of this language between LYJ and her husband. Even when he talked to us, although he professed caring for her, he spoke more the language of having done his duty for or to her, and that thus he could hold up his head to his colleagues and others. But that he has "only" done this duty of paying for and handling certain basic things makes the question of his "feeling" or rather its absence stand out more clearly. From LYJ's point of view, it is the absence or lack of this feeling that renders him so inadequate as a husband and as a caregiver.

Her brothers, while stressing duty and responsibility, also speak the language of feeling, especially as modeled by parents and especially their mother.

All of the brothers give their parents money; LYJ's husband also gives 70 yuan per month [about US$12 then] to support living and food for his son (who has been living there since 2–3 grade in primary school), and LYJ's wages go to her parents (see page 6). This in light of the Lee, Parish, and Willis [1994] paper I sent you about intergenerational support in Taiwan.

Two different stories about who did what caregiving when LYJ stayed in the hosp. When we asked father, he said it was mainly his wife and his sons (page 9). Although this is reiterated by her family, her husband says he himself played a much greater role in this than they credit to him. He says he was by her side at night and that he too cooked and sent food to her. The son criticized his father to us about not in fact being by his mother's side when he was "on duty" as a *peiban*, and not letting him, the son, go in to see his mother in the intensive care ward. *Peiban* stories (page 9). There is an example in the notes of how the grandfather and perhaps grandmother correct LuLu [Li Yu Jie's son] when he says something that they don't approve of. Here, he has said that his father spent the night by his mother's bed. The grandfather adds that *"Laolao* also spent the night by your mother's bed." The boy hadn't said this wasn't true (page 9). Brothers didn't do too much *peiban* in hospital, but they did take food.

On page 12, the old mother talks about her own work experience, in response to your question. She says that she hasn't worked outside her home very much. She worked during the Great Leap [Forward—1958–1959], which I take to be something that everyone was more or less "forced" to do. And then later she says that she "went to work in the *jiedao* factory as a temporary worker." My question is: would that have been something that she might have been encouraged strongly to do during the CR? I mean that the idea of a housewife just staying at home was something "feudal" and may have been criticized during that time, forcing women who otherwise would not have gone to work outside to in fact go. Do you think this is possible or likely?

On page 13, *dage* refers to his mother as *"xianqi liangmu."* I know this is a "virtuous wife and good mother," but could you tell me a little more about just how strong of a statement this saying is. What does it tell us, if anything, about this *dage* as a "traditional" son and about his view of his family and parents? This is a "set phrase," I know, and he uses it seriously. So, I am thinking that this suggests that he himself has pretty traditional ideas about who he is and what he should do and so on in his family. Right or not? Say more. Note that on page 14 *dage* actually refers to Kongzi and Mengzi [Confucius and Mencius] directly as important teachers of these ideas. And he says that his mother "belongs to the great mothers" (page 13). Can you tell me more about what that might mean, in the Chinese words he used?

You say on pages 13–14 that the phrase *dage* uses here is close to something Lenin said and that you learned. Could you please be more specific about this? Tell me what Lenin said, exactly, and where you learned that he said it. Is this something you yourself learned as a young man and were asked to memorize?

It is interesting that here again we have a family member saying that because of China's public health system "there are no difficulties for medical treatment charges" (page 14) at the same time that LYJ's factory could not pay the medical bills for her care and that they themselves had to collect money and pay it. They still haven't been paid back for that money. He wants not to criticize, but of course his story or their story *does* make it apparent that the system does not really work the way it is supposed to work.

There is an interesting reference to "feeling" by the *dage* on page 14 where he says that "We brothers have a feeling basis with our *dajie (ganqing jichu)*." Actually, LH, could you tell me more clearly and more specifically what *"ganqing jichu"* means in English, and what it means about their feelings for each other as a basis for being concerned about and taking care of each other.

The brothers' wives are described by *dage* as women who have been taken into their family, who have learned their lessons well from the men's parents and the kind of family relationships that obtain there, and that they behave properly as harmonious members of these men's family (page 15, top). This certainly is a traditional description of women as *waixingren*. There is an interesting moment on page 19 after LH has clarified the details of who paid for what that the matter of money and its sensitiveness comes clear. *Dage* is saying that they agreed to let his parents pay the 2,000 yuan [about US$35] then] for LYJ's medical costs, saying that their family is close and they understand each other and that their [brothers'] wives, although good, have their own "little objections" (page 19). I take this to mean that paying out all that money for the sister would not have been a popular thing with these wives.

LYJ's husband's uncle and aunt give him 15–20 yuan [US$2.60–3.50] a month subsidy (page 21). Also pay his son's school tuition (page 25).[13]

LYJ's husband is concerned about bad things said about him by them to us (page 21).

LYJ says that her husband is not even properly filial toward his old aunt and uncle who raised him (page 22). This kind of criticism of duty, we have learned, is a serious one.

LYJ's husband presents himself to us as concerned about her health and life and as a good and dutiful husband who has done his proper responsibility, but who is himself quite wronged in all of this (begin page 23). Makes an interesting presentation of himself by distinction between what he would like to do and what he is in fact able to do (page 24). "What I have done is not bad and is more than average" (page 25). Criticizes personality of his wife and how difficult she is, and her parents for letting her live there with them. "I have pressure on me" (page 25). Admits that his relationship to his son lacks (page 26), but attributes that more to his wife and her parents. Says there is "a difference in our ideas" with her parents about caregiving and what he should do; he says they expect him to do everything she asks; he demurs and says, after all, I am a man (page 27, 30). This is interesting in that I am sure he is struggling with his own sense of what a man and a husband is allowed and ought to be allowed. This comes up when we talk to him at his office and he tells us about his sense of himself and his reputation; that he is in effect embarrassed by this situation since although he is married and supports his wife, he has no "couple life." Says that LYJ originally didn't like being a housewife and wanted to live with her parents (page 30). About himself he says, "It is only me who no one loves" (page 43).

LH asks about her family's objection to him on these things and he answers in terms of responsibility. But he says he has his own objections to them (page 32). This is where he mentions that he has had no sex life with his wife for a long time (page 32). And he talks here about his moral duty to LYJ and that he has fulfilled that (pages 32ff). He says, in fact, that there is no feeling here but there is duty done. Interesting and important point. If you do your duty, then you are good, he says about himself. Interesting reference here to the social supports for his own position, especially in light of what his mother-in-law did in criticizing him to his former unit leaders for his treatment of his wife. He has been described to us [by this mother-in-law and wife] as very clever with words. Here is an example, says LH, of that use, where he criticizes LYJ's parents indirectly or implicitly, but unmistakably (page 32).

LH, please look at the top of page 43 of the notes. You are talking about LYJ's brothers and you say they are very good, "They look like real men (dingtian lide)." Could you tell me exactly what that phrase means—its literal translation, and also could you help me understand what you meant there? Check out the surrounding talk to get a sense of what your meaning at that moment might have been. Do you think you were making a contrast, implicitly or without thinking about it, with Mr. Yang?

About Yang, the mother says, "One of his biggest faults is that he always thinks he is the greatest one" (page 44). And the wife says, "In the past and now, I depend on my brothers and my parents. . . . Now I have lost my confidence in him" (page 46). "Ta bu hui zuo shi" = "he's a fool" (page 47).

Last page, LYJ says, "I found this bitter thing myself, I have to swallow it by myself too" (wo ziji zhaode zheige, wo zhi neng ziji tun). LH: I asked you here [in the fieldnotes] if the word "bitter" is missing in this but was in the original comment and in your notes. Without the "bitter" it does not seem as strong. Could you please check, and then give me the correct *Hanyu pinyin* and *Hanzi*, with tone marks?

Well, again, there is a lot here. I have written down almost everything that I think is important. I don't think I will be able to put all of these points in the written version of the chapter, especially if I focus on the duty/feeling issue and combine it with the material from Wang Su Min's story. In any case, when you have time, please look through here and let me know the answers to the questions and also what you think about what I have written. Please add things that I have missed, and correct things that I have misinterpreted.

Sorry to give you so much work.

Our love,
Joseph (and Nancy)

$$*****$$

Tianjin
13–17 August 1994

Dear Joseph:

Hi! I sent a letter to you on 8/7/1994 and I hope you have received it by now. I got your last letter just a couple of days ago because my Academy has been on holiday. I am sure it arrived here several days ago.

We seem to be able to work together even though we are 20,000 miles apart. Of course, you are working harder than I am because you have to read the notes and raise the questions. I am trying my best to answer them. I like doing it. It's just like "I love this game" in the American NBA!

About case 23 questions:

I like your idea of making the distinction between "feeling and duty" using the data from cases #29 and #23. From my own experience looking after my father, and from our research, this distinction is important to write about. It is almost the core process of caregiving work, and it structures the roles of the caregivers or other family members. In my opinion, every family member in China ought to have a moral duty to look after an old and ill relative. I mean, it should be inevitable that this duty comes to each of us. But that does not mean that everyone *can* or has to put his or her feeling into this care. And of course, there are different contributions to caregiving done by the different family members we met.

For the people involved in the care, they do it thinking of their feeling or they do it thinking of their duty; and as you know, "feeling" can go with "duty." Anyway, both feeling and duty influence the caregiving process.

Actually, when a family brings up a duty of looking after an old and ill member morally, it brings up a feeling to do it at the same time, at least those parents try to do it so. There is a Chinese saying: *yang er fang lao*. It means bringing up a son so that he will look after his parents when they get old. And in our notes you can see that some sons, like #24's and #8's second son always speak about "paying a debt of gratitude to parents for bringing us up" *(bao yang yu zhi en)*. I am sure that they are talking not only about their responsibilities for care, but also about the feelings they have. But, unfortunately, it doesn't always turn out this way because of the complexity of the relationships between these family members as well as other reasons. There are social reasons distinct from feeling and duty. And sometimes, doing one's "duty" can produce a good "feeling," but it also can turn a good feeling into a bad one. I mean that the relationship of feeling and duty may change in the process of care.

To everyone, the care for an old and ill family member is a burden. It's hard work—especially if it goes on for a long time. As I said before, it is really a sorry thing for a person to have to take this burden if he or she has no feeling to put into it. We could see this kind of person and situation in the families in both case #23 and #29.

This leads me to think or ask what is more important, feeling or duty in supporting the process of caregiving (maybe I should say "good caregiving"). My idea is that it is feeling inside and it is duty outside. Duty gives a moral limitation to a person who is involved in the care. So, it is like a power outside him pushing him to go in the care. Feeling gives an emotional limitation to a person and also pushes him to go in. It is like a power on the inside. Although there are two limitations and two powers here, a limitation and power from inside are stronger than others. It is because one is *willing* to do it with his feeling rather than to do it because of the moral pressure. Anyway, I prefer the inside to the outside. But can I just say duty is on the outside only? It is really sometimes also on the inside when duty has somehow become part of a person's thought. However, comparatively, feeling is more inside than duty is, right?[14]

This is a big question and I will tell you some of my ideas here.

First, I think your writing about #23's basic situation is correct. I will go back to the notes later and check it again. I mean those dates, the amount of money, ages, and so on.

Second, about the idea that Yang was "cheated" to marry Li. It is an important point in this case. Why? We know that Yang does not have a good feeling with his wife, Li. And we know that he complains about his situation. So, can we conclude that his being "cheated" is one of the important grounds for breaking his feelings with his wife and her family? Yes, we can.

I'll tell you a real story that happened two years ago in *Hongqiao* District. A friend of mine there told me last year. A man who was mentally ill killed his wife with a knife. This man had stayed in a mental hospital and had been taken home by his wife. His wife had just had a baby two months before that time. At his own home, which had two rooms, his wife was feeding the baby with his own mother sitting beside her. He was in the other room at the time. Suddenly, he rushed into the room where his wife, son, and mother were sitting and killed his wife with a knife. He didn't harm his son or his mother. His mother took the baby and ran outside, calling for people to save her daughter-in-law and to catch her son. But the man ran away. That night, he went back to the hospital where he had been staying and was caught.

There was a serious argument between his family and his wife's family. His wife's family seriously criticized him and his family for not telling their daughter or them about the mental illness before they were married. His wife's family said that the man and his family had "cheated" the poor woman who was killed. A policeman got involved in the argument and tried to calm the dead woman's family. Her body was not cremated for half a year because her family refused to do it until the argument was settled. On the day of the cremation, the dead woman's family members beat the husband's sister and almost hurt a policeman. This story shows that this idea of a person being "cheated" in their marriage by the other is really very serious or can be very serious. So, you can guess that Yang is unhappy about his wife's heart disease because no one told him about it before they were married.

However, third, we cannot ignore another reason, which is that looking after Li is a burden to him, a burden that can make him lose his feeling for her. As we know, Yang complained that his wife is too self-willed and spoiled by her family. Clearly, there are inconsistencies in the ways each of them see things. I don't mean that the lack of feeling between them is due more to Yang than to Li. I guess they both cause it.

Fourth, it makes me think about the "feeling" on both sides. Yang does things for his wife mainly because of his sense of moral duty toward her rather than because of his feeling. At the same time, Li is really very critical of Yang. So, can I say that Yang is a caregiver who does his duty but does it without feeling? Precisely. And we can say that his wife has no feeling for him. This situation is different from the one where one side has feeling for the other but the other has none for him or her. It makes me think about when parents are ill but they don't want to depend on their children for care. Here there is also a distinction of feeling and duty, but it does not come from a caregiver himself. It comes from both sides, from caregiver and patient. Sometimes this really happens. A caregiver likes to give care, but the patient doesn't want to accept it for a variety of reasons, including the reason that the patient has no good feelings for the caregiver. What do you think of this?

Fifth, you talk about *chumenzi* here. Li is a *chumenzi* daughter in this family but, obviously, she has come back. Is she then an example "against Chinese tradition"? Morally, she is. But this case shows us that Li depends on "feeling" between herself and her mother and the others in her family. She prefers feeling here to duty in order to save herself. In other words, she prefers her feeling with her mother to her husband's duty to help his wife. Traditionally, *chumenzi* is really a feudal idea and takes only a woman's duty to her parents-in-law as important rather than what her feelings might be. Conversely, Wang Su Min #29 is an "old virgin" and never left her own family. She has no husband to depend on. So she has to depend on another kind of duty within her own family. When you put these two women's cases together, you really have to face this issue of *chumenzi*. I guess it will be very interesting.[15]

Finally, I think you are right to say that this family tries to minimize the face-to-face conflict between Yang and Li. On the one hand, I think they are worrying about their daughter. Li is really too fragile to stand a face-to-face conflict with her husband. On the other, I should say this is somewhat influenced by Chinese culture. There is a Confucian saying: *ren wei gui, he wei gao*. It means "to bear up, to endure, is precious; harmony is high, dear." It is linked to that "face facts and you'll stay happy"—*zhi zu chang le*—that Gao's wife said. Both of these sayings inspire Chinese not to be against anything. As you know, "*zhong yong*" is a key phrase of Confucian philosophy. Actually, both "*zhi zu chang le*" and "*ren wei gui, he wei gao*" are part of this Confucian thought. *Zhong yong* means the "Golden Mean" according to the Chinese-English dictionary. It is also the title of a book of Confucian philosophy written by Zi Si about 2,000 years ago.

In Li's family they still try to keep peace, at least on the surface, although they criticize each other. I don't know how you Americans deal with it, but it takes place very often here. Interestingly, you can note that many things like bookmarks sold in the street have the Chinese character *ren* on them. This means "bearing up or enduring." Socially, it also tells people that despite being unhappy or angry about something they should not offend anyone or anything by putting their feelings out. "Okay! You just stay in that beautiful but empty room!"

Yes, the fact that those brothers don't send their kids to their mom to look after is like a contribution to the care for their *dajie*. It is because a lot of old people are looking after their grandchildren, like #9. Of course, it is a burden to look after those kids, as we know from An Wei Sen's family. So, those brothers leave some space for their *dajie*. That they often reminded us of this was to show us of this unusual behavior.

LH was really sensitive to those interviews with this family. He tried his best to protect the process of the fieldwork from pressures in his academy. He did it very well with big help of Mr. Shi.

Also, LH didn't know how to properly deal with those criticisms told to us [about Mr. Yang] and the requests [for our support and help]. It was really hard to stay balanced between Yang and Li. It was like walking on a wire with one end held by Yang and the other held by Li, with them constantly shaking it. LH mainly thought he and S[chneider] should go forward and remember what they were really interested in. He had to find a way that he and S could go and not fall down. Fortunately, they were okay; more than okay!

Here, there are two things I would like to say. One is that Li and her mom, on the one hand, said, "We shouldn't say anything bad about her husband." On the other, they really said a good deal of bad words about him. You know, this is a contradiction. But what is the background of this contradiction? I was thinking that they wanted to or were trying to wear a mask of morality in front of us. Inside, they really wanted to criticize Yang. But they think it may be against the morality of "bearing" and "harmony" to do that. Actually, the contradiction lies in their mind, and it is between morality (outside?) and their feelings (inside?). Is that right? Second, I appreciate your attempt to let both Yang and Li talk about how they saw things here. I mean about Yang's changing his unit. To put differing stories before the readers is really a good idea.

I am trying to understand your idea and your way of telling multiple "truth" points. I think your questions here are really important ones that are directly linked to your writing. My idea is that China has been a *da yi tong*, a big, unitary, autocratic country since Qin Dynasty (221–207 B.C.). Chinese people have been asked to be consistent with the national political system (forced, especially in the recent past), to accept that *only one* thought is truth, without other choices. As you know, the CR is a time typical of this in recent history. During the CR, people wore the same clothes, had their hair cut in the same ways, and spoke the same words. Anyway, there was only one choice of what was correct, and it was the one that the political head preferred. Others had to follow it. As you say, in the family the number one authority figure has been the father. Whatever he says is correct and no one can challenge it. It has been the same in a village, factory, a school, and an academy, and so on. Here LH means that the political system cooks it, the national system cooks it, a family system cooks it, and the same system cooks it every place in China. The core of the system is only one—for instance, an emperor—he controls everything and he is absolutely autocratic and "right." He himself is "truth."

But here there are two questions. One is "Who is really correct? Only the emperor? Only the father? Only those heads of the units?" The answer of course is "absolutely not." However, people do not dare to say this, especially in public. Furthermore, do people really accept or believe this? There must be some who do not. So, they leave whatever they think is right in their minds. They give space to their own thoughts, and they begin to develop a philosophy or a strategy to deal with these different ideas. The key part of this is to have everything fit together there, to mix together the "truth" with whatever they think. You could maybe use the English word "implicit" to describe Chinese people and their thinking. They cannot put their real truth out[side] of their minds. And they are used to being this way. It's familiar to them and has been this way for a very long time. Only tolerance of shifting truths can save them both in their minds and in their actions. Changing this depends on that time of rationalism to come, maybe!

Another question I have is whether two correct but different things can get along—if there are two different ideas that are both correct. (I guess this is close to your question.) You've said it to me before. We Chinese like to divide things into good or bad, one or the other. You are right! Chinese people have been taught this by the system, and they have been taught to hold onto the good and give up the bad. Over time, they have developed a habit of thinking this way. So, they would answer my question by saying "No. You cannot have two correct [but different] things at once." Moreover, they would answer your question—whether there can be *two* kinds of things that seem so contradictory fit together in one cultural tradition—in the same way: "No!" Since they can't even have two correct things fit together they couldn't accept the idea that two contradictory things could fit together. It is impossible; like water and oil. But how about in their minds? Can't they hold these two kinds of things together in their minds? LH would give you two answers: they might say "yes" according to what they are taught, and "no" according to their own thinking.

I read your ideas about truth on page 38. I am coming to understand your thinking that leaves questions of "truth" open and lets the reader think about the real situation.

I remember that we heard critical things about hospitals and doctors in #25 (He Zhiqing) family, #6 (Wu Yu Pei), and #8 (Zhang Xiufang). Mr. He's family members criticized those doctors and nurses in the hospital when He was so sick. Wu Yu Pei's daughters criticized doctors when they took their mother to the emergency room at the hospital. And Zhang Xiufang's son criticized a sickbed doctor who came from another hospital to treat his mother.

About the language of feeling. Here, Li's mom says "*huo*"—it means a good, or a thing—to describe her daughter. *Huo* here is used as a Tianjin folk saying. Usually it is used to describe a bad guy. For example, LH could say "*zheige huo*"—"*That thing!*"—to describe a person who gets in his way in the street. But Li's mother says it not in this way, not as a criticism. I guess it's like using a bad word to refer to a lovely child to show both one's hateful feeling and one's loving feeling. Does that make sense to you?

Li's mom did not work outside her own home because she had to look after her kids when they were young. You could say it was a burden. My mom once told me that she did not go to work because she had to stay at home to look after me when I was one year old during the Great Leap Forward. I know that there was much more chance for women to work outside their homes at that time because the government encouraged the people to do this. As you know, the Great Leap was a time of craziness to set up factories, so there were chances for women to work then. And I think that many people remember that time as an opportunity to work and like to remember it [see Gao 1994].

I think a man could have been criticized as "feudal" if he tried to stop his wife from going to work outside then. Husbands can still be criticized for this now. It was much worse—the criticism—during the CR, for sure. But, would a wife be likely to tell others that her husband forced her to stay at home? Probably not. I think there is an argument or discussion going on right now about whether or not it is "feudal" for a woman to stay at home. Of course, if she is forced to stay home, it certainly is something feudal. However, most couples would discuss it before making a decision. At least this is true for the people I know. Actually, I don't think there is a lot of this—wives staying at home—today.

I think the fact that *dage* says these statements about his mother to us [e.g., *"xianqi liangmu,"* etc.] shows his respect and praise for his mother. He says this seriously and refers to her working very hard and doing her work very well. And you also could see these words as a language of feelings. I mean, that he says them shows his feelings toward his mother too. His saying them then has both meanings. One is that his mother has been doing things for his father; another is that she has been doing things for his *dajie* and his brothers and for him. And we know his mother has done a lot for Li. She is a good mother for sure to look after Li the way she does.

What *dage* says is something close to Lenin's words: "The power of an example is inexhaustible." In Chinese it is *bang yang de li liang shi wu gong de.* I learned this during the CR as a slogan when I was a student in primary school. We had to memorize a lot of slogans and quotations then. We also were encouraged to learn from "revolutionary examples," like Lei Feng.

About the public health system: right! Politically, people would say one is correct, but in their minds it may not be so. This system is supposed to work. Truly, it does not work.

About feeling basis—*ganqing jichu.* This phrase is quite popular, and many Chinese in urban areas say it often. It means that if there has been feeling between people in the past they can use this feeling to get along in the future. I think the key word here is "basis." That means there is a history or a past during which people stayed together and established a feeling between them. The phrase can be used in talking to friends, family members, colleagues and "comrades," and so on. Even if a couple is divorced, they still could say that they had this basis of feeling when they lived together. In Li's family, those brothers lived with *dajie* and got along with her, and thus they can say that they have a basis of feeling with her [and see Kipnis 1997, 104–115].

It is not a popular thing for those brothers' wives to agree to give money to their husbands' sister. They are not the same as their husbands. *Dage* tries to describe his big family as a harmonious one, but I don't think it can work for everything, or in all kinds of family situations. Money is just like house, and is also a sensitive topic among family members here, especially if they don't have enough money to support siblings after they are married. It is very easy for sisters-in-law or even brothers-in-law to oppose it.

I think Yang is in a really complicated situation in his feelings. He feels alone, and he says to us, "It is only me who no one loves." I think it will be very interesting for you to hold this to write how this guy balances his feelings and his duty in taking care of Li. Generally, we can say that he has not the same kind of feeling of the other husbands we met who were looking after their wives, like #26's (Wang Xiuying) husband. But that is too simple just to leave it there. Yang is really in a situation of complicated feelings with his wife, his son, his own parents, and his parents-in-law.

He, Yang, has to learn it to be a person in an empty room. He has to put everything in his mind and fit them together, and sometimes he has to put some that he doesn't like out "properly." I mean, sometimes he has to act in ways he doesn't like.

"*Dingtian lidi*" means "of gigantic stature; of indomitable spirit" in my English dictionary. When I spoke it about LYJ's brothers I meant real men who work hard, are capable and experienced. But I think now I wasn't very serious in using the phrase when I said it. I expressed my sense that those brothers looked capable and experienced. And when I said it I didn't implicate Yang at all. Even now I do not think Yang is not a man. He is, but he feels vexed *("wo nang")*.

I will ask you if you have the sense that Yang tries to be No.1, as his mother-in-law says. Probably not, I guess. But it is possible for Yang to regard himself as good, a good husband and a good father. Doesn't he talk about his accomplishment of his duty in caring for Li? What's your idea?

Okay! LYJ said, "*wo ziji zhaode zhege, wo zhi neng ziji tun.*" What she said was incomplete. There is a saying, "*wo ziji niangde ku jiu, wo ziji he,*" that means "I made this bitter wine and I have to drink it." It is for sure that what Li says comes from that saying. She orally changes a little of it. She didn't use "bitter" but she implied it.

Well, there is a lot here, too. I hope that you will be happy with my answers. I got your letter late and I am afraid of writing back to you late. It will take nine days more or less. I hope it gives you some help when it arrives in Des Moines. Looking forward to hearing more from you! More questions and more chapters! And, thank you for your encouraging me to do it!

I got your fax on 8/15/94 yesterday morning. I am happy you both like that foot massager. Sorry to give you so much answers.

Our love to Nancy and you,
LH (LM and XX)

6

Harmony

The narration of participant observation thus turns from the researcher's struggle with his own images to focus on his struggle against the resistance that the empirical world seemingly offers. The struggle becomes a struggle to see more than mere perception allows, to see deeply, beneath the veil with which the empirical world supposedly hides itself. Thus what is first understood as the researcher's struggle with his imaging is displaced onto the spectacle itself. Now it is the spectacle that is difficult, that is resistant to penetration. The spectacle now threatens with castration, so that what comes to motivate participant observation is the desire to get as close as possible to what is observed without getting lost in it, without becoming completely absorbed in what is to be made visible. Thus, in its narration, participant observation becomes eroticized with the anxiety and excitement of the sexual scenarios of vision.

Patricia T. Clough, *The End(s) of Ethnography* (1998)

Zhang Xiufang is the name Laihua has chosen for the character at the center of this chapter, which, like the others, tries not to be such a good story that you forget it is one. She is a small woman with once-bound feet, slightly graying hair pulled back tightly into a bun, who lives in a narrow yard in one of the most desirable parts of the city, the so-called *wu da dao* or five big streets area. LH said her real name seems a bit strange for a woman her age, someone born in 1912. "It's too 'modern' and was probably given to her later. She probably just was called 'first,' 'second' or 'third daughter' and given no proper name at all." Zhang Xiufang's husband, Li Changqing, an engineer who worked in construction and had what one of his sons called "a very high salary," died just after Mao Zedong died and the earthquake came in 1976. Now at seventy-eight, suffering diabetes and hypertension, she had become unsteady on her feet and had fallen twice recently, first just outside her doorway and later, when getting up during the night. These falls, in which she sustained bruises, scrapes, and sore muscles, worried her children—four sons and one daughter—a great deal. Her first and second sons, Li Yu

Nian, fifty, and Li Yu Qiu, forty-seven, had set up an almost around-the-clock schedule of care that they shared with first son's wife and the youngest brother, Li Yu Quan, forty-four. Zhang Xiufang's daughter, Li Yu Fen, fifty-seven, who had routinely come to her mother's home twice a week for several years to help her bathe and wash her hair, now was ill herself and occupied by her own family's responsibilities. To keep a channel of communication with, and possible access to, the hospital, Zhang's oldest son had arranged for a sickbed from Main Hospital. It was just a few weeks after the old woman's last fall that we two first appeared at her door.

Now, several years later, back in Des Moines, when I think of Zhang Xiufang I see her dressed as she was that first time we met, 17 November 1990: in a traditional black jacket and pants tapering down her short legs, disappearing into small black shoes. This image—an old woman, hobbled, hair pulled back tightly, wearing a black *guazi*—still can be seen along Tianjin streets; a marker of a time both certainly past yet unmistakably still quite present. Only the most apparent of many signs of tradition that circulated around and through her, these were pieces of a mosaic of filiality and care that instructed us on some of the complexities and tensions of that cherished but elusive family harmony storied to be so central to what it means to be Chinese, even in the late twentieth century.[1]

Although local opinions might differ on the desirability of the *wu da dao* neighborhood, the old woman and her family shared the view that this indeed had been a good place to live. It also had been a good place—certainly, far better—for some of the richest and most powerful foreign colonizers and their Chinese colleagues and families who lived in Tianjin earlier in this century and at the end of the last. The particular section where the Li family lived was in the heart of what had been the British concession. A large and now busy street, called Racecourse Road or Machang Dao, snakes through the area and ends in what had been a racecourse, polo grounds, and clubhouse constructed for the wealthy foreign population.

Many of Tianjin's most powerful older cadres and party officials have lived in this section of town in former colonial buildings that their bureaus and units now own. Joseph and Nancy themselves lived in this neighborhood, quite near to the Lis, in the foreigners' apartment building at the Foreign Languages Institute, once a Catholic college run by Jesuits. But beyond state and municipal bureaus, schools, and the like, many of these houses (if they have not been torn down) now accommodate five, six, or more families, allowing only one or two small rooms for two or three generations. The Li family had come to their small yard just after 1949, and Zhang Xiufang and her husband had given birth to and raised most of their children there. Then, the Lis alone occupied the yard, at the end of a narrow *hutong* off one of the area's main streets.

Their yard was bordered on the north by four flat-roofed rooms with common side walls, all with large windows facing the south. A strip of land about eight meters wide was the yard itself, bordered on the south by a high wall. In summer, it was full of flowers, vines, and vegetables, and was partially shaded by graceful locust trees. This was indeed a good place, and since it was not "private property," the rent was very cheap; only 8.54 yuan per month (about US$1.50 in 1991).[2] The Lis's own rooms and yard were not part of a once-grand colonial house, but had been somewhat jerry-built at a time when capitalism was in decline. This meant, among other things, that the yard had no sewer connection and thus no flush toilet. At night, the Lis—and Zhang Xiufang during the day, too, like Wang Su Min—used chamber pots.

When we met old Mrs. Zhang, she and her family had long since grown accustomed to sharing the yard with two or three other families, although they had been able to retain the two most desirable rooms near the entrance for themselves. This sharing had come as a mandatory part of the reaffirmation of socialism and the critique of capitalism and private property mounted during the Cultural Revolution about which Du Li Rong and her sister spoke, in chapter 4. Such sharing also had come as a practical necessity due to the inexorable press of a burgeoning city population.

But external politics and population aside, over the course of their lives here, space inside these walls also had become more dear. The Lis had built an additional small room of roughly nine square meters extending into the yard at the middle of the south wall. This new room had one small window rather high up its north wall, which meant it received no direct sunlight and thus no natural heating or warmth from the sun in winter. When they spoke about it, the brothers described the room as "cold," "damp," and "dark." It was not a good place. Still, it was a room; a place to live and to make a small family within the larger, encompassing one. This is just what the youngest Li son, his wife, and daughter, had done for nine years, until they moved in 1989 to a larger room in a large apartment complex twenty minutes away.

When Zhang Xiufang's husband died in 1976, their first and second sons already were married and had brought their wives, and in time, their children into the yard. The Li daughter had married and left, while sons three and four were still single. All together there were nine people living in three small rooms. But perhaps most troubling, there were four Li brothers, and only three rooms in this yard.

"Our Family is Relatively Harmonious"

14 January 1991. 10:30 A.M. LH arranged for us to meet Li Yu Nian, fifty, Zhang Xiufang's oldest son at the Foreign Languages Institute on Racecourse Road where I live. We have just returned from an earlier interview with Li Yu Jie (chapter 5). Bikes hastily parked inside the foreigners' compound, we run back toward the main entrance to wait for our guest.

It's our first meeting with this *da ge* (as you know, meaning "oldest brother"), an engineer/businessman who is married with a twenty-two-year-old son who sometimes lives in his father's old room in the Li family yard. As we walk toward the front gate, in rides a middle-aged man on a motorbike, wearing a raincoat and an air of confidence that tells us this must be our respondent. As he guides his bike to a parking spot beside the guardhouse—almost every office and bureau, and certainly every school and college has one—the old men in charge eye him warily. He can't be a student; he doesn't look like a teacher; he is Chinese; he has shown these old men no respect or deference. What is his business here?

As Laihua and I move toward this stranger, the old men draw back a bit, recognizing that whatever his business, it has been pre-arranged and it involves a foreigner. It thus passes from their realm of responsibility, and they retreat back into their warmed space.

Beyond his bearing and air as a *dage*—big, oldest brother—to help us recognize him, Li Yu Nian looks a good deal like his mother and second brother, with whom we have spent three previous and quite friendly interviews. His oval face and full cheeks have become victims of gravity and age, and he looks a bit haggard. A smiling Laihua extends his hand, introduces himself, and then turns to introduce me. We shake hands and I thank him for agreeing to meet with us. As we walk to a second gate and guardhouse at the entrance to the foreigners' residence, where all Chinese are required to *dengji,* or register their name, work unit, name of the foreigner they are visiting, and purpose of the visit, along with the time of arrival and departure, I watch Mr. Li out of the corner of my eye as he talks to Laihua. In his usual way, Laihua is saying something congratulatory about the Li brothers' care of their mother, although I cannot make out all of his words.

In our translation of this interview a day or two later, Laihua will comment to me that this man "talks like a *dage . . .* like an educated man with more . . . readiness than his second brother" (the word I choose and write in brackets in my notes is "authority"; I might have written "arrogance"). We learn that he is in fact educated, having gone to one of the most respected middle schools in the city and then on to a local institute of science and technology. And he is something of a man of the world, having traveled to Holland, England, Hong Kong, and Indonesia; and is planning a similar trip back to Indonesia in the near future.[3] He strikes me immediately as also less warm and friendly than second brother Li Yu Qiu, whom we feel we have come to know best among these brothers (and who has treated us with a good deal of deference).

There is not a shred of deference in this *dage's* behavior as he enters the second guardhouse, shows his identification card, and completes the registration form, with the two older men standing over him closely inspecting what he writes. The absence of deference is notable because it is so typically present in this scene of *dengji,* where a Chinese person comes face to face with authority and is expected to assume a properly other, supplicant posture. In fact, it is the guards who begin to defer to him, as they sense the presence of an important man.

Finally settled upstairs, the three of us sit around a low table, teacups, pens, and notebooks properly in place. Laihua has given his usual brief introduction to our project and then, skillfully and with deference, of course, asks Li Yu Nian to introduce himself and his family to us, and to explain how the caregiving for his mother is organized. His face already partly obscured in a cloud of smoke from the first of five cigarettes over the course of the next hour and 20 minutes—much to our regret—*dage* begins by telling us some of what we have just told you, above—his age, work, and education. Then he continues, with what becomes something of a curious comment that, subsequently, provided me a theme for writing this chapter:

"My father died in 1976, about the 19th of September. Then, we all lived together as a big family."

This "we" does not include his older sister who, at that time, lived with her husband in Nanjing. In fact, most of the we's that he uses in referring to his siblings do not include this sister, who by her age is the actual *da* or oldest among this family's children. But from our stories thus far, you know about *chumenzi.* In the Li family it had, in effect, reduced five siblings to four brothers.

"Several days after my father died," Li Yu Nian went on, "my mother said we should separate. She said what she feared most if we brothers all continued to live together—*jiu pa you bu yukuai de shi*—was that there would be some unpleasantness—some unhappy things—in our family."

He did not treat what he had said as in the least requiring elaboration or explanation. Laihua had received the comment in the same way; as perfectly understandable. I didn't understand it, but at the time I assumed I had misheard.

"My wife and my son and I were the first to move away to our own apartment. But we continued to take care of my mother. Soon after we moved out, my third brother got married and moved to a suburb as a teacher. My second brother, his wife, and their son lived in the room next to my mother—where I lived before I left. My youngest brother soon married. They lived in that small, third room. Soon their daughter was born."

As Li *dage* spoke about this, I wondered what more he might say about the "unpleasantness" that had worried his mother. Mr. Shi and I already had heard a story from second brother about when his youngest brother and his new wife first came to live in the family yard. I remember this because I was a little surprised by what he said. You know, we Chinese say *"jiachou buke waiyong."* In English it means "Don't tell your family troubles to outsiders." When second brother told us about the conflict with his youngest brother, I was surprised, and it made me a little nervous—the same way I felt about some of the things Li Yu Jie and her mother told us about Mr. Yang, in chapter 5. I was sure it would complicate our work; make it more sensitive.

"I think my mother's health is getting worse now," *dage* was saying. She doesn't like to go out of her room; she is very afraid of falling again. For the last year, her blood pressure has been unstable, and I think she has some trouble with her heart. The sickbed was set up for her a year ago. I wanted her to go to the hospital but she refused, so this is better for her."

"What about her medical expenses?" Laihua asked. "Who pays them?"

Actually, Laihua knew the answer to this question, which was, basically, "I do." Second brother earlier had told us as much. But it was a way to skirt for the moment the question that *dage* himself had alluded to but did not pursue: the delicate business of family harmony ("some unpleasantness in our family").

"I pay all of them," he said. "It's about 30–40 yuan each month. My unit will reimburse me for half of this. My mother never had a *danwei*; she was a housewife and has no income of her own. I also give her fifty yuan each month *lingyong qian,* small change, and spend 15–20 yuan each month for the breakfast that I take to her each morning on my way to work. All together, it's about 100 yuan. *Wo xiang [zhe shi] yinggai [zuo]de.* My wife also is pretty good. She works in the same company as I do and has a direct personality. Her relationship with my mother is not bad."

Laihua stops writing and takes a sip of tea. The smoke in the room is thick, and my eyes are burning. If we open the window it soon will be too cold. Our guest uses the moment to take another long drag from his cigarette, and then asks if the smoke is bothering us. We lie; he knows. Laihua continues.

"We understand that your wife helps your mother wash her feet." This is a detail about the relationship between the *dasaozi* and her *popo*—her husband's mother—that second brother also has provided us, with great approval and praise for his first sister-in-law. He told us his mother was "a little feudal" in her thinking and didn't want any man except her husband to see her feet—including her sons.

"Yes, yes; every night after dinner. And she has no objection about the money I give my mother."

A "good wife," as we know well by now, is one who helps her husband be a "good son." Since good sons typically give their parents—and especially their mothers—money, delectable food, and other things (often in an economy of scarcity), a proper wife is one who says nothing critical about this, or, even better, encourages it. "The Chinese family" also writes the mother-son bond as "special." That this eldest son actually *tells us* that his wife does not "object to" what he gives his mother—totaling, as he says, about 100 yuan a month [then, about US$18]—may be a measure of just how demanding the haunting has become for the ghost of the *xiaozi* or filial son. But beyond what a good wife does not say, there is the matter of what she in fact does. For the wife of a *xiaozi,* be he ancient or "modern," this was quite a lot.

Still, this wife cannot be given too much credit for her propriety. It is, after all, "what she should do"; and among those two or three generation families that either live together or spend a good deal of time together, there is the delicate business of the relationship between the son's mother and the son's wife, the *po xi guanxi.* If the son praises his wife too much in the presence of his mother, or makes it a point to "choose" his wife over against his mother in some (almost any?) difference, the mother may well not be "happy," and the son thus calls his own status as a son into question.[4]

"At the present time," Li Yu Nian continued, "there is no problem about the payments to my mother. And my wife has done a lot of housework in my mother's home," revisiting and thus underlining a point we had not raised but that he wanted to make.

Laihua changes the subject: "Did you brothers make a plan for dividing up the housework and care for your mother?"

"No," *dage* said sharply, as though the question offended him. "We never discuss this. All of us make our own efforts to care for my mother relatively conscientiously. For example, my second brother recently has been sleeping there at night to take care of her; and my third brother—he is a middle school teacher who lives in the distant suburbs—comes to see my mother every other week and brings her fish and other things she likes to eat. He even suggested that he retire from his job early and move back home to take care of her. I said I didn't think we could resolve the question of housing if he did that. My youngest brother lives near my mother's home and goes there every day to cook lunch and do whatever needs doing. In the past, my sister and brother-in-law came once or twice a week to cook, and my sister would help my mother take a bath and wash her hair. Recently, her own health is not too good and she is busy helping her daughter-in-law move near her, since her son has gone to Japan. Generally, we brothers all think of how to take care of *lao taitai*.[5] Even if she is feeling fine, we go to see her."

"Yes. You brothers do a lot. But I think you pay more than the others," said Laihua, smiling.

"I have three advantages. First, my salary is higher, so I can afford it. Second, my wife supports me in taking care of my mother, and she herself also takes care of her. Third, my wife and I once agreed. Suppose we had no brothers to help us. We still should take care of her. We shouldn't demand that the others do this. In fact, when they take care of my mother, they reduce some of our burden."

"I think your mother loves you all very much," says Laihua.

"Yes. *Ta teng women.* I might say '*cun cao xin, nan bao san yue hui.*'[6] Our distribution of caregiving to our mother depends on our habit and on our conscientiousness, not on regulation. There are never any problems of finances for my mother or housework for her among us brothers. We do not regard them as important things. We brothers help each other and our relations are relatively harmonious. I think this is a heritage from my mother and father."

"Yes, yes," says Laihua, as he takes another sip of tea. By this time, my head is splitting and full of congestion from the smoke. I sit here, dumbly, hoping that the interview soon will end, valuable data or not.

"*Waixingren* are Not the Same as Children"

But it didn't. And hasn't.

"Just now you said you brothers treat your mother well. What about your sisters-in-law—do they often come to your mother's house to see her?"

It's interesting to hear Laihua ask *dage* this question. From one local son to another, it is rather bold. We already know that three of the daughters-in-law come only rarely to see Zhang Xiufang. We also know there is a family conflict over who shall have the mother's room when she dies. These matters easily are read as about filial propriety in the family—of who should defer to whom and how much; of a daughter-in-law's politeness (or its absence); and of the proper limits of a younger brother's interests.[7]

The most unmistakable mark of this conflict is that second brother, *er ge*, does not speak to his youngest brother, Li Yu Quan. Second brother told us that in an argument between them, just before the youngest brother and his wife moved out of the yard, *xiao si*—little fourth—said to him, "*Wo ma ni!*"—I curse you! As a result, he decided not to speak to his youngest brother until he apologized, and also until his youngest sister-in-law apologized for what the older brothers saw as her impolite behavior toward Zhang Xiufang—all having to do with the question of who shall control her room.

We cannot mention this to *dage* for it both would make public the conflict and the fact that second brother had told us about it. *Jiachou buke waiyong.* Clearly, it is something *dage* seems not to want to open for us. Moreover, we have said all our conversations are held in confidence. But our questioning is somewhat treacherous—as it often is—in that by it we create an opportunity for this man to lie, thinking we do not know "the truth" (but, isn't the point to wonder which truth this one, the one that we think we know, is?). He responds.

Yes. They come. "Except my third brother's wife and my fourth sister-in-law. Third brother's wife lives in the suburbs and is a teacher. She is very busy. Fourth sister-in-law comes to see my mother less because there is a little difference of views and estrangement—*fen qi ge he*—between us and her. This is still going on. Of course, my brothers and my sisters-in-law do not care for my mother in the same ways. *Waixingren* are not the same as children."

A problem "between us and her," as he puts it. It is her fault. But there is much cultural precedent here for a story about a daughter-in-law who is not "good," who does not treat her mother-in-law well, and who thus threatens family harmony. "*Waixingren* are not the same as children."

Second brother said the problem is between his youngest brother and him; that it has to do with *xiao si's* refusal to willingly vacate their mother's room after a brief celebratory period following his marriage. Zhang Xiufang had offered to move to the smaller and less desirable room so that her youngest and his wife could enjoy her space for a time after their wedding. A mother's love; and of course Li Yu Quan is the "baby" of the family. But when the time came for them to go back to the smaller room, they refused to move. Finally, after pressure from the two oldest brothers, and angry words exchanged between the young wife and the old mother, youngest brother and wife moved back across the yard. But to stake his claim, and thus create a reminder that daily could rankle his two oldest brothers, *xiao si* left some of his own furniture in his mother's room to foreshadow his and his wife's eventual return. Of course, that furniture also foreshadows Zhang Xiufang's death.

"How do you all spend the Spring Festival holidays?" Laihua asks *dage*.

He hesitates and shifts a bit in his chair. This is a clever question and is not something I would have thought to ask. It is like asking, in the United States, how do you spend Christmas or Hanukkah, Easter or Passover, except that the family expectations for Spring Festival are even more fine-grained. It seeks out the displaced details of family trouble. This is what sociologists do. At least, it is some of what we do. It feels sneaky to me, but we justify it in the name of a need to know, for the sake of "knowledge." "If we don't do it this way, we can't get the data." And getting the data is, after all, everything.

"In the past, all of us came to my mother's home on Spring Festival eve and stayed until we had to go back to work—that is about two weeks—except my sister. She only came there the second day of Spring Festival. Recently, our family members have moved to new places and things have changed. My youngest sister-in-law doesn't often join us. For instance, last year she stayed in her own home on Spring Festival eve and only came to my mother's home the morning of the first day." He doesn't elaborate. But we want to know the details of this trouble. They help us, we think, get below the surface, to the heart of the matter.

"The Tradition is Melting"

Tradition still has it that a daughter-in-law should come to her husband's family the evening before the Spring Festival holiday begins, and go to her own parents' home only on the second day of the period. So, in at least more than a few homes, daughters who are wives remain daughters-in-law first, at least on this important holiday.

"As oldest brother," LH turns the topic away from holidays, "do you often ask your brothers about their work?"

"I think about my brothers and their children only a little," *dage* says straightforwardly. "And we talk to each other about our work only rarely." He pauses a moment to snuff out his cigarette, then says: "Maybe it is because we all have our own personalities and don't want to depend on one another."

"Really?!" asks Laihua, surprised. His tone seems to give *dage* pause. He takes out another cigarette, lights it, and exhales a cloud of smoke.

"I think the major problem is personality. I remember. Once my youngest brother went to my sister and asked her opinion about changing his work unit. He never mentioned it to me. My third brother also doesn't talk to me about important things. Except for very special things—like going abroad—we brothers rarely talk to each other." He means, of course, that they do not come to him.

"This is a little strange," says LH as we stand up for a break in our work of ethnography the next night at his house. The hard chair next to his desk is making my right leg numb, and I have to go to the toilet. He continues as I walk to the bathroom. "In a normal large family like this, if they really are harmonious, you should find certain things, such as respecting old people and a lot of help exchanged between brothers and sisters. But in this family, these brothers seem only to have responsibility to and care for their old mother. There is no help between the brothers. It is a little strange."

"Oh," I say to him, thinking it may not in fact be so strange; and wanting to consider the price of this harmony before we mourn its loss too much.

Meanwhile, the interview is almost finished. We have asked Li Yu Nian all we can think to ask, and our eyes are watering fiercely. Laihua says more about how well the Li brothers take care of their old mother, and himself credits it in part to "Chinese tradition." *Dage* agrees and asks LH if he, and if the foreigner, Mr. Shi, has seen the TV series "Si Shi Tong Tang"—"Four Generations Live Together."[8] Since I don't hear this question at the time, I later find out that Laihua has answered for me: "I don't think he has seen it."

"But now the situation has changed a lot," *dage* says as he stands up and looks at the foreigner. "It's due to the problem of housing . . . of economic conditions, and so on. The tradition is melting. And I also think there is a different way of thinking between America and China. Chinese people respect older people. Kongzi inspired us to be *xiao*."

Laihua turns to me and translates *dage's* comment, and adds: "Mr. Li wonders what is the situation of caregiving for old parents in America."

This is not a time for much talk, but I hear myself saying something I have said before in response to similar questions. "In America, the situation for old people is not so good. If children or old parents have money, then the parent can go to a more comfortable retirement home or nursing home. If not, the conditions are less comfortable. Sometimes children forget their parents in such places. We do not have a tradition of Kongzi like you do here."

This of course is what they both want to hear; American children think of themselves and forget their parents. So selfish; so much individualism. But it is also too simple to be the "whole story." As my gerontologist colleague points out, gently, to me, "There are several studies that show. . . ." But as I look again and again at what I said, it occurs to me that something other than professional discourse wanted to speak me, then, there. Perhaps what I should have added was, "Compared to what you have done, Li Yu Nian, I do not deserve to be called a son." This is the guilt of a "son" who neglected his mother when she was dying . . . and alone. No amount of writing over that past (?) self can erase its outlines in the palimpsest that is the now.

"She Thinks of Me as Her Daughter"

We have marked before the important place of "the daughter-in-law" as a figure in the performance of traditional family harmony: the key relationship in her adult life was likely to be that with her husband's mother, for whom she could serve as a personal maid and substitute in routine but often arduous household tasks. If one had a "good" mother-in-law, it could be the difference between a life of relative security—within the frame of patriarchy that custom defined—and one of constant abuse and rejection, with little if any way out. These images and stories do not offer viable characterizations of common practice in the late twentieth century. But it is not difficult to see versions of the "old ways" still very much part of how mothers of the senior generation and their middle-aged daughters-in-law relate to each other. This is hardly surprising, in that filial sons and their wives both are part of the same world, haunted, albeit perhaps not equally, by our familiar ghost.

Dasaozi—again, eldest sister-in-law—could stand quite well as a late-twentieth-century representative of the generations of her forbears who took up the duties and burdens of a *xiaozi's* wife. And although she has an independence and an identity of which these women ghosts from the past could not have dreamed—she is a woman of a socialist state who has been told, publicly and officially, that she "holds up half the sky"; who has her equality in marriage affirmed by The 1950 Marriage Law and its 1980 reaffirmation[9]; she has a job and income quite separate from her husband and his family, although she is a worker in the factory and he is a cadre; she is educated and, it is said, opinionated, even within the Li family—although she has all of these resources that set her off from her predecessors, she remains unmistakably the dutiful *erxifur*—daughter-in-law—to her husband's mother, to her husband; to her husband's family, and even to her own family.

6 March 1991. 8:00 P.M. Laihua asked *dage* a week or so ago if we might talk to his wife about the care she gives his mother. He agreed, and we have an appointment to see her tonight, after she, as usual, cooks for and eats dinner with her husband and her mother-in-law.

LH and I have arranged to meet at a familiar corner and ride the last few blocks together to *dage* and his wife's new home in a high-rise apartment building perhaps twenty-five minutes away from his mother's home. It is a cold, raw night, and as we peddle into the strong north wind, I complain to my friend and try to make a joke. "God, it's cold! Tonight we need our internal heating!" LH laughs and agrees. "Yes. We need that heating!"

Finally, we find the building and the Lis's flat. It is quite large—three rooms, plus a kitchen and a toilet—and they appear to have new furniture. *Dasaozi* explains that *dage* has stayed on a bit at his mother's to be sure that the coal stove is properly prepared for the night. His second brother is in the hospital, and so this first son has asked his own son to take his brother's place, more or less, sleeping in the room adjoining his mother. *Dasaozi* brings us tea, which is hot and for which I am especially grateful. While Laihua barely touches his cup, I embrace mine with both hands, drawing it toward my chest and resting it on my bent knees so that the steam and warmth rise up around my red cheeks.

LH explains that since she is an important caregiver for her mother-in-law, we want to talk to her about what she does.

"Your investigation is far-reaching," she says, smiling. "You have talked to many family members." We wonder if this is an objection. But, as she continues, her tone is friendly and she speaks easily and quickly. I think of how different she is from Zhang Xiufang's own daughter, who seemed to us much more guarded and deliberate in what she told us about her family, which actually turned out to be very little. But then, as *dage* himself had said, *waixingren* are not the same as children. They are outsiders, with which also comes a certain license.

Dasaozi recalls how happy Zhang was at Spring Festival this year because her third son and his family came and spent much of the holiday with her. Then she explains that second brother, Li Yu Qiu, has taken advantage of his mother's recent relatively stable health to go for treatment of a chronic shoulder problem.

"Li Yu Qiu treats us very well," she adds. "He treats me like a *da jie* (oldest sister). And he likes to make jokes." She thus returns the compliments that her second brother-in-law earlier has given her, and seems to affirm that second brother behaves toward them just as he should, with the deference and praise—the face—an elder brother deserves. Her claim that second brother treats her "like *the* big sister," which is to say like his *own* older sister, is interesting in its boldness, for it seems to assert her "special" status among the "outsiders" inside this family.

LH begins to ask some of the questions I had prepared for this visit. Now, writing this text, and in a different place, these questions seem embarrassingly coy; for they ask, in a way that tries hard to deny it, things that we (think we) already know—a kind of professionally endorsed disengenuousness, just as when we met with *dage*.

"You are the wife of the oldest son in your husband's family. Does that mean something special in terms of your duties to his family, and especially to Zhang *lao*?"

Clearly, this woman knows the question is one that only a foreigner—or someone who acts like a foreigner or outsider but is not—could ask. Perhaps she thinks Laihua is asking *my* question (ventriloquism, again).

"Yes. Because of the influence of traditional ideas, I feel I should take more responsibility than the others. I mainly do . . . all the brothers are concerned about *lao taitai*. I only cook, and buy vegetables. They all like to eat what I cook. When they eat and say it is good I am very happy." I mainly do . . . no, no. Let me put it another way. All the brothers. . . .

I have practiced this next question and so I quickly begin, before LH can continue. "You do a lot for Zhang *lao*. Could you tell us in detail what you usually do—every day?"

"Yes. I go there every morning and empty the pot under her bed. I prepare warm water for her to wash her face and brush her teeth. In the past, I would stop and buy her breakfast, but then she said she wanted to have bean soup. I had no time to make that. She complained. Then Li Yu Nian took over buying breakfast for her. I think maybe *lao taitai* is a little prejudiced. What he buys is the same as what I bought, but she doesn't complain. I also go there after my work to help prepare dinner."

"Does she treat you in a special way?" asks Laihua.

"She doesn't regard me as an outsider. If she wants to say anything to me, she does. Others once told me she thinks of me as her daughter."

Dasaozi has invested a great deal in the Li family, and one of the most important tests for this first wife of several *xiao* brothers is what may be said about how she tends the relationship to Zhang Xiufang. Clearly, she cultivates the notion that she has been accepted by her "as a daughter," not as a *waixingren*. All three brothers whom we met praised her for this. Only second daughter-in-law had anything critical to say about her, but that daughters-in-law might criticize each other is hardly a surprising piece of this tradition.

"But you are a *waixingren* in the Li family," says LH. "Please tell us a little about that."

"Yes. A daughter-in-law is of course a *waixingren*. But *lao taitai* is not *very* unfair. She once criticized *dajie* her daughter. I tried to discourage her. She said that a neighbor's daughter comes to her old parents' home and spends time with them every day. I told her she shouldn't compare her own daughter to that neighbor's daughter. They have very different family situations."

"She does treat you very well, then." LH demonstrates his skill at discovery; or is it production? Or manipulation?

"Well, I think she treats the other daughters-in-law more politely than she treats me—such as Li Yu Qiu's wife and the third daughter-in-law. When they go to her house, she usually greets them more warmly and says more good words. But then this Spring Festival, third daughter-in-law came to *lao taitai's* home and spent more time and cooked more than usual. She reduced my burden. Then, when I cooked steamed bread, the dough fermented better. *Nainai* praised me and said, 'That's very good; a good omen.' I was happy about that."

Laihua asks what he would call a "difficult" question: "Does she often criticize you?" Our respondent does not seem fazed by this.

"If she wants to say something to me, she does. She feels at ease to talk to me. When what she says is not right, I don't respond. She once told the neighbors, '*Da sao* has a good temper.' I never hate her. For many years I have felt she is unfair. But actually, she treats us better than she treats the others.

"It's true. I do more. It is because she treats me like my own parents treat me. And she took care of my son for a period of time; and helped *dajie* with her two children. She has not had an easy life. But she is tough, and she likes to have things her way."

The tea seems to have worked on me and I am feeling quite warm. I take the moment LH spends looking at his list of questions to ask another that I have been rehearsing as I listen to them talk. *Dasaozi's* pronunciation is very standard and crisp, and I can understand most of what she says.

"You said your son will stay next to his grandmother tonight. Does he stay there often?"

"If Li Yu Qiu stays there, we tell our son to come back home. If he doesn't stay, we ask our son to stay. Since second brother has been in the hospital, our son has been staying there at night, although he does very little housework there. She spoils him. It's always been like that. She always told him, "It's more important for you to do your homework than to do housework."

"*Hao, hao. Wo zhidao,*" I say, proudly writing in English what I heard her say as Laihua regains the floor.

"How about your own parents now?"

"They are good. Their health is good. My father is seventy and still works although he is retired. My mother is sixty-nine. She is healthy and she walks faster than I do. My two brothers live near them, and they both respect and obey them. They help with daily things, like buying coal, vegetables; and they also help with the housework. *Wo yi xin dou pu zai Li jia.* I devote myself heart and soul to the Li family. I usually go to see my parents every three of four weeks."

"You are a member of three families: your own big family, your husband's family, and your own small family. This means a lot of responsibility for you. How do you do all this?"

"Among these three families, I do more in my mother-in-law's family. Before Spring Festival, my mother went to visit *lao taitai.* My mother told her, 'I ask my daughter to come here. I don't need her; let her help you. If she does anything wrong, you should criticize her.' "[10]

We've been here now over an hour and seem to have exhausted most of the questions we prepared. I try to look at my watch without drawing attention. It's 9:15. Laihua says:

"I think you are a direct person."

"I like to talk. If what I say is wrong, I'll correct it. If I meet trouble, I stop talking."

"In that kind of situation, when you meet trouble, what does your husband say to you?"

"He says, 'Don't say more—don't argue with *lao taitai.*' Mostly, I only want to explain what I meant. He says, 'It's better for you not to explain. You needn't explain it.'"

We go back to the topic of her own family. "You have no time to look after your own parents. Perhaps you give them money?"

"Yes. I asked my brothers to look after our parents, but I give them a lot of money—more than 50 yuan each month. I know my parents like to buy gifts for my brothers' children. They often tell them, 'These gifts are bought by your aunt!' I am the first child in my own family and here I am the first daughter-in-law."

Laihua returns to a "productive" question. "How do you all spend Spring Festival?"

"Usually, with *lao taitai.* She likes that. On Spring Festival eve we drink some wine and make dumplings together. This is a tradition. This year, third brother and his family came and stayed five days. They brought and cooked many things. Usually, they can't come or can't stay because they raise chickens."

"What about the fourth brother? Did he go to Zhang *lao's* home on Spring Festival eve?" Laihua tries to get to "the problem," again in our treacherous way.

"No. He came the next morning and ate dumplings filled with vegetables. This is also a tradition.

"Fourth brother's wife has a big difference with second brother. And so does he. If his second brother was there, fourth brother wouldn't come into the room, for sure. But he wanted to eat those traditional dumplings. He said he especially wanted to eat them since I was cooking."

Riding away from the interview that night, I recall Laihua saying "She told us a lot about that trouble. It was very good." Our strategies had paid off; we were getting "deeper" into the truth of this challenge to family harmony.

"That big disagreement is caused by the house. Fourth brother once said that his wife planned to ask *nainai*—"mother," spoken from her husband's position—to live permanently in that little room across from her own room, and that fourth brother and she should live in *nainai's* room. You know, really. Is that possible?"

Laihua presses on: "Did fourth brother's wife go to Zhang *lao's* home during this Spring Festival?"

"This time she didn't. But fourth brother's daughter goes there often—at lunch and on her way home from school. *Lao taitai* loves her very much. She is the only granddaughter in the family, and *lao taitai* enjoys very much having her come."

Wait, I think to myself. She is the *only* granddaughter?! Zhang Xiufang's daughter has a daughter, a granddaughter who once lived with her grandmother for a time in the recent past when she was sick. But in the calculus of the *xiaozi*, through which *dasaozi* speaks, this daughter's daughter does not count as a granddaughter.[11]

"Have you tried to mediate this big difference between Li Yu Qiu and his youngest brother?" LH asks.

"Yes. Once I tried. But Li Yu Qiu is a little stubborn. He said, 'Fourth brother's wife is not polite. They should criticize themselves for this. Until they do, I won't speak to them.' I tried to talk to him again about it this Spring Festival. He said 'Maybe later.' I want everyone to be happy. Actually, fourth brother is quite a good man, but as long as his second brother is in *lao taitai's* room, he won't go in. Otherwise, he does a lot there."

"Does Zhang Xiufang know about this," I ask, seeming to surprise them both by speaking.

"She once talked to me about it. She said '*xiao si* talks nonsense and isn't polite; he's a gossip—*ta shi chezi*—and says things he shouldn't say.' She also said that Li Yu Qiu is stubborn."

Just then we hear the front door open and look to see Li Yu Nian coming in, back from his mother's home. It's 9:30 and time to stop. Tonight, we agree, we have gotten a lot.

"It's Just My Personality"

Family stories that are said to come from the distant past—but of course which work in the present—of China's "traditional" culture of children's "absolute obedience" to their parents likely would give little attention to a daughter-in-law, save as a negative model detailing one source of family disharmony.[12] Surely, seeking out the *views* of daughters-in-law to construct an image of the family of their husbands would have been even more rare. But in the modern traditional family, daughters-in-law and the ways they take up the remnants of these responsibilities do count for more. The way a daughter-in-law positions herself in the folds of these old ways can make a great difference in today's success of the culture of *xiao*. For all the "stickiness" of these traditions of patriarchy and male dominance in late-twentieth-century families, this success, when it happens, is likely due much more to the willing participation of these women than ever before. This makes *dasaozi's* apparent embrace of her position in the Li family all the more notable in considerations of the persistence of the familiar forms.

But the Li family has other daughters-in-law whose views on these traditions, as well as their own mundane practices of family, offer an appreciation of just how precarious this edifice of the *xiaozi* seems to be. In terms of the traditional model, some of their views and actions certainly would be considered "against tradition." But by another standard, one that seeks to understand how the culture of the *xiaozi* is maintained in the late-twentieth-century, what they do and how they see their positions might well be said to be another piece—along with that provided by *dasaozi*—of what keeps those traditions alive. Zhang Xiufang's second and fourth daughters-in-law, although we never met or talked to the latter, thus provide us occasions to further complicate our story of a modern traditional family and the performance of *xiao* around the care of an elderly parent.

12 January 1991. 2:00 P.M. It's been more than a month since we visited anyone from the Li family. We want to talk to the wife of Li Yu Qiu, the second son, who has taken to spending the night at his mother's home, sleeping in her bed to ensure against her falling again in the night. When they inquired as to how he managed this, he told the researchers that the demands of his job as a warehouse clerk were "light," that his wife was gone most of the day at her relatively high-paying job in Tanggu, part of a special economic zone on the coast; and that, in any case, she and their sixteen-year-old son were able to manage at night without him.

For most of her married life, this woman had lived in the Li family yard as *ersaozi,* or second daughter-in-law, and she apparently more or less did what she should do as a second son's wife. This would have included being apprentice to her first sister-in-law in taking care of Zhang Xiufang and ministering to the senior Lis, all while raising her own child, going to work, and no doubt helping care for her nephews and nieces.

But now *ersaozi* lives a quite different life. In a new, two-room flat with kitchen and bathroom, on the sixth floor of a high-rise in a developing area of the city, she, her husband, and son, along with *dage* and *dasaozi,* are part of what might be called a new, rising middle class in Chinese cities: certainly not "rich" but certainly with more comfortable lives than when they were small and more comfortable than most others living in the city. And virtually all of the new-found luxury of space and material goods in this small Li family is due to her job success rather than to her husband's, or to any help obtained from his family. In fact, when the two researchers made their last visit of 1991 to the Lis, second son virtually had stopped working, saying that his salary was not worth making the trip to his unit to collect. He still had not returned to his job in 1993. It was *her* work unit that had made the new flat available to them, and it was they who sent her on a recent training trip to Japan, where she had been able to acquire the state-of-the-art video and television equipment that sat on new, floor-to-ceiling stylish furniture in their flat. Her husband had told Mr. Shi and Wang *laoshi* that because of her work schedule, she now had little time to come to his mother's home. And while he added, quickly, that she had done a lot of housework for his mother in the past, it was clear that this woman now was more or less free from that set of routine responsibilities; duties that *dasaozi*, her husband, second and fourth brothers continued to embrace.

I went to look for Mr. Li Yu Qiu a few days ago at his mother's home to arrange for Mr. Shi and me to visit his wife. We are to meet him this afternoon at the front gate of the Foreign Languages Institute, and he will lead us to his home where his wife has been recovering from breast surgery. Anyway, Mr. Li Yu Qiu arrives just at 2:00 and we three set out in the crowded afternoon traffic.

I had been thinking that we should take Li's wife a small gift since she is recovering from that operation. Although I didn't talk to Mr. Shi about it, I made a plan to stop along the way and buy some oranges; the ones in the market look pretty good these recent days. On the other side of the street I notice a fruit seller with some oranges, and I ride toward him.

"Wang Xiansheng! Wang Xiansheng!" Mr. Li calls out to Laihua as he slowly maneuvers his bike through the traffic after him. "No need to buy anything. No need!"

Laihua ignores this and proceeds to pay the seller 5 yuan 50 fen for the bag of oranges, which he then hooks over his handlebars. I have stopped across from this scene, and as I watch I feel a little embarrassed not to have thought of this kindness. Laihua the good, I think to myself.

As Mr. Li turns the key and opens his apartment door, we hear a woman's voice. "Ah! You've come!" We step into the narrow hallway just as a door across from us opens. Pang Xinping, second son's wife, stands there looking quite healthy.

"Welcome!" she says, with a broad smile. "It's cold here by the door. Come into this room where it's warm; have some tea." She and her husband lead us into a small room with a low "modern" glass table and a sofa and chairs arranged around it. On the table is a plate of fruit and tea cups readied for hot water. As I take off my coat, Laihua gives Pang Xinping the oranges. "We wish you good health," he says.

Gradually, we settle ourselves around the table. Li Yu Qiu and Pang Xinping sit on a stool and a chair, to our right; we on the sofa, in front of the table. The afternoon sun makes the room warm and bright. Laihua says the familiar sentences about the research and introduces me as an American sociologist who has studied how people live with chronic illness in America.

"Yes, yes. I know," Pang Xinping says enthusiastically. "My oldest sister lives in America—in Hawaii. They have two children; one has a Ph.D. Brother-in-law teaches at the University of Hawaii. Now they all are Americans. My oldest sister wants us to move there; she especially wants my son—he's in high school now—to go to school there."

We both stare somewhat slackjawed at Pang as she speaks so easily and with such smiling animation. It seems that she, too, "likes to talk," and we each find this a most promising development.

"There are five sisters in my family. Now, one is trying to get a visa for America. She is forty-five years old and has just come back from Japan where she went as a technician for a corporation. She learned math and is now studying metallurgy.

"My *dajie* and brother-in-law once told us that America is very developed, and that American young people are very lovely and warm. My niece there is in love with a boy. In fact, she has two boyfriends at once— one Chinese and one American! My sister said, 'I prefer that American young man'! But a colleague said that competition there is very keen. If someone has no ability, or doesn't work hard and only depends on the 'rice bowl,' he will have a hard time."

I'm never quite sure what to say in the face of such glowing comments about "America"—and they are not hard to hear from the Chinese I have met in Tianjin. Mostly, I want to say, "But. . . ." Yes, I think to myself. It is "developed." "Lovely and warm" young people—what to say about that? And the girl's mother prefers the American boyfriend? That sounds unusual, for sure. I ask LH what the word for "competition" is and then say, "Yes. The competition in America is very keen. I think Chinese people, especially Chinese young people, who go there have to work very, very hard." This is something I feel quite sure of from knowing the experience of some of my former Chinese students. It's also something I can say, in a more or less recognizable way, in Chinese.

Laihua has taken my talk as an opportunity to frame a spontaneous question. "Mr. Li told us that his sister's son has gone to Japan, but that his grandmother is not happy about that. Have you told her that you want to send your son to America?"

Li Yu Qiu responds. "My sister believes when children grow up they should be independent from their parents. My mother hates to part with her children and grandchildren. She wants all of her children and grand-children beside her, especially at her age."

"Older people always have some old ideas," Pang Xinping adds, quietly.

"My mother was only unhappy when she heard that my sister's son had gone to Japan," says second brother.

"Yes. She also knew that she couldn't call him back, in any case," *ersaozi* says.

Li Yu Qiu, the good son, then speaks a familiar line, with what sounds like a combination of resignation and nostalgia: "Now the family is not like the old Chinese family. Then parents told children to do something and they did it. The tradition is melting."

"But there is a regulation," Pang Xinping says, somewhat insistently. "We can't wait until after he goes to college; that would be too late. We should send him abroad after high school."

"Yes," says Laihua. "I know about that regulation too."[13]

"As long as our son is capable of going, we should agree; and we shouldn't ask him to wait," *ersaozi* continues.

Second son mumbles to the Chinese researcher, "We haven't discussed this before." A call to comrades for help, perhaps. In any case, the topic shifts.

It is clear to the researchers that this woman and her husband are not in the same place on some of these issues. She presents herself as ori-ented to the new, to change; to the outside. She stresses her connection to Japan and the United States. He, while not rejecting such possibilities for his own son, recalls the old ways, and says later that perhaps they will wait to send their son to America until after his mother dies. That way, they will not add to her unhappiness. The researchers have found an-other interesting difference to exploit.

The Chinese sociologist pauses to check his jotted translation of one of the foreigner's questions, then says: "Li Yu Qiu works very hard taking care of his mother. He spends almost every night sleeping there. We wonder what you think about all the time he spends doing these things." LH has waxed virtually bold here.

"*Nainai* is not sick just half a day or a single day," Pang says. "It's all the time now, and she has gotten worse." This question seems not to have given her the pause that the foreigner thought it might.

"When we moved away, she cried and was unhappy. Then, there was no one in her room to take care of her at night. When we lived there, I did that. Now she can't walk, and she fell and hurt herself. Oldest brother and sister-in-law take care of her at supper and at breakfast, but I can't help her now. I work as a cadre at Xingang. I get up at 5:30 and leave for work at 6:30. I come back at 6:30 at night. It's dark when I leave and when I return. I can't manage the family's things—not even my own family's things. I told Li Yu Qiu, you go there; help your mother at night. At first, he wanted to sleep in the room *next* to his mother—where we lived. I told him if he did that there was no reason to go. I asked him, 'If she falls, how will you stop it?'"

As I watch Pang Xinping talk and Laihua scribble furiously in response, I think of how articulate and intelligent she seems. Although her husband, second brother, is certainly not the opposite of those adjectives, I say to myself, "Here is another very competent woman married to a man who seems less so." Certainly, he seems a kind man . . . principled—we know—and responsible; even perhaps a moralist of sorts; but connected to the past; looking backward rather than forward. And I can't help thinking of him as a "mama's boy." Perhaps it's that he sleeps in his mother's bed; or, that he seems actually to believe his mother's story that his partial deafness was caused by his own tears running into his ear when he was a baby; or that he, ironically, like his youngest brother, seems content to stay by his mother's side, watching her—and television—and doing housework rather than "making something" of himself. I was never like that, I think to myself. Was I?

"Sometimes *lao taitai* is very superstitious," *ersaozi* is saying to Laihua. "She told me that a fortune teller said she would live with her second son in the future."

Li Yu Qiu looks surprised and says, almost to himself, "This is the first time I have heard that!"

"But I think this isn't possible," his wife says. "Our apartment is on the sixth floor. She can't climb the stairs. So I said to him, you go there. Take care of your mother."

Laihua and I stop here in our writing and rewriting work to refurbish our tea and coffee and take a stretch. "I think both big brother and Li Yu Qiu and their wives invite Zhang Xiufang to come live with them because they are good children," I say. "But also because they know she cannot or will not do it."

"You are right," says Laihua as he pours water from the thermos into the recycled glass jar he uses as his "at home" teacup. This we have learned before, from other families. Children and parents should be close, but not too close, an arrangement that also seems to be the preferred pattern in the United States (see Kinsella 1994, Conner 2000). And even when they cannot be acted upon, good words from children to parents should be said. But, back to inscribing the data.

Pang Xinping sets out on her own topic. "I like it when people come here and have a good time. I have many friends and I like to get together with them. I'd like to do more of it, but I am so busy with work."

Just then, there is a knock at the door. It is *dajie* and her daughter, who have come to talk with us—as planned—and to see second brother's new house. As Li Yu Qiu goes into the hallway to greet them, Laihua turns to *ersaozi*.

"You are very good to help take care of his mother," he praises her.

"No, no. It's just my personality. I also treat my colleagues warmly, and I like to help other people. I don't pay attention to trifles."

Laihua looks up from his notebook as he translates the Chinese into English for me to edit and write down. "This is evidence of a kind of person, a kind of personality—*xing ge*—an 'open' and 'optimistic' one."

"Yes. It's hard to imagine that she has much in common with her mother-in-law," I say, belying my misunderstanding of the limited space allowed for such trifles in Chinese family life.

"He Stays with His Mother at Night . . . He's a Model"

We create two more opportunities to talk to *ersaozi*, which marks our sense that she has interesting and important things to say not only about herself but about her husband's family. It seems that she will say things that others might not; things that her husband might wish she would keep unspoken.

24 January 1991. 2:00 P.M. We are back at Li Yu Qiu's house, with his wife and, unfortunately, her mother. She is a clear-eyed, seventy-two-year-old woman with a lot of energy and a lot to say. But we had planned to ask Pang some "sensitive" questions about the Li family, and we clearly cannot do that in her presence. Moreover, we spend a lot of time being polite, talking to her and about her life situation. This is enabled by her daughter, who seems to help keep the focus on her mother who, with her daughter, seem to turn the focus on us. It is we who feel like "pandas," curious objects of attention who are expected to perform. On the road back home, we share our frustrations and lay plans to return and, somehow, avoid such interruptions.

During the conversation with *ersaozi*'s mother, Laihua did ask if she knew about Zhang Xiufang's situation.

"Yes. I know about it," she said. "Her sons treat her good. Her first son is good. He (pointing to second brother) stays with his mother at night, and helps her get dressed and go to the toilet. His sister is in the hospital now and can't go there."

"Do you think there is a difference between daughters and sons and how they take care of their old parents?" asks Laihua, following up the comparison she has implied but also reiterating an abiding interest we have.

"Yes, there is a little difference. Daughters usually are more careful. Sons aren't. If a son marries a good wife, they can treat his old parents well. If he can't find a good wife, they can't. Sometimes that happens. It's the traditional way. *Lao taitai's* situation is pretty good. Her sons treat her good. This is also a result of their wives supporting them. Otherwise, sons can't really help their old parents very much."

Although we complained about the time we spent on Pang Xinping's mother, it did give us a chance to ask one of the prepared questions—about what second brother does for his wife's family. Laihua, recognizing this, says to Li Yu Qiu: "Your wife has taken care of your mother in the past. Have you also helped your wife's family?"

I told Mr. Shi later that this was a bold, direct question. I was a little nervous about it. What would we do if Mr. Li could say nothing? His mother-in-law was sitting there to hear what he said. I think perhaps Mr. Shi expected him to say he didn't feel a duty to his wife's family. But he didn't.

"My wife and I are the same. When her mother was in the hospital in the late 1970s, I stayed beside her while her son tried to arrange a transfer to another hospital. It was against the regulations, so we had to do it secretly. I carried her from her bed to the stretcher, and then took her to the ambulance where her son was waiting. She was very heavy! Before we got married, my wife's fourth sister was in a serious accident in Baotou. I went there with my wife and helped bring her back. Her younger sister once had a liver inflammation, and I also stayed beside her in the hospital. Of course, when my mother and sister have been sick, my wife also takes care of them. Even when the nephews got sick, she took care of them. She has done her duty."

27 January 1991. 2:05 P.M. This is our third appointment to speak to second brother's wife. Laihua asked Li Yu Qiu if anyone else will be there. He said no.

It's early afternoon, just after the two-hour post-lunch rest, as we knock on the door, six flights up. Pang Xinping greets us, again with a broad smile, and ushers us into the warm room. Second brother has been called away, she explains, to help the family of a good friend who died suddenly last week. It is just the chance we hoped for—to speak to his wife alone. As we settle in the familiar space, after some talk about foreign films showing on TV, Laihua moves directly to our questions.

"You are a member of two big families, your husband's and your own. You also have your own small family. How do you meet all these responsibilities?" She smiles and pauses a moment or two.

"Yes. Now there are three families. My mother generally doesn't need much help. Her health is good and she has enough money. My brothers and sisters are better at this than I am. They take care of her more than I do. Ever since I was a child, I have liked to play—even sports. I can't do a lot of housework, so I just go to see her; perhaps I'll buy something to take, but I don't help her a lot.

"As for *lao taitai,* we lived with her for a long time, but I don't help her much now. I have a good temper and I don't pay attention to trifles, so there are no bitter conflicts between us. I can't cook, so I usually buy something for her to eat and take it there.

"In my own small family, I put more energy on my son. We have to encourage and help him with his studies. Before, I concentrated less on him. Now I pay more attention to him."

"We understand that you lived with Zhang Xiufang in that yard for a long time." Laihua wants just to gesture in this direction, hoping it will be sufficient to generate her talk.

"Yes, but when we lived there *lao taitai* could take care of herself. We ate together, but then she didn't need someone beside her all the time. Compared to others, she and I have the best relationship. Perhaps that is because of my personality. We never quarreled. Generally, I don't quarrel with people."

"When you lived there, did Li Yu Qiu ask you to take care of his mother?"

"No. He often didn't know what I did. Now, *dasaozi* mainly cooks for *nainai. Dajie* has helped her mother a lot. Usually, she went there once a week and helped clean her mother's room. As daughters-in-law, no matter what we do, we always should be polite. It's the same for sons-in-law. If these *waixingren* can be concerned about their parents-in-law and not quarrel with them, that is the best.

"Whoever has old parents, they should care for them. I have never been forced to do this for *lao taitai.* Actually, I have a rather faint idea of family. When I was younger and wanted to take the college entrance exam, I was not allowed to because I had a 'bad' family background.

When I graduated from high school, it was the time of the Socialist Education Movement.[14] I went to work in a factory as a lathe operator and worked there for twenty years. I studied Japanese with a colleague in that factory and that is how I got the job in Tanggu in the Special Economic Zone. There was a party committee document that said if a person could pass a special examination, they could change their unit and go to work there. A friend told me about it and said, 'If you pass, you can change your work and your fate!' I passed and went to work there. Actually, I didn't want to study a foreign language. I wanted to be a doctor. . . . Now, when I think of that time in the past, I am sad. I was unlucky and missed my chance."

"When you were doing this, did other people help you?" Laihua wonders.

"No one helped me." The sound of her voice makes me stop writing and look up. *"Meiyou ren bang wo!"* There are tears in her eyes, which she quickly wipes away.

"Don't cry," says Laihua, quietly. "Anyway, you were lucky."

"I am not lucky," she disagrees. "And I always feel sad about these things. Now I can only put my hopes on my son. I feel bored most of the time. I watch television only because I feel bored and there's nothing to do. I really admire my older sister in America. She's doing something important."

I can sense that Laihua is uncomfortable that Pang is upset. He raises his head and shoulders away from his notebook and drinks tea, then leans back on the sofa. "This furniture is very good," he says as he nods toward a large cabinet on the far wall. "Very beautiful." I bob my head and repeat, "Yes. Very beautiful." She smiles. We go back to the topic.

"Do you ever talk about your own experiences and feelings with your mother-in-law or your sisters-in-law?" As I hear this question from my young colleague I am a little surprised and impressed. I'm sure he knows or can guess the answer. I can too, but it isn't a question I would have thought to ask; and it isn't an "easy" one.

"No. I don't talk about these things with *lao taitai,* and I also rarely talk about them with her family members. And we sisters-in-law don't talk about these things. We all are busy, and there is nothing really worth talking about. I don't talk much in the Li family."

"Does Li Yu Qiu talk about these things with you?"

"He doesn't concern himself too much with these things, but he supported me a lot and was very happy when I got the new job. Usually, people in the Li family do not concern themselves with me and my affairs, but the youngest brother and his wife admire me a lot. They told me that if our son does well in his studies, it is because of me."

"What do you think of your youngest sister-in-law?" *More* respect for Laihua as an interviewer—such a direct question about a "sensitive" topic!

"She is not a bad person," Pang says, pausing. "She is direct and honest. She and *popo* once quarreled about the disagreement between her and *dage* over the house. Mainly, this conflict is between *dage* and fourth brother. Li Yu Qiu knows this thing really is his little brother's responsibility, and he respects his big brother and wife very, very much.

"The feeling between the youngest brother and his wife and me is more real, more sincere. They are more honest than *dage* and *dasaozi*, and they treat *nainai* good too.

"Actually, *dasaozi* and *lao taitai* have a bad relationship. *Dasao* often can't stand to hear what *nainai* says. If *popo* says one sentence of criticism to her, she would answer with three sentences of criticism back. I am the opposite. If *popo* said ten sentences of criticism to me, maybe I would say only one back, and it also would be a sentence that would agree with what she said. Yesterday, I went there to see *nainai*. She encouraged me not to go to work. Sometimes she criticizes *dasao* to me.

"Li Yu Qiu and I have different opinions about the youngest brother and his wife. He knows what they did is not right, and he is very stubborn." Pang Xinping stops and sighs.

"He's very honest, really, but he has no brain in his head. He's always foolish in these things. Don't you think so?!"

"No, no!" protests Laihua, as a chuckle grows and is quickly but ineffectively stifled, thus acknowledging her point. Seeing them both so bemused over what's been said, I chuckle too, although I have missed the characterization of her husband on which their shared laughter rests.

More sips of tea; shifting in our seats; a cough. And then:

"*Waixingren* have a special relationship in their spouses' families. Can you tell us something about these relationships in the Li family?"

"I think *popo* and we sisters-in-law understand these relations. We can't ask very much of each other—*shei ye buneng yaoqiu bieren tai gao.*"

"This is exactly the right way to express these relationships," LH says to me as he straightens up in his chair and fiddles with a paper clip on his desk.

"Hmmm. What is the opposite of this, then?" I ask.

"Blood relationships—people can ask a lot of each other—endless things."

I think he really might have meant "expect" rather than ask, for if one actually has to "ask," it is a mark that the obligations have not properly been attended to by the hearer.

"In the past," I ask, "even sometimes they could ask their lives?"

"Yes, that's right. But what is more important is not the request but what is done without having to ask—what is given." Right, I think.

"Do you feel any pressure that you should take care of your *nainai* more?" asks LH.

"No. I have no such pressure. They all know I have returned to work and am very, very busy," she responds.

"Do they always help you then?"

"No. They do not help me, and there is not much help given between the brothers, either."

"Do you daughters-in-law ever talk about how to care for *lao taitai*?" Laihua asks.

"No, but *dasaozi* complains more, and says she has to work harder in taking care of *lao taitai* and that they spend more money. At the same time, *lao taitai* criticizes her. The youngest brother's wife complains less. Sometimes *dasao* is a little narrow-minded. I talk to her about this and she feels better."

"What do you say?"

"I say, 'You do more than others; everyone can see this. You are criticized because you are close to *lao taitai*.' She feels better."

"Have you seen youngest brother lately?"

"Just yesterday when I went to *nainai's* house he was there. He said he had planned to come see me after I got out of the hospital, but didn't know our address."

"Really?" LH asks, somewhat surprised.

"Yes. But he is also very afraid of his second brother. There really aren't any reasons Li Yu Qiu doesn't talk to his youngest brother and his wife. *Lao taitai* knows this but she can't resolve it either. Especially, she can't control Li Yu Qiu. *Dage* is also afraid of him. He once was called a model in taking care of and saving other people and neglecting himself. During the Cultural Revolution, he saved a child who had fallen through a hole in the ice. He has a good reputation for this among his colleagues at his unit. Really, he's a model."

"My Mother Tells Me Everything"

After we met *dasaozi* on 3 March, we had no contact with the Li family for two months. We had given up the idea of interviewing the third son

and his wife. They lived far away and seemed to have little directly to do
with taking care of Zhang *lao*. We had not, however, given up hope of
meeting the youngest son, Li Yu Quan, who with his wife seemed to be
the object of such moral indignation by second brother and *dage*. But,
obviously, we couldn't use our usual connection, Li Yu Qiu, to help us.
How to get to *xiao si* without causing suspicion that we were, so to
speak, looking for trouble/truth?

Finally, at the beginning of May, and after discussing this problem
repeatedly, Laihua one day stopped by the Li family yard, "just to see who
might be there." *Xiao si* sometimes cooked lunch for his mother, if second brother wasn't around. LH had learned just a few days before that Li
Yu Qiu was in the hospital. We were lucky. Not only was youngest brother
there, but he agreed to meet us for an interview a few days later. At last,
we thought, we can make this story complete.

10 May 1991. 9:30 A.M. We coast to a stop at the familiar spot beside
the alley door to the Li yard. Bikes parked and locked, I hang back a bit so
Laihua will be sure to take the lead. As we knock, open the gate, and step
Into the yard, a man opens Zhang Xiufang's door and steps out toward
us. He and Laihua already have acknowledged each other, and the man's
face, remarkably similar to his second brother's, tells me this must be
xiao si. After LH introduces us and we go in to greet his mother, youngest brother suggests we move to the next room, which he calls *"dage's*
room," to talk.

As we find our seats in the next room, I begin to relax a little. I was
apprehensive about meeting this fourth brother. He had become something of an aggressive troublemaker to me, as I seemed to be seeing him
through second brother's eyes. I had allowed myself to think we would
ask him directly about the conflict, even though I knew better. I worried
about how he would respond and about the conflict with his brothers.
Since the opportunity to meet him had developed so quickly, and since
we were heavily involved with interviews in two other families, we did not
really have time to formulate a particular strategy for the interview.

My young colleague was proceeding with the familiar description of
the project and had asked Li Yu Quan to tell us about himself and his
carework for his mother. He had begun to respond. I wrote a description
of the room and how we were seated, relying on LH to get what he said.

"I am a worker at the Number 3 Coal Processing Factory in Tianjin.
I'm forty-four years old. My wife works in a bank near here. She is a cadre
and is thirty-nine. I have a daughter in primary school. She is eleven.

"Yes," says LH. "We once met her here. She is lovely and your mother likes her very much!" The level of tension in this small space seems suddenly to decline.

"That's right! Among our generation, she is the only granddaughter [yet again!].

"My work schedule now is light because I haven't been feeling well. There is some problem with the oxygen in my blood. I work only from 2:00 to 6:00 in the afternoon, and I come here every morning at about 9:00 and stay until 2:00 when I go to work."

"What do you do here, ordinarily?"

"Whatever needs doing, really. I usually pour out my mother's pot, straighten up the room. Whatever I meet, I do. I also go buy vegetables and cook lunch for us."

"What do you usually cook?" More "easy questions" to get us started, I think to myself.

"Usually, common foods. Whatever she likes to eat, I cook. I think my brothers and [first] sister-in-law don't cook better than me."

"Who pays?"

"Basically, I pay. It all together comes to about 50 yuan a month, but most of it I eat myself. *Dage* buys breakfast for my mother, and they come to cook dinner."

"What about other money? Do you give your mother extra money each month?"

"Yes. I give her 20 yuan as *yueqian*—monthly money. That's the least amount from any of us, but they all have more income than me. Anyway, *lao taitai* doesn't spend much money."

Mr. Shi asks a question here. I wrote it down: "Who decides how much *yueqian* each of you will give your mother?" *Xiao si* understands and says: "We give whatever we want . . . or whatever she needs. I know what the others give her because I am the youngest. My mother tells me everything."

"I understand," says Laihua. "What do you and your mother talk about when you are here together?"

"Mainly we talk about who has come to see her, where they are going; who has brought things for her. We talk about relationships among the neighbors. Gossip. That sort of thing."

"Does your mother often criticize you?" I wonder where he is going here; I'm sure he knows. In any case, I continue writing about his questions, my own puzzlement, and Li Yu Quan's facial expressions as he hears and then responds to the questions. He has a broad and open face, and smiles easily. I feel a little foolish when I think of my apprehension about him, and I began to wonder if I have been too quick to accept second brother's characterization of him as a destroyer of family harmony. Perhaps we've overdramatized it.

"Basically, my mother doesn't criticize me. But I don't give her any reason to criticize me. She often asks me to eat the fruit and food that my brothers buy for her. I feel a little embarrassed to eat it, but she always asks me to. I think this shows that she loves me very much."

We pause as Laihua writes. *Xiao si* looks at me and says, *"Chou yan ma?"* as he holds out an opened pack of cigarettes. Luckily, I have been here before. *"Bu hui,"* I respond. *"Xiexie."* Literally, it's "I don't have the capacity to smoke," meaning that I never have, or may as well never have. Laihua resumes, smiling to himself.

"Does your mother criticize others in front of you?" It occurs to me that Laihua is trying to get at the nature of this son's family position relative to his old mother, and he is moving on the assumption that the youngest child, and especially the youngest son, likely has a "special" and protected place in his mother's heart. Of course, this son himself has suggested as much.

"She doesn't. She doesn't criticize other people to me. She doesn't evaluate how we brothers and sister and *waixingren* take care of her. She only tells me who comes here, what they do, and so on. She doesn't judge others as good or bad."

When we translated this interview the next afternoon at Mr. Shi's apartment, I told him I really didn't believe what *xiao si* said here. This topic was a little sensitive in the interview, but it would be very hard for Zhang *lao not* to judge and criticize the others when she talks to her youngest son. He has told us they talk about the other family members. She is an old Chinese woman, a mother with all these sons. It would be normal for her to criticize the others to him. I think he doesn't want to say anything that might criticize his mother, especially to us. And remember, *dasaozi* said the old woman called her son "a gossip."

"Do you feel that the caregiving work you do for your mother is a burden for you?" Laihua asks *xiao si*.

"No, I don't. I only work half a day in my unit. Besides that, I have nothing else to do and I have nowhere to go. I don't have any hobbies. I feel good staying beside *lao taitai*." As he says this, fourth brother begins to laugh, then adds: "I do all the housework in my own family. I am like a *jiating funan!*" A family househusband!

Laihua chuckles with him, and tries to take advantage of their shared good will.

"What does your wife think about your caregiving for your mother?" Fourth brother treats this question in a relaxed but skillful way.

"She supports me, but she herself comes here very rarely. And she meets housework here even more rarely. Her unit can't do without her. She is very busy."

"Who does the most caregiving work among you children?"

"My oldest brother and sister-in-law. We respect them even more because of this. My second brother is the second. He's sick a lot of the time, but does his best to come here. He can't do any housework . . . I mean he isn't good at it."

"Maybe you are the third in line?" asks LH.

"Yes. My sister comes here one day a week. This is the same as in the past. Why? A son should take more responsibility."

We can hardly resist following this one. "Please tell us more about that," Laihua says, quietly.

"Since I was a child, my parents have loved me the most. Now my mother is old and sick. I should look after her. This is what I should do. The others also do their duties, and I don't object to what they do."

To sustain this, LH says: "Please tell us about how the *waixingren—dasaozi, ersaozi,* and so on—take care of your mother."

"My oldest sister-in-law really does it good. She is the best, and sets a good example. Third and second sisters-in-law are very busy with their work, and their own families. They only come to see my mother or buy her something. My wife doesn't buy things for my mother, but she says, 'You buy what *lao taitai* likes to eat.' Brother-in-law also sometimes comes here. *Dage* and *dasaozi* set a good example."

From these comments, one would not guess that there is any tension between *xiao si* and his two oldest brothers. Laihua focuses a bit with a familiar question.

"Do you and your brothers talk about how to look after your mother?" The reply is also familiar.

"No, we haven't. Generally, we all have done our duties. Beyond that, we don't talk about it."

"What about the relationship between you brothers?" asks Laihua, in a last effort to open up this question.

"Well, it isn't like what is shown in films. I mean, we are relatively harmonious. They all talk more to each other. I talk to them little. I am a worker. I can't talk. I have no ability to talk. When I do talk to them I feel ignorant, dumb."

"Like there is a wall between you?"

"Yes. I feel the same when I talk to my wife and her colleagues. I don't really like to make friends. I don't see many people. My situation is like the folk saying: 'lao po haizi re kang tou.' I'm not sociable."[15]

Giving LH a break here, and also keeping myself alert, I shift in my seat and signal that I am about to say something. I ask a question that I've of course been preparing as I listen.

"Sometimes in China I know things are hard to get. Things you need. If you have to find a back door to solve this kind of problem, do you ask your brothers for help?"

"I don't really need anything," he says, directly. "And I don't like to ask them to help me. I have one room. I think my living is pretty good."

Laihua professes surprise, and he says to me, later, that he thinks perhaps xiao si is being a little ironic when he says this is a pretty good situation.

"Really? You have only one room?"

"Yes. Just one. It's in that large complex off WuJiaYao street."

Another opening to ask about housing, and LH takes it, pushing as he does.

"How did you get that room?"

"It was assigned by my wife's unit. Before that, we lived in that room across the way."

"From what we know, your brothers live in new apartments. We visited your oldest and second brothers' homes and they are pretty good." But fourth brother will not take the bait.

"Since we got married, we lived in that room—for nine years. My brothers just recently got those new houses. That room across the yard was impossible. The roof leaked, and there were other problems. Although we lived there, we were only tolerating it. Because there is no sunshine there, I think my daughter's eyes are bad."

"Yes." Laihua acknowledges. "It would be hard to live there for such a long time with three people."

Mr. Shi asks another question at this point. About fourth son going to the countryside, which is something Mr. Shi is always interested in. I think in this family, the effects of that are very clear on this youngest son compared to his older brothers.

"When did you go to the countryside, and how long did you stay?" Mr. Shi asks.

"I went in 1969 . . . I herded cattle in Inner Mongolia . . . for 5 years. Later, I went to a small village in Hebei Province, where I stayed for three years. That was my parents' home town. Then I was assigned to deliver coal to people's homes here in Tianjin. I was glad to come back to the city. Later, I went to the Number 3 Coal Processing Factory and that's where I work now, unloading coal from trains."

"Hmmm," Laihua says. "It was not an easy time. When you were in the countryside, did your family help you?"

"My mother sent me 10 yuan every month. That wasn't a small amount back then. My brothers didn't give me money. They didn't have much either. What they did have they gave to my parents."

"When you came back, and before you got married, where did you live?" Again, Laihua asks about housing.

"Then, I lived with my second brother in this room. When he got married, my father built this little room."

"Ohhhhh. Yes," Laihua responds. "It sounds like you were held back by the Cultural Revolution. You had no chance to go to college." He speaks appreciatively about this situation because he himself was in it, although he also escaped it. Fourth brother did not.

"Yes. They all graduated from colleges or universities. I wanted to be a student there too, but I couldn't. I graduated from middle school in 1966. When I was assigned to a job, it was in the countryside and the Cultural Revolution was beginning."

7

The Ghost of the *Xiaozi*

The Master [Confucius] said: In serving his parents a filial son renders utmost reverence to them while at home; he supports them with joy; he gives them tender care in sickness; he grieves at their death; he sacrifices to them with solemnity. If he has measured up to these five, then he is truly capable of serving his parents. He who really loves his parents will not be proud in high station; he will not be insubordinate in an inferior position; among his equals he will not be contentious. To be proud in high station is to be ruined; to be insubordinate in an inferior position is to incur punishment; to be contentious among one's equals leads to physical violence. As long as these three evils are not uprooted, a son cannot be called filial even though he feast his parents daily on the three kinds of choice meat.

Hsiao Ching: The Canon of Filial Piety (1961)

My God, My God. Why have you forsaken me?

Matthew 27:45

[T]o write about invisibilities and hauntings . . . requires attention to what is not seen, but is nonetheless powerfully real; requires attention to what appears dead, but is nonetheless powerfully alive; requires attention to what appears to be in the past, but is nonetheless powerfully present; requires attending to just who the subject of analysis is.

Avery Gordon, *Ghostly Matters* (1997)

I think it was sometime in middle school—we called it junior high—that I first heard jokes that would begin, somewhat like the above, "Confucius say." But these jokes never had anything to do with how to be a good son. Instead, what Confucius said were "proverbs" that were always sexual, by which of course I mean heterosexual/sexist and genital. Women were the objects of sexual looking, penetration, and pleasure by and for men; men were the sexual doers, or at least voyeurs, with occasional word plays on the supposed Chinese pronunciation "ong" to allow attention to the remarkable action and/or state of "dongs." Confucius was supposed to be some sort of Chinese wise man, and I think the image of Charlie Chan from TV films came to mind (one Chinese image was then as good as another, and I didn't know about Fu Manchu). I knew he was different from us, and it seemed that his "wisdom" carried a mixture of the sinister and the salacious, although the words I used probably were "sneaky" and "dirty." He was, after all, an "Oriental."[1]

Little did I know that there really were books filled with passages that began "Confucius said"; or that what Confucius was thought to have said once had such enormous importance in the world beyond Des Moines (yes, I was in Des Moines even then; and no, the idea that there might have been Chinese immigrants there too who did care about what Confucius had said didn't occur to me); nor did I suspect that the *last* thing he likely would have been reported to have said was something readable as sexually salacious. I didn't think of the jokes I heard and repeated as racist, as a denigration or insult to an other culture or to people who had and still used what "Confucius said" as a resource for producing their lives and selves. But neither did I think that about the much more prevalent jokes I then regularly heard and told about "Negroes"—but that mostly wasn't the word we used then either. And I certainly did not think that whatever Confucius may have said would ever have anything to do with me, save as a pretext for another titillation among the many that define male puberty and adolescence. I didn't imagine then that one day I would find myself so taken with, and conflicted over, his descriptions of what a son should do and be, and so concerned to do and be just that. After all, divorce had early divided my parents, and my "real" father was mostly a distant and ineffectual, albeit friendly enough, figure. An "alcoholic," and thus "unreliable," he came into town one Sunday a month to take me to supper at a local restaurant. My mother's brothers—uncles George and Carl—were sometime-fathers who impatiently instructed me in the working-class manly recreations of hunting and fishing.

*****

I cannot remember exactly when I first heard the name Kongzi—that's how we say his name in Chinese: the family name "Kong" with the character *"zi,"* which itself means "son." My memories are very different from what Joseph has written above. I was surprised that he could see Kongzi as "sinister and salacious," and I don't understand about the jokes when he was young. What a difference between the real Kongzi and those ideas!

In 1965–1966 I was in the first grade. Before that, I was too young to know about his writings. I think we read a story then about a descendant of Kong named Kongrong who gave his elder brother, rather than himself, the first bite from a pear. It's called *"Kongrong Rang Li"*—"Kongrong Gives Up a Pear." The story is that he was offered a pear but said that since he himself was younger than his brother, he should ask his brother to enjoy it first. This story is even popular today and children still study it. I'm sure we studied it before the Cultural Revolution began in the summer of 1966. After that, when our school started again in 1967, we only studied Mao's writings and revolutionary ideas. It was what "Mao said" then that seemed to matter. My classmates and I studied and memorized quotations from the Chairman's "little red book."[2]

But I do remember that I learned some of Kongzi's ideas from my grandfather, my father's father, when I was eight or nine years old. He would say to me, when I had done something naughty, "You should learn and follow the *ren* and *yi*." I didn't really understand the meanings of these words then—they just meant to be good, to do the right thing. My grandfather's lessons stayed with me, but it was only later that I connected those ideas to Kongzi, and learned that *ren* especially means that one should be kind to other people, that one should restrain his own desires, and that you should sacrifice yourself for other people. *Ren* is something closely connected with "collectivism." (I'm sorry. I want to use an English word that is just the opposite of "individualism," but I can't think of the word. It's close to collectivism [a common English translation of this word is "benevolence"].) *Yi* means that one should be just and fair to other people, and that you should be generous and tolerant to your friends.

My grandfather was careful not to use Confucius' name. During the CR I recall seeing posters in the streets with pictures of Confucius and a lot of criticisms written below them, although I really didn't understand what it was about. There also were films that criticized Confucius and Mencius. That's when I began to learn that Kongzi was not a good person. *Ren* and *shan* or kindness, were criticized a lot because they were key parts of his theory of human nature, a theory held by the *dizhu jieji*—the landlord class. Then, *ren* and *shan* could be good only if they were directed toward the people, not if they were used toward class enemies. I learned that landlords and capitalists were very ugly and terrible.

When I was in junior middle school—about 1974—there was a movement to criticize Lin Biao and Kong.[3] Confucius was called a reactionary. But that's when I really began to learn stories about his life, and it also was when I memorized many of his quotations from an ancient book called *San Zi Jing* or "three-character teachings."[4] I still remember some

202 The Ghost of the Xiaozi

of them today. We had to learn these sayings because they were politically bad and were supposed to be objects of class struggle. Now I realize that Lin Biao used these quotations for his political purposes. I also knew that Kongzi had many names; some were good and others not so good. Most of the time then, people were told or encouraged to call him "Kong *lao er*." Remember, Kong had an elder brother, so he himself would be the second child, which, informally, in Chinese is *"lao er."* It means, literally, "respected second," but the meaning then was meant to be just the oppo-site—that he is not really all that respected.

This all gradually changed after the CR, and especially after 1978. Now, Confucius is supposedly respected as a great thinker, scholar, and educator, but I don't think common people take it as especially important to read or study his teachings.[5] Actually, just before I first wrote this in the spring of 1993, Xiao Xue, my six-year-old daughter, asked me about Kongzi because she was trying to write a Chinese saying that is Confu-cian. I told her about the phrase and what it means. So far, in preschool and in primary school, she has not studied any writings by Confucius even though she already is in the second grade. But she knows something about him from readings the teacher assigns for students to do outside of class. Students, and especially those like my daughter who are in better schools, now have many reading assignments that talk about Chinese history and traditional morality, so perhaps she will learn more about what Kongzi said.

*****

Patricia Clough is the first person I remember saying that sociologists should pay attention to ghosts.[6] I don't mean she is the first one who ever said it—although she may have been—but she is the one who got me thinking about haunting as relevant to sociological work. Clough (1998, 15–28) had been working out and on a critical examination of the dis-avowed and denied operation of oedipal sexual desire in realist ethnogra-phy in the human sciences, and especially in sociology and anthropology. She talked about how the conventional ethnographic narrative is haunted by a familiar masculine story of quest, of challenge and threat, and, fi-nally, of conquest over or in the feminized space of "the other," all in the name of the ethnographer producing true stories. She said it was an all-too-familiar tale of power, pleasure, and domination written in the lan-guage of scientific realism, and that the former clearly haunted the latter, if one allowed oneself to see/feel it. She called for the end of ethnography in its familiar forms, as such, having critically examined its ends. She wrote about the haunted space of conventional realism in sociology; but her book has haunted me into writing this book and out of doing more of that kind of sociology.

More recently, and also through a feminist, poststructuralist, and psychoanalytic critique of human science, but especially of sociological method and writing, Avery Gordon (1997) has written an entire book about ghosts and haunting. I rely especially on Gordon's discussion to try to say—as simply as I can—what it is about ghosts and haunting that makes me see them as promising ideas/discourses for the present stories, and for a rejuvenated sociology that tries to be more honest about telling stories about others.

One of the most important resources Gordon takes from psychoanalysis (and the vision is critically selective, as both her feminism and sociology would require) is the idea of the unconscious, although—luckily for us—not quite in the way Freud himself would have it.[7] We here want to use the unconscious as a mark of movement, in Gordon's (1997, 46) words,

> into another *region* or field where things are *there and yet hidden,* where things *stand gaping,* where the question of how we present a world, our own or another's, becomes a question of the limits of representation. We enter a kind of disturbance zone where things are not always what they seem, where they are animated by invisible forces whose modes of operation work according to their own logics. The world of the unconscious is far away from that of the contemporary social scientist whose scientific covenant is precisely to ward off the mythological, the place where things stand gaping. . . .[8]

It marks a movement toward, an openness to, "that which is not seen, but is nonetheless powerfully real" in what people say and do.

Gordon also uses Freud's essay on the uncanny to help get at what the experience of ghosts and haunting possibly could be about.[9] To put it no doubt too simply, the uncanny refers to a movement in which the familiar (*familia?*), the homely, suddenly seems, feels strange, even alien; often frightening; certainly unsettling. The uncanny also comes in one's sense of being involved in the operation of "fate" (51), and, in Freud's (1955b, 241) own words, is a feeling especially common for people "in relation to death and dead bodies, to the return of the dead, and to spirits and ghosts." And of course, it is not at all "clear": "There is something there and you 'feel' it strongly. It has a shape, an electric empiricity, but the evidence is barely visible, or highly symbolized" (Gordon 1997, 50).

The experiences that we might mark as evidence of the unconscious and the uncanny are precisely the sort that social science, which also is to say reason, ignores and dismisses as not "empirically viable." That is, while sociologists can position themselves relative to ghosts and haunting as folk terms and practices invoked and embraced by those whom they study—by "others"—the scientist, at minimum, reserves judgment on or "brackets" the ontological status of such notions for himself or herself.[10] More likely, the scientist takes up a position of unabashed skepticism toward such fantastic objects, taking them as marks of "primitive," less critically aware, "less educated" people[11] whose lives and conduct are to be "explained" or "made clear" by the scientist. Most importantly for us, conventional sociology and its methods are seen as simply not subject to the operation of such ghostly presence. Indeed, from this view, such things are not real.

Sociological storytelling, like the operation of reason in and through "educated" people more generally, relies on a model of vision that makes observability and the real coterminous (but see Phelan 1993, 1–33). One "looks out" onto or into "the world," and reports what is there. This model also denies the importance of "feelings" as a source of insight into the real. More likely, feelings are taken to be threats to accurate perception, as a source of "measurement error." The real is there to be seen by anyman or anywoman who looks with a clear eye, which is to say with the correct method and subjectivity. Just who else the observer/scientist is should be irrelevant to what is seen and see-able.

Psychoanalysis, by contrast, makes the one who sees—and feels—of prime importance in attempting to understand the story that is told. And as a mode of social criticism and analysis, rather than as therapy, it makes all stories always shaped by—but not always easily understandable in terms of—multiple encounters and experiences with others in the teller's past psychic and social life. Unlike scientific realism, then, psychoanalysis allows a space for ghosts and for haunting, both in the lives of those about whom sociologists write and in the lives of sociologist-analysts themselves. Conventional psychoanalysis limits the significance of the relational dynamics between analyst and patient/client to "the problem of transference-countertransference," and in its canonical, even "postmodern," texts defines the feminine as always—and, most problematically—a space of lack or absence. Gordon wants us to be alive to the importance of these connections as they operate to shape the stories that emerge out of the encounters between "researcher" and those whom he or she "studies," especially in the practice of ethnography. As she puts it, allowing ghosts and haunting into one's work and life often changes the subject and object of analysis and attention. Indeed.

Gordon says that since Freud was interested primarily in creating "an official science" of the individual psyche rather than exploring the mobile interfaces between the social and the psychic, he offers us less insight into the *social* bases of the unconscious, and into haunting and ghosts, than some of his earlier writing suggests he might. He gave great explanatory importance to repressed infantile sexual desires—the infantile complexes—that could trouble the emotional health of adult life. Those who were haunted by unsuccessfully negotiated childhood sexual desire, typically in certain of their family relationships, became patients, the sick people psychoanalysis sought to treat and to heal.

Gordon the postmodern sociologist and feminist critic is more interested in drawing our attention to Freud's own early appreciations that ghosts could, and, typically do, come from the very experience of life with others in society. These latter ghosts come not from pathology but rather from the ordinary course of people's lives with and through others in sociocultural context; in short, from "the real." And they come to disperse, trouble, open, and make fluid and multiple any tightly ordered and sovereign center that presumes to know fully who one is as well as what one does and why.[12] "The important thing about ghosts," then, Gordon (1990, 498) says, "is the haunting they do."

Whether one responds to such troubling or haunting as something to lament or puzzle over, or even enjoy, depends on a great variety of considerations. Among students of human society, the nature of one's relationship to the words "modernism," "postmodernism," and "poststructuralism" might be a good indicator of the direction of this reaction. For those who see themselves, finally and first, as defenders of modernism's founding institutions—and science with its "subject" certainly would be among them—the kind of messy multiplicity that such a "social unconscious" allows only serves to denigrate and destroy the promise of true knowledge and social progress that the Western enlightenment ushered in and that some feel now to be embattled. For these defenders, taking ghosts and haunting seriously could only mean a de-based sociology and lessened knowledge. In short, it would be disastrous. And for people who don't spend a lot of their time thinking about such things, who are struggling to "get on with it" in the present of a modern society coming apart at the seams (and, in truth, these can be one and the same person or body), ghostly matters are likely seen, if at all, as not welcome.

But for Gordon, and for us, and we hope for all who would propose to tell true stories about others as a practice at the heart of what they do, opening our eyes to the possibility of seeing the play of multiple, contradictory, and transgressive desires and feelings that interweave our work and the positions we take up in the world can only enrich—if, admittedly, make less "clear"—what we write and say about the others located both inside and outside our selves. When I said earlier that this might yield a more "honest" sociology, it was not meant to suggest that conventional work is necessarily "dishonest." Rather, allowing the presence of ghosts in our own work ought to make us more appreciative and aware of their presence in the work and lives of those whom we set out to know and write about. It is indeed the project of "the true" that we take on in writing as experts on social life that would seem to put a burden on us to at least explore how an embrace of the unconscious can contribute to a more vital sense of the games of "knowledge production" that we play.

✶✶✶✶✶

Young children like Laihua's daughter apparently once knew quite well what "Confucius said," or, at least, what he was alleged to have said about how to be good, good to one's parents, and hence a respectable human being (see Hamilton 1984, 411–414; 1990, 92–97). Children learning and repeating and following "what the Master said"—and in an unmistakable sense of course this is to say "what the Father said"—is a very long-lived practice, one that "we" (the particular we in question is almost irrelevant for the point) know well. That Mao Zedong had supplanted Confucius during Laihua's time in middle school possibly can then be read as a mark of continuity that helps us appreciate the reappearance of Kongzi in his daughter's reading assignments in 1995. The place of the Father abhors a vacuum, and seems always to tell a story of impending chaos should that occur.

Still, all "fathers" are not the same. What Mao said, in substance if not, finally, in form, was perhaps one of the most sustained attacks on "actual" fathers and mothers, and on sons' and daughters' obedience to them, that the figure and legacy of Kong have faced. This official attack on then-unwanted "feudal ideas," which certainly included the teachings of The Master, was not the first to emerge from within the Middle Kingdom, even in this century. There was the May Fourth Movement of 1919, which "New China" seeks to read as its own forerunner; and, more recently, and with greater resonance for the West, there have been the criticisms from within China that have followed upon "the opening," "modernization," and "the democracy movement."[13] But for generations, and certainly well into the present century, Chinese children—and especially the children from elite families—studied texts of conversations between

"the Master" and his disciples as guides for being. And in terms of continuity and longevity, which is to say in terms of the maintenance of a
certain very "real" family order as the center of things, this discipline
prevailed.[14]

The Master's words that open this chapter come from one translation
of what is said to be the most influential of these texts, the *Xiaojing, or
Hsiao Ching*, in another romanization. *Xiaojing*, the canon or classic of
filial piety, is considered by some to be one of the "great sacred texts" of
ancient China. The conventional story of this sacred text is told in the
editor's preface to a 1961 English translation. Paul K.T. Sih (1961, ix–x),
then Director of the Institute of Asian Studies at St. John's University in
New York, a Catholic university, writes:

> The systematic teaching of filiality in China to the very young is done by means of
> the Confucian Classic of Filiality or the *Hsiao Ching*. In this classic we find the
> sphere of *hsiao* extended to embrace almost everything that is desirable in hu-
> man conduct. We do not know exactly who is the author of the *Hsiao Ching*. In
> literary form, it consists of conversations between Confucius and Tseng Tzu, one
> of Confucius' most famous disciples. This poses a problem regarding the author-
> ship. The work was not mentioned in the *Analects*. It was first referred to in the
> *Spring and Autumn of Mr. Lü* (Lu-shih Ch'un Ch'iu, a compilation of various
> schools of thought made under the direction of Lü Pu-wei who died 235 B.C.).
> This book exalted filiality to a degree that exceeds its importance in the teaching
> of Confucius.
>
> Most probably, the *Hsiao Ching* was written sometime between the time of
> Mencius and the establishment of the Han dynasty, or roughly between 350 and
> 200 B.C. One thing is clear: The doctrine of filiality had great influence during the
> Han dynasty. The posthumous titles of the Han emperors, for instance, are all
> prefixed by the word *"hsiao,"* indicating the particular importance that was given
> to this ideal.
>
> The *Hsiao Ching* did not become one of the Thirteen Classics until the T'ang
> dynasty (618–906), the "Augustan Age of Chinese Letters." There are two re-
> censions of the text, one of eighteen chapters and one of twenty-two. The eigh-
> teen-chapter edition was used by Hsüan-chung (713–755), an emperor of the
> T'ang dynasty, to produce the T'ang edition commentary on which the present
> translation is based.

This book exalted filiality to a degree that exceeds its importance in the
teaching of Confucius. Its eighteen chapters are very short; the Chinese
and the English texts each covering only nineteen pages.

> The capacity of a person to be a good husband, a faithful friend, or a loyal citizen
> is seen in the first and most intimate of all human relationships—that of a child to
> his parents. If one is unfilial at home, he will not likely assume the duties proper
> to a citizen. A radical disorder has [thus] shown up at the source of all order, and

this first disorder, if not corrected, must necessarily breed further trouble for the person, for those about him, and for the entire society. On the other hand, if a person is a loyal, responsive child, this indicates a sound inner disposition of soul that will inevitably manifest itself in the entire complex of human relations. (Sih 1961, v)

Confucius' five directives on filiality for a son invited a list of five "don'ts," which is credited to "Mencius (372–289 B.C.), a disciple of Tsu-ssu who was Confucius' grandson." Paul Sih continues, quoting a description of these from an ancient source:

The first is laziness in the use of one's four limbs, without attending to the nourishment of his parents. The second is gambling and chess playing, and being fond of wine, without attending to the nourishment of his parents. The third is being fond of goods and money, and selfishly attached to his wife and children, without attending to the nourishment of his parents. The fourth is following the desires of one's ears and eyes, so as to bring his parents to disgrace. The fifth is being fond of bravery, fighting, and quarreling so as to endanger his parents. (Sih 1961, ix)[15]

And, finally:

In short, filiality is considered as the virtue of all virtues. The greatest joy for a Chinese son is to serve his parents when they are old. On the other hand, there is no greater sorrow than to be unable to render such service. Po Chu-i, a famous Chinese poet of the Tang dynasty, wrote a poem called "Swallow." He described the sorrowful and lonely feeling of the parent swallows when they found that the young swallows flew away from the nest. Philosophically, the poet remarked: "Please don't feel so sorry. You must reflect. Now you know how much your parents suffered when you yourself flew away from them." This sentiment actually reveals the hardest part in human life. Parents raise their children; educate and encourage them to be mature and independent. However, when they do grow up and become independent, they want to be free and to get away from their parents. Herein lies the dilemma which calls for a higher expression of filial piety. . . . If the center of the Western family is found in the relationship of husband and wife, the center of the Chinese family is found in the relationship of father and son. The West is concerned more for the youth than for the aged, while China is concerned more for the aged than for the youth. (Sih 1961, vii–viii)

This is quite a tribute indeed, coming as it does from a late-twentieth-century, apparently ethnic Chinese academic son, who seems also to be a Roman Catholic and an American. But perhaps it is, after all, not too surprising that the filiality that so concerned Confucius also would be relevant to Catholicism and Christianity, which themselves have had quite a lot to say about "the Father" and "the Son" in the intervening millennia.

Indeed, this translator of the *Xiaojing* is Maryknoll Sister Mary Lelia Makra, herself an immigrant to America, seeking to serve the Father. She is storied and stories herself and her translation work as follows, helping us see again that daughters—or "brides"?—too, have been *xiao*, fully committed to unity and harmony in the name of the Father.

As a New York taxicab wove through heavy Broadway traffic on a winter evening in 1911 it conveyed a seven-year-old immigrant girl on the last phase of a journey over land and sea, from the plains of her native Hungary to the plains of America's great Midwest. The young passenger, Elizabeth Makra, did not dream that twenty-two years later, as Sister Mary Lelia of the Maryknoll Sisters of St. Dominick, she would be leaving America on a longer and more perilous journey to do active missionary work among the Chinese in Manchuria.

From 1933 to 1941 Sister Mary Lelia labored in Japanese occupied "Manchukuo." When the United States entered the war, she was repatriated to her adopted country and shortly afterwards assigned to the Panama Canal Zone. . . .

In 1946 I was reassigned to North China by way of Peking, where it was planned that at Fu Jen Catholic University I would do graduate work in Chinese before proceeding to Manchuria. With the threatening tide of communism such a move was deemed inadvisable. Consequently the locale was changed and the work was done at the Catholic University of America, Washington, D.C. between 1947–49. . . .

It has long been my secret desire that this translation of the *Hsiao Ching* might bring about not only a dissemination of the noble ideas it contains but also that it might serve as some measure of proof that the conclusions reached by classical Chinese philosophers, aided only by natural reason, are in reality a segment of the whole Truth. And it is my fervent prayer that publication at this time will help speed the day when East and West shall meet in the unity of the Revealed Truth.

Sister Mary Lelia Makra

Maryknoll, New York
July 15, 1960

Hsiao Ching (1961, back cover and xiv)

Much might be said about the relays between the ancient "sacred text" of China and the texts and practices of filiality in Christianity and Catholicism and beyond in the present (see Bellah 1970). Indeed, our book itself might be one item in the dense web of texts that such circulations constitute.

It seems safe enough to say, in reference to the above, that enthusiasm for filiality has spread far beyond the land of Kong. And although it is clear that we, or, at least one of us, have more than a little doubt about the glories and harmony of filiality, Professor Sih's and Sister Makra's words invite just the sort of connection our text has gestured, again and again, toward. Indeed, he calls the *Xiaojing* "an important human document of great significance for our own times"; and says "[W]e are in need of the teachings contained in this classic" (Sih 1961, x, xi).

But all fathers are not the same. Gary Hamilton (1984, 1990) makes a fine-grained argument that none other than Max Weber missed just this point in his comparative study of patriarchy and the nature of domination in premodern China and the West. Hamilton elaborates and extends Bellah's (1970) more general argument that the nature of the connection between fathers and sons in Christianity-influenced as compared to Confucian-influenced cultural practice has important implications for an understanding of the how domination, in general, works on the ground. The difference that Weber apparently couldn't see, presumably because he was looking from the familiar-as-universal, is that between the Western notion of *patria potestas* or "the father's power" (Hamilton 1984, 405) and the Chinese notion of *xiao*. Although conventionally translated as "filial piety," Hamilton (1984, 407) says, after Jamieson (1921), that *xiao* is more insightfully read as:

> "filial duty or submission . . . the respectful submission to the will of the father, which is assumed to arise naturally out of the relationship." *Patria potestas* means power; *xiao* means obedience. "*Roman law emphasizes the domination of the father, which implies duty and obedience on the part of the son. Chinese law looks at it from the opposite point of view; it emphasizes the duty and obedience of the son, which implies power on the part of the father to enforce it.*"

Moreover, Hamilton (1990, 95) argues, this is not merely a matter of sons and daughters submitting to their fathers and mothers, but rather a matter of *everyone*—from highest to lowest—subjecting themselves to the demands of the "roles" or the social positions in terms of which they are defined or come to exist. Indeed, he insists, mundane competence itself is defined in these terms:

> Humanness resides in roles. The treasured qualities of life can only be gained by the careful cultivation of roles, by finding the person that lies within roles. Humanness rests upon the denial of strictly individual desires and unique selves and, more generally, upon the studied negation of personal magic, that is, upon the negation of what Weber called charisma. Humanness in China is intrinsically social and relational, and not psychological and individual, as Westerners have so often viewed it. (1984, 413)

For Confucius' *xiaozi*, then, the operative slogan most definitely is not "the personal is the political." It's easy to appreciate Weber's mistake. *Zhe shi wo yinggai zuode!*

*****

The metaphors of hauntings and ghosts seem especially helpful here in thinking about the many-layered intersections of family, filiality, and subjectivity. They acknowledge the presence of past experience and intimate relationships actively alive in the now of cultural practice, often in ways that are difficult if not impossible for us to put directly and clearly into words, even to ourselves.[16] They help us acknowledge the presence of something "powerfully real" but often "not seen." Gordon (1997, 46) uses Foucault to help her speak about this kind of connection, or, "a certain common field for psychoanalysis and social anthropology, a promise, more accurately, of 'the possibility of a discourse that could move from one to the other, . . . the double articulation of the history of individuals upon the unconscious of culture, and of the historicity of those cultures upon the unconscious of individuals' (Foucault 1973, 379)." These readings of Freud encourage us to pay more attention to what Gordon calls the social significance of his ideas . . . like the importance of ghosts and hauntings in our lives.

The words "ghosts" and "hauntings," when compared to "the unconscious," are likely more familiar, more alive for us. This seems especially so when talking about things "Chinese." For instance, our sense is that if one says "the unconscious," or, as it has been rendered in Chinese, *"qian yi shi,"* meaning "hidden, latent or submerged conscious,"[17] or "subconscious," it might well be read/heard as "Western," and thus other to that which is Chinese. If, however, one says—at least, in Tianjin—"ghosts," "spirits," "the dead," and "hauntings"—*youling* or *gui* or *guihun; hun* or *shen* or *guishen; gui* or *wangren;* and *wuchang* or *heibai* or *yang fu ti,* respectively—not to mention "ancestors," *zuxian*—there surely will be something "Chinese" to talk about; something familiar, even if "feudal," "old-fashioned," "superstitious," and "not 'real.'"[18] Ghosts, it can be said with some confidence, and China, have a certain resonance.

You have seen this already in the excerpts from Maxine Hong Kingston's book, *The Woman Warrior,* subtitled *Memoirs of a Girlhood among Ghosts.* Historian R. David Arkush and literary scholar Leo O. Lee (1993) have collected travel writings in which well-known Chinese intellectuals and writers offer their observations about life in the United States from the mid-nineteenth century to the present to readers back home in China. They title their book, drawing on a characterization by Fei Xiaotong, the foremost anthropologist and sociologist in twentieth-century China, *Land Without Ghosts*. The land *with* ghosts, of course, is China.

The editors comment more generally on the dualisms at work in the texts they collect that seem to be an inevitable aspect of other-ing:

> Chinese views of America have mirrored the process of China's own self-defini-
> tion during the painful historical transition from tradition to modernity. In their
> writings about America, generations of Chinese have voiced concerns about their
> own country. Not only did they seek in America values and ideals that they hoped
> to see realized in China, they also felt the need to reaffirm their Chinese identity
> by means of an implicit contrast with less attractive American features and cus-
> toms, such as weak social and family ties. (Arkush and Lee 1993, 300)

As for who has seen "the other" more clearly, Arkush and Lee conclude, drawing on their larger familiarity with American writings on China[19]:

> Throughout, we would argue, the Chinese can claim the more rational degree of
> understanding. Americans have tended to be more ethnocentric than the Chi-
> nese, showing less respect for Chinese than Chinese accorded American culture.
> . . . Genuine intellectual respect for Chinese culture has been rare among Ameri-
> cans, and Americans have not felt the need to understand China on a profound
> level, as the "other" culture that poses a viable alternative to their own. However,
> as several Chinese intellectuals have observed, what is lacking in this land with-
> out ghosts—the missing element in the Americans' self-confident and dynamic
> national character—is precisely a shadowy sense of national crisis that would
> provoke greater introspection and self-examination. (302–303)

"They" have weak social and family ties. Ours are strong; "we" are known for that. "They" are "modern," not haunted by ghosts; "we" not only are a land *with* ghosts, but we know them . . . well. And while it may be that Americans have "seen" China all too much as "other," Arkush and Lee here might be read to invite us to treat Freud's ideas as a possibly legitimate resource with which to think about things Chinese. They seem to say "we Americans" could use some ghosts. Or, perhaps, it is that we might try harder to know those that we always already have.

This isn't to say that accepting such an invitation is without risks of reading too much, or too little into this bridge from Chinese ghosts to Freud's unconscious. Some of Fei Xiaotong's observations included in Arkush and Lee's book help us be wary here; but help us, nonetheless.[20] After taking a Ph.D. in anthropology in London, under one of the noted founding fathers of the discipline, Bronislaw Malinowski, Fei spent a year— 1943–1944—in the United States, and part of it at the University of Chicago. There he planned to work on a book manuscript, and was given the office of sociologist Robert Park, who had been his teacher in Beijing during a 1932 visit, but who then had gone south for the winter by the time Fei arrived.

The section of the Arkush and Lee translation of Fei's text where he talks about his arrival at Park's office is called "A World without Ghosts." Two things about Fei's comments seem relevant. First, he talks about ghosts and spirits as very material presences—first, in terms of Park's office "chair," his "nameplate" on the door, the "old books lining the walls, even the air in the room" (Arkush and Lee 1993, 176); and, later, as his story turns to boyhood memories in China, to "dark and desolate rooms" in his family home, an image of his dead grandmother completing her daily kitchen routine—he *saw* her; of her room, with every item still in its proper place, as when she was alive. He insists that "to a child like me brought up in a small town, people and ghosts were equally *concrete* and *real*. . . ." (178, emphasis added).[21] Second, Fei conflates history, tradition, and ghosts in a way that leaves very little space for precisely what Freud made so central, the psyché itself.[22] Fei's view is a joining of "history" and "the past" that is full of nostalgia, which, it seems important to note, is not present in Hong Kingston's recollections noted earlier. "[G]hosts," he says, "symbolize belief in and reverence for the accumulated past" (179). It is perhaps no wonder that a woman might experience such ghosts quite differently from a man.

Arkush and Lee write Fei to say of his thoughts about leaving Park's office untouched, so he could work in the presence of his spirit:

> There is here a sort of historical causal connection: because of a past memory the present takes on a significance greater than anything in the current situation. My strong desire to have the name left on the door arose out of a need for concrete, living, moving history. . . . [T]his lingering past . . . is the "tradition" of which I have written. . . . (176)

When his American academic hosts insist on the importance of their own connection to and reverence for their ancestors and history by reference to the presence of their photographs in the room and the preservation of dairies, Fei observes:

> [B]ut I still feel their regard for tradition is to a greater or lesser extent *conscious, intellectual,* and *artificial*. It is not the same as ours. The reason I feel this way is that I have found Americans do not have ghosts. When tradition is concrete, when it is part of life, sacred, something to be feared and loved, then it takes the form of ghosts. This is equivalent to the statement by <<Durkheim>> that God is the representation of social cohesion. (177, emphasis added)

There is no evidence to be found here that Fei had read Freud on the uncanny, or that the, by implication, "not conscious," "practical"?, and "real" encounter with "history" that he suggests characterizes Chinese experience has much if anything to do with the unconscious. Haunting in Fei's version seems more likely to produce "a pleasant nostalgia" than it is to unsettle.

But, still, perhaps Fei had not been fully captured by Durkheim's rationality. There are threads in his text, at least the English text, that might be pulled. In the last paragraphs of the translation, Fei is shown to turn to questions of differences in the nature and quality of relationships between "us"—we Chinese—and between "them"—the Americans—and of the implications of these differences for encounters with ghosts. Disdaining the transience and superficial quality of social encounters in America—there is too much movement there—they/he write/s: "With interpersonal ties like these, naturally they seldom see ghosts after death. . . . Always being on the move dilutes the ties between people and dissolves the ghosts" (180). There is insufficient permanence in connections between people, and between people, places, and things to give ghosts a chance to grow and be nourished, Fei laments; not like "the kind of relationship I had with my grandmother, living interdependently for a long time, repeating the same scenes, so that these scenes came to seem an inalterable natural order" (180). He has moved back to social relationships as the fertile soil for ghosts, a connection Gordon underlines in Freud, although he still can see only "friendly" spirits and hauntings emanating from the long, secure, stable, and "natural" ties that he wants to mark as "Chinese." He thus cannot seem to imagine, or bring himself to write, the possibility of "the Chinese family" as other than an object of nostalgia.

In the penultimate paragraph, however, Fei allows some small space for an "Oriental" appreciation for ambiguity, albeit unnamed as such. Complaining about how brightly Americans seem to light their rooms, he comments, via Arkush and Lee:

> Living in such rooms gives you a false sense of confidence that this is all of the world, that there is no more to reality than what appears clearly and brightly before your eyes. I feel the attitude of Westerners toward the unknown is very different from that of Orientals. They think of the unknown as static, waiting for people to mine it like an ore—not only not frightening, but a resource for improving life in the future. They are very self-assured. (181)

Fei contrasts this with "We Orientals," who "have more reverence for the unknown" and "for fate," which "makes us content with our lot . . .

aware of human limitations, and keeps our eyes fixed on the humanly attainable" (181). Could it be, then, that the "unknown" here is the same unknown of which Gordon speaks? An unknown that is "not seen" but "powerfully" and, even, disturbingly "present" in "the real"?

If we move with this, as we have here, it seems that central to the relevant "past" that these material presences—these ghosts?—effect is the cluster of duties and obligations—practices—that constitute the subjects of (at least) family life and relationships. Ways of doing that constitute ways of being and ways of valuing that one is expected to know and follow. As such, then, to speak about the ghosts and hauntings of people in Chinese space is to invoke a "family resemblance" to the sort of thing that Foucault and Gordon mean by a "cultural unconscious" (cf. Rofel 1999, 217–276). Not a small part of what we are doing here, then, is to invite you to take your own step—to move, too—using and being used by the materials we have woven together; to see what can be done.

*****

This attention to fathers and sons in the context of ghosts and the unconscious clearly solicits the question of whether we might read these relationships as oedipal, after Freud. The best response to this question seems to be a refusal of the yes/no option in favor of asking another question: how productive might it be to try to read *xiao* through Oedipus? Where might it take us?

I was following references, trying to find something that spoke to me about the machinery of filiality in "modern China"—actually, I was looking for *any* reference to Freud (they are hard to find, but see Yue 1999)—when I picked up political scientist and sinologist Richard Solomon's book, *Mao's Revolution and the Chinese Political Culture* (1971). On page 29 I was stunned to read, as a section heading, "OEDIPUS WAS AN UNFILIAL SON." My breath caught in my throat. My God, I thought, at last. But it was not quite as I had expected. Instead of reading *xiao* through oedipus, it was a Confucian indictment of Oedipus, and from an American political scientist!

I tried to read it aloud as it might sound in Chinese. *"Aodipusi meiyou xiaozi!"* I read it then also as . . . it felt like . . . an indictment by a chorus of Chinese and English voices, of . . . me and of what I want here to write. And Solomon (1971, 37–38) did mean to startle and decenter "the Western reader" (Weber, too?) toward being "more conscious of some of the distinctive aspects of Chinese social life," and toward being "aware of certain biases he brings to the study of China given his own cultural background, which lays such stress on individual autonomy." And if I felt it as criticism, it arguably is also criticism of the cultural assumptions on which the story and figure of Oedipus move, which is to say of an active and vital presence in "family culture" today (see Edmunds 1985). Perhaps, then, "we" are haunted here by at least two ghosts with rather different concerns: those of the *xiaozi* and those of Oedipus as well.

Solomon's provocative claim serves his chapter's purpose, which is to highlight the intimate connection between family and larger polity, not only in Chinese life but in "Western" politics too.[23] By linking the Greek myth of Oedipus to the lessons of the *Xiaojing*, Solomon helps me understand some of my ambivalence about my own F/fathers, filiality, caregiving, and the sorts of masculinities that seem to be connected to them. But Solomon doesn't cite Freud, even once.[24] After all, this is (masculine) social science.

He says, somewhat grandly, that from this comparison we might gain insight into "the solution of the fundamental political problem of human life, the tie between dependent son and powerful and disciplining father" (Solomon 1971, 36). Mothers and daughters, if they are as charitable as the Taiwan women Margery Wolf stories, may find such a claim amusing, but it does signal the importance Solomon gives these cultural narratives in distilling practices that are today alive in both Chinese and Western space. More inclusively, he frames the issue as "the difficulties of relations between the weak and strong," solved "through an institutional patterning of the human life cycle" (28–29).

Solomon draws his story of Oedipus, King of Thebes, from the fifth-century B.C. play by Sophocles, the same source Freud used (see Edmunds 1985, xx). It tells of Oedipus, the fated son who as an infant is sent away by his regal parents in hopes of avoiding the oracle's terrible predictions that he will come later to murder his father, the king, marry his mother, himself become a courageous and revered king, but bring himself and his people dishonor and desolation through arrogance, pride, and transgressive incest. This is a political tale *par excellence,* says Solomon, and one of wide appeal. He speaks to his fellow readers with masculine gusto: "Oedipus appeals to the Horatio Alger in us, for he was a 'high achiever,' a self-made man who, though rejected by his family, used his intelligence to outwit the Sphinx that had terrorized Thebes and thus, by his own determination, rose to great power and fame" (Solomon 1971, 29). Isn't this the kind of man "we all" are taught to emulate "here"? High achiever. Self-made. Impervious to rejection. Clever. Brave. Successful. Having forgotten Freud, Solomon also forgets to add: and with a healthy libido; surely, a would-be king.

But this son promised trouble for his family from the beginning. Although a father must try to discipline his son so he can "become a participating member of society," this discipline leaves resentment, even hatred, "and a desire to 'do in' the one who first forced denial or restriction of the pleasures of life" (30). The problem of power and conflict, of the pursuit of aggressive individual desires, would be "solved" by banishment. But, of course, that didn't work. The oracle's prophecy came true nonetheless. The son would challenge his father's authority, act on his sexual desires for his mother, and think foremost of himself. This undermines, to say the least, the family harmony that might have been, if only. . . . If only it were not for "Western individualism" and its stress on the key place of the self-directing and autonomous "actor," says Solomon (31).[25] The story is, he says, "a metaphorical expression of the Western life cycle." It's the way with sons, and families. It's the way with a certain kind of masculinity that "we" know quite well. But, we should ask, is it "fated," as with Oedipus? Could it be otherwise? "Can we talk" to this ghost, as Gordon suggests?[26]

As for "the Chinese," they have faced "the same" father-son, dominant-subordinate problem, says Solomon, but have managed it within the family and the society in a rather different way. It is filiality—obedience, duty—rather than banishment that is operated to secure the threatened family and social harmony in the face of the potential struggle between the more and the less powerful, the high and the low. And there, it seems, it *has* "worked." There we have no tragedy, with a would-be filial son as protagonist. To recall Paul Sih's (1961, vii) words about children in his preface to the *Xiaojing*: "[W]hen they do grow up and become independent, they want to be free and to get away from their parents. Herein lies the dilemma which calls for a higher expression of filial piety. . . ." And, Solomon notes, it is not in a play, a publicly presented drama, that these tensions are drawn out, and thus dissipated, as in ancient Greece and "the West." Rather, they are, from very early in a child's life, given little if any space for existence at all. It is toward the higher goal of family and social harmony and propriety, effected through careful study and memorization of model texts, that the *xiaozi* always strives. Aggression against the father—or elder brothers, for that matter—seems simply not to be storied at all.

*****

Some 1,600 years *after* the *Xiaojing* is said to have been written, filiality was given an apparently needed cultural "transfusion" of "'new' blood" by another set of texts thought to have originated during the Ming dynasty (1368–1644 C.E.)—the Ming and Qing period, up to 1912, apparently being a high point of filiality and its institutionalization in China.[27] *The Book of Filial Duty,* on which Solomon draws, is a collection of twenty-four brief stories and commentaries about children, virtually all sons, and how they nourished and cared for parents when they were alive, and, even after they were dead. The images of the *xiaozi* that they offer contrast pointedly with those of Oedipus, a one who seemed, single-mindedly—as if "fated"—to pursue his own, individual desires. We here include translations of two such texts to provide a sense of just what a man might be asked to do to be a son.

Number 1
The Filial Piety that Influenced Heaven

Yü Shun, the son of Ku Sou, had an exceedingly filial disposition; his father, however, was stupid, his mother perverse, and his younger brother, Hsiang, very conceited. His actions are related in the *Shang Shu,* in the *Chung Yung,* and in the works of Mencius. Those who speak of him say that Shun cultivated the hills of Li (in the province of Shansi), where he had elephants to plough his fields and birds to weed the grain. So widespread was the renown of his virtue that the Emperor Yao heard of him, and sent his nine sons to serve him, and gave him two of his daughters in marriage, and afterwards resigned to him the imperial dignity.

Of all those whose virtue and filial duty deserve to be illustrated, Shun is preeminent; and his example, in obeying his parents, is worthy of being handed down to posterity, through myriads of ages. Once he was in great danger in a well, into which he was commanded by his father to descend, and his brother cast down stones upon him; again, he was in a granary, when it was set on fire; but from these, as well as from many other dangers, he escaped unhurt. He fished, burned pottery, ploughed and sowed, with great toil on the hills of Li. He laboriously performed all these duties, but his parents were not affected, while his brother Hsiang became more insolent and overbearing. His parents alleged crimes against him, but Shun could not find that he had done wrong; he loved and revered them, though they did not requite him with affection. His feelings were grieved at these manifold troubles, and with strong crying and tears he invoked Heaven.

His perfect sincerity was effectual to renovate his family; his parents became pleasant, and his brother more conciliatory and virtuous. Heaven also considered his excellency to be great, and regarded him as truly good, thus establishing his reputation so firmly that it was perpetuated to, and influenced, succeeding ages. Even Confucius is regarded as elevated but a little above Shun, and I would praise and extol them both to coming generations.

Number 4
Clad in a Single Garment, He was Obedient to his Mother
During the Chou dynasty lived Min Sun, a disciple of Confucius, who in early life lost his mother. His father subsequently married another wife, who bore him two children, but [she] disliked Sun. In winter she clothed him in garments made of rushes, while her own children wore cotton clothes. Min was employed in driving his father's chariot, and his body was so cold that the reins dropped from his hands, for which carelessness his father chastised him; yet he did not vindicate himself. When his father knew the circumstances, he determined to divorce his second wife; but Sun said, "Whilst mother remains, one son is cold; if mother departs, three sons will be destitute." The father desisted from his purpose; and after this the mother was led to repentance, and became a good and virtuous parent.

The filial piety of the renowned Shun influenced Heaven, whilst that of Min renovated mankind. If Heaven be influenced, all below it will be transformed; if men be renovated, from them will spring a power able to cause their families to become good. In all ages men have exhibited a great love for their wives; but dutiful children have often met with unkindness. Min carefully concealed all his grievances, and refused to indulge in any complaint; even while suffering severely from cold and hunger, he maintained his affection unabated. During the long period which he endured this oppressive treatment, his good disposition became manifest; and by his own conduct he was able to maintain the harmony of the family unimpaired. His father and mother were influenced by his filial devotion; and his brothers joined in extolling his virtues. All his friends and acquaintances, with united voice, celebrated his merits; and the men of his native village joyfully combined to spread the fame of his actions. The memory of his agreeable countenance and pleasing manners was perpetuated to the remotest ages; and his example was in many respects like that of Shun, whose parents were equally perverse.

Chen (1910, 33–34, 37–39)

Oedipus, indeed, was not a filial son if these sons are the measure. Each time I read these short tales, still, I feel a combination of incredulity, anger, and a bit of derision; the same sentiments I felt around my misunderstanding of the proverb about the *xiaozi* at his father's bedside in a very long illness, noted in chapter 2. I feel sure that Laihua would not respond to them this way. I think that he would respect Yü Shun and Min Sun, allowing of course that "times have changed," coupled with a sense of his own inadequacy as such a son to his father and mother. When I would ask him, as I often did, about his parents and his relationship to them, Laihua always said something like, "I am always sad to think about them, that I don't have them here to take care of. I am so unlucky." They were a gap, an absence in his life; as though, he said, he had been "cheated by fate." But still, he "thought of them all the time." They, and he, were here, together. It is very hard, he said, because "I don't really have them here to take care of." After all, he is still a son.

The stories of Yü Shun and Min Sun and the others that accompany them write subjectivities that sometimes seem to these eyes hard to imagine, not to say emulate. I find it difficult to read myself into these storylines. I don't want to. I do want to. But perhaps this difficulty comes from positions long taken in other stories, from other places, that know Oedipus, the "high achiever" and "self-made man," all too well. Or perhaps this trouble comes from attachment to abstractions, like "fairness" and "equity" toward individuals, and even "love," which certainly are not central to the filial family. And, although Solomon does not mention it since he speaks the masculinist language of universal knowledge and truth, it is not a small matter that we are here talking about men, about masculinity, and how, properly, to produce it. Finally, I want to know more about the emotional quality of the attachment between the *xiaozi* and his father. Where can I see the *feeling* between them? Indeed, as we asked in chapter 5, what is the place of this feeling in the intersection of duty and care? It is not a surprising question, coming as it does from Des Moines, asked of "the Chinese" sons. But, of course, it is not really being asked of them at all.

To insist that this is "about masculinity" rather than about "the strong versus the weak," or about "power," as Solomon does, seems to bring matters into sharper focus; makes the contradictions, for me, more uncomfortable; harder to displace, and thus possibly more productive. After all, it was Joseph who sought to produce himself as a son to that third father, whose name he himself took; it was Joseph who so wanted to serve and please the *person* of that father; to take care of him when he was sick; to win his approval and love. For it was precisely that personal approval and love that made him, there/here, a real son. He was the father then who helped Joseph be a man, and who seemed, indeed, to love him too. But Joseph was a "good son," who willingly took up subordination, weakness toward—which helped produce—that fatherly strength; he was deferent and did not, for the most part, challenge. And he often thought of what a model—or, was it a burden?—he was for his two younger brothers. Surely, there was pleasure in that. But, some did wonder, in effect, "what kind of a *man* is this?" Where, they seemed to ask about him, was Oedipus?[28] Was he acting too much "like a woman" to this father? Was he, then, too "filial"? He had, though, fought the second, would-be father for his mother's love—though he lost—and so he knew a bit about oedipality, too.

Solomon underlines the cultural difference here: "[U]nlike Oedipus, who rewarded his rejecting parents with an inexorable, fate-driven vengeance of death and violation of social taboo, Yü continued a life of toil on his family land and returned his parents' rejection with reverence for them and sincerity in his lifelong social obligations as a son. His reward was the moral renovation of his family through his own example: 'His parents became pleasant, and his brother more conciliatory and virtuous'" (32). In Min Sun's case, while an archetypal "evil stepmother" and his father and brothers abuse his devotion, the exemplary son remains true to the requirements of his position. *Zhe shi wo yinggai zuode!* This is what I should do! While the torment for Oedipus's transgression was guilt and shame, an *internal* suffering; for the *xiaozi* it is torment from the *outside* and is often described as quite physical, but this comes, not as punishment for any wrongs done, but simply as a matter of fate. As the story says, "dutiful children" often meet unkindness. The character of the father in these dramas must be harsh, distant, and cold. Almost effaced. For how else would the *xiaozi* accumulate the resources necessary to become, to *be*; and to be so widely revered for it, to boot? And this, all in the name of proper obedience, not to the *person* of the father, but to the requirements of one's position as son. The father-son bond in the land of Kong was not (is not?) an emotional one (either), but a means to the higher aims of family and wider social harmony.[29] Mothers, outsiders to this calculus, were "in charge" of nurturance for both sons and daughters.

As Solomon notes, there is a symmetry of interests to this pattern that rewards perseverance, in that

within the *interdependence* of the family the son reciprocates the nurturance he receives in his childhood dependency by nurturing his parents in the dependency of their old age. . . . [T]hus for the filial individual, life comes full circle. The filial son in this sense remains a "son" as long as he lives; he never breaks out of his original social matrix to establish an independent life. (1971, 37)

For to do so would constitute a self-banishment. The good son knows that one day he too will "have" a son (note how daughters are invisible here, but, in fact "there") or a son-substitute, who will "enable him to enjoy the pleasures of dependent old age."[30] And mothers? They will depend on loving sons (again, daughters remain invisible) who give them nourishment and priority—at last—over their own wives.

There is a darker possibility alluded to in the tales of Yü and Min, and that Solomon makes explicit in reference to what he calls "perhaps the [Chinese] equivalent of the Oedipus myth." This is the story of Hsüeh Jen-kuei, a soldier during the Tang dynasty who was renowned for his skills in battle, especially with bow and arrow. Sent by the emperor to fight far away, he finally returns home for a reunion with his wife, whom he left, pregnant, some eighteen years before. Nearing his home, he sees a young man shooting wild birds by a river. Impressed by the youth's skill, he challenges him to a contest, touting his own acuity. But when the youth accepts the challenge, Hsüeh, without warning, shoots him rather than the birds, commenting that he could not let another (man) live who was better than he with bow and arrow. Continuing home, he happily greets his wife but is suspicious of her professed fidelity during his absence when he notices a pair of men's shoes under the family bed. The tragedy of the tale is revealed when his wife chides him, explaining that the shoes are those of their son, born just after her husband departed, and who at the moment is out by the river, hunting birds. Says Solomon: "Hsüeh Jen-kuei's actions suggest the father's reluctance to let the son grow to his own maturity; his unwillingness to be challenged by him. Hsüeh's doubts about his wife's fidelity reveal a tension in the father-son relationship born of the particularly intense mother-son tie" (35), also to be found in the other stories of filiality. Rather than the son killing the father and marrying his mother, as with Oedipus, the father here kills the son in a contest over name and reputation, in which the sexual and emotional relays between mother and son are referenced.[31] What might such a story teach a son about his father?

Good. Faithful. Loyal. "Heroic-ly" loyal. Responsive. Persevering. Bearing. Self-denying. Self-sacrificing. Family. No sex. Well, no libido. Discipline. Dead. But renowned. What kind of a *man* is this? Here he is figured in the modern version of the ancient Chinese pictograph that is the word "*xiao*":

Like most Chinese characters, this one is composed of separable parts called "radicals," each conveying meaning and/or clues to vocalization.

Xiao's two components are arranged vertically: on top is the element that represents an old man. Beneath is the figure of a son, *zi*. The essence, then, of filiality is the son bearing—in service to—the father.[32] Could this son learn from Oedipus? Should he? Yes, he could, but the subject, that son, indeed would have to change, and in ways that are already all too familiar.

*****

Sun Longji (also Sun Lung-kee) is an American-educated ethnic Chinese who took a Ph.D. at Stanford University in 1985 by writing on early twentieth-century Chinese intellectuals and shifts in their thinking and writing between the May Fourth period and the 1930s. One of his central concerns in that work is the image of the Chinese individual or subject to be found in selected literary texts of the period. Sun had written a considerably more controversial book about the nature of the Chinese individual, in Chinese, several years earlier that goes by the English title, *The Deep Structure of Chinese Culture*.[33] One of the first things to note about this title is its seductive promise to provide us a key to, the essence of, "Chineseness." We should of course beware even as we are seduced by the promise.

Sun does not paint a particularly attractive picture of this essence. In fact, it is a rather devastating portrait.[34] And he writes in the idiom of the totalizing category, if not the stereotype. All of which is to say, once more, that orientalism is alive and well, even when somewhat displaced.

Drawing loosely on and, certainly, with his own reading of psychoanalytic language and frame, he concedes that writing the book was a "personal catharsis" that helped him "outgrow my own cultural heritage" (Sun, quoted in Barmé and Minford 1989, 32). A rather far cry from much of the personal politics of cultural critique common in the postcolonial academy these days, there is a resonance with the texts of the *xiaozi* such that we want to quote Sun on the kind of man this filial son might be—or be imagined to be. While warily considering the description of his own cultural demons, you may want to note and perhaps resist the Western, liberal masculine humanism in his discourse, which no doubt provides a foundation for his angst toward this other in him.

[T]he Chinese "individual" is organized and motivated by the "other" (if not the "nation" then the "family"). The Chinese "individual" per se does not possess the capacity to "unfold" his own potentialities fully, to give himself a willed shape. Even in a so-called free environment like Hong Kong, I find individual development skewed, and more often than not in a "somatized" direction. Such an individual may look after his own interests very well and, within the framework of Chinese social obliga- tions, may even be indulgent towards others, but nonetheless he is un- aware of himself as having a "purpose," and in all likelihood regards himself as an instrument of others. I believe the archetypal model for this kind of interdependence to be Chinese generational relationships. They generate a kind of human being who is not fully aware of the fact that he belongs first to himself, and only then to the world at large; he tends to become the private property of the "family" and its surrogates, thus giv- ing rise to a kind of "selfless" selfishness . . . (Sun, quoted in Barmé and Minford 1989, 31–32).

The whole network of social relationships serves as a womb (family, social group, collective, state). And no man, in the sense of man with a strong ego, has ever been born in China. As Lu Xun [one of the most famous early twentieth-century intellectuals and social critics in China] remarked: "True manhood has not yet been created in the Chinese world." The Chinese self is permanently disorganized. It has to be defined by leaders and collectives. Clinging to the mother's womb is the norm in Chinese culture . . . (34).

In existentialism, a man "exists" by virtue of retreating from all his social roles and searching his own soul. . . . By contrast, a Chinese fulfills himself within the network of interpersonal relationships. . . . Strip him of his relationships, and there is nothing left. He is not an independent unit. His existence has to be defined by his acquaintance. This concept of man is best exemplified by the primary Confucian con- cept of *ren*. *Ren* may roughly be translated as humane. The Chinese written character is made up of two components, "man" and "two," and denotes essentially a bilateral relationship. Only in the presence of an- other person can our "humanity" be displayed. . . . This Chinese con- cept of man forms the basic substratum, the deep structure, of Chinese culture and has remained unchanged up to the present day (though ex- tended to the domain of the collective) . . . (Sun, quoted in Barmé and Minford 1989, 163).

Conventional Chinese culture leaves little room at all for self-realiza- tion. To be a man, one must create oneself—one must make a work of art out of oneself—out of one's body, one's appearance, one's mind, intel- lect, passion, and will. Man can be something higher. Man must tran- scend man . . . (165).

The Chinese as a whole show a marked tendency towards oral fixa- tion. In the Chinese language, population is expressed as "number of mouths" *(renkou)*. The Chinese tend to relate to the world with their mouths . . . (Sun quoted in Barmé and Minford 1989, 226; and see Yue 1999).

The older generation constantly treat the younger as babies, whose sexual organs are not yet developed. They never disclose anything about sex, with the result that the young remain ignorant and bewildered . . . (226–227).

To maintain social harmony they must "desexualize" the individual, that is, make him unaware of his own sexuality. This also helps to maintain harmony between the generations.[35] If any individual is allowed to be an independent being, he will eventually break away from his elders. This is the basis of Freud's theory of the Oedipus Complex . . . (227).

Chinese tend to oralize their sexuality. It is assessed in terms of whether it injures or benefits the health. Sex, like food, strengthens the body, but too much of it, like too much food, is harmful, especially to the genitals. Such a concept inevitably leads to the suppression of sexual desire in men, and hinders them from full development as human beings with a normal sex life. If a man is not fully developed as a mature being, it will be impossible for him to produce other "men." Lu Xun once remarked: "(The Chinese) as a rule are tools for the production of children. They are not fathers of 'men'. Even if a Chinese has children, he himself is still not a 'man'" . . . (228).

Sun Longji's objections aim at qualities that define the model filial son. For him, it appears that the *xiaozi* not only could but should take a lesson or two from Oedipus, as well as from the French Revolution, the European Enlightenment, the Judeo-Christian tradition, and even late-twentieth-century, Western hegemonic masculinity. Sun's reactions against traditional Chinese masculinity might well be shared by others who embrace these dominant discourses of "humanity" and even the nation-state in late modernity (see Duara 1995 and Rofel 1999). And the twentieth-century debate on the relationship between tradition and modernization or progress in China speaks to some of these same qualities (see, e.g., Su and Wang 1991). We might say that such recurrent debates themselves could be read as evidence of the ghost of the filial child, haunting the children of successive presents. *Zhe shi wo yinggai zuode!*

While Joseph's hesitance and ambivalence over the images of this "good son" make him sympathize with some of Sun's complaints, his disdain for the particular pleasures and horrors of the story of Oedipus, and its generalized version appropriated by Freud to describe family dynamics and mature masculinity, prevent him from seeing that as an option for producing caring yet mobile and human, "agetic" people. And some of what Sun disdains in his heritage, we two see both as recuperable and to be recommended. The sense of self as always already shared with others; always at least joint, and always socially contingent, with a healthy dose of humility, are elements of Sun's disdainful characterization of "Chinese" that we would want to hold. Still, "suppress the self; follow the rites—*ke ji fu li*"[36]—are not.

So, the question of whether the *xiaozi*, the filial child, *should* learn from Oedipus is the far more important one, not least because today it seems to be so much more likely. At the end of the "Second Christian Millennium,"[37] with the so-called global witness of the "defeat of communism and socialism and triumph of international capital," we would hope this answer is "no." Oedipal masculinity, in the context of *xiao*, appears to us a disastrous lure for today's sons—and daughters—of Kong. Rather, we might better consider Gordon's (1997, 49–50, 58–60) hopeful, but admittedly difficult, advice, that we engage these two ghosts—the *xiaozi* and Oedipus—in conversation, that we talk to them about what else is possible for us, not just in our relationships to fathers and mothers— where neither ghost offers us much hope for movement—but with each of the several others within and linked to each of "us." Are these relationships, after all, so fated, so "natural"? Could they be otherwise? Can we imagine how?

8

Reflextion. Diffraction.
Criticism. Sociology. Science?

I am sick to death of bonding through kinship and "the family," and I long for
models of solidarity and human unity and difference rooted in friendship, work,
partially shared purposes, intractable collective pain, inescapable mortality, and
persistent hope. It is time to theorize an 'unfamiliar' unconscious, a different
primal scene, where everything does not stem from the dramas of identity and
reproduction. Ties through blood . . . have been bloody enough already. I believe that there will be no racial or sexual peace, no livable nature, until we learn
to produce humanity through something more and less than kinship. I think I am
on the side of the vampires, at least some of them. But, then, since when does
one get to choose which vampire will trouble one's dreams?

> Donna Haraway, *Modest_Witness@Second_Millennium.*
> *FemaleMan©_ Meets_Oncomouse™* (1997)

To the extent that sociology is wedded to facticity as its special truth, it must
continually police and expel its margin—the margin of error—which is the fictive.
But these facts are always in imminent danger of being contaminated by what is
seemingly on the other side of their boundaries, by fictions. Like a taboo that is
always being approached in the act of avoidance, when sociology insists on finding only the facts, it has no other choice but to pursue the fictive, the mistake it
seeks to eliminate.

> Avery Gordon, *Ghostly Matters* (1997)

Seek truth from facts.

> Deng Xiaoping

The opposition of private and public that has allowed sociology to enhance its
authority by making public what is first described as private is an opposition that
can no longer ground social criticism. The vulnerabilities of observation become
the vulnerabilities of a rereading that, rather than being displaced onto the observed, are returned to the reader and writer. And this is not a matter of urging a
fixed identity between reader and writer—only women writing only about women,
for example—although this corrective is to be expected. Rather, it is to urge a

reconsideration of the privilege given observation and "factual" descriptions as the basis of criticism. It is to urge a social criticism that gives up on data collection and instead offers rereadings of representations in every form of information processing, empirical science, literature, film, television, and computer simulation.

Patricia T. Clough, *The End(s) of Ethnography* (1998)

Working at the borderline of what is and what no longer is [sociology] . . . one also knows that if one crosses that border, if one can depart from where one is, one can also return to it more freely, without attachment to the norms generated on one side or the other. So the work effected would constantly question both its interiority and its exteriority to the frame of [sociology]. . . .

Trinh T. Minh-ha, *Visualizing Society* (Chen and Trinh 1994)

Last chapters are supposed to do something special. They should tie together, draw out themes that have come before but perhaps remain implicit; mark coherence; say "what it's all about"; effect a closure that then can become grounds for another opening, usually for "more research" or "future needed work" that returns thought to a disciplined space. Last chapters usually turn back into the folds of earlier texts in order to bring the past into the present and then look toward a "better" future. And while not exactly requiring the conventional narrative's "happy ending," they do, well . . . close. You almost can hear the (hoped-for) sigh of pleasure as the last page/s is/are turned. For this particular book, you might anticipate this, given its incomplete, fragmented, "disturbed," and contradictory make up. "Now," you might hope, "at least/last, they will tell us what they really have been up to."

But if you have been reading this book from the beginning, you might have prepared yourself not to hope the usual reader's hope for a last chapter that does these familiar things. You might suspect that after dragging you through all of this, we hardly can give up (on) the ghost/s at this point. We hardly can say, now, "So, here is what we really meant; here is how the data on caregiving in Tianjin fit together into a 'meaningful whole'; and here is what you should do, or think about doing, when you write true stories about others." One might have learned by now that it can't be a question of banishing ghosts—a familiar fantasy linked to closure and totality—but rather of seeking to engage them, to let them help us wonder how to move (on), but differently.

A dissatisfied reviewer of a draft of this chapter, although generally positive toward the book, complained:

I'll be rude here. I don't think last chapters should be about themselves; they should be about the story just told and the next story to be told. The story just told is given in the first full paragraph on page [231]—what this ethnography was supposed to be, and what it became. So, I want this chapter to be about that paragraph, not Joseph's and Laihua's reflections on Clough, Haraway, Latour, and others. I want an old-fashioned JS essay on guilt, nostalgia, family, death, and caregiving . . . read through what is already here. . . . I want Joseph and Laihua to return to the thrice-told tale model of Wolf [1992], and think about three clear and cleanly divided texts, each of which reflexively folds back on the other.

Granted how pleasurable, compelling and, certainly, relevant an "old-fashioned essay" on guilt, nostalgia, family, death, and caregiving could be (aside from whether or not JS could in fact produce such), it is the very form in which this is imagined that gives me pause; that would seem not to fit, especially here. And while the allusion to Wolf's recent "model" of writing experimental ethnography does gesture toward a new form (at least as our reviewer characterizes it), her own assessment of the promise of "post-" work, on balance, does not. In fact, her text (a word she treats with derision) arguably takes up a position rather squarely against our project and practice. Indeed, Denzin (1997, 219) characterizes Wolf's position as holding "a commitment to objective inquiry and to a belief that there is a world of intersubjectively constituted facts out there ready to be discovered by the ethnographer" as grounds for truth. For better or worse, the "old-fashioned essay" and Wolf's "model" cannot help us here.

Still, this is the last chapter. What sort of note might we think to strike in this last linear position in a collection of texts we have wanted to call something like "an ethnography coming apart at the seams" at a time when the seams of so many ordered ways of life, so many "texts," here and in innumerable else wheres—including even Tianjin and Des Moines—seem to be straining ever more obviously, wanting, in a sense, to "come apart" but hesitating at the wonder, "What then?" The fear of dis-order is strong, especially for those who have known so little of centeredness and prerogative in their pasts and past lives. While such reference, for North American academics, may conjure images of African-Americans, the poor, and women—the familiar categories of race, class, and gender—almost all of the people I met who lived and grew up in mid-to-late-twentieth-century China seemed quite prepared to choose *against* disorder and for some version of "harmony"—even increasingly "modern" harmony/History—if given the option (see also Duara 1995, 3–50; and Rofel 1999). In such subaltern experience, the "play" and promise of deconstruction and ambiguity can quickly fade, especially if they are reduced to caricature—as they so often are—by critics' glib, mocking asides that reality is "mere fiction" and that "there is nothing outside the text."

The thrill of the possibility of endless de-centering—"continuous revolution"?—that deconstruction allows is, of course, fickle. Worse, it is designed not only to be disloyal, but to tell the world the secrets of those who have the temerity to use it. For when we deploy it, or it deploys us as its ostensible agents, we accept, although often without realizing it fully, the impermanence, the fragility, and the thoroughly interested and made-up quality of our own momentarily "safe places." Deconstruction does, eventually, "bite the hand that feeds/operates it." It is a machine in which there is no place to hide. All pauses to "make a point" and "get somewhere" immediately call out to, solicit, the full force of its destabilizing flow. In this it shares much with what has been called radical or full reflexivity in the critique of knowledge production practices.

Whether we speak of the more obvious stories of the subordination of women, people of color, the poor, those whose sexual desires and identities are deemed "perverse"; or of those perhaps less obvious stories, of the characters in so many family dramas, of wives and mothers; of children, daughters and sons; of husbands and fathers, who live lives in which the seams are felt to be so clearly under strain that they surely must—it is hoped/feared—burst; for them, the politics of deconstruction can seem, finally, as too mobile, too "relative," and not quite serious enough; of limited use for someone wanting to "get somewhere," to "make a difference" in the world, or in worlds already too full of injustice, suffering, and pain (cf. Mascia-Lees et al. 1989; Smith 1993; Caplan 1988/1989; Wolf 1992). Some might say that the play of signifiers, and a skill to see where to pull on a thread that is, inevitably, there to be pulled such that any fabric, any world, any solid ground can be revealed as always already woven, "cooked" and not "raw"; as "made up" and thus relative to the ways of world-making employed; some might say that this finally stops too short of a moral and ethical engagement with whatever worlds the embodied operator of this deconstruction machine of writing and discourse inhabits. It's an exciting place to visit, but you wouldn't want to live there. You couldn't. It moves too fast. And it's much too cool (as a relative of "cold").

But the option not to "travel," not to visit or inhabit a "there" (even while at home) to sample the local/global "color" as it whizzes by is also less available to more people today (see Kaplan 1996). Perhaps you couldn't live with this machine, but perhaps, increasingly, you couldn't live without it, either, for its workings are hardly relevant only to a tiny, white male, first-world academic elite with literary pretensions, as some of its critics seem to suggest. Rather, the flux, ambiguity, contradiction, and instability of lives lived in the widening and complex flow of international capital, nation, and technoscience are, arguably, embodiments of the terror, disorientation, and occasionally the thrill of deconstruction as a description of, if not a program for, post/modern "experience" and the subjectivities it produces.

*****

The real story of this ethnography was supposed to be about the myriad ways that Chinese children sacrifice themselves to take care of their elderly and ill parents. It was to be a story of praise and guilt; praise for all of the hard work, perseverance, loyalty of Chinese sons and daughters that I first met in the "modern" hospital ward; and guilt from and critique of the way American adult children seem to shift this work and burden off onto various professionals, paraprofessionals, and salaried others in places that are called "homes" but are not. And it was to be some sort of critique of the more diverse ways we care, or not, in the sophisticated ultra- and postmodern "West" as seen from "deeper" and much longer-lived "traditions" of care and connection in "China." It short, it was to be a story driven by a largely unacknowledged masculine nostalgia and memory-work (see Kaplan 1996, 33–37, 57–64). And although not clear to me at the outset, it was a story intimately connected to my own life as a son who abandoned his mother . . . or, at least left her at a time of need, to make looking for, and then after, a father the center of his identity even as he began to realize that was a world, a subject, he could not live with/in either. And, although only recently somewhat more apparent to me, this was to be a story provoked by a nostalgia not peculiar only to me and my "present" but to Laihua and to various versions of masculinity at the end of the millennium "in China" as well.[1] No doubt, one of the "grounds" on which Laihua and I could stand so comfortably together—and with many of the people we interviewed—was that of family, filiality, loyalty, and a nostalgia for an imagined "past" when these things were more pure, more real, and when we could be more sure that we were indeed "good" sons, people, "subjects." But as I came to appreciate, with each next writing—from proposals to fieldnotes to memos to letters to paper-and-chapter drafts—the narratives of modern social science require disciplines that do not well serve such a conception; the direct and "self-conscious" (autobiographical) story, written in a "clear prose style," eludes the writer who has come not only to "believe in" ghosts but to listen closely for what they suggest.

The social science story that this book might have been could not have taken ghosts seriously. It was to be a true story based on scientific facts and data, carefully collected in detailed fieldnotes made from many interviews and observations with real, living people that would uncover the *social* machinery of their lives and selves; that is, it would be about what was, ostensibly, common to them; shared, "the same" and, of course, "really there." It would be a story in which much data from "the field" would have been used to ground empirical generalizations about caregiving as mundane work done, much in the style used by Anselm Strauss and colleagues, although it would not be especially interested, pacé Anselm, in constructing any "general theory." It would not have spoken about the intimate connections between what I wanted and needed as a man/son and the kind of sociology I have done. And it would have been "very respectful" of, if distanced from yet dependent on, "the Chinese."

But in the very process of planning and carrying out *that* study, Joseph began to listen to ghosts, although he didn't realize that was what he was doing and he didn't think about it using that metaphor. Like more and more stories of research told in the human sciences these days, the subject/s and the field/s of/in the fieldwork initially planned began, as a result of such listening, to change, to move (e.g., Krieger 1991; Gordon 1990; Clough 1998, xi–xiii).

I don't know quite how the travel to China, first as a spouse and middle-school English teacher and then as a professor of sociology at a key university, and finally as a sponsored researcher and then again as a professor at an elite university in Hong Kong, helped this movement; loosened things up; or opened my ears as much or more than my eyes. I am sure it was critical. But such travel has had as much or more to do with a sense of absence or emptiness in my own all too secure and "successful" bourgeois life in late-twentieth-century United States than with potential "research findings" and "knowledge" that were crying out to me for discovery "in China." There was, then, from the beginning, a displacement at work.

As I look at my notes and memos from several years ago on "Why China?" and "Why now?," questions that I have repeatedly asked myself and that others have asked me, there is considerably more attention given to what I felt I didn't have "here" than any particular thing drawing me "there," save of course for its "difference," distance from many pieces of that here, and "it" being virtually synonymous with "the unknown." After all, I had read nothing about China when I decided to apply for the Fulbright to teach the sociology of "American Social Problems" in Beijing during the 1985–1986 academic year (which, of course, is quite consistent with Fulbright expectations). I could and did use the "social problems" angle as a professional justification to myself and to others, since I had done some work on that, but that exhausted my "legitimate" grounds. Also, by the way, my father had just died shortly before my wife and I decided to go/run.

To search the "Why?" for that initial and then subsequent repeated travel from Des Moines to China—first for two years of teaching, 1985–1987, with annual returns every subsequent summer for several weeks until 1990–1991 when the year-long fieldwork was done; followed by Laihua's visit to the United States in 1992, and then my returns to Tianjin in 1993, 1995, and 1996, punctuated by two years in Hong Kong 1996–1998, not to mention the substantial traveling I did while living there—comes much closer to what Mills (1940) called "motive mongering" than a setting forth of conventional "real reasons." Still, some mongered motives seem more insightful and productive, which is to say disturbing, than others. And the more I have read of the links between colonialism and the history of the human sciences, about the deep skepticism toward the Enlightenment and "liberal" notion that knowledge will lead to freedom and that power means only oppression (but, of whom?); the more I thought about "our" personal investments in holding fast and boldly to the presumption of a rational, choosing "center" of consciousness surveying the world from the I/eye, and the constant "resourcing" that is required to keep that I/eye secure (Sofoulis 1988, cited in Haraway 1991, 198); and the more I considered the claim that these things seemed so often to be structured by and with gender. . . . Well, the more, then, the "motives" set out in postcolonial-and-feminist writing seemed good candidates for consideration (since, in any case, it would be a "mongering" of such motives). How to read/tell a story of a white, Protestant, heterosexual, middle class, middle-aged male, very "American" sociologist/academic from Des Moines at the end of the century—which is to say, more or less, someone from the "center"—who goes off to China knowing next to nothing about anything "Chinese," stays, returns repeatedly to "do research" and "write about it," and, in effect, never quite comes back "home"? (Luckily, he had tenure before he went.) How to understand what it was Joseph was, has been, doing there/here? An escape? And/or a search? A denial?

You already have come across this question and various partial answers throughout the book. In the spirit of Mills's critique of motives as explanations for behavior, and Spivak's disabling of the phrase "I choose because . . ."—at least as innocent usage—and framed by my preference for more "dark" than "bright" readings of human conduct, it seems to me that recent writing in postcolonial theory offers up a rich resource of speculations about such "Whys?," questions that of course might be asked (at least) about any/all ethnography, done "at home" as well as "away."

With respect to the whys of travel, study, observation, authenticity—a term that seems close in meaning to "the true"—and knowledge about others, all operated, as Trinh might say, "from the center," Caren Kaplan (1996) offers up a rich set of possibilities in her recent book, *Questions of Travel: Postmodern Discourses of Displacement,* where she critically interrogates the notions and images of travel and displacement that have seemed to define the Euro-American "modern." Kaplan (1996, x) says that like most modern westerners, she herself "was brought up to believe that distance gives needed perspective, that difference leads to insight, and that travel is quite figuratively 'broadening.'" At the same time, she admits that travel "can be confusing, distance can be illusory, and difference depends very much on one's point of view." She wants to draw on the bourgeois familiarity with and desire for "travel" to bring up a set of issues that usually remain in the shadows: travel's links to "a more postmodern moment of destabilized nation-states, cultural and economic diasporas, and increasing disparities of wealth and power" (xi). She notes, not surprisingly, that some of the students exposed to her analysis complain that she has "ruined" their "next vacation," for these latter questions, and others like them, are never part of travel brochures and, in general, are rarely juxtaposed with the "fun" and "broadening" that "travel" is said to provide to relatively affluent moderns. Certainly, these were not matters that I had considered at my initial sojourn to and life in China. Moreover, none of my mid-twentieth-century U.S. training in academic sociology had encouraged me to consider them as relevant to my professional interests.

Although much of Kaplan's analysis is of travel writing, literary criticism, postmodern cultural theory, and feminist theory, I read her discussion of self-imposed exile, nostalgia, and tourism as having a lot of resonance for my critical reconsideration not only of "Why China?" but also for much that defines conventional ethnography and sociology practice. First, there are her comments, drawing on Renato Rosaldo's critique of the violence in what he calls "imperialist nostalgia" (quoted in Kaplan 1996, 34). Unlike (but also like) a longing for (re-membered) experiences from a person's childhood, imperialist nostalgia emerges from a history of cultural domination and is hardly innocent. At its heart, of course, is a paradox: one's own "group" has destroyed, changed irreparably, or otherwise altered practices and persons of another "group" or place, only to mourn these losses and the change that has resulted. This mourning sets off an endless but finally futile search to assuage it. The paradox provides an ideological discourse that disconnects those who now mourn this loss from an appreciation of their own "collective and personal responsibility" for and implication in this loss.

Euro-American moderns thus often look to "the past" by looking to another country or culture where this "lost" reality and authenticity might be found, due to its "difference" (read "less-developed state") from the life at the center/s. Kaplan quotes Dean MacCannell from his book, *The Tourist: A New Theory of the Leisure Class* (1976), to say that "For moderns, reality and authenticity are thought to be elsewhere: in other [past] historical periods and other [older] cultures, in purer, simpler lifestyles" (Kaplan 1996, 34–35). Of course, anthropologists are familiar with such claims as part of their self-critique, which has been central to the development of postcolonial criticism. Sociologist-ethnographers may be able to avoid interpellation here, thinking it all has to do only with those whose objects of study exist "far away" in time and/or space. But "the field" need not be so distant, nor travel so far for these characterizations to interest us. And although just what "modern" might mean is often quite open, the human/social sciences and (techno)science more generally would seem surely to qualify (but see Latour 1993).

As I read Kaplan about writers who see actual if not self-imposed exile to a place away from "home" as a requirement for aesthetic and even realist insight, I could hear familiar descriptions of the importance of "making strange" that which is familiar to the sociologist who studies people and practices "at home." We already have alluded to the importance of distance between the object of study and the analyst/scientist for the conventional practices of scientific realism, and I read Kaplan's critique of the fantasies of distance and separation for "clear" vision into the quality of literary texts as quite relevant to me and to those practices.[2] Says Kaplan: "When detachment is the precondition for creativity, then disaffection or alienation as states of mind become a rite of passage for the 'serious' modern artist or writer. The modernist seeks to recreate the effect of statelessness—whether or not the writer is, literally, in exile" (36). It is, she says, precisely the accomplishment of "exilic displacement" for the "modern writer" and, arguably, the social scientist/ethnographer, that legitimates a "point of view" and casts him or her into a desired "professional domain." For the ethnographer, of course, it is the peculiar combination of being both "up close" to "the real" and "far away" at the same time, in a "field" set off from "home" that is so strikingly seductive.[3] And in Kaplan's discussion of Euro-American literary criticism of mid-century, I could read lines strikingly similar to Clough's (1998, 15–28) and others' criticism of masculine realist narrativity as central to the ethnographic genre: "[Self-]Exilic perspective becomes a vocation and a virtue, a reminder that writers with 'great vision' take us with them through the shoals of loss and, having paid a terrible price, will lead us back into the safe harbour of reunion. A return is always possible in the distant future . . . but assimilation is never represented as conducive to literary production" (Kaplan 1996, 37). To "go native," then, is to lose completely one's professional credentials and (masculine) subjectivity. Writing of Malcolm Cowley's (1982) *Exile's Return: A Literary Odyssey of the 1920s*, Kaplan notes just how gendered (masculine) the trope of expatriation and authorship as exile in such work is and how central it is to "imperialist nostalgia—the melancholic quest for substance while erasing or violating the object of concern" (45).

Another theme from Kaplan's discussion that has more than passing resonance to the now-accumulated critique of ethnography and to broader themes central to much interpretive and symbolic interactionist sociology as well is what she calls the "hypervaluation . . . of 'experience'" (46). As we know, "being there" is absolutely central to the authority of the conventional ethnographic eye/I and the credibility of what it sees (indeed, to securing the place of the I of "us all"). That I would "be on the ground in 'China'" in 1985 seemed central to the imagined gain, the worth, of what I could see and tell about, what I could "get." Identifying such travel as tourism—a term usually abhorred by the serious scholar at work as irrelevant to what he or she is doing "there"—Kaplan draws again on MacCannell: "The value of 'such things as programs, trips, courses, reports, articles, shows, conferences, parades, opinions, events, sights, spectacles, scenes and situations of modernity' are determined by 'the quality and quantity of experience they promise'" (quoted in Kaplan 1996, 46). And that which is prized above all else as object, there, of course, is the experience of "otherness." With this focus on experience of the other, Cowley's modern expatriates "see 'others' or 'otherness' but do not yet divine their own role as actors in the production of the world they believe they are simply observing" (quoted in Kaplan 1996, 47). While I do not want to understate the extent to which what is being called "new ethnography" in sociology and the human sciences has repudiated this sort of unreflective and nonreflexive position, I also feel sure that it remains quite secure and, for the most part, unacknowledged in (at least) more than a few "methodology courses" in "modern" graduate programs in sociology around the world, not to mention in some recently published ethnographies. Like the authors of the realist novel of the nineteenth century, and the "classic" anthropological ethnographies of colonialism, this genre of Euro-American travel writing is quite explicitly gendered male (Kaplan 1996, 54).

While my own apparent but initially unrecognized search for some sort of "rootedness" and identity in the "more fundamental" family relationships in China clearly moved under or through the discourse, "the sign," of "research" and a search for "knowledge," its nostalgia seems to have been a mix of just the sort of things that Kaplan and those whose writing she critiques here address. My disdain for the "market" and the "modern" in China, registered superficially in reactions to what I and other "visiting scholars" called "rampant commercialism," "ugly clutter," "McDonaldism," and "no respect for their own past" seems, arguably, to be part of the sorts of remarkable tourist reactions Kaplan describes. Similarly, Rey Chow (1993, 1–10) notes the rather incredible criticisms from some Western scholars disappointed that modern Chinese art and literature are simply "not Chinese enough" for them; not sufficiently authentic. These reactions are precisely what Rosaldo means by "imperialist nostalgia." This reminds me of my almost breathless excitement at the prospect of getting "inside" the private if not secret domains of "ordinary Chinese family life," where the fantasy of this sought-for authenticity might be realized (see Kaplan, 59–61). "For the tourist," says Kaplan, "a souvenir or photograph, developing relationships with indigenous people, documenting customs, manners, and landscapes, or learning a language will serve to mark the portals of 'entrance' into the 'authentic'" (60). Once this authentic past is secured and materialized (including its representation in printed texts), it then can be what Donald Horne, in *The Great Museum: The Re-Presentation of History* (1984), has called "museumized" and commodified for repeat visits and use (see Kaplan, 59).

Finally, in an elaboration of Erving Goffman's insights about "front" and "back stage" social spaces and the performances they occasion, MacCannell differentiates the kinds of penetrations of the other space, in search for the authentic, that tourists and many ethnographers and sociologists hope for. Kaplan represents MacCannell:

> [S]tage 1 is the front region, the "kind of social space tourists attempt to overcome or get behind"; stage 2 is a touristic front region that appears to resemble a back region, even deliberately decorated as a back region for "atmosphere"; stage 3 is a front region that openly simulates a back region (this is the most

ambiguous stage); stage 4 refers to a back region that is "open to outsiders"; stage 5 is a back region that is organized in recognition of visits from tourists; and stage 6 is the ultimate social space that motivates the traveler's imaginary, the ideal, uncontaminated back region. (60)

It is of course to this last space that the tourist, and, arguably, the theorist/analyst as well seek free access. For the theorist not only wants to "see the sights" but, in effect, "to possess them and his fellow sightseers through his superior knowledge" (63). Kaplan notes that such searchers often develop a sharp eye for what they see as "'false' back regions," set up by locals to thwart just such penetrating vision. She adds that the difficulty of discerning one sort of region from the other "only adds to the intensity of the quest." This is indeed a familiar story.

Of course, it is possible that my readings of myself and my earlier ethnographic practices are vulnerable not only to charges of idiosyncrasy but incompetence. My seeing myself in Kaplan's characterizations may be due to my own misunderstanding of what "real ethnography" is and my sloppy "methods" for doing it. Perhaps the entire project here is due to that. While I cannot, finally, be the one to speak to these questions, I would claim that the relays I felt between this criticism of modern tourism and travel writing and my memory of "why?" relative to China, family caregiving, and filiality—and to my position as a "qualitative," or "symbolic interactionist fieldworker"—have a historical specificity and location outside me and, as such, can be a legitimate part of the current critique of human science work. What Kaplan urges, given this kind of critique of ethnography, in particular, is that since we write to represent we cannot imagine our work as other than central to questions of power, but we must ask ourselves "What kind of power? Exercised in what ways? to whose benefit? and to whose loss?" (61). Frankly, I also was not thinking of such matters when I began my travel to "China," although I was, certainly, "interested" in them.

*****

There was traveling of a different sort also to be done in this project that, increasingly, confounded the familiar assumptions and fantasies just discussed. Avery Gordon (1990, 495) writes helpfully of a movement, a displacement that can occur in the psychoanalytic encounter between analyst and client:

An acknowledgment in the transferential relations in any analytic encounter suggests that our field is often not what we thought it was—that the real is subject to

and is the subject of reversals, displacements, and overdeterminations, that the
real is just (but not only) a powerful and fascinating story. . . . If the fields that
are bound up and continuous with (the fields that overdetermine) any analytic
encounter are not just other academic fields . . . then the "real story" is always
a negotiated interruption. Traversing fields, the story must emerge out of the field
of forces that really attract and distract the story-teller.

Like Gordon's (1990) writing of her own distractions by a ghost, the
"real" story in this book has been disturbed and displaced—but, certainly,
not erased—by attempts to listen to and take account of things that usually are excluded from sociological storytelling and ethnography, not to
mention storied masculine lives. Gordon suggests to ethnographers and
sociologists that the analytic encounter she references has something to
tell us about the encounter between the ethnographer and the people and
situations she or he encounters in "the field/s" and in the writing that
follows and accompanies them.

What started out more than ten years ago as an imagined fairly straightforward, real sociological story about family caregiving as collective work
managed by adult children in the shifting space of an urban Chinese city,
quickly got very complicated. You might say it became a space crowded
by ghosts, most of which were not peculiar to Joseph or to any single
person. The more Joseph wrote, while reading, elsewhere, of the power
of reflexivity and the crises surrounding representation, reality, and the
telling of others' lives, the more haunted that space became. The more he
tried to say what he meant about giving care, about caring, caring for—or
what he thought he or the words and phrases he used (or used him)
meant—the more he had to write in order to get this meaning "right." The
more he wrote, the more he knew he had to write, toward selves he was
only beginning to "see" or hear and about meanings that wouldn't "hold
still" where he had put them. Truly, sometimes it felt more like torment
than haunting. At others, the ambivalence, uncertainty, multiplicity, and
openness have offered the most fulsome pleasures.[4] It is in the context of
these appreciations that the "old-fashioned essay" that our reviewer wanted
JS to write here came to seem both impossible (itself a fantasy?) and, for
me, dishonest (a word that should be put under Derrida's "erasure," never
to be used as though it were fully possible and unproblematic).

And while I do not want to make conversations with the ghosts of
mainstream or "modern" sociology a centerpiece of this writing, in trying
to link this text to current discussions of the place and nature of ethnography in the human sciences (the familiar professional move), it seems
important to acknowledge how productive the hauntings by those ghosts,

and our ongoing encounters with them, have been for this project. More-over, those encounters have not been unlike similar encounters with "the (Chinese) family," with filiality, Oedipus, "tradition," hegemonic mascu-linity, feminism, and science. Indeed, all of these ghosts or families of ghosts have haunted this text and much other current work in sociology and beyond. This implies, quite rightly, that continued movement in eth-nography and sociology today must *negotiate* its way in fields more nu-merous and diverse than its conventional or mainstream forms are usually prepared to acknowledge or allow, including, of course, those very con-ventional forms, practices, and subjects themselves. This "negotiate," here and by Gordon, should not be read to mean "persuade," "becalm," "con-vince," "overcome," or "get through unchanged." It definitely does not imply a unity or harmony or "integration." Similarly, rather than think of this movement in fields as enabling a "going beyond" or "filling in gaps" or offering something "new"—favorite modern phrases—it seems prefer-able to be more modest; to think in terms of how what we do opens up ways of seeing and thinking that can or might then become productive, making possible yet more movement and re-positioning to places "else-where," but which resists reinscribing domination under the sign of the "postmodern" (cf. Kaplan 1996, 65–100), which is precisely what some of its feminist critics have warned about. This is about not only how we might do sociology and ethnography differently, but how the subjects of these doings—those very "we's"—must, necessarily, also change in the process and in ways we cannot exactly see.

But my enthusiasms for the "posts-" might be heard by some to come too close to ignoring morality and ethics since it seems sometimes to suggest that movement itself—the loved/hated deconstructive "play"—is to be privileged above all else, neglecting the question of which of the many possible "movements," "openings," "linkages"—themselves surely not neutral words—might be preferable, even if only temporarily so. Which of these are worth pursuing, worth living/working for? Although this can bring us to a full stop—there are so many, and "choosing" one can be risky in all sorts of ways (professionally and "personally")—we cannot avoid making such selections, such "cuts" or "inscriptions," as Clough (1998, xxiii) has called them, even if we want to. And "morality" and "ethics" complicate the plural pronoun itself, making "we" immediately problematic for the violence it so easily can do to movement and differ-ence (in truth, so even within an "I"). What morality? Whose ethics? Where and when? What kinds of subjects of what kinds of sociologies and ethnographies might we want to encourage and perform?

*****

The feminist critic of science Donna Haraway writes as one who cannot afford to ignore morality and ethics, but as one who also appreciates much about the de-centering moves in the reading and writing technologies I have been calling "post-." What makes Haraway's work so relevant to the recent debates around the future of ethnography and, at least, sociology is this simultaneous embrace of explicit attention to the morality and ethics of our "professional" positioning even as she calls for a seriously humble yet "strongly objective" presence that yearns to embody something she calls, after Sandra Harding, "a successor science."

Haraway has written much sharply insightful and critical analysis of the workings of science and technology—or, what she calls "technoscience," thus marking their inseparability—in the late twentieth century. Although she and her science-studies colleagues seem often to take the natural sciences and cybernetics as their prime topics of study, I long have read this work as being "about" sociology too, a move I take to be consistent with these authors' arguments and intentions. After all, we sociologists have fashioned ourselves, for better or worse, as social *scientists*. And Haraway (1997) endorses this reading in her most recent book, *Modest_Witness@Second_Millennium. FemaleMan©_Meets_Oncomouse™: Feminism and Technoscience*.

She takes up, among other questions, the practice of reflexivity as a resource to help those who study science and knowledge production move away from both what she calls, after Sharon Traweek, the "culture of no culture" and the so-called masculine "modest" witness that define modern science as cultural practice and subjectivity, on the one hand, and the agonistic, struggle- and war-framed metaphors of some of the "best" recent work in science studies, on the other. For Haraway, the problem with this latter work, most notably represented by Bruno Latour's (1987) *Science in Action* and some other actor-network writing, is that while it has masterfully made visible the "modest" figure of the detached, objective scientist thought to be the transparent medium who operates "the scientific method" to uncover and convey the facts and truths of nature, it draws all too heavily as resource on the very figures and practices, the very stories, that it takes as its topic. As she puts it, "The story told is told by the same story. . . . It is the only game imagined" (Haraway 1997, 34). And this is a familiar story indeed: of male heroic action on the battlefields of "Man's" progress in the strategic but very serious games of knowing and appropriating "nature" in the entwined stories of the West.

Haraway, seemingly never at a loss for the brilliantly critical phrase, calls this "heterosexual epistemological erotics" (33).[5]

For the antiracist feminist Haraway, "The self-contained quality of all this is stunning. It is the self-contained power of the culture of no culture itself, where all the world is in the sacred image of the Same" (1997, 35). It is not the sort of game she would choose to figure her vision of a different sort of science, one that would break free of the "culture of no culture" and heroic stories of allies, struggles, enrollments, wars, and victors as the measure of the truth of such a science in the "Second Christian Millennium," a characterization that she does not intend in praise of this religious referent, which she takes to be typically ever-present but also unspoken and thus given. Moreover, she argues, these stories (re)enact worlds after their own images. A critical analysis of science done with this science turns out to be not quite critical enough.

But neither is Haraway persuaded that the kind of radical reflexivity encouraged by Steve Woolgar, Latour's co-author in the early and impor-tant ethnography of scientists at the bench, *Laboratory Life: The Social Construction of Scientific Facts,* offers much help toward a desired suc-cessor science. Although Latour and Woolgar (1979) worked together in the earlier book, they since have parted ways on this question of the utility of "extreme" reflexivity, the former seeing it as an infinite regress that always "return[s] the boring thinking mind to the [center] stage" (Latour 1988, 173). Woolgar, by contrast, has become a leading champion of radical reflexivity within science studies and has offered friendly but telling criticism of selective relativism in social constructionist arguments both within and outside that specialty. In these arguments, Woolgar says that the reflexivity and relativism have been "gerrymandered" to serve the interests of the analysis, which, he insists, is also subject to the deconstructive force of its own arguments (see Woolgar and Pawluch 1985; Woolgar 1988b; Grint and Woolgar 1995). It is another case, he might say, using Haraway's metaphor, which she borrows from Shapin and Schaffer (1985), of the "modest" witness disappearing from the scene of knowledge production in order to effect the telling of truth. He who makes knowledge cannot appear in this story.

At the heart of his call for a thoroughgoing reflexivity in the study of how knowledge is done, Woolgar holds a very bright light on the process of representation, which is considered by some today to be beset by cri-sis. To speak about representation, of course, is to speak about some-thing that is hardly peculiar to science. Rather, representation—to re-present—is a thoroughly mundane and ubiquitous routine in any language/

meaning-relevant practice involving beings, both human and nonhuman. It is about, says Woolgar (1988a, 30), "the means by which we generate images (reflections, representations, reports) of the object 'out there.'" To get a sense of just how mundane this particular game is, he might have added "talk" to his list of images, after Melvin Pollner's (1987) early insights into this problem for sociology. For to "talk about" some thing is to take the thing talked about as in fact there to be talked about, or, at the least, to offer it up as a candidate for such object-hood (and see Garfinkel 1967, 31–34).

Woolgar links representation closely to another idea (and object!) that has become anathema to constructionist writers in human studies, including feminism, cultural studies, and virtually all of the "post-" positionings: essentialism. Stripping his discourse to the essentials, he says that this "is the idea that discrete objects exist independent of our perception of them" (1988a, 30). There are, of course, important specifications of this notion of essentialism that Woolgar's definition leaves out, but he wants to argue that what almost all constructionist and related critiques of science and knowledge production practices leave out is a thoroughgoing deconstruction of their own reliance on what he calls "the ideology of representation." This surely would be a criticism he might make of Latour, just as Haraway does.

The problem to which this ideology is connected, says Woolgar, is that we can never be sure that the thing we take to stand in for the absent ("lost"?) object—that which we "speak"/write about—is a true, valid, proper representative of that object itself (as though, of course, there were an "object itself," a view Haraway [1997, 136–137] characterizes as "a fetish"). The connection that representation makes between mark and object, between signifier and signified, is always haunted, it seems, (at least) by the question: what is the warrant for the link proposed? And anxiety here is only heightened by the fundamental constructionist or interpretive point that the representation, reading, marking, perception, record, report, indicator, and so on might be other than it is. In short, multiplicity and variability in such inscriptions over time, place, observing machine, observer—the very stuff of relativism—make us doubt essentialism and the ideology of representation even more. That this dilemma is reminiscent of Derrida's (1976) famous discussion of deconstruction and logocentrism is of course not by chance. In science we are very much in a game of language/meaning/writing, not to mention subjectivity and desire. These all must be explicitly a part of Haraway's figure of a truly modest witness.

Once one begins to walk down the constructionist *and* deconstructive path, to think this way, these and other of what Woolgar calls "methodological horrors" surely will be met.[6] Moreover, once these horrors have been encountered and their ubiquity in and implications for any sort of analysis are appreciated, it is very difficult simply to retrace one's steps back to a ground that is safe and solid enough to support the old epistemology-ontology dualism, although the powers of denial are, as we know, amazingly resilient. This, surely, is one source of the fear that engaging such questions can, might, lead to silence, which of course has its own associated subject-ive terrors (and see Pollner 1991).

For there is a third element that defines this ideology of representation that remains in the shadows (itself a familiar metaphor here) in order for the machine to work: the agent of representation himself or herself; the one who effects the connection that is said to exist "in fact," "in nature," between the object there and its mark here. Haraway names this figure "the Wizard of Oz," and the name does seem apt. He is of course the "modest" witness of conventional scientific practice. But, it's you and I, too; doing science or not. Please remember the ubiquity of this game of re-presentation.

Woolgar rightly anticipates the question—and has faced it in fact more than a few times—of why one would want to embrace such a criticism and the kinds of writing technologies that might flow from it. First, it is important to see that in joining his problematic we will not be speaking about "solutions." That's the wrong question altogether, which is part of his sense that the dilemma is not a moral problem, that is, not something "bad" to be done away with or hidden in the closet. It simply is. And, he says, if we want to appreciate the implications of "discourse" for social analysis, we cannot become embroiled in hopeless attempts to get outside it to "the real," as though discourse itself were somehow not real.[7]

From the above and many other recent critiques of science, it seems clear that the hope of an Archimedian point outside language/meaning and representation is a discredited fantasy.[8] Rather, Woolgar invites us to pursue this issue in the spirit of an "interrogation" of representation rather than trying either to explain it (or any thing) or escape it (1988a, 94). After more than a decade of making this argument, Woolgar (Grint and Woolgar 1995, 302) recently has written, in a tone of exasperation, that we might, following Kant's suggestion, *sapere aude* or "dare to know" or see the workings of our own hands in the making of our worlds. If there is a god or goddess in "the machine" of our various technologies, including our writing technologies, that brings us the truth and solution/salvation, we surely have put it there.[9]

Second, given the centrality of representation and essentialism to our mundane lives—and our general obliviousness to these workings—Woolgar argues that these are themselves a fitting topic (object!) for study. In a discussion of ethnography as a recently much-used research strategy in science studies, he distinguishes what he calls "instrumental" from "reflexive" ethnographies, and especially encourages the latter (1988a, 91–94). Instrumental ethnographies—while perhaps providing valuable insights or "news" with which to challenge dominant (and, it is usually assumed, flawed) understandings of the object—are those that keep the analysts' own world-making practices in the shadows. If we are interested primarily in the ways of knowledge and truth, such ethnography stops short of this aim; it still is operated by the "modest" Wizard of Oz, behind the screen (or, inside the "black box") of representation.[10]

With reflexive ethnography, ways of knowing, believing, and of course persuading—our own no less than others'—are themselves the primary objects for study. This involves more than appreciating the importance of the "rhetoric of inquiry" in making a particular (disciplined) inquiry "better." While the instrumental ethnographer would want to tell, for instance, "what the Arawak are really like," Woolgar insists:

> [T]here is more to ethnography than just showing what, say, the Arawak are really like. . . . Nor is the intention to add this piece of collected culture to a stockpile of stories about other "primitive" peoples. . . . Nor, again, is the point to use a picture of the Arawak to speak to theoretical concerns about the character of primitive peoples in general. Instead, the strategic value of reflexive ethnography is that it provides an occasion for reflecting upon, and perhaps reaching a greater understanding of, those aspects of our own culture which we tend to take for granted. . . . *[T]he critical target is our own ability to construct objectivities through representation.* These representational activities include *the ability to adduce evidence, make interpretations, decide relevance, attribute motives, categorize, explain, understand and so on.* (1988a, 92–93; emphasis added)

For Woolgar, such stories of the very process of knowing are the "most useful" ones we might tell. They constitute, he says finally, given the intimate connection between representation and writing, "an ethnography of the text" and textualization. And given his earlier discussions of the benefits to sociology and ethnomethodology of taking referential or "radical" reflexivity seriously, Pollner (1987, 1991) would seem to agree.

But for Haraway, the antiracist, feminist, and socialist critic of technoscience, this is not enough. She accepts Woolgar's critique but wants more. She does not discount the importance of reflexivity's disturbing attention to representation, or its revelations about the enormously important figure of the "modest" witness who operates it. In fact, quite the opposite. It is possible to read a very strong resonance between Haraway's criticism and Woolgar's more narrow focus on the agent of representation (see especially, Haraway 1997, 23–25, and her discussion of gene fetishism, 144). But after you tell us that epistemology is dead, that all knowledge claims are relative and contingent, that all the objects we try to know about are inseparable from our ways of knowing them— that ontology, too, is problematic—what more, Haraway seems to ask, will you say? It is full reflexivity's repeated ending with itself, in an ongoing deconstruction of attempts, Woolgar might say, to "get somewhere," that Haraway finds to be, finally, more of the Same. For her, this relativism is the twin opposite of the familiar totalizing discourses of science. Both are enemies of the kind of stories and attendant figures Haraway would urge us to write and speak.

Her reading is that Woolgar's position leaves all knowledge claims as "equal," which is to say equally contingent, and that his silence on what to make of this is an abdication of responsibility that long has defined the culture of no culture of conventional science. Even Woolgar is thus a much too "modest" witness to enable us to engage him in his *own* local, situated, and surely noninnocent knowledge games; this "self-vision as the cure for self-invisibility" is a "cure," Haraway says, that too much resembles the "disease" it aims to resist (33). Whereas Woolgar sees some of his constructivist and feminist colleagues suffering a "failure of nerve" in their hesitance to embrace a full reflexivity, Haraway says that it is Woolgar and the position he encourages that are all too timid. Where, after all, is *he* in all this, his *own* "game"? She solicits the figure of a credible *mutated* modest witness of knowledge who will dare not only to know, but to know from a particular *body*, in a *place*, at a *time*; "for" some worlds and not for others. For Haraway, to dare fully to know is thus truly risky business.

Rather than Woolgar's version of reflexivity, Haraway prefers Sandra Harding's "critical reflexivity" and "strong objectivity"; Deborah Heath's "modest interventions"; and her own "situated knowledges" as ways toward, as she puts it, "another e-mail address" (1997, 36, 45). She collects these preferred meanings in the metaphor of "diffraction" to help focus her desire for a new kind of science and knowledge. "The point," she says,

> is *to make a difference in the world, to cast our lot for some ways of life and not others*. To do that, one must be in the action, be finite and dirty, not transcendent and clean. Knowledge-making technologies, including crafting subject positions and ways of inhabiting such positions, must be made relentlessly visible and open to critical intervention. (36; emphasis added)

You have to *care about* the worlds or possible worlds that your own work, your own *kind* of work, is making. You cannot be "clean"; you must be "in the action," for, of course, you always already are. You cannot be on the "side-lines," un-related. It is an all-too-familiar place for social scientists. There is no Archimedian point, no innocent vision; no eavesdropping device by which to "listen in" without implication on the conversations of lives actually lived. The positions you take up/that make you up "must be made relentlessly visible" and open to critique.

Diffraction and troping cause things to change course, to swerve, but according to what visions, and in what directions? Although a fan of hypertext and the endless linking it privileges, Haraway warns that "Communication and articulation disconnected from yearning toward possible worlds does not make enough sense" to warrant this practice. The problem, she says, is that this technology does "not suggest which connections make sense for which purposes and which patches we might want to follow or avoid" (1997, 127). But it does bring us to the edge of the question. If we can make "all possible connections," or, at least all of those that are possible within the given net before us, rather only than those convention would suggest, then what choices shall we make? For whom? Toward what ends, and with what consequences? We might even begin to think about possible worlds outside the net itself.[11]

Haraway draws on bell hooks's notion of "yearning" to help her embody this point. Yearning is as much about one's heart and soul as about one's head; it is about feeling, desire, longing . . . for "barely possible worlds," often long-denied; worlds where the "modern" metaphors of freedom and justice, and a reduction of human suffering, are still alive and well. She and hooks want us to hold onto these figures, not as "putative Enlightenment foundations" (Haraway 1997, 191) but rather as bright beacons from serious yearning for what might be possible. Please remember. She is talking about science, and, by extension, social science, and sociology. She wants us to ask ourselves how our work, our ethnographies, go beyond reflection and self-visibility to help tell altered, "material and semiotic" stories that seek to make better worlds for living beings. This storytelling is a modest intervention, she says, but one well worth making: *to see our sociological ways of telling stories as always a doing, an un-doing, a re-doing of worlds* (45; and see Game 1991).

A fundamental difference between Woolgar and Haraway here is that she wants us still to see science, a successor science, and the kinds of situated knowledges it might produce as "worth living for," as worth doing, even after she has taken quite seriously the sort of critique Woolgar makes. Woolgar, by contrast, says that an ongoing deconstruction/

interrogation of science and its core metaphors of true knowledge and reality and the "self" in representation—what one might call a "critical wide-awakeness" toward these doings—is all that is possible, and, presumably, also worth living for—although, importantly, he never says so.

Although he, too, insists that claims of certain knowledge—epistemology—are no longer possible, Woolgar may have enclosed himself within just the space that he takes as his target of deconstruction. We might say that he is still haunted by the ghost of the epistemology/ontology that he has deconstructed. Since certain knowledge has been deconstructed, all that is left for us is to interrogate how we still strive, always unsuccessfully, for certain knowledge (see Grint and Woolgar 1995, 302). It is as though if one wants to speak, to think, about producing true knowledge, we must speak only from within the space that has denied its possibility, a space that itself seems to be "owned" by the progeny of Boyle's "modest" witness.[12] It is indeed a well-known "e-mail address."

But Haraway, unlike Woolgar, is not concerned with certain knowledge or its impossibility. She speaks repeatedly of "strong knowledge claims," after Harding's notion of "strong objectivity"; and "situated, local knowledges." These are not about certainty, closure, and universalism; and they definitely do not refer primarily to the hermetic operations of the seminar room and the culture of the Same.

> To see scientific knowledge as located and heterogeneous practice, which might (or might not) be "global" and "universal" in specific ways rooted in ongoing articulatory activities that are always potentially open to critical scrutiny from disparate perspectives, is to adopt the worldly stance of situated knowledges. . . . From the standpoint of situated knowledge, strong objectivity—reliable, partially shareable, trope-laced, worldly, accountable, noninnocent, knowledge—can be a fragile human achievement. (1997, 137–138)

Part of a barely possible world she yearns for, this knowledge would be relevant for what she calls worldly human collective projects of freedom, justice, and democracy; against domination and racism, that require commitment, responsibility for one's witnessing, and an always open engagement of contestation and critique. This is a space of risk, which, she says, should be the space of ethnography itself:

> [T]o study technoscience [and "human science"?] requires an immersion in worldly material-semiotic practices, where the analysts, as well as the humans and non-humans studied, are all at risk—morally, politically, technically, and epistemologically. "Ethnography," in this extended sense, is not so much a specific procedure in anthropology as it is a method of being at risk in the face of the practices and

discourses into which one inquires. To be at risk is not the same thing as identifying with the subjects of study; quite the contrary. And self-identity is as much at risk as the temptation to identification. One is at risk in the face of serious nonidentity that challenges previous stabilities, convictions, or ways of being of many kinds. An "ethnographic attitude" can be adopted within any kind of inquiry, including textual analysis. Not limited to a specific discipline, an ethnographic attitude is a mode of practical and theoretical attention, a way of remaining mindful and accountable. Such a method is not about "taking sides" in a predetermined way. But it is about risks, purposes, and hopes—one's own and others'—embedded in knowledge projects. (1997, 190–191)

And it is a space where the word "commitment"—it is such a powerful word—and hooks's "yearning" are as important as "deconstruction." But how to put these together—yearning, commitment, and deconstruction? Remember, Haraway talks about barely possible worlds and how our stories might help bring them about (or not). She wants us, in these stories, to look into the mirror, perhaps more carefully than usual, in the hope that you will see something more than, something different from, the Same that mirrors so readily help us always to see. To look in the "mirror" and see some other thing. She wants us to think seriously about metaphors other than the mirror and, perhaps, of connectors or links defined in terms other than sight (I think of Trinh's suggestion of "listening nearby").

By contrast, Woolgar's recommendation for reflexive ethnography seems to stop short of the words "commitment" and "yearning" and the images they conjure. With him, we still are very "clean" in our reflexive ethnographies of representation and essentialism. In a defense against the charge that a fully reflexive constructionism leaves us unable to choose among competing knowledge claims, where all claims are "equal"—which is to say they all are equally contingent and "relative" in their un/certainty—Grint and Woolgar insist this is in error. But what they say in defense of their view speaks volumes in the context of what Haraway says about the kind of work they and we typically do.

They deny the claim that a "strict" or fully reflexive constructionism leaves one with no grounds for choosing among claims. This is simply wrong, for "The constructivist does not assert that all claims have equal status; instead he or she asks which claims attract the most significant support and why?" (Grint and Woolgar 1995, 302). For those intimate with constructionism's theoretical warrants, this is indeed a familiar position. But this is a disappointing response; and it leaves me sympathetic with Haraway's desire for more. Following Woolgar's earlier writing and criticism, John Kitsuse and I have argued for just the sort of position Woolgar here offers, what we called "strict constructionism" to mark it as different from the "contextual constructionism" many were writing in social problems theory. In short, we chided our colleagues for a "failure of nerve" at the precipice of what Grint and Woolgar here call "post-essentialism" (see Kitsuse and Schneider 1989). In Grint and Woolgar's version, it is the analyst's job to ask which claims succeed and why, treating all claims as, in principle, equally worthy or not. No longer can one adjudicate knowledge claims, as in conventional science, based on empirical evidence about the object in question. The analyst is "on the sidelines," clean; above the "dirty" action. While these constructionist claims might deconstruct the "naturalness" of entrenched and powerful truths long endorsed as "the way things are," Haraway is right to find them wanting as a worthy example of her successor science. It seems, simply, too much of more of the Same. It does accomplish some important things, but they are not enough.

   Grint and Woolgar say that the claim that social change requires an epistemological realism might best be understood as a pragmatic appreciation of the power of the "rhetoric of truth" in these knowledge games people play. But, they add, there is ample evidence that truth and realism are no "guarantee" of the desired conduct or change. Perhaps realism confines us to a politics that sees criticism as the only viable form of political action: "non-criticism is all too easily identified with a lack of politics" (305). Perhaps we should think about "an alternative form of politically relevant inquiry," they suggest; one "that moves us beyond merely political radicalism." They apparently mean this as a gesture toward the radicalism of a full reflexivity and a politics that it might enact. But just what that might look like is indeed unclear . . . or all too familiar.

   They end their discussion by returning to the question of what any particular technology or "thing" really is, saying:

> What the [a] thing actually is . . . is not something that any kind of detached, objective, or realist analysis seems capable of constructing. What it is depends on who is describing it, although not every account of it is equal: self-evidently, the eco-feminist account is not powerful enough to persuade political leaders completely to abandon the technology [in question]. But this is precisely why post-essentialism can provide resources for those seeking to change the world rather than just account for it. If Foucault is right that truth and power are intimately intertwined, then those seeking to change the world might try strategies to recruit powerful allies rather than assuming that the quest for revealing the truth will, in and of itself, lead to dramatic changes in levels and forms of social inequality. (Grint and Woolgar 1995, 306)

So, here the circle is closed, or perhaps we should say connected to precisely the metaphor that Haraway has turned away from: Woolgar seems to have "returned" to Latour and the actor-network images of science in action as an agonistic contest of struggle, of victors and vanquished; of power and allies, with the analysts themselves once again transparent. Almost as an afterthought, Grint and Woolgar close by saying, in effect, that we here should take heart. If the world is, after all, made up, we can strive to make up new worlds more to our liking. But, sadly, they never use "we"; they never include themselves in this serious game of yearning for such worlds. This inclusion, which is at the very heart of Haraway's anxiety and hope for another and "better" e-mail address in the Second Christian Millennium. For the mutated modest witness she imagines, "we" is the operative and crucial pronoun, tenuous and always fraught as it is. We cannot look for a god or goddess in any machine to save us, to stand behind our serious claims about the world and the true stories we try to tell about others. We must take her notion of witnessing quite seriously:

> Witnessing is seeing; attesting; standing publicly accountable for, and psychically vulnerable to, one's visions and representations. Witnessing is a collective, limited practice that depends on the constructed and never finished credibility of those who do it, all of whom are mortal, fallible, and fraught with the consequences of unconscious and disowned desires and fears. (Haraway 1997, 267)

We must ask ourselves—and speak publicly about—what our commitments are or, perhaps more to the point, might be; and for what we yearn in the sociology and ethnography that we do. Our work may or may not "make a difference" in the world by creating difference patterns; we may get stuck in the reflexivity that Woolgar so prizes. But our work should not be free from questions where "you" and "we" always include us and not only them. After all, we ethnographers and critics are "members" too (Schneider 1993b).

*****

Well. That felt dangerously like a closure, didn't it? How to resist these seductive pleasures of unity that come with exhortation and certainty (even, twisting a notion from Spivak, "strategic certainty") about what kind of "science," what kind of sociology/ethnography "'we' should do," given Haraway's spirited and appealing advice? How to shape and pursue work that one hopes—for how else can you think of such an aim—will "make a difference" for "better lives for living beings" in particular worlds? How, also, to turn away from what Clough (2000, 172) names the "autoethnographic and emotional realism" characteristic of some recent developments in ethnography without turning back toward the disappearing and none too modest witness as the one/s who, finally, speaks/writes "knowledge"? On the other hand, how to end here without just stopping? Like so much in this book, "we"[13] too yearn here for things that supposedly are incompatible or contradictory. For instance, Haraway's visions for a successor science that is worth living for but whose contours now can be seen only in faintest outline, on the one hand; pursued with the doubt, distance, anxiety, and openness that an abiding appreciation of the "deconstruct-ability" of one's own position/s (of any and all sorts) always brings, on the other. Passion, caring, commitment, and courage; doubt, modesty, partiality, and self-other criticism and scrutiny.

The figure of contradiction itself can import a logic to be resisted if one is to move in this space/time that Haraway has so forcefully named. Contradiction implies an opposing dualism, a dichotomy in the face of which one cannot have both. You must choose one *or* the other; not *both, and.* But this "both, and" is one of the engines of this book: to ask, repeatedly, "Why not 'both, and'?" Why not true stories that ask no privileged warrant for our attention and consideration; stories that do not have to bear the burden or ultimately impossible mission of vanquishing all contenders so as to be deemed "the one" and only (sounds a bit like hegemonic masculinity, doesn't it)? Why not a successor science or sociology that might scandalize some of its founding fathers and their filial progeny by the very forms its practice and texts can take?

As has been suggested already, the more Joseph read and thought about the radical reflexivity that Woolgar and Pollner describe; and the more he understood what deconstruction and poststructuralism imply about any "ground" or foundation; the more he listened to various (mostly but not exclusively) feminist calls for an ethnography and a sociology that aims to "make a difference" (or "difference patterns") in the world; the more he appreciated what Clough and Gordon might mean by a sociology in which ghosts are taken seriously as relevant to so-called members and analysts alike; and the more he saw in some recent ethnography a return to a realist vision and voice that are unmistakable relatives of standpoint epistemology, and thus, indeed, "more of the Same," the more it seemed to him that the partiality, anxiety, locatedness and contingency that Haraway uses to characterize her figure of a mutated modest witness in knowledge projects, along with Clough's (1998, 2000) hopes for sociology as a "social, cultural criticism" asking no privileged warrant seemed just the places, the "grounds," from which he could, at least momentarily, speak/write.

The "now" in which this particular ending is done does seem to be, at least for some, a time/space "in-between"; constituted more by the temporary and mobile than by certainty and absolute conviction . . . or even absolute commitment.[14] Any attempt to embrace too tightly this "space between" or to "stand there" too long surely teaches just how unstable and unsure it and its subjects are. This is felt as such especially if one desires assurance about how we in the human sciences will work and be "in the future." Although some of us, borrowing Haraway's phrase, may be searching for another e-mail address for our work and lives, this does not imply we can say what that address will be. "Bad neighborhoods," both globally and locally, or, from Clough (2000), "glocally," might be easier to describe than the clearly desirable ones. Indeed, the very notion of "a good place to live" if that implies a "settling down" might be met with some skepticism (cf. Pollner 1991). "Home" and "family" are not, as Haraway's comment in this chapter's epigraphs implies, the operative metaphors in this now, unless of course the versions offered seek to unsettle if not throw into crisis the very meanings those terms have come to have, "here" as well as "there." Trying to imagine and begin to effect queer homes and families is more what this in-betweenness seems to imply, both "in China" and "in the West."

There is much to recommend in Haraway's call for a critical ethnography as "a method of being at risk in the face of the practices and discourses into which one inquires" (1997, 190), a way of working that "is not about 'taking sides' in a predetermined way. . . . [b]ut . . . about risks, purposes, and hopes—one's own and others'—embedded in knowledge projects" (191). Trying "to know about" worlds in the ways she suggests is, and should be, risky; thinking about ethnography as a way of producing a "map" not for describing those worlds but rather for intervening in them in particular, meliorative ways, is an enormous challenge.[15] It may not be quite right for all, surely, but it will work productively for some. And it does seem productive for sociologists and others who long have moved under the sign of "the social *sciences*" to hold onto her mutated modest *witness* as a familiar if sometimes difficult "neighbor." Without denying the potential productivity of the turn to a full poetics as a kind of sociology (e.g., Richardson 1994; and see Denzin 1997, 199–227), and refusing decidedly to treat "data" as an unproblematic term, Haraway insists that *witnessing* is at the center of anything that could be considered a "successor science." "Being there" in or "listening nearby" the worlds and subjects we write and that write us is a part of science practice that I want to retain. But, like Haraway, I want to read this as a blurring and a rejection of the familiar "observation" and "description" as embodiments of this witness without denying the subject/agent of the knowledge produced. To insist on this figure of the witness is to insist on a subject position or agent in knowledge that is always responsible although not, in fact, fully accountable for what she sees, hears, senses, feels, and, finally, conveys about the worlds and lives and others created in the resulting "stories" (which may well not be narratives, per se, as the films of Trinh Minh-ha demonstrate). Fraught and always compromised as it is, we sacrifice too much if we turn away from the aim of telling true stories about the worlds and subjects we fashion. In her trenchant critique of but deep love for the best that science can become, Haraway invites us to imagine what sociology too might become. Such a move also might bring a serious interrogation of what the true itself could become (and, it seems, always already has been).

The only bit in Haraway's vision that I would call "seductive," as in appealing to desires that easily can draw me toward it but that might not, finally, be quite what they seem, is her insistence that our ethnographies and work must "make a difference" in the world. I love the idea and aim but it feels risky to me in a way that is different from the other risks she recommends. Rather than threatening what one already might have, it seems to promise more. Such promises are of course what desire is about, and so, perhaps, especially at this point, we might invoke her notion of modesty to help keep us off center. I manage this moment by looking to Clough for a cooler, perhaps sadder, sensibility about the subjects we are and might publicly become. It is with this hesitation about Haraway's yearning, but stopping well short of the disappearing act that Woolgar effects in his reflexive ethnography, that I would like to end or stop here, in this now.

The desire that our work make living beings' lives better in the worlds we learn from and with uses language that for many academics in the humanities and social sciences is full of a nostalgia that is easily misread as something I think she does not quite say; or, perhaps she does say but that means in multiple, conflicting ways. The left political sympathies of many in Haraway's audience, especially if they came of professional age in the second half of the twentieth-century in the United States, can easily aid an all-too-familiar reading of this phrase, "to make a difference." The fantasied figure of the engaged scholar at "the barricades of revolution" or pressing for "radical social change," fighting against domination, helping subalterns resist—wherever these barricades and subalterns might be and in whatever version they might be materialized—can still make more than a few academic hearts skip a beat. While Haraway does not imply that the kind of politics in the knowledge projects she hopes for can be those of the past—ideologically unified, "community"-based, global, social movement carried, liberal to radical to "Marxist" or in the name of "Woman," and so on—it may be all too easy to convince oneself that, of course, *our* work" does, finally, make the difference in the world toward which she gestures.[16]

The very popularity, dispersion, and work of this phrase "to make a difference" far beyond the critical study of technoscience and knowledge projects makes me uneasy about it as a spoken and heard part of what a different sort of ethnography and human science might be. I am looking at a page from a Sunday newspaper insert that pictures Newt Gingrich and offers his accompanying text, pledging that "It doesn't matter if you're left or right—we can all come together on Make a Difference Day."[17] Gingrich, the text continues, will "tell Make a Difference Day stories" on his daily radio show, "The Age of Possibilities." A series of steps tells readers how they can play a part in the upcoming Make a Difference Day: "You may want to help the elderly, clean up a river; teach children or gather food for the hungry. Act alone or enlist your whole family, club, class, office, or town." And there is a website: www.makeadifference day.com where you can find out more. The full-page advertisement seems to be sponsored by the Coca Cola Company ("Coke is like family. You can never have enough"); and Wal-Mart is a participating company. "Making a difference" clearly does not mean only what Haraway hopes, and this, surely, is not the "different e-mail address" she has in mind.

Yet, it is what this "Make a Difference Day" subject seems to share with Haraway's mutated modest witness who also wants to make a difference that both calls me to it and gives me pause. And it is perhaps this witness as key to any imagined successor science that convinces me not to stray too far from a critical Woolgar-like reflexivity that keeps the writer/ethnographer/sociologist "front and center" in whatever stories are told. Among all those whose work I have read to help me to this place, now, no one more than Patricia Clough has made it clear to us just how fraught this subject (at least) of knowledge is; how vulnerable it is to dispersal and disarray; how drawn it is to any nostalgia for the fantasy of a centered and secure voice, a present being; a ground on which to stand as though "the one." Perhaps this nostalgia is even greater for academics, intellectuals, in America than for those to whom Gingrich appeals, looking out at us with a kindly and soft face, framed by his open hands, on which we see watercolor "tattoos" of other, helping hands emblematic of this organized commitment to "make a difference." For it does seem we academics not

infrequently feel compelled to respond to anticipated charges of "isola-
tion from the 'real world,'" "irrelevance," "ivory tower elitism," and "im-
practicality" in and for the work that we do as human science scholars
and intellectuals. We do seem often haunted by our own voices demanding that we, in our knowledge projects, "make a difference."

From Clough's poststructuralist and psychoanalytic positions, this desire is both inevitable yet always to be deferred. The fantasy of wholeness
and presence would seem to be central to the subject who makes a difference in the particular world in question (although the grandest fantasy of
course is to make this difference in "the world"). This would be true no
less for those of us who speak in the privileged discourses of "knowledge
production" and in any version of science, in particular. The presumption
that the one who speaks/writes does indeed know is enormously seductive and assuring of a centered place and unified voice. Indeed, like writing, and even like the caring Laihua and I were so interested in seeing in
others and in ourselves, it is something to be loved . . . but not with the
blindness that this love often brings with it. Throughout this book, it is
possible to see a movement toward and away from this sort of voice and
sense of presence as "the one." Finally, it seems, it is something one
cannot escape short of silence, disappearance, death. It is an acknowledgment of this place "in-between" that provides a possibility for speak-
ing/writing ethnography and other critical studies of culture that seems
preferable to the pledge to "make a difference," less because one rejects
the possibility of readers/writers turning one's texts toward "better worlds"
than for an appreciation of just how seductively repetitive this desire is.
Standing somewhat uncomfortably with (or at least near) critics of the
post- discourses, we should see that the "autoaffection" Clough describes,
from Derrida, which the human subject has for a sense of stable, present
self, should not—for it cannot—be denied in our writing about others, our
selves, and the worlds we craft. It is a matter of (our) life, finite though that
is. Iain Chambers (1994, 25–26) underlines this complexity, invoking
Nietzsche, but with a hopefulness that is his own:

> As Nietzsche insisted, there are no facts, only interpretations. Just as the narra-
> tive of the nation involves the construction of an "imaginary community," a sense
> of belonging sustained as much by fantasy and the imagination as by any geo-
> graphical or physical reality, so our sense of our selves is also a labour of the
> imagination, a fiction, a particular story that makes sense. We imagine ourselves
> to be whole, to be complete, to have a full identity and certainty not to be open or
> fragmented; we imagine ourselves to be the author, rather than the object, of the
> narratives that constitute our lives. It is this imaginary closure that permits us to

act. Still, I would suggest, we are now beginning to learn to act in the subjunctive mode, "as if we had" a full identity, while recognising that such a fullness is a fiction, an inevitable failure. It is this recognition that permits us to acknowledge the limits of our selves, and with it the possibility of dialoguing across the subsequent differences. . . . This fictive whole, this "I", is, as Nietzsche would have it, a life-preserving fiction, one that conserves us, and saves us from the discontinuities of the unconscious, from schizophrenia, self-destruction and the entropy of madness. It is this knot, the interminable tying together of the stories across the "resistance to identity at the very heart of psychic life," that holds us together.

Falling silent as I hear Haraway call me to "make a difference," I might turn to something closer to Clough's call for an ethnography and sociology that aims to be a cultural criticism akin to that she identifies in the films and writing of Trinh Minh-ha:

Indeed, Trinh's works seem to be a proposal for a cultural criticism which is deeply resistant to conceptions of culture as universal or whole. She rather prefers to recognize cultures as fluid and mobile; therefore the critic is committed to engagement with generalities and particularities of the local and global, drawn into various configurations both by the worldly intensities—the political, the economic and the social—and by desire moving through the critic, making her a critic. (2000, 170)

While this figure of the critic as imagined by Clough and Trinh and much written here may not exactly be recognizable as Haraway's mutated modest witness in a successor science, it surely would help social science, sociology, ethnography, as well as its subjects and objects and thought, to move else where.

Notes

Preface

1   Taking a longer historical view might make it somewhat easier, say, from the mid-nineteenth century forward to the successful Communist revolution in 1949. See Chow (1998, 149–167) and Duara (1995) for helpfully nuanced comments about how "China" does and does not fit the postcolonial narrative that has emerged from India and other histories.

2   The National Academy of Science's CSCPRC (now the Committee on Scholarly Communication with China), was a prestigious Washington-based funding body that seemed usually to give research support only to those in China studies, but whose materials encouraged nonsinologists from "the disciplines" to apply for support.

3   This is the argument some feminist critics of "postmodern" or experimental ethnography have made about how these practices de-center their own "coming to voice" (see, e.g., Mascia-Lees et al. 1989).

Chapter 1

1   Understandings of "translation" are indeed seductive for ethnographers, and are relevant not only to encounters where observer and observed appear literally to be speaking different languages. Thinking that one "knows the language" of the other can lead too easily to assumptions of equivalence of meaning and full "understanding," which itself is surely a piece of the colonial space out of which the knowledge machine of anthropology grew. For critical and theorized recent discussions of translation, see Trinh (1989, 54; 1992, 113–136), Chow (1995, 182–192), and Spivak (1992).

2   One of the most frequent targets of this criticism is the conventional disciplinary divisions of the arts and sciences, and especially the human sciences. Anthropology, given its more intimate connection to Western Enlightenment projects of colonialism, has seen such critique earlier than sociology, but the skepticism about the past verities in the social sciences is now pervasive. See Lemert (1995), Game

(1991), Game and Metcalfe (1997), Clough (1998), and Denzin (1997) for particular instances of this critique and as calls for a different sociology. And see Reed-Danahay (1997) for a collection of recent anthropological texts that further stretch the definitions both of anthropology and ethnography.

3 Clifford (1986, 1988) calls for ethnographies that seek and embrace "partial truths"; but Haraway (1991, 1997) insists, with Harding (1991), that not just any partiality and locatedness will do. Rather, it must be a knowledge that is also embodied, critical, passionate, and relevant to social transformations away from and against domination and in the direction of freedom, justice, and antiracist ways of living. We say more on Haraway's vision in the last chapter.

4 Stacey (1990, 1996) has written a good deal on the tumult in and new forms of family life in the late-twentieth-century United States.

5 The issue of standpoint epistemology, the idea that true knowledge comes from being in and seeing from a particular personal and social experience, is a vexed question among feminist and other poststructuralist writers. For a pointed exchange on this question, see Clough (1993a, b) and Smith (1993). See also Denzin (1997, 53–89).

6 Crapanzano (1992) offers a strong and clear statement of these connections in ethnography. And see how Game and Metcalfe (1997) elaborate the intersections of these terms in academic sociology.

7 Indeed, this "givenness" of the "there" there is at the heart of virtually all thought and, certainly of all inquiry. Pollner (1987, 1991) offers a wonderfully lucid and accessible discussion of this point that in certain respects parallels Derrida's (1972) distinction of the signifier and signified. For examples of work on the rhetoric of science and scholarly inquiry, see Nelson, Megill, McCloskey (1987). For an early sociological appreciation of rhetoric in science, see Gusfield (1976).

8 The roots of this position often are traced back to Weber's famous essay "Science as a Vocation" (see Gerth and Mills 1946).

9 Shapin (1994) offers a fascinating examination of the social conditions on which claims of true knowledge have rested, examining their connections to what he calls civility in the emergence of modern science in seventeenth-century England. The figure of the proper gentleman—as in the person of Robert Boyle—was crucial, Shapin argues, to the anchoring of the credible.

10 Game and Metcalfe (1997, 128–130) argue that one of the most profound consequences of the displacement of the Author as the source of meaning in a text is its similarly decentering impact on the former interpreting reader/subject, who himself or herself now has to move into this void as a new sort of reader.

11 Thanks to my linguist colleague, David Umbach, for helping me with these directions.

12 For well-contexted and detailed discussions of this period in rural settings, see Madsen (1984), Chan, Madsen, and Unger (1992), and Kipnis (1997).

13   There is a growing and varied list of autobiographical accounts of Cultural Revo-
     lution experience by people who took up various positions in the dramas of the
     time. See, for instance, Yang (1997), Chang (1991), Gao (1987), Heng and Shapiro
     (1983), Yue and Wakeman (1985). Also, see Chan (1985).

14   Latour (1988) suggests this as a prudent strategy for any sociologist, quite oppo-
     site to that which we follow here.

15   It is a comment on academic publishing in China today that we had to pay 25,000
     yuan to cover publishing costs (roughly $3,038 in 1998 U.S. dollars), even at a
     respectable publisher.

16   The characterization of writing as "transformative" rather than representative we
     take from Game (1991, 1–36) and Game and Metcalfe (1997, 87–105).

17   There is an accumulating discourse around HIV-AIDS that takes as interesting
     the combination of care and caregiving and masculinity as part of a larger dis-
     course on relations between men, and on men as givers of comfort and support.
     It emerges against a background of assumption that such positioning and practice
     is more "naturally" feminine, and that men are not expected to be "expert" at or
     especially "interested in" caregiving that involves touch and the subordination of
     one's own bodily practice to the interests and comfort of another. The notion is,
     perhaps, that it smacks too much of subservience and service, which, again, have
     been and are written in and through the feminine. This notion is something we
     want to resist, although we are simultaneously subject to it.

18   Game's (1991, 79–85) and Game and Metcalfe's (1997, 146–148, 152–154)
     discussions of Hélène Cixous's critique of Hegelian desire and its incessant return
     to the self at the expense of the other holds out hope for a self/other relationship
     that thrives on difference kept alive, but, as she says, also kept "very close."

Chapter 2

1   We noted earlier some of the conventions of proper scientific writing as discursive
    and rhetorical strategies for presenting a text as connected to a "larger research
    project" focused on the natural world, cast as independently awaiting the scien-
    tific gaze. The present chapter is filled with conventions, such as this citation to
    earlier published work by Strauss and colleagues, that connects "the research"
    and the present text to a collection of already existing texts that mark the intellec-
    tual and scientific territory within which authors typically seek to locate their own
    publications and identities. This is a piece of the "inter-textuality" about which
    literary analysts write in their discussions of the textual web or grid in terms of
    which any particular text might be read. Beyond making connections to previous
    work that has been "accepted" in the profession (by its very publication), such
    citation practices and methodological conventions also constitute a performance
    of proper scientific modesty (cf. Haraway 1997, 23–39). This chapter, and subse-
    quent sections of the book where we effect a conventional scientific, observa-
    tional, and analytic position are usually marked by these tropes, including the

presence of footnotes, in which authors develop arguments and/or commentary seen to be collateral or subsidiary to those in the "main text"—an interesting division in and of itself (see Landow 1992, 64–70). Footnotes are also often the location for "the personal" in those social scientific texts that conform more completely to conventions of objective and distanced analysis.

2　Symbolic interactionist sociology, especially as found in the research traditions and writing after G.H. Mead (1934), of Everett Hughes (1971), Herbert Blumer (1969), Anselm Strauss (1959), and Howard Becker (1973, 1986), is the intellectual terrain out of which most of my earlier thinking, teaching, and writing come. I moved toward this tradition of work from a structural-functional and quantitative graduate school curriculum and dissertation because I thought it offered a much more "human" and interesting way to do sociology; a chance actually to meet and talk to the people I said I was studying. It applauds the personal of the sociologist as a repository of ideas and experiences out of which research questions may be formed, in no small part because of the assumed insight an "insider" vision can provide for understanding locally produced meanings. Hence, the move to study interactions and relationships around illness and caregiving seemed a theoretically warranted one for me. This tradition also directs sociological attention to the careful, painstakingly detailed description of how people do things together in natural settings, which is to say in their mundane and everyday lives. An understanding of meaning as it is created and deployed in these local settings is everything. The deductive view of scientific explanation sometimes found in research/writing that combines a "macro" theory and quantitative data manipulation techniques aimed at answering the "Why?" questions is here resituated in the "How?" questions, which are answered by reference to the detailed description of processes of symbolic interaction—meaning construction and use—between people, captured in and through fieldnotes and interviews made by the researcher himself or herself while in "the field." Here, the social is seen as repeatedly and ongoingly "built up" out of and in these interactions *in situ*. Although it has not always been appreciated, this vision of the social as jointly constructed by and in moments of dynamic interaction has various affinities with many recent "post-" debates over how to imagine the social, including the view of writing as creative and transformative/performative contained in Game and Metcalfe (1997). The conventional ethnography contained in this chapter clearly bears the marks of these symbolic interactionist assumptions and their attendant writing practices.

3　Note here the pretense of the "good, democratic foreigner" siding with "the common people" against an oppressive régime. This is an almost irresistible position for sociologists, given our "love of the other" and professed distaste for narcissism. "With their selfless desire to serve the external love object (the disadvantaged, the oppressed), sociologists have often presented themselves as the very model of the more advanced, civilized and masculine 'anaclitic' type whom Freud contrasts with the feminine narcissists" (see Game and Metcalfe 1997, 66).

4　Given the importance sometimes attributed by non-Chinese writers to using "connections" as a "Chinese way" of doing things, I should note that it was only through my own connections, quite intentionally nurtured, that I was able to be introduced to hospital leaders and, finally, given entrée to the hospital. And, as such, my presence there rested on informal rather than formal, official grounds, such as those described by Wolf (1985), Judd (1994), and Kipnis (1997). The "up" side of this sort of access is that it might well be considerably easier and quicker to obtain, and may be more wide-ranging; the "down" side is that it rests on those persons to whom one is connected and so can easily dissolve in the face of "trouble," as described in the following note. For another unofficial, almost clandestine, strategy of doing research in China see Yuen's (1998) study of informal networks among rural women in a south China village.

5   This mantra, finally, did not "save me," as I ran afoul of the extreme skepticism and authority of a head nurse whom I encountered one night on the ward during the late shift. She apparently had not been involved in the discussions about my presence and project and reacted with great alarm when she saw me and what I was doing. After expressing her concern to municipal officials, who, apparently, also had not been consulted, hospital leaders asked me to stop coming onto the ward without a public health bureau host accompanying me, "for fear of disturbing the patients." It was a request I could hardly effectively refuse, and so I decided to terminate the fieldwork. Fortunately, and I did feel that way at the time, I already had gotten enough data—almost four months worth—with which to write a credible research paper.

6   *Peizhu*, translated literally as "accompany stay," is also used to refer to family members and perhaps speaks more accurately to what I here describe. It was only later in the project that I discovered this other usage, and so I decided to retain the somewhat less specific term, *peiban*. This is the kind of cautious and anticipatory comment one often finds in ethnographic writing. It seems clearly directed to would-be critics who have more and better Chinese language skills than the writer.

7   Interestingly, these conversations almost always reiterated the theme that since I was a foreigner in this "natural" Chinese space, there would be many things that people there would be trying to hide from me; and that it would be very difficult for me to get at "the truth." And assurances about my being capable of getting this truth call for the kind of characterizations offered here about the setting and my strategies for negotiating it as a scientific observer. You, as scrutinizing reader, need to know how careful I was in anticipating various problems and circumstances in the field that might cloud or distort my vision and judgment with regard to what was happening there.

8   We sociologists, or perhaps it is inherent in the position of the "objective observer," delight in the "discovery" of contradictions—gaps between what we see to be true and what we are told is the case by those local to the scene under study. This kind of irony plays a central part in perhaps all scholarly analysis, and evidences one of the most familiar flows of power that we regularly produce. This is sometimes rendered in the language of the obfuscating effects of ideology operating on local eyes, whereas the objective observer is positioned above or outside ideology, a place from which the Truth can be discerned. But theory itself can be a discourse that obfuscates, excluding those not familiar with it, including the "lay" or non-professional reader, who, through its use, is shown to be naive and probably in need of just the knowledge that theory offers up. Atkinson (1990,

158) helpfully points out that this production and use of irony is both at the heart of ethnography/sociology and, of course, is entirely a matter of writing.

9   Realist descriptions of the research site such as this paragraph offers are typical features of ethnographic research. They are intended to give the reader a sense of place, a detailed "picture" of the "there" within which to locate the unfolding story of the ethnography that is to follow. Such descriptions are essential to the *vraisemblance* or reality-effect of the ethnographic text, and are important to the production and maintenance of reader credibility in the text (see, e.g., Atkinson 1990, 62). Novelists consider this problem of verisimilitude to be a matter of textual, rhetorical strategy; a question of tropes and "stage setting." The difference between such a view and that common among most social scientists is a clear example of what it means to talk about writing that treats language as though it were "transparent." To "us," it's seen often as "just good description."

10   Of course, this is precisely what I was looking for so it is hardly surprising that I was "struck" by it.

11   While this sort of unpaid labor might be attributed to socialist/party ways of conduct, sociologists of work in the United States have noted how various private and public organizations and institutions alike seem to rely on large amounts of unpaid and unrecognized labor for their continued operation (see Bucher and Stelling 1977).

12   Throughout this chapter I quote the Chinese family members and patients I spoke to in English as closely as possible. Some readers of earlier versions of this chapter objected to this "pidgin English," as they called it, suggesting that it demeans the Chinese speakers. I—the foreign I who was "there"—feel quite the opposite. In fact, to edit their English into smooth and standard form would seem to dismiss their efforts to learn and speak English, as if to say their English was "so bad" it couldn't be understood "as English." We have by this time learned a good deal about the régime of "standard English" within the United States and Britain, and how it marginalizes other ways of speaking/writing in this language. Moreover, I was, from the beginning of the project, quite surprised by how much I, then having only very rudimentary skills in Chinese, was able to learn from these people who, without exception, told me they "could not speak English." Finally, to the extent that these "data" are taken to be informative about a "there," they are testimony that one need not have mastered Chinese language to pursue a project such as this. To nonsinologists like me approaching China, it may be an encouragement.

13   Notice here, and earlier, the way that material "from the field"—data—are used in the text. This amalgamated quotation from these two doctors is set as a block of type separate from the surrounding text. The words attributed to *peiban* and doctors in the hospital that appeared earlier in the text are set off by quotation marks; and the long extract from my fieldnotes is similarly distinguished as a different and particularly important kind of text. Notice how detailed the notes are, and how much I try to avoid judgment and evaluation in the words used; I am the instrument of observation and I must "get it right"—This is parallel to the way

quantified data are used in other social science and natural science texts as well. The form and practice is to mark the presence of "the world" (see Mulkay 1985) in this text, which purports to be about that world, and the credibility of which depends on readers such as you being convinced of that. Typically, the words of the scientist/observer are omitted from the conversations that are alleged actually to have taken place, masking further the interactive and produced nature of the encounters between the researcher/observer and the others with whom he or she is said to have spoken "in the field" (see Latour 1988; Atkinson 1990, 158).

14   The kind of analysis you see in the sentences before the parentheses, here, is a familiar one in ethnographic and qualitative writing in sociology more generally. It is a sort of "explanation" of the "facts" of the permission signing form. One thing to note about it is how it draws on a shared sense of the plausible as a device to make the account credible. I didn't actually ask any of these children about permission-form signing they had done or were to do. Yet in the text here, there is a sort of implication that this account of anguish in complying with the doctors' requests is based in data obtained "in the field." Such accounts convince as though by reference to a there, but the actual work is done textually, here, and through an assumed intersubjectivity between writer and reader. Even if we had data to "back it up," the textuality of the persuasion here would remain. The aim in making this point is less to say that such an account be rejected, but rather simply to draw attention to the mechanisms through which such analyses operate. Watch for it in what follows, if you like.

15   This translation of the "saying" above is not quite correct. It should be that even a filial son, a *xiaozi,* could not be expected to care for a father whose illness lasted a very long time. It is, in other words, an "excuse" for the son, under such circumstances, to reduce this burden of care. After an earlier version of this chapter was published, Charlotte Ikels pointed out this error to me. At first I was chagrined, but upon looking at how I used the incorrect translation, I realized that it served my own needs quite well—it seemed in short clearly to be a willful misreading. As such, it was an opportunity that, given the aims of this book, I hardly would want to "correct."

16   Note, again, how an "empirical" image has been abstracted from the pages and pages of notes and interviews made, and here brought forward as theoretically interesting and providing an occasion for explanation. What is the logic of this selection?

17   My introduction to the *danwei* system came with reading Henderson and Cohen (1984) before I went to China. While their book helped me understand the hospital I visited, my concerns are considerably more narrow than theirs. Henderson and Cohen do note the presence of family members in the hospital, but they do not discuss in detail their work or their relationships to medical staff.

18   Kipnis (1997, 26–27), in his examination of the intimate relationship between feeling or human feeling—*ganqing*—and relationships with others—*guanxi*—discusses what might be called the performative qualities of emotion in relationships among the people in the north China village he calls Fengjia. "Doing" the proper

feeling for one's position relative to an other as people jointly construct and reconstruct their relationships through time, Kipnis argues, is an intimate part of what relationships, connections, *guanxi*, "feeling," is.

19   Yang (1986, 128-135) describes several kinds of relationships that can obtain between people based on "the degree of personal emotional and moral commitment," on the one hand, and "the degree of gain-and-loss calculation and interest at stake," on the other. So-called *hou men[r]* contacts thus might easily be set off from the more general *guanxi*, which can include ties of intimacy and deep commitment.

20   The circumstances for peasants are less supportive in that since they have no *danwei* to support them, they have to bear the costs of medical care themselves. For peasants who have increased their incomes dramatically since the reform, however, this might not represent the burden it would for those who have not. By 1999, virtually all patients in China were paying more, both in absolute and relative dollars, for hospital care than they had a decade earlier.

21   Henderson's (1989, 206-210) paper on modernization in Chinese medical care helps us put this remark in the context of general trends of the rising cost of hospital stays, contributed to especially by those—such as this man's father—whose *danwei* pay most or all of the costs of care. At the same time, she reports, part of the western and modernizing model, especially found in cities, is an attempt to increase turnover of patients, reducing the average length of stay. This pressure exerted by doctors and hospital officials is especially strong for those who lack some form of subsidy. The *jiating bingchuang* or family sickbed program through which we gained access to the families studied in 1990-1991 was said by some to have been set in hopes of moving convalescing patients from hospital to home and in keeping marginal, chronic patients stabilized there rather than bringing them to the hospital for acute episodes provoked by lax or misdirected home care.

22   A moment I read as emblematic of this is seen in Zhang Yimou's 1992 film, *The Story of Qiuju,* which tells of a peasant woman who seeks justice for a wrong done her and her husband by a village party secretary. As Qiuju and her niece prepare to visit the home of a high public security bureau official in advance of the bureau considering her appeal from a lower-level ruling, they realize they cannot meet him without taking gifts, especially ones that will remind him of Qiuju and her plea. There is no explicit conversation between Qiuju and her niece about trying to influence his decision with these gifts—and it would be considered unseemly to suggest as much. Still, there is no mistaking their hope that the gifts will make the public security bureau chief "favorable" toward Qiuju's appeal.

23   Given the gift exchange calculus that Yang (1986, 1994) has described, and details from the present study, it was not surprising to have heard stories of surgeons receiving rather large gifts of money (*hong bao*) from family members in advance of surgeries performed. Although I did not hear any first-hand accounts of this, it was brought up often in discussions with other foreigners about medical care in China. Chinese who commented on this said that "it was more common" in the

recent past but that crackdowns on corruption in the hospital had reduced its occurrence. It apparently has not disappeared.

24   The nationwide campaign against "spiritual pollution" (especially from the United States) had begun in the fall of 1986, just before I started this project, and was a regular item in local news stories.

25   It would be disingenuous in the extreme to suggest that this model of knowledge of and desire for the other, for difference, is peculiar to the human sciences. It surely is not, but, rather, is said to characterize western philosophy and thought, examples of which are as easily available in literary fiction as in scientific fiction (see Game 1991, 3–38, 65–89).

Chapter 3

1   Similarly, all work unit and hospital names, as well as anything we took to be too identifying of the particular people we met, also have been changed. Laihua has chosen pseudonyms for family members consistent with naming practices popular among their respective generations. In Gao Changping's case, his given pseudonym means "prosperous and smooth," which are quite apt adjectives, it seemed to us.

2   "Cadre" is a common English rendition of the Chinese *ganbu*, meaning official or administrator or person with authority. There has been an elaborate ranking of levels into which *ganbu* in China fall, with the heads of the party and government at the top. Its full range would include university teachers, and thus does not always mean the same as "party official." Local wisdom once had it that anyone with any significant authority in any Chinese work unit likely also would be a party member. While this might be more likely among explicitly governmental units (e.g., possibly neighborhood, district, city and above units), it would be less of a "sure thing" among intellectuals, although the higher the ranking and the more the authority, the greater the likelihood of *"ganbu"* also meaning party member. Given Mr. Gao's past and current privileges, we assumed that he was.

3   Conventional qualitative methods textbooks and discussions of ethnographic practice often speak of "key informants" and others "in the field" on whom researchers especially rely for insights into local cultural space and practice. Sometimes there is an acknowledgment of the dynamics that operate to produce these relationships between researcher and "key informant" (see Clifford 1983b; Rabinow 1977), but more commonly these relationships seem either to be unrecognized and/or untheorized. To "theorize" such relationships would be to ask how they emerge, the investments and tactics the parties involved pursue in order to sustain, or in some cases end, them; and how the relationship itself becomes a condition for knowledge production. It would require us to talk about desire for an other and what that desire seeks; how it operates in this case. Sometimes, key informants become collaborators and even co-authors; sometimes local research assistants become key informants and more, as in our case. But usually we don't talk about the flows of desire and attraction/repulsion between observers and

those who are both observed and who themselves operate as observers in service of the knowledge project (but see Reed-Danahay 1997).

We visited seventeen different families in our project, but you will meet only a handful of the people we met and hear only segments of our stories about them. Which figures you meet and what stories you hear have a lot to do with our personal attractions to some of the people we met. In Mr. Gao's case, it seems apparent that we two men "liked" and respected him; he was highly educated, a professional; a careful and precise thinker, and highly articulate not only about his own family situation of care but also about a variety of social and political moments through which he and his family lived. He also seemed to adopt what we both, although it was unspoken between us at the time, felt was a "politically correct" position on the question of daughters and their relative worth in family life. Not surprisingly, we felt he and his family "liked" us too; our interviews with them all were friendly and long. This was not always the case in our relationships with the people we met, many of whom you do not meet here. This is not to say of course that the only criterion for writing subjects and lives here is that we enjoyed cordial relationships with them, but these relationships were far from minor in shaping our investments of time and energy in them and in the "records" we made and writing we subsequently have done.

4 We asked Gao exactly what the colleague might say to his acquaintance in General Hospital. Gao said, "It's very simple. He would say 'This is the leader of our company.'" He chuckled, and his wife added, "They wouldn't say a lot."

5 The fixing of responsibility for death and/or injury—in hospitals and medical work and in Chinese society more generally—sometimes involves a complex process in which what may seem to be excessive avoidance is displayed. Given the nature of the legal and insurance infrastructures in China, however, and the importance often given to "harmony" or at least some sort of consensual understanding of the questions "who is responsible?" and "has enough reparation been exacted?" one comes to appreciate measures such as those Gao and his wife faced here and that we noted in chapter 2 in the intensive care ward. Gao said he explained his sleep apnea to the sanitarium doctors, and that it could improve naturally. He also assured them that he would not hold them responsible were he to have an episode and die during his stay. The leaders refused to accept his word. Given the great increases in medical costs, and the interests of all sorts of parties in China in profit, the financial outlay for a death and its consequences for a family could be very great, as we saw in a few cases of which we had direct knowledge. And that burden is even greater now that state units face rising costs and shrinking profits. Recently, the government has announced a massive plan to move most of these state enterprises into the private sector.

6 For a discussion of the modern history of what sorts of persons could effectively speak scientific truth, see Shapin and Schaffer (1985), Shapin (1994), and Haraway's (1997, 23–48) critique.

7 Although there is a good deal of comment on how this may be changing with the rise of the market and the economic reforms begun in the early 1980s, it is far too early to suggest that the party and one's relationship to it are unimportant consid-

erations in the distribution of privilege in today's China, especially since that positioning itself can be entrée to various "markets," including capital.

8   See Duara's (1995, 147–176) discussion of how the "History" of "'modern' China" has dramatically re-written the meaning of "feudalism"—*fengjian* in Chinese—in the twentieth century, in service of the nation-state and its subject.

9   Such a branch office, given the size and importance of Tianjin in China's economy, likely would have been a quite desirable posting for a young university graduate.

10 Peasants' lives in China's countryside have not been organized in terms of state work units, but rather by various collective arrangements, sideline production organizations, and, most recently, the "responsibility system." See Kipnis (1997, 123–146) for a recent discussion of these changes in one north China village.

11 After a few interviews, he presented us a large table he had made with two sheets of yellow paper that contained all of his hospitalizations, their dates, the diagnoses, and other details. Unsolicited, it was quite helpful in sorting out some of the details of his complex medical story.

12 That Gao would decry the current importance of "money" is not surprising, for on that criterion alone he likely would not be able to reproduce the care he had enjoyed.

13 But Kipnis (1997, 24) suggests this may be a culturally specific—and perhaps especially "American"—reading of the particular amalgam of the material and "feeling" that defines Chinese relationship practices and the subjects they require and create. He notes that the expectation that the material somehow degrades the sincerity or honesty of feeling is a familiar logic in the West but that these distinctions are considerably less clear in the calculus of social relationships in China, both in the past and in the present.

14 The depth and breadth of this support was underlined by Gao himself: "My unit is pretty good. It is in good financial condition, and it has relatively few members [employees]. It especially has fewer older members, and among them, the number of patients is even smaller. So, they can support those of us who get sick. There are no limits at my unit. For instance, other units redeem members' medical expenses at a fixed percent. The people in those units have to queue up and can then redeem only a part of their costs. At present I can redeem 100 yuan a month in regular fees. My usual fees now are comparatively low. Here, for example, is a receipt for only 3 yuan. It is for my medicine last month. The charge for my sickbed from the sanitarium is only 9 yuan a month, so it's all very cheap. Plus, when I went back to work in 1987, my work time was flexible. I stayed in my unit half a day and was at home the other half. I didn't have to take reduced salary. This is another way that my unit looked after me. Of course, I worked on things from my office during the half day I was at home. I have no difficulties in redeeming my medical fees, even though the expenses at the sanitarium are great."

15 In 1978 the central government issued a document (No. 104) concerning a "temporary method of worker retirement due to illness." This document did not directly

mention the problem of a shortage of jobs for the growing number of urban youth seeking to return to their homes from the countryside, coupled with the job needs of younger urban youth then graduating from high school. Rather, it encouraged workers not yet at but nearing retirement age to give their positions to their children. This kind of solution helped the government deal with this growing demand and potential problem while simultaneously allowing parents, paraphrasing the doctor quoted in chapter 2, to "do what they like to do"—namely, sacrifice themselves for the benefit of their children, further cementing the asymmetries already built up between parents and child over the course of their lives together. Although we do not suggest that these parents thought of the possible benefits to themselves in giving up their jobs to their children stuck in the countryside, we merely point out yet another example where national policy and so-called traditional family practices fit nicely together, apparently to serve both government and individuals. In 1985, another document was issued officially halting this "temporary" option.

16   Rey Chow (1995, 155) offers an interesting reading of a quite parallel expression—*zuo gei waiguoren kan*, "such and such is done 'for the eyes of the foreigner,' with 'foreigner' usually meaning those from the advanced industrial West." Her point is to underline the concern with capturing the gaze, the attention, of some valued other as a mark of one's own worthiness.

Chapter 4

1   This *laoshi*, which means teacher in English, is also used after one's surname as a way to convey respect. See also Kipnis (1997, 32) for a discussion of this word's usage to imply honor via the figure of kinship.

2   This critical positioning with regard to gender and the position of women in Chinese cultural space has been foreshadowed earlier. It goes beyond the "neutrality" that conventional ethnography encourages. It is subject to the criticism that a voice of white Western male privilege engages in a kind of cultural imperialism in taking up such a position relative to things "Chinese"; an argument also made currently by leaders of the Heung Yee Kuk, a male-dominant lineage council resisting (significant local) criticism of their male-only inheritance practices in Hong Kong's New Territories. But such positioning need ask for no epistemological privilege, which is the usual defense based on "method" in scientific work, but rather should be judged on moral-ethical grounds that clearly are not the exclusive property of "the West."

3   This sort of "have it both ways" position seems to be similar to what Gubrium and Holstein (1997, 97–114) describe as the "analytic tensions" at the "border of the real and the representational" (109); as a positioning—as we have suggested—"of the moment"; that is, as one that sociologists at the end of the century can be invited seriously to embrace.

4   Which it seems sometimes is translated as "filial child" even though the first dictionary definition of the character *zi* commonly is "male child."

5   When we began the project in the early fall of 1990, it had not occurred to me that we should give each of the families we visited a gift. Sometimes the obvious is the last thing thought of, if at all. In any case, Laihua, in a meeting before we began our visits, explained where some of the roughly US$5,000 that I had agreed to pay to the Tianjin Academy of Social Sciences for their support and cooperation would go. When I indignantly asked what "this 'gifts' line in the budget of my money" meant, he quietly pointed out that it meant of course gifts for our cases. Oh yes, of course, I thought. This led ultimately to our "going shopping" at the local Friendship Store to find something suitable. We left with "17 copies" of a royal blue table lamp, lashed to our bicycles. We also, again at Laihua's suggestion, bought *"liuge pingguo"*—six apples—for each patient and family as we began our visits. These six apples conveyed, as Laihua explained, wishes for harmony and smoothness—just what we needed in our work and relationships with our new acquaintances and with each other.

6   The word *bai* can be translated as "to embody respect," and this *bai nian* ritual at Spring Festival, likely more common in the countryside, involves people coming to one's home, sometimes performing a quick *ketou* (kowtow) to the residents and offering good wishes for the new year (see Kipnis 1997, 77–79).

7   We footnote Hong Kingston's text to say that in at least one village in Guangdong Province about which we learned from Susanne Chan through her current fieldwork there, twentieth-century daughters who left, and especially those who went to Hong Kong, were expected to send back money to their families for support, although they themselves were not expected to return to the village. Personal communication, 1997.

8   We borrow this characterization from the title of a 1987 film by Carma Hinton and Richard Gordon, *Small Happiness,* in which Hinton and a collection of rural Chinese women tell their lives as part of this particular weave of discourse/practice.

9   On this intersection of Chinese family practices and business, see also Hamilton and Chen (1991), Kipnis (1997, 147–164), Redding (1990), and Wank (1995).

10   "Trust And Prosperity: The Role Of Chinese Family Enterprise In Economic Development," given as the inaugural T.T. Tsui Annual Lecture at the University of Hong Kong, 3 February 1997.

11   The notion of power as outlined by Foucault seems relevant: power as a dynamic, mobile resource for movement; as "positive" as well as "negative"; as moving in and through discourse/practice in the lived world; and as always linked, connected, to other positions of discourse/practice in those worlds, with their own potentials for similar sorts of deployments. This notion of power fits well the image suggested by Margery Wolf in the segment quoted from her paper "Chinanotes" (1990), where she describes the "uterine family" and the agendas and interests women took up in the face of a male world of ostensibly much greater "significance." This sense of power is also indexed by the commonsense, usually male-espoused, notion that women "control" family or domestic matters.

All of the conditions and qualifications on women's power in family life to the contrary notwithstanding, Foucault might encourage a careful examination of just what women are able to do with/from these positions in terms of withholding and/or shaping the terms of their cooperation and responsibilities.

12   Quoted in Croll (1995, 32), from the *North China Herald*, Shanghai, 10 February 1931. We have modified the form in which this poem is presented by Croll.

13   Quoted by Croll (1995, 13) from the *Nu Jie*; emphasis added.

14   Croll takes these from the *Nu Jie*—Precepts for Women—and *Nuer Jing*—The Classic for Girls—and *Lie Nu Zhuan* or biographies of filial daughters. She draws on the *Book of Changes*, section XXXVII, trans. J. Legge, and on I.B. Lewis (1919, 8) *The Education of Girls in China*, New York; see Croll (1995, 13–14) and her citations (194 nn.7–10).

15   Adapted and supplemented from Croll (1995, 13–14), from *Nuer Jing*.

16   See Croll (1995, 14) and her citation to Ayscough (1975).

17   "Family" ought not be thought of only as a physical space with genetically linked people in it, or as activated only upon the co-presence of these individuals in a local site. Rather, family and one's location in it seems present in diverse scenes and segments of life in Chinese communities, such that one—and especially if one is a woman—can only with difficulties often involving pain and dislocation really get free from it or beyond its discursive grasp/régime/(but could we say comforts?). This of course is not completely unfamiliar to women who are "not Chinese," but it surely is a considerably less viable characterization of men—and perhaps of men and women—in certain social worlds not so marked (for a discussion of family as a mobile site, see Gubrium and Holstein (1990). As a possible exception to this "rule," see Silber's (1994) discussion of *nüshu* or women's script used exclusively by women in certain areas of Hunan Province to communicate with each other. Quite aside from whatever additional relationship practices might have occurred, Silber writes about the sentiments of love and friendship expressed among these women in this special writing in the context of strongly competing family and marital obligations.

18   Croll does note the oral traditions very popular among these and other young women that told stories about warrior women who were both filial and fierce in their bravery and physical prowess in battle to protect and defend family and name. One of the most often mentioned figures from such tales is the fearless Hua Mulan, which we take up later in this chapter.

19   Laihua here offers a characterization that does appear consistent with much sentiment on differences in work opportunities and other aspects of life between men and women in China. Xu (1996, 383–384) summarizes this situation as follows: "The post-Mao reforms have opened up certain new economic opportunities for Chinese women and men, but women's position in relation to men has not improved significantly. In some areas regression is conspicuous. Obviously, when women are being bought and sold openly as sexual objects and birth

machines; when they are bring forced into prostitution; when they are being subjected to rape and sexual and physical abuse in marriage, as well as sexual harassment in the work place; when concubinage in its contemporary versions and betrothal-marriage are reemerging, no equality between the sexes exists." She then offers citations of stories published in China to ground these claims (see Xu, 409 n.11).

20 While the comments about privilege and access to resources that we made in the discussion of Gao Changping's situation and in chapter 2 on *peiban* seem borne out in various ways in the story of this family's caregiving situation, we found it notable that Wu *lao's* children seemed to have to work much harder at getting "special treatment" for her. Of course, the thousands of people who have none of the kinds of associations and resources to draw on that Gao and Wu had are likely to experience even greater difficulty in dealing with access to a regular hospital bed (see Henderson 1989).

21 But here is another opportunity to underline the importance of reading across disciplinary boundaries, in this case into autobiography and fiction writing. Well before the recent attention to writers such as Amy Tan (1989, 1991) and, earlier, Maxine Hong Kingston, there were autobiographies and short stories available that spoke voices of women's lives and experience, albeit they were, admittedly, few and hard to find; and perhaps almost impossible to find in English translation, as Croll suggests.

22 These include not only the books by Wolf (1968, 1972, 1985) and Croll (1983, 1989, 1995) but also work by Barlow (1989, 1993, 1994); Chan, Law, and Kwok (1992); Chang (1991); Gilmartin et al. (1994); Hershatter (1997); Honig and Hershatter (1988); Judd (1989, 1994); Mah (1997); Mosher (1993); Pearson and Leung (1995); Rofel (1999); Yang (1997); Yue and Wakeman (1985); Zito and Barlow (1994).

23 See Wolf (1968, 216–217).

24 Wolf's text is a nice example of a "postmodern" one, and it seems to us ironic that she has written a book (1992), in which she questions and fundamentally rejects the potential for postmodern ethnography to contribute significantly to our understandings of both *what* we tell stories about and *how* we do it.

25 See also Dai (1995), who links this characterization to a contemporary play by Bai Xifeng, "Here Come the Old Friends with Wind and Rain" in *Bai Xifeng juben xuan* (Selected plays of Bai Xifeng), Beijing: *Gongren chubanshe* (Workers Publishing House). n.d.

26 There is the more recent story of "iron girls" from the Cultural Revolution period, although these images seem today to have fallen on hard times, and are reported to be the object of popular ridicule, caught in a complex of discourses on just what the proper image of "the 'real' Chinese woman today" might be, with "western feminism" often used as an all-purpose source of Chinese women's "problems" and confusions" in love and sexuality (see Barlow 1989; Xu 1996, 404). On images and stories of "iron girls" seen from a later time, see Honig and Hershatter (1988, 23–26, 30–31); Dai (1995, 263), and Croll (1995, 70–72, 99–101).

27 See Allen (1996), who cites some of the more recent versions of this ancient story, said to date from the early Tang period (sixth–seventh centuries C.E.). In Allen's paper there are references to several recently published versions of this story; and in a Hong Kong bookstore Joseph found a volume in the Asiapac Comic Series in English titled *Hua Mulan: China's Sweetest Magnolia* (trans. Wang Jian, Singapore: Asiapac Books, 1996). A publisher's note inside reads: "In our efforts to promote Chinese culture, we would feel regret should we fail to present through our comic series Hua Mulan, the *only* woman warrior in the history of China, or even the world, in terms of disguising herself as a man in order to join the army for her invalid father. Whilst Hua Mulan succeeded in relieving her father of his military obligation, she had invariably put herself in the forefront of not only the battlefield but women's contention for equal capability. She unconsciously spearheaded the effort to challenge the traditional notion of male superiority in a given scenario." But Allen argues, as do we, that this fundamentally is a tale of domestication, of a return home rather than a story of martial achievements. Finally, the recent Disney film, *Mulan*, represents the greatest global dispersal of this story and the images associated with it, although with the addition of an explicit heterosexual and romantic politic inflecting it in ways that reduce further the likelihood that it might be read as a critique of conventional gender arrangements.

28 We thank Pang Bingjun for this translation of the Hua Mulan text; and thanks to Susanne Chan for finding the text in Chinese and for the initial translation used in our class at the University of Hong Kong.

29 I am indebted to Bronwyn Davies's (1989, 1993) writing on the importance of stories and how they create positions for subjectivities that then become important resources for how children and others can imagine themselves as gendered beings. I saw the Hua Mulan story as most probably operating very much in this way.

30 The suicide apparently is not a common feature of the Mulan story versions that Allen (1996) has surveyed, although he argues that from the earliest versions of the story there are intimations of an unrequited or lost heterosexual romance.

31 Until about 1994–1995, PRC citizens who went abroad were allowed upon return to use their passports to gain entry to special stores where they could buy various foreign-made household appliances and goods that were not generally available to urban consumers. Purchases had to be in foreign currency and prices were somewhat lower, it was said, than they would be if these items were available elsewhere. Those who had been abroad longer were allowed to buy more items.

32 As a postscript to one of the threads of this story, in 1997 Li Rong's daughter, then twenty-three, left Tianjin to study in Finland—no doubt after several unsuccessful attempts to secure a visa to the United States, where she has several relatives. Although "further study" was ostensibly the aim, her mother clearly implied to LH that she would not come back to Tianjin. When he told me this, I thought how happy her mother must be to have succeeded in at least ensuring that this daughter will not be one of those "heavy, deep-rooted women" of whom Hong Kingston wrote, who stay behind "to maintain the past against the flood,

safe for returning." I wanted to read more into this information than it alone would allow. I found it hopeful, for this young woman and for others, although for her mother it would have to be both bitter and sweet, for it meant that she would have no daughter to care for her as she had for her mother.

Chapter 5

1 The production of theory in qualitative social science most familiar to Joseph is based in the inductive procedures set out by Strauss and Glaser in a series of books on "grounded theory" spanning two decades (see Glaser and Strauss 1967; Glaser 1978; Strauss 1987; see also Charmaz 1983). See also chapter 2, notes 2, 3. For a non-grounded-theory methods text that bears a family resemblance to it as well as offering friendly glances toward the postmodern, see Emerson, Fretz, and Shaw (1995).

2 If the plural pronoun does this totalizing work, the "I" does it with a vengeance that is even more easily missed. As our later invocation of Freud suggests, all of what "we" say here about "we" can be said about "I," including its similar fictionality as a centered place outside the text.

3 In the many computer files associated with this project there is indeed a folder called "LH's Story," a collection of autobiographical texts Laihua wrote during the time he first visited the United States and lived with Joseph and Nancy Schneider. There is no such file called "Joseph's Story," at least not that Joseph knows about.

4 A noted sociologist who does research in contemporary China bristled in a seminar Joseph attended at the University of Hong Kong in spring 1997 when he questioned a research practice that used covert observation of consumers in retail shops and department stores. The defense offered was in terms of "if we don't do this, we can't get the data we need." Joseph thought, unfortunately only later, to wonder why and by whom it was "needed."

5 For China, see Wolf (1992) and Mirsky (1994), although they are not the most unfriendly of critics. Among sociologists more generally, including those who do more interpretive work, Denzin (1997, 250–273) has summarized pointed resistance to and criticism of such writing.

6 The page numbers referenced here and below refer to a copy of the full texts of the fieldnotes for cases #23 and #29. Once we planned to include these in an appendix of this book, for readers' reference, but costs and space constraints changed our minds. We leave the page numbers in place to mark the close reading that typically privileges fieldnote writing in conventional ethnography.

7 "Baomu" in English means nurse or housekeeper—one who takes care of, attends, others. Yangcun is a countryside village near Tianjin.

8 Throughout these letters, and in the fieldnotes as well, "traditions" and "customs" are often used uncritically as resources in order to affirm what speakers are "talking about," and to account for or explain this or that course of action. Although

the preferred theoretical position on what "norms" are and how they "work" in social life held by Joseph is an ethnomethodological one, which is to say that such use should be a topic for the social analyst to study—how "members" deploy and invoke such language resources uncritically—it is clear that he and Laihua are themselves also members in that they variously use such notions as "Chinese traditions" and you/we "Americans" unproblematically as interpretive resources in their own sense-making activity. One sort of scene in which the resources of "tradition" and "custom" are commonly invoked by the people we met and talked to is when a speaker wanted to mark the "Chineseness" of what was being discussed or explained, and, usually, their own position "here" as distinct from that of the American foreign researcher and his "culture," "country," or way "there." This sort of marking of difference is also apparent in these letters.

9   We have edited out the sections of the letter that respond to Joseph's earlier questions about Gao Changping and matters in that chapter, many of which you already have read there.

10 Joseph's idea here, taken from various studies, is that when socialism came to China, women's social position relative to men began to improve. He seems to want to credit socialism *per se* for at least some of this change. On this question and its complexity, see Barlow (1994), Brugger and Reglar (1994), Gilmartin et al. (1994), Honig and Hershatter (1988), Rofel (1999), Stacey (1983), Wolf (1985).

11 Li Yu Jie is the youngest patient we spoke to. Doctors at the sickbed office urged us to include her both because of the seriousness of her illness and the "specialness" of her caregiving situation.

12 Here is a nice example of how Joseph takes "Chineseness" to exist independent of the practices that mark and bring it into being; then he asks Laihua to "explain" this "Chineseness" to him. One might ask if this is an "honest" question from Joseph to Laihua. One answer is "partly yes and partly no." On the one hand, Joseph may have asked the question to get a sense of what Laihua would say—as insight from an "insider" for his own writing of this quasi-authoritative text; on the other, he likely did not intend to use Laihua's answer as fully "authoritative." Such authoritative answers of course are themselves part of what we, in the present text, are "worried about."

13 Our estimate of these 1991 costs for a year of schooling at this particular school is about $5,900 *renminbi* or US$1,035.

14 This discourse of inside/outside is somewhat risky for one who usually moves in what might be called a "Western" cultural space. The "inside" to which LH refers may or may not be as familiar as it seems to such a reader, given the difference between Western moral and philosophical conceptions of the person, on the one hand, and those that have obtained in Chinese social and cultural life, on the other. See Kipnis (1997, 108) for a discussion of this from his fieldwork in a north China village and for discussion (105–108) of a controversy involving Potter and Potter (1990) and Kleinman and Kleinman (1991) on the place of feeling or emotion in Chinese life.

15   Anthropologists Judd (1989) and Kipnis (1997, 28–32) note today's rural daugh-
     ters and their sense of commitments to and connections with their parents upon
     and well after marriage, further complicating the "reality" of *"chumenzi."*

Chapter 6

1   David Y.F. Ho (1996) has studied the presence and practice of filial values in the
    Chinese diaspora as well as in the PRC. He concludes that while the influence of
    filial traditions among Chinese populations is of course considerably less than it
    once might have been, there remains a good deal of allegiance to the *discourse* of
    filiality in these populations.

2   Most housing property in Tianjin and in other Chinese cities after the revolution
    has not been owned by the dwellers, but rather by the state, usually administered
    through a work unit and municipal district management housing stations or *fang
    guan zhan.* Commonly, monthly rental fees for the space have been paid to the
    work unit, and the units then pay the state, the city, or the district. These rents
    paid by individuals historically have been low in most cities. In Tianjin, beginning
    in about 1980, work units began to construct and assign new housing for their
    workers. This of course placed an enormous financial burden on most units, and,
    in any case, it usually could not fully meet existing demand. Over the past decades
    there have been several rent reforms in which monthly charges to individuals have
    increased, and a small but growing number of people have been given the option
    of buying their apartments from their work units, but for sums that often are well
    beyond the means of many families. Laihua notes that his own apartment—two
    rooms in a high-rise with kitchen and bath, heat, and cold water—would in 1995
    cost between 7,000–10,000 yuan to buy, roughly US$875–$1,250 at that time.
    This opportunity has come about in part as an attempt by struggling *danwei* to
    increase their incomes at a time when the state sector faces increased competi-
    tion from private and joint-venture enterprises and falling revenues (Seth Faison
    [1996] writes in the *New York Times* that a recent China government survey
    reports that only 28 percent of state-owned industries realized a profit in 1995
    and that the Deputy Prime Minister, Wu Bangguo, reported that the debt-to-asset
    ratio for state-owned industries was at 80 percent; and see Wang 1992). And
    rents continue to rise. This means that people are in some sense being "urged" to
    buy their homes by these increasing rents. Data from the Tianjin Housing Man-
    agement Bureau obtained in late 1995 show that beginning in 1996, rents in the
    kind of area where the Li family lives will be charged at a rate of 1 yuan per square
    meter of space per month. Housing rents in the entire urban district in which *wu
    da dao* is located will be calculated at this rate, which represents a substantial
    increase even from 1992, when the rate was .136 yuan per square meter.

3   In August 1993, when we returned to visit this family, Li Yu Nian had gone to
    Indonesia for a two-year contract period of work and consultation. His second
    brother then told us that he was preparing to return in a month or so, with his
    boss, for his son's wedding. This oldest brother seemed to have been able to
    loosen the dictates of the saying *fumu zai bu yuan zou:* if parents are alive, one

shouldn't go far away. But this, after all, was a modern son, and he had his brothers and their wives, not to mention his own wife, who could take up his duties toward his mother, in his absence.

4   At least by the traditional calculus of what a son is and what he should do, about which we say more in the next chapter. These matters are linked closely to notions of face (see Kipnis 1995, 1997; and Gabrenya and Hwang 1996).

5   A rather formal phrase that translates into English as honored, respected wife (notwithstanding that Zhang's husband had then been dead some fifteen years).

6   This is part of a Tang dynasty poem by Meng Jiao that Li Yu Nian used to express the relationship between his mother and her sons. This poem, *You Zi Yin*, is meant for one who prepares to travel far away, as his kind mother sews clothes for the trip. The mother loves her son very much, and her son should remember and acknowledge her when he is away, with this verse.

7   The shortage of housing space in China's urban centers is hardly news. The increased magnetism of cities as places to earn more money, coupled with often high rural unemployment rates and the financially strapped condition of many state-subsidized work units makes the demand for adequate housing in cities great. Housing can become an issue in which family harmony is severely tested—as was the case in Wang Su Min's family. Although the square meter living space per person in Tianjin city almost doubled between 1980 (3.6) and 1993 (7.0), population density in greater Tianjin in 1994 was 825 people per square kilometer. But in the district where Zhang Xiufang lives, population density *(changzhu renkou)* was in 1994 a whopping 47,895 persons typically staying or living in one square kilometer (*Tianjin Tongji Nianjian* 1995, 119, 39; *Tianjin Fangdichan Shichang* 1993, 21).

8   This series was based on the novel by the same name written by Lao She in the 1940s and tells a story of Beijing residents living under Japanese occupation. It first aired in 1985. Perhaps Li Yu Nian chooses to mention it here because of its title's relevance to his own comments.

9   By reference to these Marriage Laws we do not suggest that they have assured or produced equality between men and women. At the same time, their existence as official documents and their interpretation, widely disseminated in propaganda, as giving women certain official discursive prerogatives in their relationships with husbands, should not be ignored as a resource for women toward variously improving their circumstances.

10   I was disgusted that her own mother would say this to her daughter's mother-in-law. But I should remember that language is itself a form as well as a substance, both of which can "mean" and "do." A Chinese friend chided me, saying, "It is true that a daughter's mother, often out of traditional courtesy, asks the mother-in-law to scold her daughter if she does anything wrong or unsatisfactory. Today, this is mere courtesy. Usually, the mother-in-law refrains from criticism even in a traditional *xiao* family because she understands this is no longer the old society."

11 We should note that the changes in such notions of who counts as inside and who outside are apparent in what might be taken as a great fluidity in naming practices. It is not difficult to find families in the city in which all grandchildren seem to be considered as equals, and all grandmothers have become *"Nainai,"* a privileged term traditionally reserved for the paternal grandmother. By that calculus, maternal grandmothers were *"laolao"* in north China or, more formally, *"wai po,"* literally, "outside grandmother" (or most informally, *"popo"*). Similarly, daughters' children have been called *"bai yan er"* or *"bai yan,"* which means "white eyes," coming from *"bai yan er lang,"* "white-eyed wolf," somehow taken to mean that the "white-eyed wolves" will take from you and finally leave you with nothing; they have no gratitude and there is no reciprocity. Now, although the name still is used, these children seem to be loved equally.

12 See Munro (1977, 135–157) for a discussion of the importance of models, both positive and negative, in modern Chinese cultural practice.

13 This 1990 regulation from the China Educational Committee (document 14, 1990) made it more difficult for Chinese college graduates to get permission to go abroad for graduate study from the local units to which they were assigned. It also made it more costly. A college graduate was required to work for five years before he or she could apply to go abroad if they were paying with private funds or if they were supported by a school abroad. If he or she wanted to negotiate this regulation, the per-year fee for missed work/service was 2,500 yuan. Graduates from master's degree programs also had a five-year commitment, but their per-year fee, if successfully negotiated, was 4,000. For Ph.D. graduates the fee was 6,000. But again, the existence of the document should not be taken to mean that it was enforced or evenly enforced. Great variability in how units put these regulations into effect are common. But the question of a so-called brain drain of China's brightest and most educated young people and scholars during the 1980s, with many being very slow to return—if at all—apparently has received a good deal of attention in both China and abroad (see Maddox and Thurston 1987, and Orleans 1988, 109–111). One source has it that the number of Chinese students and scholars in the United States increased well over 200 percent between 1985 and 1989 (from 12,000 to 40,000; see Madsen 1995, 151; and Harding 1992, 150, 367). After the Tiananmen Square demonstrations were brutally crushed by authorities in June of 1989, the United States government granted extensions of stay to many of those already in the United States. It seemed that the U.S. requirements for a student visa became more demanding at the same time that the Chinese government made it almost impossible for a "common" Chinese student to gain local permission to go abroad for study.

14 The Socialist Education Movement, launched by Mao Zedong in 1963, has been identified by Richard Baum (1975) as something of a "prelude" to the Cultural Revolution. Although aimed toward a rectification of party cadres in the countryside to make them more credible and effective stewards of the socialist revolution and to turn them away from various "revisionist" practices, the movement arguably is the beginning of what was to become a wrenching ideological battle throughout Chinese society between Maoists and all "others" (see also Madsen 1984,

67–72). Pang's mention of it here, in the context of her "bad" background, is to offer an account for why she did not continue on for further, and ultimately professional, education after high school.

15   The balance of this common expression, which Li Yu Quan does not say, is *"sanshi mudi yi tou niu,"* which, all together in English, is: "A wife, child, and a warm bed; 30 mu of land and a cow." In short, all I need to be content are life's fundamental pleasures.

Chapter 7

1   Fu Manchu is a more sinister character that appeared in several films produced in the United States during the 1920s and early 1930s (and resurrected in a 1968 film) that spoke to the fears of and desires for the exotic, Asian other in America (see Moy 1993, 106–114). My memory of Confucius and Charlie Chan as "salacious" and "sinister" seems to mix the sexual stereotypes used to figure Chinese at the end of the last, and during the present centuries in the United States. Moy argues that it has been the exoticized and highly eroticized image of the Chinese woman that has been seen as the more worrisome sexual threat to white America. The Chinese male, although equally as deceiving and treacherous, often has been portrayed as sexually impotent and feminized in the face of "real" American masculinity. These latter images, Moy notes, should be read in the context of their service to a larger quasi-colonial and certainly imperial discourse of "America" and its proper role in international morality and politics. Again, see Moy (1993); on the overlap of nation and sexuality, see Parker et al. (1992).

2   Some of the most forceful and direct of the Chairman's exhortations and writings about revolutionary struggle and glory were drawn together into a small red book titled, in English, *Quotations from Chairman Mao Tse-Tung* (Mao 1966), first published in 1964 (Teiwes and Sun 1996, 201). Subsequently, it became a bible of sorts for Red Guards and the ideological canon of the Cultural Revolution.

3   For an analysis of Lin Biao the revolutionary and his fate, see Teiwes and Sun (1996); for historical and social accounts of the Cultural Revolution, see, for instance, Yan and Gao (1996) and MacFarquhar (1974, 1983, 1997).

4   About this book during "Ming and Qing times" Hamilton (1984, 411) writes: "The *Three-Character Classic (Sanzijing)*, a book the barely literate could read and one that beginning school children memorized, features *xiao* above all other virtues."

5   On this continued presence of the Confucian past in the "modern" present of China, see, for instance, Duara (1995, 89) and Chow (1993, 104–106, 112).

6   She specifically suggests this after a discussion of a similar suggestion by Gregory Ulmer (see Clough 1998, 136).

7   Gordon (1997) argues that Freud in his "mature" and later writing on the unconscious, writing that ironically has much to do with the psyche's encounter with the social, "gives up the ghost." She means that in his desire to make secure his

science of the psyche, Freud relies on his theory of drives and ancient archetypes to account for ghosts and haunting as the return of repressed personal and early life experiences of the individual, treating the haunting that occurs in common social reality as a matter of misperception and subject to "reality testing," which is to say irrelevant to the unconscious as he conceived it. She says: "Freud leaves us with an extraordinary restriction of the haunted field. After having dragged the human sciences into all these ghostly affairs, Freud's science arrives to explain away everything that is important and to leave us with adults who never surmount their individual childhoods or adults whose haunting experiences reflect their incorrect and childish belief in the modes of thought of their 'primitive' ancestors. After getting so close to so much, he forgets his own important lessons about the transferrential field and about the fundamental insight the discovery of the unconscious inaugurated: 'we do not know those things we think we do' (Mitchell and Rose 1982, 4). Freud gets so close to dealing with the social reality of haunting only to give up the ghost and everything social that comes in its wake" (Gordon 1997, 57). For Gordon, the uncanny is about "being haunted in the *world of common reality*. To be haunted . . . is an enchanted encounter in a disenchanted world between familiarity and strangeness. The uncanny is the return, in psychoanalytic terms, of what the concept of the unconscious represses, the reality of being haunted by worldly contacts" (55).

8   "Stand gaping" is from Foucault's (1973, 374) *The Order of Things*. Gordon has used a long quote containing this phrase just before her comments, quoted above. The Foucault quote is as follows: "In setting itself the task of making the discourse of the unconscious speak through consciousness, psychoanalysis is advancing in the direction of that fundamental region in which the relations of representation . . . come into play. Whereas all the human sciences advance toward the unconscious only with their back to it, waiting for it to unveil itself as fast as consciousness is analyzed, as it were backwards, psychoanalysis, on the other hand points directly towards it, with a deliberate purpose—not towards that which must be rendered gradually more explicit by the progressive illumination of the implicit, but towards what is there and yet is hidden, towards what exists with the mute solidity of a thing, of a text closed in upon itself, or of a blank space in a visible text. . . . [P]sychoanalysis moves toward the moment . . . at which the contents of consciousness articulate themselves, or rather stand gaping."

9   The two key Freud sources Gordon uses are his essays "The Unconscious" (1955a) and "The Uncanny" (1955b).

10 This move is central to the position of "objectivity" that defines the scientific stance. One is not to take up an evaluative or ethical posture toward the practices and beliefs of those whom one studies. One's job is simply, it is said, "to describe" and "analyze." Aside from the difficulties of actually maintaining this posture in the mundane work of doing social science, there is also the question of, as Gordon says, what "the field" in question is. That is, in a field of contested views about not only what is but what should be, such a "detached" posture would hardly be seen as "objective." It would seem that only from outside that field, but from inside another that encompasses the former—which is to say professional

social science—could such a posture of objectivity be sustained as a practical matter. That is, the kind of bracketing that is at the heart of scientific realism is effected through an unmistakable flow of power and difference on the question of what is, in fact, the Truth.

11   As Gordon (1997, 31) shows, Freud himself uses the characterization "supposedly educated" to refer to "us," now, today; in the "modern" and non-"primitive" world who do not believe in ghosts and haunting, while, simultaneously, with no apparent irony, offering up an example of his own uncanny experience.

12   Although, Gordon (1997, 42) says, Freud "will disappoint" the desire to open more widely our social scientific thinking about human experience in society, "at least he," citing Spivak (1985, 257), "problematizes any statement of method that would begin, putatively, 'I choose because . . .'."

13   On the May Fourth movement, see, for example, Schwarcz (1984). As to the question of May Fourth as a legacy to xin Zhongguo—"New China"—some recent Chinese democrats—no doubt among others—dispute this; see Barmé and Minford (1989); see also Duara (1995, 147–176). And see the debates around the critique of "tradition" in China contained in the Heshang television series of 1988 and 1989 (Su and Wang 1991).

14   Bellah (1970, 96) compares the nature of the father-son relationship in Christianity and Confucianism. Among many provocative observations, Bellah speculates that Mao's attack on family and reverence for one's own father and mother came in part from a Christianity-influenced (non-Chinese) communism that held out a higher, transcendental authority—perhaps later personified by Mao himself—beyond that of one's own family and father. Although Bellah says this influence was a parody of true Christianity, where "the Heavenly Father" transcends the authority of one's earthly father, a positing of the ultimate, the transcendent, opens the possibility of disillusion and fragmentation of belief if and when that Father is doubted, or, surely, as in the case of Mao, shown to have feet of clay. Such a view seems congenial to analyses by some who study post–Cultural Revolution morality and religion in China, and who speak of a moral vacuum or malaise there during this time of what we might call "fallible fathers." See, for example, Madsen (1984, 1995).

15   Taken by Sih from the James Legge 1893 translation of Mencius, Book IV, Part II, Chapter 30 (The Chinese Classics. Oxford: Clarendon Press). The importance of "nourishment" here is linked both to food and broader care and support, although the particular importance of and concern with food is a storied part of Chinese cultural space. To locate the mother's breast as a central image in this chain, and to a "special" emotional connection between children and their mothers in later life around supplying them with their "favorite food," as nourishment, is, it seems to us, not far-fetched (see Yue 1999, 1–29, 289–292). That some deny this as having any sexual component is an interesting reading.

16   Lisa Rofel (1999, 20, 48–49, 165) offers a resonant reading of how what she calls "postsocialism" in China today is troubled, disturbed, resisted by the memories and stories of a cohort of women silk workers who remember themselves as

"socialist heroes" of an earlier time, and in some sense thus against the new masculinity of the (post)modern market sphere of risk and individualism.

17 Problems of translation in moving Freud's writings into Chinese have been particularly troublesome, with sometimes amazingly divergent and surprising results. See Blowers (1994, 42–43) for a discussion of this as well as of the reception of Freud's ideas in China.

18 See Duara (1995, 147–176) for a detailed discussion of the richness of meaning and practice marked by "feudal" or *fengjian* before its modernist and socialist rewritings in this century.

19 Two widely noted sources of writings on China by Americans that they cite are Cohen (1978) and Isaacs (1980).

20 All details of Fei's visit come from those supplied by Arkush and Lee (1993, 171–81).

21 In this regard, although in some senses "worlds away" from Fei's memories, it is worth pointing out that, at least in Hong Kong, there is a lively genre of "ghost story" films set in both the past and present, in which, ghosts and spirits take on very corporeal and material form. This discourse of ghost-as-material-presence occurs also in films that might not easily be located in this genre. See Ho (1999) on Ann Hui's films; and see Teo (1997, 219–229) and Hammond and Wilkins (1996, 89–106) on Hong Kong cinema ghost genre.

22 Kleinman (1986; 1988, 100–120) has raised the question of whether what Western psychiatry calls "depression" exists in China and in what form. Kleinman, a medical anthropologist, uses fieldwork and other data to argue that what in the west is called depression gets rendered as "neurasthenia" in China, seen in Western eyes as vaguely defined complaints about bodily aches and pains. Kleinman concludes that these psychic disturbances are mediated by culture and displaced onto the body. The relevance here would seem to be that, according to this view, the psyché is not a very elaborated or expansive space under this sort of cultural mediation. Given its history with "individualism," perhaps we should not be surprised.

23 Although he does not call his work ethnography, Solomon (1971, xi) here describes his book and the study in which it is "grounded" in just the sort of oedipalized language Clough (1998) has noted: "The present study of China and her twentieth century revolution was initiated in the hope that through the techniques of social science analysis—interviews using controlled sampling procedures and structured questioning, psychological projective tests, content analysis of published documents, and interpretation of data on the basis of social theory—it would be possible to come to some understanding of the Chinese revolution on Chinese terms. However, given the facts that China has not been open to direct observation, and that she has presented a constantly changing face to the foreign world over the past two decades, this has been no easy task."

24 The closest we come is a reference to a paper by Muensterberger (1951): "Orality and Dependence: Characteristics of Southern Chinese."

25 Or, as Duara (1995, 3–33) might say, one that is "self-conscious" in "History."

26 Might this have been some of what the creators of the television series *Heshang* were trying to do (see Su and Wang 1991)?

27 Hamilton (1984, 414–418; 1990) suggests, through a codification of subordinate's responsibilities to "the father" position rather than to an increase in the "power" of the father-as-person, that *xiao* or filial piety became *more* rather than less important toward the end of the dynastic period in China. One implication of Hamilton's argument would seem to be that at the time of the fall of the Qing empire in 1912, filiality likely was a very important part of routine Chinese life at all levels, hence making its presence in today's China and in Taiwan and Hong Kong less surprising.

28 Of course, they wouldn't have asked it that way, but I suspect you get the point.

29 Bellah (1970, 95) underlines this as one important difference between Confucian and Christian father-son relationships (and notes that the ancient Hebrew family was, in many ways, similar to the ancient Confucian family in this regard). Whereas in Christianity, even with "God the Father," relationships have been storied as very much about connections between an individual person and a father, Confucian father-son ties, Bellah says, involve "submission not in the last analysis to a person but to a pattern of personal relationships that is held to have ultimate value." Hamilton draws on Bellah and offers a detailed examination of the differences in Western and Chinese patriarchy—in contrast to Weber's reading—of *patria potestas* in the former tradition and *xiao* in the latter. Bellah argues that "Western patriarchy emphasizes the ultimate supremacy of persons, whereas Chinese patriarchy emphasizes the ultimate supremacy of roles" (1970, 92) and one's duty, obligations, to their demands and their emotions (see also Kipnis 1997, 104–115).

30 Hence what might be called a practical aspect to the preference for sons over daughters, who, as we have seen in chapter 4, "could not be counted on"; although, of course, they were.

31 Apparently, one usual translation of "Oedipus complex" into Chinese is *lian mu qing jie,* with an English rendering, according to Blowers (1994, 42), of "romantic/sexual love of mother." What is not mentioned in this Chinese phrase, what perhaps cannot be mentioned, is the crucial other bit of the oedipal story—the conflict with and hatred of the father. Bellah (1970, 90), who respects Freud's insights about family and power, suggests it is only after a father is dead, in the sometimes violent and emotionally excessive mourning rites, that we might find expression of the tensions and ambivalence that would seem to "us" to be inevitable in conventional Chinese father-son filiality.

32 See the *Hsiao Ching* (1961, 45 n. 9).

33 To our knowledge, this book, written in 1983 (Sun 1991), has not been translated into English. We first learned of it through reading translated segments contained in Barmé and Minford (1989), and all pages quoted here are from that

source. According to Kipnis (1997, 187), the book has been published in Chinese as *Zhongguo wenhuade "shenceng jiegou" (The "Deep Structure" of Chinese Culture)*, second edition (Hong Kong: Ji Xian She, 1987).

34 For a similarly harsh and personal view, see B. Yang (1992).

35 Michael Harris Bond (1991, 63–64), a Hong Kong–based Canadian psychologist and widely known for his research and writing on Chinese personality and culture, addresses the question of heterosexuality, but from a rather different but nonetheless relevant angle. Linking his comment to the work of historian Frances Hsu, Bond traces the particular difficulties and complexities in interactions between Chinese men and women to the "importance of the father-son bond." While filiality draws the son to the father's authority, says Bond, "the sex drive pulls sons away" from their parents. "It also interferes with the father's involvement in the activities of the son," by turning the son's attention to his wife. Finally, Bond says, admitting sexuality more openly into family life would destabilize family power "by humanizing the parents with desires shared by their adolescent children." Instead, silence about sex, coupled with traditions of filiality lead to—and here he is drawing on his science—"an avoidance of contact(s) with the opposite sex before marriage, ignorance about the biology of sex, low levels of sexual activity, and a widespread morality about sexual propriety."

36 Fei (1992, 66, 74) so quotes Confucius to describe characteristics of traditional Chinese social relationships.

37 A phrase Haraway (1997) uses to mark the present/future.

Chapter 8

1 Lisa Rofel (1999) argues that the current "postsocialist" moment in China is a time for popular repudiation of the alleged emasculation under which generations of Chinese men are said to have suffered, first in the duties of Confucian filiality and the imperium, and then from the socialist state and Maoism's Cultural Revolution, where gender's "natural" divisions were supposedly erased but "in fact," so it is now held, denied. In the face of this repudiation, the often-heard comments from people we met that, as Li Yu Nian put it in chapter 6, "the tradition is melting," suggest that the search for fathers and a subject of filial duty, as well as a palpable sense of lost or reduced "social connection," may be even more alive among older men and women in China than in the United States.

2 The parallel between the sociologist who studies "social texts" (assuming that one is able to consider this as a viable notion) and the literary critic who examines "literary texts" has for some time seemed to me quite productive.

3 In some "new ethnography" written recently in sociology, it is said to be precisely the absence of distance and separation that is the legitimating position, as in what is called "auto-ethnography" and in some work developed by Carolyn Ellis (e.g., 1995b) and others in the sociology of emotions. This work requires the "expression" and examination of the ethnographer's own feelings, emotions, and

selves in social space. While I respect the presence of the ethnographer in these texts, it appears to be a figure who has direct access to his or her feelings and emotions as a voice of the authentic, "really real" person that these authors say is typically denied in social scientific writing. While distance is thus in one sense collapsed and a reflective eye is turned on the position from which knowledge comes, scientific realism is nonetheless retained in what bears an unmistakable family resemblance to standpoint epistemology and to the unimpeachable authority of "experience" (see Denzin 1997, 53–89; Gubrium and Holstein 1997, 57–74, 107–108, 197–198; and Clough 1997, 2000, 170–184).

4   As suggested, the heady quality of this sense of dispersion I have felt and spoken about has to be connected to having enjoyed the centeredness and security of an embodied voice and identity of diverse superimposed privileges: male, white, bourgeois, heterosexual, first-world, "American," highly educated, tenured college professor, "healthy," "the norm," and so on. As Trinh's words at the epigraph of this chapter might suggest in paraphrase, with a little help from Roland Barthes, if one starts with these it is both easier to "go prospecting" in uncharted territory as well as to return to these places of security with less commitment to them. These pleasures may well not be so available for those moving from less privilege or struggling to sustain a center from which such movement can make sense, just as Wolf (1992) and some other feminists have noted. Granting this point does not mean, however, that the resulting politics of such criticism necessarily dis-serves "women" or shores up established regimes of domination.

5   As Duara (1995, 3–84) makes clear in his discussion of these familiar themes in the dominant narratives of "Enlightenment History" and the nation as the subject of this History in twentieth-century, "modern" China, Haraway's critique can be made to travel quite well, and with productive results, far beyond the United States, Britain, and Western Europe.

6   These are familiar to ethnomethodologists. Woolgar (1988a, 32–33) names them as indexicality—multiple readings/representations of allegedly the same event/object imply multiple events/objects; inconcludability—we can always ask for further definition, clarification, specification of terms; and reflexivity—each half of the representational couple elaborates, refers back to, what the other means, is. The account and the object are thus inseparable.

7   On this point, see Woolgar's (1988a, 73) discussion of Dorothy Smith's (1978) well-known study of "K's" mental illness and its textualization.

8   "There is nothing outside the text."

9   In a highly schematic but very powerful characterization of what he calls "splitting and inversion," drawn from his research with Latour on laboratory scientists, Woolgar details how the ideology of representation typically *begins* with a document ("data"), from which it creates an object that is cast as antecedent (rather than a consequent) and causal to the document, followed by a "forgetting" of how these connections have been forged by the agent. This "rewrites history" so that the "ontological foundation" of the "discovered object" is secured. Crucial here is

the erasure of the key place of the agent (see pp. 68–69). See also Pollner's (1987, 108–112) reference to Merleau-Ponty's notion of "retrospective illusion" to mark the place of forgetting in mundane ontology more generally.

10   In a provocative discussion that appreciates the place of radical reflexivity in sociological and human science inquiry, Pollner (1991, 372) distinguishes two kinds of reflexivity that always have been present in ethnomethodology: an "endogenous" sort that focuses attention on the mundane practices by and through which social reality is unreflexively accomplished or constituted by "members" in various scenes and settings of social life; and "referential" or "radical" reflexivity, where the distinction and distance between those designated as "members" and those marked as "analysts" falls away, and the analytical work of inquiry itself is seen as similarly constitutive. It is the latter that Woolgar names as distinctive of "reflexive ethnography." Finally, as Pollner argues, to accomplish a truly referentially reflexive inquiry is impossible in that its "grounds" are continually thrown into crisis. Nonetheless, Pollner mourns what he sees as the disappearance of this "impossible" reflexivity in both ethnomethodology and sociology for the insights and "imagination" that are lost.

11   But the very notion of "making a choice" may itself be more nostalgic than we like to admit, an anachronism in the televisual and cybernetic worlds of global capitalism in which so many live and where the idea of "an individual" making "a choice" may be seen more accurately as an advertising ploy than a reflection of the humanist's autonomous subjectivity. Not only do "choices" whiz by at very high speeds, leaving no space for "making," but the "agent" of choice is often a machine-human hybrid where all "choices" already have been scripted. Clough (2000) places these considerations at the center of her new work. See also Ang (1996, 162–180).

12   To be fair to Woolgar, he does note that "truth" is always the result of processes of knowledge production, and thus social and contingent, rather than that which comes before and must be sought out. "Knowledge claims are deemed to be true as a result of a particular concatenation of social relationships: truth is the ex post shorthand for agreement on a state of affairs; facts become true (facts) by virtue of actors' beliefs; beliefs are not caused by true facts" (Grint and Woolgar 1995, 304). An appreciation of this would seem only to push him closer to Haraway's view of the kind of knowledge that might be produced in a successor science.

13   In writing this "we," I again tried to think how to avoid the passive voice—which obscures authorship that is still very much here—but without also using the rather formidable plural pronoun, which seems easily more "grand," larger, grounded, "bluff" and imposing than a writing position inscribed by the fingers of two hands should be. The use of quotes here was the "cheap" solution. Surely, this should not be taken to be the literal "Joseph and Laihua." Haraway does not seem to struggle so much with her we's.

14   This implies neither chaos or nihilism, which are the all-too-familiar retorts from the heart of modernism toward such ideas. But it does mean a lot of hard work,

false starts, being wrong, serious mistakes, and quite different notions of authority; and probably a lot more committees.

15   I am reminded here of Foucault's (1977, 154) remarkable statement, "knowledge
is not made for understanding; it is made for cutting." And see Haraway (1997,
135) for this notion of maps as tools for intervention. As to whether or not this
intervention always should then be pursued by the "map makers"—that is, become their practical project—is, I think, a very open question.

16   This difference seems not especially to be about having created or aiming to
create a body of critical scholarship, per se, although that might be an open
question within the frame provided by Haraway's vision. I think here of Wolf's
(1992, 14) rather remarkable assertion about the effects of her research and
writing: "I may not have always gotten it right, but Taiwanese *women* were taken
seriously as agents because of my research and writing." It would indeed be interesting to pursue just which "Taiwanese women" this claim might describe, where,
when, and how. This pursuit would not challenge the somewhat more modest
claim that her work has been enormously important among scholars and writers
on Chinese women in the twentieth century. What isn't clear is just how that falls
out in terms of what Haraway imagines by her "making a difference."

17   This from *USA Weekend*, 3–5 September, 1999, p. 13, contained in the *Des
Moines Sunday Register*, 5 September 1999.

Bibliography

Abel, Emily K. 1991. *Who cares for the elderly? Public policy and the experiences of adult daughters.* Philadelphia: Temple University Press.

Allen, Joseph R. 1996. Dressing and undressing the Chinese woman warrior. *Positions* 4:343–379.

Anagnost, Ann. 1997. *National past-times: Narrative, representation, and power in modern China.* Durham, NC: Duke University Press.

Anderson, Marston. 1990. *The limits of realism: Chinese fiction in the revolutionary period.* Berkeley: University of California Press.

Ang, Ien. 1996. *Living room wars: Rethinking media audiences for a postmodern world.* New York: Routledge.

Arkush, R. David, and Leo O. Lee, eds. 1993. *Land without ghosts: Chinese impressions of America from the mid-nineteenth century to the present.* Berkeley: University of California Press.

Atkinson, Paul. 1990. *The ethnographic imagination: Textual constructions of reality.* London: Routledge.

Ayscough, Florence W. 1975 [1937]. *Chinese women, yesterday and today.* New York: Da Capo.

Barlow, Tani E. 1989. Introduction. Pp. 1–45 in *I myself am a woman: Selected writings of Ding Ling,* ed. Tani E. Barlow. Boston: Beacon.

————, ed. 1993. *Gender politics in modern China: Writing and feminism.* Durham, NC: Duke University Press.

————. 1994. Politics and protocols of *funü:* (un)Making national woman. Pp. 339–359 in *Engendering China: Women, culture, and the state*, ed. Christina K. Gilmartin, Gail Hershatter, Lisa Rofel, and Tyrene White. Cambridge: Harvard University Press.

Barmé, Geremie, and John Minford, eds. 1989. *Seeds of fire: Chinese voices of conscience.* New York: Noonday Press.

Barthes, Roland. 1974. *S/Z. An essay*, trans. Richard Miller. New York: Hill and Wang/Noonday.

Baum, Richard. 1975. *Prelude to revolution: Mao, the party, and the peasant question 1962–1966.* New York: Columbia University Press.

Bauman, Zygmunt. 1976. *Toward a critical sociology.* London: Routledge.

Becker, Howard S. 1973. *Outsiders: Studies in the sociology of deviance.* New York: Free Press.

————. 1986. Telling about society. Pp. 121–135 in *Doing things together: Selected papers.* Evanston, IL: Northwestern University Press.

Beijing Foreign Languages Institute. 1983. *The pinyin Chinese-English dictionary*, ed. Wu Jingrong. Beijing: Commercial Press.

Bellah, Robert N. 1970. Father and son in Christianity and Confucianism. Pp. 76–99 in *Beyond belief: Essays on religion in a post-traditional world.* New York: Harper.

Billeter, Jean-François. 1985. The system of class-status. Pp. 127–169 in *The scope of state power in China*, ed. Stuart R. Schram. London: School of Oriental and African Studies.

Blowers, Geoffrey. 1994. Freud in China: The variable reception of psychoanalysis. Pp. 35–49 in *Applying psychology: Lessons from Asia-Oceania*, ed. G. Davidson. Carlton, Victoria: Australian Psychological Society.

Blumer, Herbert. 1969. *Symbolic interactionism.* Englewood Cliffs, NJ: Prentice-Hall.

Bodde, D. 1953. Harmony and conflict in Chinese philosophy. Pp. 19–80 in *Studies in Chinese thought*, ed. Arthur F. Wright. Chicago: University of Chicago Press.

Bond, Michael Harris. 1991. *Behind the Chinese face: Insights from psychology.* Hong Kong: Oxford.

Brown, Richard Harvey. 1977. *A poetic for sociology: Toward a logic of discovery for the human sciences.* New York: Cambridge University Press.

———. 1987. *Society as text: Essays on rhetoric, reason, and reality.* Chicago: University of Chicago Press.

Brugger, Bill, and Stephen Reglar. 1994. *Politics, economy and society in contemporary China.* Stanford: Stanford University Press.

Bucher, Rue, and Joan G. Stelling. 1977. *Becoming professional.* Beverly Hills, CA: Sage.

Calhoun, Craig. 1994. *Neither gods nor emperors: Students and the struggle for democracy in China.* Berkeley: University of California Press.

Caplan, P. 1988/1989. Engendering knowledge: The politics of ethnography. *Anthropology Today* 4(5):8–12, 4(6):14–17.

Chambers, Iain. 1994. *Migrancy, culture, identity.* New York: Routledge.

———. 1996. Signs of silence, lines of listening. Pp. 47–62 in *The post-colonial question: Common skies, divided horizons,* ed. Iain Chambers and Lidia Curti. London: Routledge.

Chan, Anita. 1985. *Children of Mao: Personality development and political activism in the Red Guard generation.* Seattle: University of Washington Press.

Chan, Anita, Richard Madsen, and Jonathan Unger. 1992. *Chen village under Mao and Deng.* Berkeley: University of California Press.

Chan, Cecilia, C.K. Law, and Rita Kwok. 1992. Attitudes of women toward work in socialist and capitalist cities: A comparative study of Beijing, Guangzhou, and Hong Kong. *Canadian Journal of Community Health* 11:187–200.

Chang, Jung. 1991. *Wild swans: Three daughters of China.* New York: Anchor.

Charmaz, Kathy. 1983. The grounded theory method: An explication. Pp. 109–126 in *Contemporary field research,* ed. Robert Emerson. Boston: Little Brown.

Chen, Guafeng. 1987. Top expert warns of shortage of doctors. *China Daily* (March 31):1.

Chen, Ivan, trans. 1910. *The book of filial duty*. New York: Dutton.

Chen, Nancy N., and Trinh T. Minh-ha. 1994. Speaking nearby. Pp. 434–451 in *Visualizing theory: Selected essays from V.A.R. 1990–1994*, ed. Lucien Taylor. New York: Routledge.

Chow, Rey. 1993. *Writing diaspora: Tactics of intervention in contemporary cultural studies*. Bloomington, IN: Indiana University Press.

———. 1995. *Primitive passions: Visuality, sexuality, ethnography, and contemporary Chinese cinema*. New York: Columbia University Press.

———. 1998. *Ethics after idealism: Theory-culture-ethnicity-reading*. Bloomington, IN: Indiana University Press.

Clifford, James. 1983a. On ethnographic authority. *Representations* 1:118–146.

———. 1983b. Power and dialogue in ethnography: Marcel Griaule's initiation. Pp. 121–156 in *Observers observed: Essays on ethnographic fieldwork*, ed. George W. Stocking, Jr. Madison, WI: University of Wisconsin Press.

———. 1986. Introduction: Partial truths. Pp. 1–26 in *Writing culture: The poetics and politics of ethnography*, ed. James Clifford and George E. Marcus. Berkeley: University of California Press.

———. 1988. *The predicament of culture*. Cambridge: Harvard University Press.

Clifford, James, and George E. Marcus, eds. 1986. *Writing culture: The poetics and politics of ethnography*. Berkeley: University of California Press.

Clough, Patricia Ticineto. 1993a. On the brink of deconstructing sociology: A critical reading of Dorothy Smith's standpoint epistemology. *Sociological Quarterly* 34:169–182.

———. 1993b. Response to Smith's response. *Sociological Quarterly* 34:193–194.

———. 1994. *Feminist thought: Desire, power, and academic discourse*. Cambridge, MA: Blackwell.

————. 1997. Autotelecommunication and autoethnography: a reading of Carolyn Ellis's *Final Negotiations. Sociological Quarterly* 38:95–110.

————. 1998 [1992]. *The end(s) of ethnography: From realism to social criticism.* New York: Peter Lang.

————. 2000. *Autoaffection: Unconscious thought in the age of teletechnology.* Minneapolis: University of Minnesota Press.

Cohen, Warren I. 1978. American perceptions of China. Pp. 54–86 in *Dragon and eagle: United States-Chinese relations, past and future,* ed. M. Oksenberg and R. B. Oxnam. New York: Basic Books.

Conner, Karen A. 2000. *Continuing to care? Older Americans and their families.* New York: Falmer Press.

Cowley, Malcolm. 1982 [1951]. *Exile's return: A literary odyssey of the 1920s.* Harmondsworth: Penguin.

Crapanzano, Vincent. 1992. *Hermes' dilemma, Hamlet's desire: On the epistemology of interpretation.* Cambridge: Harvard University Press.

Croll, Elisabeth. 1983. *Chinese women since Mao.* London: Zed Press.

———— 1989. *Wise daughters from foreign lands.* London: Pandora Press.

———— 1995. *Changing identities of Chinese women: Rhetoric, experience and self-perception in twentieth-century China.* Hong Kong: Hong Kong University Press.

Dai, Jinhua. 1995. Invisible women: Contemporary Chinese cinema and women's film, trans. Mayfair Yang. *Positions* 3:255–280.

Davies, Bronwyn. 1989. *Frogs and snails and feminist tales: Preschool children and gender.* Sydney: Allen and Unwin.

————. 1993. *Shards of glass: Children reading and writing beyond gendered identities.* Sydney: Allen and Unwin.

Davis, Deborah. 1992. Urban families and the post-Mao state: Politics and the patrilineal tilt. Paper presented at Family Process and Political Process conference, sponsored by the Institute of Modern History, Academica Sinica, Taiwan.

————. 1993. Urban households: Supplicants to a socialist state. Pp. 50–76 in *Chinese families in the post-Mao era,* ed. Deborah Davis and Stevan Harrell. Berkeley: University of California Press.

Davis-Friedmann, Deborah. 1991. *Long lives: Chinese elderly and the communist revolution.* Stanford: Stanford University Press.

De Bary, William T. 1970. Individualism and humanitarianism in late Ming thought. Pp. 145–248 in *Self and society in Ming thought,* ed. W.T. De Bary. New York: Columbia University Press.

Denzin, Norman K. 1997. *Interpretive ethnography: Ethnographic practices for the 21st century.* Thousand Oaks, CA: Sage.

Derrida, Jacques. 1972. Structure, sign, and play in the discourse of the human sciences. Pp. 247–272 in *The structuralist controversy,* ed. Richard Mackey and Eugenio Donato. Baltimore: Johns Hopkins University Press.

————. 1976. *Of grammatology,* trans. Gayatri C. Spivak. Baltimore: Johns Hopkins University Press.

Duara, Prasenjit. 1995. *Rescuing history from the nation: Questioning narratives of modern China.* Chicago: University of Chicago Press.

Edmunds, Lowell. 1985. *Oedipus: The ancient legend and its later analogues.* Baltimore: The Johns Hopkins University Press.

Ellis, Carolyn. 1995a. *Final negotiations: A story of love, loss, and chronic illness.* Philadelphia: Temple University Press.

————. 1995b. Emotional and ethical quagmires in returning to the field. *Journal of Contemporary Ethnography* 24:68–98.

Emerson, Robert M., Rachel I. Fretz, and Linda L. Shaw. 1995. *Writing ethnographic fieldnotes.* Chicago: University of Chicago Press.

Fabian, Johannes. 1990. Presence and representation: The other and anthropological writing. *Critical Inquiry* 16:753–752.

Faison, Seth. 1996. Why China is ready to cool off. *New York Times,* January 2:C9.

Fei, Xiaotong. 1992 [1947]. *From the soil: The foundations of Chinese society [Xiangtu Zhongguo],* trans. Gary G. Hamilton and Wang Zheng. Berkeley: University of California Press.

Fingarette, Herbert. 1972. *Confucius—the secular as sacred*. New York: Harper.

Foucault, Michel. 1973. *The order of things: An archeology of the human sciences*, trans. Alan Sheridan. New York: Vintage.

————. 1977. Nietzsche, genealogy, history. Pp. 139–164 in *Language, counter-memory, practice: Selected essays and interviews by Michel Foucault*, ed. Donald F. Bouchard. Ithaca, NY: Cornell.

————. 1980. *Power/knowledge: Selected interviews and other writings by Michel Foucault, 1972–1977*, ed. Colin Gordon. New York: Pantheon.

Freedman, Maurice. 1958. *Lineage organization in southeastern China*. London: Athlone Press.

————. 1961. The family in China, past and present. *Pacific Affairs* 34:323–336.

————. 1966. *Chinese lineage and society: Fukien and Kwangtung*. London: Athlone Press.

————. 1970. Ritual aspects of Chinese kinship and marriage. Pp. 163–187 in *Family and kinship in Chinese society*, ed. Maurice Freedman. Stanford: Stanford University Press.

Freud, Sigmund. 1955a [1915]. The unconscious. Pp. 161–215 in *The standard edition of the complete psychological works of Sigmund Freud*, volume 14, trans. James Strachey. London: Hogarth Press

————. 1955b [1919]. The uncanny. Pp. 218–252 in *The standard edition of the complete psychological works of Sigmund Freud*, volume 17, trans. James Strachey. London: Hogarth Press.

Gabrenya, William K., Jr., and Kwang-Kuo Hwang. 1996. Chinese social interaction: Harmony and hierarchy on the good earth. Pp. 309–321 in *The handbook of Chinese psychology*, ed. Michael Harris Bond. Hong Kong: Oxford University Press.

Game, Ann. 1991. *Undoing the social: Towards a deconstructive sociology*. Toronto: University of Toronto Press.

Game, Ann, and Andrew Metcalfe. 1997. *Passionate sociology*. Thousand Oaks, CA: Sage.

Gao, Xiaoxian. 1994. China's modernization and changes in the social status of rural women, trans. S. Katherine Campbell. Pp. 80–100 in *Engendering China: Women, culture, and the state*, ed. Christina K. Gilmartin, Gail Hershatter, Lisa Rofel, and Tyrene White. Cambridge: Harvard University Press.

Gao, Yuan. 1987. *Born red: A chronicle of the cultural revolution.* Stanford: Stanford University Press.

Garfinkel, Harold. 1967. *Studies in ethnomethodology.* Englewood Cliffs, NJ: Prentice-Hall.

Gerth, Hans H., and C. Wright Mills, eds. 1946. *From Max Weber: Essays in sociology.* New York: Oxford University Press.

Gilmartin, Christina K., Gail Hershatter, Lisa Rofel, and Tyrene White, eds. 1994. *Engendering China: Women, culture, and the state.* Cambridge: Harvard University Press.

Glaser, Barney G. 1978. *Theoretical sensitivity.* Mill Valley, CA: Sociology Press.

Glaser, Barney G., and Anselm L. Strauss. 1967. *The discovery of grounded theory.* Chicago: Aldine.

Goldman, Merle, and Denis Fred Simon. 1989. The onset of China's new technological revolution. Pp. 1–22 in *Science and technology in post-Mao China*, ed. Denis Fred Simon and Merle Goldman. Cambridge: Harvard University Press.

Gordon, Avery. 1990. Feminism, writing, and ghosts. *Social Problems* 37:485–500.

———. 1997. *Ghostly matters: Haunting and the sociological imagination.* Minneapolis: University of Minnesota Press.

Gornick, Vivian, and Barbara K. Moran, eds. 1971. *Woman in sexist society: Studies in powerlessness.* New York: Basic.

Grint, Keith, and Steve Woolgar. 1995. On some failures of nerve in constructivist and feminist analyses of technology. *Science, Technology, & Human Values* 20:286–310.

Gubrium, Jaber F., and Andrea Sankar. 1990. *The home care experience: Ethnography and policy.* Newbury Park, CA: Sage.

Gubrium,. Jaber F., and James A. Holstein. 1990. *What is family?* Mountain View, CA: Mayfield.

————. 1997. The new language of qualitative method. New York: Oxford.

Gusfield, Joseph R. 1976. The literary rhetoric of science: Comedy and pathos in drinking driver research. *American Sociological Review* 41:16–34.

Hamilton, Gary D. 1984. Patriarchalism in imperial China and western Europe: A revision of Weber's sociology of domination. *Theory and Society* 13:393–426.

————. 1990. Patriarchy, patrimonialism, and filial piety: A comparison of China and Western Europe. *British Journal of Sociology* 41:77–104.

Hamilton, Gary D., and E. Chen, eds. 1991. *Business networks and economic development in east and southeast Asia.* Hong Kong: University of Hong Kong Press.

Hammond, Stefan, and Mike Wilkins. 1996. *Sex and zen and a bullet in the head: The essential guide to Hong Kong's mind-bending films.* New York: Fireside.

Haraway, Donna. 1991 [1988]. Situated knowledges: The science question in feminism and the privilege of partial perspective. Pp. 183–201 in *Simians, cyborgs and women: The reinvention of nature.* New York: Routledge.

————. 1997. *Modest_witness@second_millennium. Femaleman©_meets_Oncomouse™: Feminism and technoscience.* New York: Routledge.

Harding, Harry. 1992. *A fragile relationship: The United States and China since 1972.* Washington, D.C.: Brookings Institution.

Harding, Sandra. 1986. *The science question in feminism.* Ithaca, NY: Cornell University Press.

————. 1991. *Whose science? Whose knowledge? Thinking from women's lives.* Ithaca, NY: Cornell University Press.

Harrell, Stevan. 1993. Geography, demography, and family composition in three southwestern villages. Pp. 77–102 in *Chinese families in* the post-Mao era, ed. Deborah Davis and Stevan Harrell. Berkeley: University of California Press.

Henderson, Gail. 1989. Issues in the modernization of medicine in China. Pp. 199–222 in *Science and technology in post-Mao China*, ed. Denis Fred Simon and Merle Goldman. Cambridge: Harvard University Press.

Henderson, Gail, and Myron Cohen. 1984. *The Chinese hospital: A socialist work unit*. New Haven: Yale University Press.

Heng, Liang, and Judith Shapiro. 1983. *Son of the revolution*. New York: Random House.

Hershatter, Gail. 1997. *Dangerous pleasures: Prostitution and modernity in twentieth-century Shanghai*. Berkeley: University of California Press.

Hinsch, Bret. 1990. *Passions of the cut sleeve: The male homosexual tradition in China*. Berkeley: University of California Press.

Ho, David Y. F. 1996. Filial piety and its psychological consequences. Pp. 155–165 in *The handbook of Chinese psychology*, ed. Michael Harris Bond. Hong Kong: Oxford University Press.

Ho, Elaine Yee Lin. 1999. Women on the edges of Hong Kong modernity: The films of Ann Hui. Pp. 162–187 in *Spaces of their own: Women's public sphere in transnational China*, ed. Mayfair Mei-hui Yang. Minneapolis: University of Minnesota Press.

Honig, Emily, and Gail Hershatter. 1988. *Personal voices: Chinese women in the 1980s*. Stanford: Stanford University Press.

Horne, Donald. 1984. *The great museum: The re-presentation of history*. London: Pluto Press.

Hsiao Ching: The Canon of Filial Piety. 1961. Trans. Mary Lelia Makra. New York: St. John's University Press.

Hsu, Francis L. K. 1971. Psychosocial homeostasis and *jen*: Conceptual tools for advancing psychological anthropology. *American Anthropologist* 73:23–44.

Hu, Shih. 1919. *Chung-kuo che-hsueh shih ta-keng* [An outline of the history of Chinese philosophy]. Shanghai: Commercial Press.

Hughes, Everett C. 1971. *The sociological eye*. Chicago: Aldine.

Ikels, Charlotte. 1990a. The resolution of intergenerational conflict: Perspectives of elders and their family members. *Modern China* 14:379–406.

———. 1990b. New options for the urban elderly. Pp. 215–242 in *Chinese society on the eve of Tiananmen*, ed. Deborah Davis and Ezra F. Vogel. Cambridge: Harvard University Press.

———. 1990c. Family caregivers and the elderly in China. Pp. 270–284 in *Aging and caregiving: Theory, research, and policy*, ed. David E. Biegel and Arthur Blum. Newbury Park, CA: Sage.

———. 1993. Settling accounts: The intergenerational contract in an age of reform. Pp. 307–333 in *Chinese families in the post-Mao era*, ed. Deborah Davis and Stevan Harrell. Berkeley: University of California Press.

Isaacs, Harold R. 1980 [1958]. Scratches on our minds: American views of China and India. White Plains, NY: M.E. Sharpe.

Jamieson, George. 1921. *Chinese family and commercial law*. Shanghai: Kelly and Walsh.

Judd, Ellen R. 1989. *Niangjia:* Chinese women and their natal families. *Journal of Asian Studies* 48:525–544.

———. 1994. *Gender and power in rural north China*. Stanford: Stanford University Press.

Kaplan, Caren. 1996. *Questions of travel: Postmodern discourses of displacement*. Durham, NC: Duke University Press.

King, Ambrose Y.C. 1981. The individual and group in Confucianism: A relational perspective. Paper presented at the Conference on Individualism and Wholism, York, Maine, June 24–29.

King, Ambrose Y.C., and Michael H. Bond. 1985. The Confucian paradigm of man: A sociological view. Pp. 29–45 in *Chinese culture and mental health*, ed. Wen-Shing Tseng and David Y.H. Wu. Orlando, FL: Academic Press.

Kingston, Maxine Hong. 1981a. *The woman warrior: Memoirs of a girlhood among ghosts*. London: Picador.

———. 1981b. *China men*. London: Picador.

Kinsella, Kevin. 1994. Aging and the family: Present and future demographic issues. Pp. 32–56 in *Aging and the family: Theory and research*, ed. Rosemary Blieszner and Victoria Hilkevitch Bedford. London: Praeger.

Kipnis, Andrew B. 1995. Face: An adaptable discourse of social surfaces. *Positions* 3:119–148.

———. 1997. *Producing guanxi: Sentiment, self, and subculture in a north China village*. Durham, NC: Duke University Press.

Kitsuse, John I., and Joseph W. Schneider. 1989. Preface. Pp. xi–xiii in *Images of issues: Typifying contemporary social problems*, ed. John I. Kitsuse and Joseph W. Schneider. Hawthorne, NY: Aldine de Gruyter, 1989.

Kleinman, Arthur. 1986. *Social origins of distress and disease: Depression, neurasthenia, and pain in modern China*. New Haven: Yale University Press.

———. 1988. *The illness narratives: Suffering, healing and the human condition*. New York: Basic.

Kleinman, Arthur, and Joan Kleinman. 1991. Suffering and its professional transformation: Toward an ethnography of interpersonal experience. *Culture, Medicine and Psychiatry* 15:275–301.

Kondo, Dorinne K. 1990. *Crafting selves: Power, gender, and discourses of identity in a Japanese workplace*. Chicago: University of Chicago Press.

Krieger, Susan. 1991. *Social science and the self: Personal essays on an art form*. New Brunswick, NJ: Rutgers University Press.

Landow, George P. 1992. *Hypertext: The convergence of contemporary critical theory and technology*. Baltimore: Johns Hopkins University Press.

Latour, Bruno. 1987. *Science in action: How to follow scientists and engineers through society*. Cambridge: Harvard University Press.

———. 1988. The politics of explanation: An alternative. Pp. 155–176 in *Knowledge and reflexivity: New frontiers in the sociology of knowledge*, ed. Steve Woolgar. London: Sage.

————. 1993. *We have never been modern*, trans. Catherine Porter. Cambridge: Harvard University Press.

Latour, Bruno, and Steve Woolgar. 1979. *Laboratory life: The social construction of scientific facts*. Beverly Hills, CA: Sage.

Lau, D.S. 1979. *The analects*. New York: Penguin.

Lee, Yean-ju, William L. Parish, and Robert Willis. 1994. Sons, daughters, and intergenerational support in Taiwan. *American Journal of Sociology* 99:1010–1041.

Legge, James. 1960. *Confucian analects. Chinese classics*, volume 1. Hong Kong: Hong Kong University Press.

Lemert, Charles. 1995. *Sociology after the crisis*. Boulder, CO: Westview.

Lewis, I.B. 1919. *The education of girls in China*. New York.

Liang, Shu-ming. 1974. *Chung-kuo wen hau yao-i* [The essential features of Chinese culture]. Hong Kong: Chi-Cheng T'u-Shu Kung Hsu.

Lin, Yu-ming, ed. 1985. *Hua Mulan de gushi* [The story of Hua Mulan]. Pp. 1–2 in *Zhongguo ertong gushi xuan* [Selections of Chinese tales for children]. Hong Kong: Art's Publishing Company.

Lin, Yusheng. 1974–1975. The evolution of the pre-Confucian meaning of *jen* and Confucian concept of moral autonomy. *Monumenta Sinica* 31:172–204.

MacCannell, Dean. 1976. *The tourist: A new theory of the leisure class*. New York: Schocken.

MacFarquhar, Roederick. 1974. *The origins of the cultural revolution, 1: Contradictions among the people 1956–1957*. New York: Columbia University Press.

————. 1983. *The origins of the cultural revolution, 2: The great leap forward 1958–1960*. New York: Columbia University Press.

————. 1997. *The origins of the cultural revolution, 3: The coming of the cataclysm 1961–1966*. New York: Columbia University Press.

Maddox, Patrick G., and Anne F. Thurston. 1987. Academic exchanges: The goals and roles of U.S. universities. Pp. 119–165 in *Educational exchanges: Essays on the Sino-American experience*, ed. Joyce K. Kallgren and Denis Fred Simon. Berkeley: University of California, Institute of East Asian Studies.

Madsen, Richard. 1984. *Morality and power in a Chinese village*. Berkeley: University of California Press.

———. 1987. Institutional dynamics of cross-cultural communication: U.S.-China exchanges in the humanities and social sciences. Pp. 191–213 in *Educational exchanges: Essays on the Sino-American experience*, ed. Joyce K. Kallgren and Denis F. Simon. Berkeley: University of California, Institute of East Asian Studies.

———. 1995. *China and the American dream: A moral inquiry*. Berkeley: University of California Press.

Mah, Adeline Yen. 1997. *Falling leaves: The true story of an unwanted Chinese daughter*. London: Penguin.

Mao, Tse-Tung. 1966 [1964]. *Quotations from chairman Mao Tse-Tung*. Peking: Foreign Languages Press.

Marcus, George E. 1994a. The modernist sensibility in recent ethnographic writing and the cinematic metaphor of montage. Pp. 37–53 in *Visualizing theory: Selected essays from V.A.R. 1990–1994*, ed. Lucien Taylor. New York: Routledge.

———. 1994b. What comes (just) after "post"? The case of ethnography. Pp. 563–574 in *Handbook of qualitative research*, ed. Norman K. Denzin and Yvonne S. Lincoln. Thousand Oaks, CA: Sage.

Marcus, George E., and Michael M.J. Fischer. 1986. *Anthropology as cultural critique*. Chicago: University of Chicago Press.

Mascia-Lees, Frances E., Patricia Sharpe, and Colleen Ballerino Cohen. 1989. The postmodernist turn in anthropology: Cautions from a feminist perspective. *Signs* 15:7–33.

Mead, George Herbert. 1934. *Mind, self, and society from the standpoint of a behaviorist*. Chicago: University of Chicago Press.

Mills, C. Wright. 1940. Situated actions and vocabularies of motives. *American Sociological Review* 6:904–913.

Mirsky, Jonathan. 1994. The bottom of the well. *New York Review of Books*, October 6:24–29.

Mitchell, Juliet, and Jacqueline Rose, eds. 1982. *Feminine sexuality: Jacques Lacan and the école Freudienne.* London: Macmillan.

Moore, Charles A. 1967. Introduction: The humanistic Chinese mind. Pp. 1–10 in *The Chinese mind*, ed. C.A. Moore. Honolulu: University of Hawaii Press.

Moroney, Robert M., Paul R. Dokecki, John J. Gates, Kelly Noser Haynes, J.R. Newbrough, and Jack A. Nottingham. 1998. *Caring and competent caregivers.* Athens, GA: University of Georgia Press.

Mosher, Steven W. 1993. *A mother's ordeal. The story of Chi An: One woman's fight against China's one-child policy.* New York: Harcourt.

Mote, F.W. 1972. *Intellectual foundations of China.* New York: Knopf.

Moy, James. 1993. *Marginal sights: Staging the Chinese in America.* Iowa City, IA: University of Iowa Press.

Muensterberger, Warner. 1951. Orality and dependence: Characteristics of southern Chinese. *Psychoanalysis and the Social Sciences* 3:54–65.

Mulkay, Michael J. 1985. *The word and the world: Explorations in the form of sociological analysis.* London: Routledge.

Munro, Donald J. 1977. *The concept of man in contemporary China.* Ann Arbor, MI: University of Michigan Press.

Nelson, John S., Allan Megill, and Donald N. McCloskey, eds. 1987. *The rhetoric of the human sciences: Language and argument in scholarship and public affairs.* Madison, WI: University of Wisconsin Press.

Ong, Aihwa. 1993. On the edge of empires: Flexible citizenship among Chinese in diaspora. *Positions* 1:745–778.

Orleans, Leo A. 1988. *Chinese students in America: Policies, issues, and numbers.* Washington, D.C.: National Academy Press.

Parker, Andrew, Mary Russo, Doris Sommer, and Patricia Yaeger, eds. 1992. *Nationalisms and Sexualities.* New York: Routledge.

Pearson, Veronica, and Benjamin K.P. Leung, eds. 1995. *Women in Hong Kong.* Hong Kong: Oxford University Press.

Phelan, Peggy. 1993. *Unmarked: The politics of performance*. New York: Routledge.

Pollner, Melvin. 1987. *Mundane reason: Reality in everyday and sociological discourse*. Cambridge: Cambridge University Press.

———. 1991. Left of ethnomethodology: The rise and decline of radical reflexivity. *American Sociological Review* 56:370–380.

Potter, Sulamith Heins, and Jack M. Potter. 1990. *China's peasants: The anthropology of a revolution*. Cambridge: Cambridge University Press.

Rabinow, Paul. 1977. *Reflections on fieldwork in Morocco*. Berkeley: University of California Press.

Redding, S. Gordon. 1990. *The spirit of Chinese capitalism*. Berlin: de Gruyter.

Reed-Danahay, Deborah E., ed. 1997. *Auto/ethnography: Rewriting the self and the social*. Oxford: Berg.

Richardson, Laurel. 1994. Nine poems: Marriage and the family. *Journal of Contemporary Ethnography* 23:3–14.

Rofel, Lisa. 1999. *Other modernities: Gendered yearnings in China after socialism*. Berkeley: University of California Press.

Rorty, Richard. 1979. *Philosophy and the mirror of nature*. Princeton: Princeton University Press.

Said, Edward W. 1978. *Orientalism*. New York: Pantheon.

Schneider, Joseph W. 1988. Disability as moral experience: Epilepsy and self in routine relationships. *Journal of Social Issues* 44:63–78.

———. 1991. Troubles with textual authority in sociology. *Symbolic Interaction* 14:295–319.

———. 1993a. Family care work and duty in a "modern" Chinese hospital. Pp. 154–179 in *Health and health care in developing countries*, ed. Peter Conrad and Eugene Gallagher. Philadelphia: Temple University Press.

———. 1993b. Members only: Reading the constructionist text. Pp. 103–116 in *Reconsidering social constructionism: Debates in social problems theory*, ed. James Holstein and Gale Miller. Hawthorne, NY: Aldine de Gruyter.

Schneider, Joseph W., and Peter Conrad. 1983. *Having epilepsy: The experience and control of illness*. Philadelphia: Temple University Press.

Schwarcz, Vera. 1984. *The Chinese enlightenment: Intellectuals and the legacy of the May fourth movement of 1919*. Berkeley: University of California Press.

Shapin, Steven. 1994. *A social history of truth: Civility and science in seventeenth-century England*. Chicago: University of Chicago Press.

Shapin, Steven, and Simon Schaffer. 1985. *Leviathan and the air-pump: Hobbes, Boyle, and the experimental life*. Princeton: Princeton University Press.

Sih, Paul K.T. 1961. Editor's preface. Pp. v–xi in The *hsiao ching*, trans. Mary Lelia Makra. New York: St. John's University Press.

Silber, Cathy. 1994. From daughter to daughter-in-law in the women's script of southern Hunan. Pp. 47–68 in *Engendering China: Women, culture, and the state*, ed. Christina K. Gilmartin, Gail Hershatter, Lisa Rofel, and Tyrene White. Cambridge: Harvard University Press.

Smith, Dorothy E. 1978. K is mentally ill: The anatomy of a factual account. *Sociology* 12:23–53.

———. 1993. High noon in textland: A critique of Clough. *Sociological Quarterly* 34:183–192.

Sofoulis, Zoe. 1988. Through the lumen: Frankenstein and the optics of re-origination. Ph.D. dissertation. University of California, Santa Cruz.

Solomon, Richard H. 1971. *Mao's revolution and the Chinese political culture*. Berkeley: University of California Press.

Spivak, Gayatri Chakravorty. 1985. The rani of Sirmur: An essay in reading the archives. *History and Theory* 24:247–272.

———. 1992. The politics of translation. Pp. 177–200 in *Destabilizing theory: Contemporary feminist debates*, ed. Michele Barrett and Anne Phillips. Cambridge: Polity.

Stacey, Judith. 1983. *Patriarchy and socialist revolution in China*. Berkeley: University of California Press.

————. 1990. *Brave new families: Stories of domestic upheaval in late twentieth-century America.* New York: Basic.

————. 1996. *In the name of the family: Rethinking family values in the postmodern age.* Boston: Beacon.

Strauss, Anselm L. 1959. *Mirrors and masks: The search for identity.* Glencoe, IL: Free Press.

————. 1987. *Qualitative analysis for social scientists.* Cambridge: Cambridge University Press.

Strauss, Anselm L., Shizuko Fagerhaugh, Barbara Suczek, and Carolyn Weiner. 1985. *Social organization of medical work.* Chicago: University of Chicago Press.

Su, Xiaokang, and Luxiang Wang. 1991. *Deathsong of the river: A reader's guide to the Chinese TV series* heshang, trans. Richard W. Bodman and Pin. P. Wan. Ithaca, NY: Cornell University, East Asia Program.

Sun, Lung-kee. 1985. Out of the wilderness: Chinese intellectual odysseys from "May fourth" to the "thirties." Ph.D. dissertation. Stanford University.

————. 1991. Contemporary Chinese culture: Structure and emotionality. *Australian Journal of Chinese Affairs* 26:1–41.

Tan, Amy. 1989. *The joy luck club.* New York: Putnam.

————. 1991. *The kitchen god's wife.* New York: Putnam.

Teiwes, Frederick C., and Warren Sun. 1996. *The tragedy of Lin Biao: Riding the tiger during the cultural revolution 1966–1971.* Honolulu: University of Hawaii Press.

Teo, Stephen. 1997. *Hong Kong cinema: The extra dimension.* London: British Film Institute.

Tianjin fangdichan shichang [Tianjin real estate market]. 1993. Tianjin: Nankai daxue chubanshe [Nankai University Press].

Tianjin tongji nianjian [Tianjin statistical yearbook]. 1995. Beijing: Zhongguo tongji chubanshe [China Statistical Publishing House].

Trinh, T. Minh-ha. 1989. *Woman, native, other: Writing postcoloniality and feminism.* Bloomington, IN: University of Indiana Press.

————. 1992. *Framer framed*. New York: Routledge.

————. 1996. The undone interval (in conversation with Annamaria Morelli). Pp. 3–16 in *The post-colonial question: Common skies, divided horizons*, ed. Iain Chambers and Lidia Curti. London: Routledge.

Tronto, Joan C. 1993. *Moral boundaries: A political argument for an ethic of care*. New York: Routledge.

Tu, Wei-ming. 1985. *Confucian thought: Selfhood as creative transformation*. Albany, NY: State University of New York Press.

Wang, Hui, and Wang, Laihua. 1990. *Laonian shenghuo fangshi tan mi* [The life style of the elderly]. Tianjin: Tianjin People's Press.

Wang, Laihua. 1992. *Ba qiye cong "ban shehui" zhong jiefang chulai* [Liberating factories from non-production costs]. *Lilun Yu Xiandaihua* [Theory and Modernization] 5:15–19. Tianjin.

Wang, Laihua, and Joseph W. Schneider. 1993. Home care for the chronically ill elderly in China: The family sickbed in Tianjin. *Journal of Cross-Cultural Gerontology* 8:331–348.

————. 1998. *Loudou: yi xiang dui laonian ren jiating zhaogu he jiating guanxi de shehuixue yanjiu* [Funnel: A sociological study of family caregiving for the elderly and of family relationships]. Tianjin: Tianjin People's Press.

Wang, Lin Ren. 1986. *Dui yiyuan peizhu tanshi wenti zhi guanjian* [View on visiting patients in the hospital], trans. Sun Binghe. *Zhongguo yiyuan guanli zazhi* [Journal of Chinese Hospital Management] 23:192.

Wank, David L. 1995. Bureaucratic patronage and private business: Changing networks of power in urban China. Pp. 153–183 in *The waning of the communist state: Economic origins of political decline in China and Hungary*, ed. Andrew G. Walder. Berkeley: University of California Press.

Wolf, Margery. 1968. *The house of Lim: A study of a Chinese farm family*. Englewood Cliffs, NJ: Prentice-Hall.

————. 1972. *Women and the family in rural Taiwan*. Stanford: Stanford University Press.

————. 1985. *Revolution postponed: Women in contemporary China.* Stanford: Stanford University Press.

————. 1990. Chinanotes: Engendering anthropology. Pp. 343–355 in *Fieldnotes: The making of anthropology,* ed. Roger Sanjek. Ithaca, NY: Cornell University Press.

————. 1992. *A thrice-told tale: Feminism, postmodernism and ethnographic responsibility.* Stanford: Stanford University Press.

Wong, Siu-lun. 1985. The Chinese family firm: A model. *British Journal of Sociology* 36:58–72

————. 1988. *Emigrant entrepreneurs: Shanghai industrialists in Hong Kong.* New York: Oxford University Press.

Woolgar, Steve. 1988a. *Science: The very idea.* London: Tavistock.

————, ed. 1988b. *Knowledge and reflexivity: New frontiers in the sociology of knowledge.* London: Sage.

Woolgar, Steve, and Dorothy Pawluch. 1985. Ontological gerrymandering: The anatomy of social problems explanations. *Social Problems* 32:214–227.

Xu, Xiaoqun. 1996. The discourse on love, marriage, and sexuality in post-Mao China: A reading of the journalistic literature on women. *Positions* 4:381–414.

Yan, Jiaqi, and Gao Gao. 1996 [1986]. *Turbulent decade: A history of the cultural revolution,* ed. and trans. D.W.Y. Kwok. Honolulu: University of Hawaii Press.

Yang, Bo. 1992. *The ugly Chinaman and the crisis of Chinese culture.* Sydney: Allen and Unwin.

Yang, Mayfair Mei-Hui. 1986. The art of social relationships and exchange in China. Ph.D. dissertation. Department of Anthropology, University of California, Berkeley.

————. 1989. The gift economy and state power in China. *Comparative Studies in Society and History* 31:25–54.

————. 1994. *Gifts, banquets and the art of social relationships in China.* Ithaca, NY: Cornell University Press.

Yang, Rae. 1997. *Spider eaters: A memoir.* Berkeley: University of California Press.

Yeatman, Anna. 1994. *Postmodern revisionings of the political*. New York: Routledge.

Yue, Daiyun, and Carolyn Wakeman. 1985. *To the storm: The odyssey of a revolutionary Chinese woman*. Berkeley: University of California Press.

Yue, Gang. 1999. *The mouth that begs: Hunger, cannibalism, and the politics of eating in modern China*. Durham, NC: Duke University Press.

Yuen, Yuet Hing, Cynthia. 1998. Regulation, negotiation, and resistance: Rethinking women's experiences of the reform in rural south China. Master of Philosophy thesis, Department of Sociology, University of Hong Kong.

Zhong, Shi. 1985. An investigation into irregularities in hospitals. *Chinese Sociology and Anthropology* 27:36–48.

Zito, Angela, and Tani E. Barlow. 1994. *Body, subject and power in China*. Chicago: University of Chicago Press.

Author Index

Author Index

Subject Index

Studies in the Postmodern Theory of Education

General Editors
Joe L. Kincheloe & Shirley R. Steinberg

Counterpoints publishes the most compelling and imaginative books being written in education today. Grounded on the theoretical advances in criticalism, feminism, and postmodernism in the last two decades of the twentieth century, Counterpoints engages the meaning of these innovations in various forms of educational expression. Committed to the proposition that theoretical literature should be accessible to a variety of audiences, the series insists that its authors avoid esoteric and jargonistic languages that transform educational scholarship into an elite discourse for the initiated. Scholarly work matters only to the degree it affects consciousness and practice at multiple sites. Counterpoints' editorial policy is based on these principles and the ability of scholars to break new ground, to open new conversations, to go where educators have never gone before.

For additional information about this series or for the submission of manuscripts, please contact:
Joe L. Kincheloe & Shirley R. Steinberg
637 West Foster Avenue
State College, PA 16801

To order other books in this series, please contact our Customer Service Department:
(800) 770-LANG (within the U.S.)
(212) 647-7706 (outside the U.S.)
(212) 647-7707 FAX

Or browse online by series:
www.peterlang.com